POL $2.00
W9-CHE-854

CRIME VICTIMS
An Introduction to Victimology

Contemporary Issues in Crime and Justice Series
Roy Roberg, San Jose State University: Series Editor

Crime and Justice: Issues and Ideas (1984)
Philip Jenkins, Pennsylvania State University

Crime Victims: An Introduction to Victimology (1984)
Andrew Karmen, John Jay College of Criminal Justice

The Police in American Society (1985)
Harlan Hahn, University of Southern California

Sense and Nonsense about Crime (1985)
Samuel Walker, University of Nebraska, Omaha

CRIME VICTIMS

An Introduction to Victimology

Andrew Karmen
John Jay College of Criminal Justice

Brooks/Cole Publishing Company
Monterey, California

To everyone whose suffering
is needlessly intensified or prolonged
because of ignorance about crime victims
or a lack of commitment to them

Consulting Editor: Roy Roberg

Brooks/Cole Publishing Company
A Division of Wadsworth, Inc.

© 1984 by Wadsworth, Inc., Belmont, California 94002.
All rights reserved. No part of this book may be reproduced, stored in a retrieval system, or transcribed, in any form or by any means—electronic, mechanical, photocopying, recording, or otherwise—without the prior written permission of the publisher, Brooks/Cole Publishing Company, Monterey, California 93940, a division of Wadsworth, Inc.

Printed in the United States of America
10 9 8 7 6 5 4 3 2 1

Library of Congress Cataloging in Publication Data

Karmen, Andrew.
Crime victims.

Includes bibliographical references and index.
1. Victims of crimes—United States. 2. Reparation—United States. I. Title.
HV6250.3.U5K37 1984 362.8'8'0973 83-27117
0-534-02997-3

Sponsoring Editor: *Henry Staat*
Production Editor: *Penelope Sky*
Manuscript Editor: *William Waller*
Permissions Editor: *Mary Kay Hancharick*
Interior and Cover Design: *Katherine Minerva*
Art Coordinator: *Rebecca A. Tait*
Interior Illustration: *John Foster*
Typesetting: *Instant Type, Monterey, California*
Printing and Binding: *The Maple Press, York, Pennsylvania*

Foreword

The Contemporary Issues in Crime and Justice Series introduces important topics which until now have been neglected or inadequately covered, to students and professionals in criminal justice, criminology, law, psychology, and sociology.

The volumes cover philosophical and theoretical issues, and analyze the most recent research findings and their implications for practice. Consequently, each volume will stimulate further thinking and debate on the issues it covers, in addition to providing direction for policy formulation and implementation.

The public is increasingly aware of street crimes and their impact, and the fear of becoming a victim of crime increases accordingly. This fear has produced a renewed interest in crime victims and their plight, both within and outside of the criminal justice system. Strong emotions have been aroused by the media, by politicians, and by special interest groups as they rush to assist these recently "discovered" victims; the result has generally been an impassioned and sensationalized approach to the subject. Thus, Andrew Karmen's scientifically objective study of the myths and realities pertaining to crime victims is both timely and refreshing.

Karmen's work focuses on victims of street crimes—murder, rape, assault, burglary, larceny, and motor vehicle theft—primarily because such crimes scare the public, preoccupy the police, and capture the attention of politicians. Furthermore, street crimes victimize specific people, usually individuals or families. How do these people become victims? What can the criminal justice system do for them? Should the system be adjusted to serve the victim better? Karmen addresses these and other significant questions from a victimologist's perspective, studying how the police, courts, and related agencies treat victims, and greatly enriching our understanding of what it means to be victimized.

While the subject matter is highly sophisticated, the reader is drawn easily into the discussion by Karmen's fluent and informative style, excellent use of examples, and sensible organization of complex materials. I have no doubt that *Crime Victims: An Introduction to Victimology* will inspire continued inquiry into the important issues it raises.

Roy Roberg
San Jose State University

Preface

This is the first systematic, comprehensive, and up-to-date introduction to a new and rapidly developing branch of criminology. I trace the emergence of victimology; analyze the public's growing concern for the plight of crime victims; discuss the current exploitation of the victimization experience by business interests; and describe the losses that burden victims of various kinds of street crime. I investigate the bitter controversy surrounding "victim blaming," and examine the many sources of conflict between victims and the criminal justice officials and agencies that are supposed to help them. I review the promises and pitfalls of restitution by offenders, and of state compensation programs. I conclude with analyses of the struggle for victims' rights and services, of the search for an informal alternative to criminal justice processing, and of the recurring impulse toward vigilantism. Throughout the text, I strive for objectivity while examining emotionally gripping subjects, and present both sides of passionately debated issues. I summarize the most significant research and theorizing in the field, and furnish the latest available statistics.

My own experiences as a victim of street crime are as relevant to my research and writing as my professional interests and my credentials as a criminologist. So far, I have been robbed twice by knife-wielding assailants. My home has been burglarized. My car was stolen and only the chassis recovered. Thieves have taken batteries, wheel covers, stereos, and other valuables from my cars on too many occasions to enumerate. But more significant to my becoming a victimologist is my firm conviction that the field is fundamentally humanistic. As an applied social science, victimology is dedicated to the relief of suffering and the prevention of harm and loss. I encourage all who yearn to do something positive about the crime problem, and who share a commitment to social justice, to explore the potential of victimology as an area for research, theorizing, and action.

As I complete this project, I want to acknowledge the assistance of a number of people. At John Jay College of Criminal Justice in New York

City, I benefited from insightful comments by my colleagues Edward Sagarin, David Sternberg, Fred Kramer, Sidney Harring, and Donal MacNamara. At Brooks/Cole Publishing Company in Monterey, California, Henry Staat, Cindy Stormer, Bill Waller, and Penelope Sky have my thanks. Various chapters were constructively criticized by Gilbert Geis, University of California at Irvine; Roy Roberg, San Jose State University; Brent Smith, University of Alabama, Birmingham; and by C. Ron Huff, J. L. Barkas, and Herman and Julia Schwendinger. Of course, I take full responsibility for the value judgments, interpretations, and controversial positions in the text, as well as for any errors or omissions.

Andrew Karmen

Contents

CHAPTER 1

The Rediscovery of Crime Victims and the Rise of Victimology

The Discovery of Crime Victims

The concept *victim* can be traced back to ancient cultures and the earliest languages. Its roots lie in the religious notion of sacrifice. In the original meaning of the term, a victim was a person or animal put to death during a ceremony in order to appease some supernatural power or deity. Over the centuries, the word has picked up additional meanings. Today, in everyday usage, the term embraces all those who experience injuries, losses, or hardships due to any and all causes. There are accident victims, cancer victims, flood victims, and victims of discrimination, among others. Crime victims are persons or entities that suffer because of illegal acts. Direct victims experience the act or its consequences first hand. Indirect victims share the suffering and losses but were not immediately involved or harmed.[1]

This book focuses almost entirely on victims of street crimes (murder, rape, robbery, burglary, larceny, and motor vehicle theft). There are many other categories of lawbreaking: crimes in the "suites" by high government officials against their "enemies" or the general public, and by corporate executives against their company's competitors, workers,

[1]Some victims and their supporters do not like the term *victim*, because it conjures up images of pain and helplessness. They prefer the term *survivor*, because it is future oriented and carries connotations of successful adjustment and continued existence. But *survivor* will be used in this book only to refer to people who are related to murder victims; survivors are indirect victims of a crime.

or customers; white-collar crimes by employees against their employers or by citizens against government programs; syndicate rackets run by mobsters; crimes without complainants ("victimless crime" to some, "vice" to others); political crimes, including acts of terrorism; and status offenses committed by juveniles. These other types of crime are serious and merit attention from scholars, law enforcement agencies, and concerned citizens. But they are not the lawless deeds that come to mind when people talk about the crime problem or express fears about being victimized. Street crime scares the public, preoccupies the police, and captures the notice of politicians. It has tangible victims, usually individuals or families. The other kinds of crime sometimes harm abstractions (like the public order or national security), or impersonal entities (like the U.S. Treasury or General Motors), or vaguely defined collectivities (like consumers or taxpayers). It's harder to grasp who the victims are in these cases, and it's also more difficult to derive any meaningful descriptions or measurements of them. A wealth of statistical data has accumulated about street crime's victims. For these reasons, then, this book concentrates on individuals who have been harmed by acts of violence and theft.

The study of crime and its victims is all about conflict. The nature of the victim–offender relationship is not characterized by equality, symbiosis, or mutual benefit. On the contrary, the interpersonal interaction is usually asymmetrical, parasitical, exploitive, oppressive, and destructive. The street criminal and the victim play roles and follow a script that resembles the dynamics between predator and prey, victor and vanquished, winner and loser, even master and slave, if only temporarily while the crime is in progress. The criminal law recognizes these inequities and injustices.

All laws prohibit specific acts and threaten penalties in the interest of saving victims from harm. Some laws are controversial because disagreements erupt over who is actually served by the rules and who is actually harmed. But laws forbidding acts of interpersonal violence and theft appear to be universal—present in all societies and necessary for every social system's survival. Any lack of consensus concerns how to handle the lawbreakers and how to aid the victims.

Since the recognition of an officially designated victim is a basic prerequisite for the enactment of legislation, the passage of every law reflects the discovery of a particular kind of victim. The laws prohibiting what are now called street crimes are among the very oldest on the books. Victims of murder, rape, robbery, assault, and theft were recognized and placed under the protection of the law centuries ago.

But over the past two hundred years, something happened. Victims found themselves belittled as pitiful losers in a world of "might makes right" or scorned as casualties in a jungle of cut-throat competition. Worse yet, victims felt themselves to be abandoned and adrift even within the criminal justice system, which ostensibly was set up to serve them. Starting in the 1960s, a critique of American society emerged in which crime victims were pictured as "invisible" or "forgotten." The indictment of the neglect shown toward victims by society in general and by the criminal justice system in particular was based on the following arguments: In colonial times, criminal acts were considered to be primarily injuries to individuals, rather than threats to the social order. Today, the situation has reversed. Crimes are interpreted as hostile attacks against the state (representing all the people). The extent of the victims' suffering is of secondary importance. Before the American Revolution, victims were the central figures in the criminal justice drama. The criminals' fates were closely tied to their wishes. Now victims are merely bit players, upstaged by the government's prosecutors, and their testimony is presented as just another piece of evidence in the state's case against the accused. Offenders of the past had to repay victims three times as much as they damaged or stole. Today, reimbursement is a minor concern. Convicts are sentenced according to different priorities: deterring crime through punishment or rehabilitating troublemakers via treatment. The protection of society and the interests of the government overshadow the demands of victims that they be restored to financial and emotional health. Offenders are provided with lawyers, housing, food, medical care, recreational opportunities, schooling, job training, and psychological counseling. Victims must fend for themselves. At best, victims are the forgotten persons within the crime problem; at worst, they are harmed twice, the second time by a criminal justice system more intent on satisfying the needs of its constituent agencies and officials than of the directly injured parties. Ironically, victims were better off hundreds of years ago (McDonald, 1977).

A widespread acceptance of this indictment has inspired the rediscovery of crime victims.

The Rediscovery of Crime Victims

After centuries of neglect, crime victims are being rediscovered in many societies. In the United States, the signs are everywhere. The plight of victims is front-page news. High-powered advertising campaigns are directed at victims and people afraid of becoming victims. Social movements rally to the side of crime victims. Their needs and wants are discussed, debated, and accommodated in legislatures, police stations, courthouses, hospital emergency rooms, and college classrooms.

In the rush to respond to recently rediscovered victims, scientific objectivity is often discarded. The suffering of victims is being exploited by some mass media representatives hungry for sensationalized news and gripping dramas; by profit-seeking outfits looking to sell questionable products and services to desperate people; and by social movements searching for tragic examples to rally public opinion behind their causes.

Scientific objectivity requires that an observer seek neutrality. Biases, either for or against, are to be avoided. Propaganda, whether in the form of advocacy or criticism, has no place. Since the study of crime and its victims is a value-laden pursuit that arouses intense passions, objectivity is hard to attain and even more difficult to maintain. But it is worth striving for, because its opposite, subjectivity, thwarts attempts to accurately describe and explain what is happening. Whenever controversial issues arise, it is best to present a balanced view by examining both sides.

The Mass Media: Portraying the Victim's Plight

Today, everyone is "familiar" with the crime problem either from direct, first-hand experience or from indirect, second-hand accounts by mass media outlets. The media of mass communications (television networks, radio stations, newspapers, magazines, books, and films) are saturated with reports about criminal incidents involving deception, loss, injury, suffering, tragedy. The flow of news items and eyewitness accounts emanates from an inexhaustible source—a crime-ridden society. Given this flood of information, the general public is in a position to become expert about what it is like to be a victim. Yet the media's coverage of crime's impact can be misleading instead of enlightening.

At its best, crime reporting in the media can explain in precise detail how victims react. By painting a picture that is faithful to the facts, journalists make it possible for an audience to transcend its own limited experience to see emergencies, crises, and adventures through other people's eyes. Skillfully prepared stories can effectively convey the drama and raw emotion arising from lawless acts. Nonvictims can better understand and empathize with the responses of victims when they are presented with accurate information, well-founded interpretations, and keen insights.

Unfortunately, the mass media's images are often distortions of reality. The exotic and peculiar are presented as the norm, or as commonplace. For example, the media's roving eye has a notoriously short span of attention. In its quest for items considered to be newsworthy, a TV station or newspaper might highlight a set of incidents culled from a much larger sample (furnished by police reports). For a week or so, lead stories might dwell on the murder of taxicab drivers. Then, poisonings due to criminals' tampering with products (such as cyanide-laced medicine capsules) might grab the headlines. A few days later, a rash of shocking cases in which teenage girls are abducted and raped seizes center stage. These events are then superseded by a series of outrageous slayings of elderly widows by young robbers. The procession of grisly, depressing, and infuriating news items about the crime problem never ceases (although, eventually, the subjects begin to be repeated).

Several consequences of media coverage of the victim's plight have become evident. First of all, false impressions, fallacies, and stereotypes (caricatures, over-simplified descriptions, uncritical judgments) are disseminated. If these myths about crimes and victims do not originate from the mass media's coverage, then they are certainly reinforced by news reports and dramatizations of similar events. (See the items in box 1-1.)

Secondly, the barrage of murder and mayhem laid down by the mass media exacts a toll on those who are exposed to it. For instance, life—according to many TV shows—is nasty, brutish, and short. The side effects of consuming this steady diet of violent fare tossed out as information and entertainment are shifts in attitudes. Heavy viewers of television tend to become increasingly concerned about the crime problem in general, and more wary of strangers in particular. Those who watch television excessively are more likely to harbor unrealistically high levels of fear about their own chances of joining the ranks of crime victims (Gerbner, in Waters, 1982).

A desire for commercial gain is the root cause of the media tendency to depart from accurate portrayals of the victim's plight. Media outlets are profit-oriented businesses. Shocking news sells newspapers and attracts viewers. Gripping accounts, colorful phrases, memorable quotes, and other forms of media "hype" (hyperbole, or exaggeration) are useful devices to build the huge audiences that sponsors want to reach with advertisements.

Two types of sensationalism in the depiction of victims are found in media portrayals. The first involves understating the intensity of a victim's reaction to harm. The second type is a distortion of the opposite kind, in which the victimization experience is overstated or blown out of proportion to the actual damage done. Both understating and overstating are forms of exploitation intended to take advantage of the victim's situation in order to serve some ulterior purpose.

Understating the victim's plight. Understating occurs whenever the effects of criminal acts on victims are overlooked, dismissed, or belittled. The most stark examples emerge when fictional characters, whether "macho" men or "super heroes," shrug off the emotional repercussions of a beating, a brush with disaster, or the death of a loved one.

A more subtle and insidious kind of downplaying of the victim's plight occurs routinely in mystery stories, police dramas, and westerns. There is a tradition in novels, plays, and movies of treating victims as part of the background and using their problems as a pretext for telling a much more interesting tale: the life story of the villain. This disparaging of the victim as a minor character overshadowed by a powerful, intriguing central figure, albeit an evil one, was sharply condemned by a critic in a review of a "docudrama" about a mass murderer who was put to death in the electric chair in 1981:

BOX 1-1 *Myths and Realities about Crimes and Victims*

Government-sponsored surveys and studies have produced findings that contradict some widely held beliefs. The following popular misimpressions are corrected by data derived from social science research projects.

- *About a crime wave sweeping the nation:*
  Myth: Crime is rising by leaps and bounds.
  Reality: The incidence of violent crime and theft just about kept pace with population growth throughout the 1970s and into the early 1980s.
- *About the prevalence of violent crime:*
  Myth: Most crime victims have been harmed by acts of violence.
  Reality: The vast majority of victims have experienced acts against their possessions that did not involve threats or force directed at them.
- *About where street crime takes place:*
  Myth: The larger the city, the larger the likelihood that its residents will become crime victims.
  Reality: The rates of assault, theft, and burglary have been relatively lower for people living in the nation's largest cities (one million or more residents) than for those inhabiting smaller cities.
- *About reporting crime:*
  Myth: Most victims tell the police about the incidents.
  Reality: Slightly less than half of all street crime victims inform the police.
  Myth: Black and Hispanic victims are less likely than others to report crimes to the police.
  Reality: Members of these two minority groups are just about as inclined to inform the police as other victims.
- *About the degree of concern over crime in the neighborhood:*
  Myth: Crime ranks as the most important problem in the neighborhood to residents of large cities.
  Reality: Environmental problems (trash, noise, overcrowding) generate just about as much concern as the threat of crime.
- *About the favorite targets of criminals:*
  Myth: The elderly are victimized more frequently than people of other ages.
  Reality: Teenagers and young adults are victimized much more often than older people.
  Myth: Women are more likely than men to become victims.
  Reality: Except for rape and purse snatching, men are victimized at higher rates than women.
- *About the danger posed by armed robbers and assailants:*
  Myth: A victim is more likely to be injured during an armed robbery or assault if the offender is wielding a gun rather than some other weapon.
  Reality: The victim's odds of being injured by an armed offender are lower if the weapon is a gun rather than a knife, club, broken bottle, or the like.
- *About resistance by the victim:*
  Myth: Victims are inclined to use force and draw weapons to repel attackers.
  Reality: Although victims defend themselves in a majority of rapes, robberies, and assaults, passive methods (seeking help, running away, hiding, pleading) are tried more often than fighting back.
- *About getting hurt:*
  Myth: Crime victims usually wind up in the hospital.
  Reality: Relatively few victims of rape, robbery, or assault get hospital care, either in an emergency room or as inpatients.

SOURCE: Adapted from *Myths and Realities about Crime*, by the National Criminal Justice Information and Statistics Service. Washington, D.C.: U.S. Department of Justice, 1978:1–32.

> Norman Mailer is a writer daring, generous, and exquisitely attuned, but it can hardly be said that he's bled tears of compassion in his work for those at the whipping end of cruelty; his sympathetic interest has always been with the neighborhood thugs who rough up the grocer, the orgy master, the psychopath, the aspiring Sade—with the beaters, not the beaten. To Mailer's credit, he did try to capture the sweet mundane homeyness of Gilmore's victims in his book, but there is something dutiful about these sections—you sense Mailer's eagerness to move on to the lurid rumble of Gary Gilmore's mind where the angels of Karma are being readied for takeoff.
>
> Shockingly, Gilmore's victims are barely given a glance in the TV version. Although Gary's cousin Brenda pays lip service to the grief of their families, the victims are little more than human props; once dispatched by Gilmore with a minimum of fuss, their lifeless bodies become mere stepping-stones on his trek into self-apotheosis. Their corpses are without glamour, and rugged glamour is finally what *The Executioner's Song* is about. . . .
>
> Stardom seems to be Gary Gilmore's true transcendence—his death set into motion cover stories, television specials, a best selling book, this made-for-TV mini-series: the machinery of pop immortality. Gary Gilmore's cagey soul absorbs Mailer . . . but the victims had souls, too, souls perhaps as far-venturing as Gilmore's, and they deserved better in life and film than this casual, callous snuffing (Wolcott, 1982: 72–73).

The most blatant examples of dismissing the victim's suffering for exploitive purposes crop up in horror films. The latest genre, called "splatter movies" in the trade, mix suspense with bloody carnage in a profitable formula. Catering to their audiences' appetite for high body counts, these low-budget productions feature nightmarish monsters and crazed ghouls running amok, relentlessly pursuing their helpless prey, who are eventually done in in the most sadistic and painful ways possible—perhaps skewered, hacked to pieces, or ground to a pulp (Rovin, 1982).

The most callous real-life instances of disregard for the victim's plight occur in on-the-spot interviews with grief-stricken survivors of violent crimes. Overzealous reporters have been condemned for maintaining a death-watch vigil at a kidnap victim's home or for shoving a microphone in the face of a bereaved, dazed, or distraught person. In such cases, there is a lack of balance between the public's right to know and the victim's right to be left alone (from unwarranted publicity, scrutiny, prying). When reporters turn a personal tragedy into a media event and then a public spectacle, splashed across the front page or as a lead story on the six o'clock news, the invasion of privacy represents the ultimate dismissal of the seriousness of the event to the injured party (Briggs-Bunting, 1982).[2]

Overstating the victim's plight. The other tendency, equally exploitive of victims, is to distort media coverage in the opposite direction: to

[2]To avoid this type of exploitation, no names of actual victims will be presented in this book.

overestimate the risk of becoming a victim, to exaggerate the degree to which the victim suffers, or to overstate the reactions of the victim to the experience.

An example of overrating the dangers people face appeared in a news magazine's lead story, entitled "The Plague of Violent Crime" (Press, et al., 1981: 46–54). The cover photo is a close-up of the barrel of a loaded gun, pointed straight at the reader. The caption substitutes the term *epidemic* for the equally misleading description, *plague,* of the title. Both expressions liken crime to a contagious disease that, by implication, may sweep across the landscape and claim just about everyone as its victims. An even greater exaggeration of risks surfaces in a section headed "Slaughter":

> Another frightening difference in the crime picture is that life now seems pitifully cheap. Law enforcement officials think they have witnessed a shift toward gratuitous slaughter. "It used to be 'Your money or your life,' says an assistant Bronx district attorney... Now it's 'Your money and your life.'"

Felony murders (homicides committed during the course of robberies or other serious crimes) are tragic events. But how often do they occur? Is it accurate to report that it used to be "Your money *or* your life" but today it's "Your money *and* your life"?

Each year, the Federal Bureau of Investigation (FBI) publishes its Uniform Crime Report called "Crime in the United States." The 1981 edition disclosed that 21,860 people were homicide victims in 1980. Nearly 11 percent of them died at the hands of robbers (in those cases where the police could establish a motive for the killing). Victims reported 548,809 robbery incidents to the police departments across the nation that year. More than half a million people were robbed, but, statistically speaking, "only" 2,361 were murdered during holdups. Mathematically, 0.4 percent of all robbery victims were killed during the course of the crime in 1980. Given this figure, it is irresponsible journalism to give the impression that robbers routinely murder their victims "these days" when 99.6 percent of them do not.

Homicide does not claim many victims when compared with less than lethal crimes like robbery or assault. The risk of being murdered is far from uniform; it varies sharply for different groups of people. (See the data in box 1-2.)

To many people, when discussing crime, the "way it used to be" was back before the crime wave of the early 1960s into the early 1970s. Comparable statistics (about the motives of murderers, as surmised by the police after investigating the cases) are not available for the "quiescent" 1950s. But impressionistic evidence demonstrates that even during the "good old days" journalists were magnifying the threat posed by robbers who took both the victims' money and their lives:

> The hoodlum will bash in your head with a brick for a dollar and ninety-eight cents. The police records of our cities are spotted with cases of "murder for peanuts" in which the victims, both men and women, have been slugged, stabbed, hit with iron pipes, hammers, or axes, and in a few cases kicked to death—the loot being no more than the carfare a woman carried in her purse or the small change in a man's pocket (Whitman, 1951:5).

Exaggeration of the victim's plight has been a problem within crime reporting for many years. The unusual has been presented as commonplace because stories with shock value sell well.

Many misimpressions about how former victims and potential victims are reacting to crime could be drawn from the overstatements that appear in a newsmagazine's feature article, entitled "The People's War against Crime" (1981: 53–56). It proclaims that "a surge in lawbreaking is stirring deep fears across the land," with the result that private citizens and businesses are undertaking an "unprecedented" array of self-defense efforts. "Fed up with being victimized by crime, harried Americans are doubling up their fists and fighting back." The story dramatizes the dreary obligation of riding around the neighborhood on patrol as "scouting the enemy." "More and more residents are prowling for troublemakers in their own radio-equipped cars." A section of the article entitled "Safe at Home—Behind a Set of Iron Bars" summarizes its theme as "worried property owners are seeking fortresslike security with guns and gadgetry." A photo caption explains how special training can turn the family pet into a fierce guard dog. The problem with news accounts like this is that they portray the actions of a relative few as if they were the typical responses of the vast majority. The reporters fail to point out the actual proportions of individuals, families, and businesses that are reacting to the fear of becoming victims in such drastic ways.

At about the same time that this sensationalized article was written, a public opinion poll was conducted (Gallup, 1981: 8). It asked a nationwide sample of people in all walks of life about the crime prevention measures they were employing, or had undertaken, as a result of their concerns about being victimized. Only 5 percent had installed a burglar alarm, and another 5 percent had joined a neighborhood crime watch group. Just 13 percent had bought special locks, and 16 percent had purchased guns for self-defense. Twenty percent reported that they were keeping a dog for protection. (Some people had taken several of these precautionary measures.)

The poll results show that, if a so-called "people's war" has broken out, few people have enlisted so far to resist the "enemy" of criminal invaders in the ways described in the article. The vast majority of the population has not heeded the call to arms. The cover story may have served its purpose of boosting magazine sales, but it failed in its mission to accurately portray the degree to which victims and fearful nonvictims are reacting.

BOX 1-2 Who Gets Murdered?

During the last twenty years, murder rates have been rising, whereas clearance rates (the percentage of cases solved by arrest) have been dropping. As a result, public concern has been growing. But certain people have a lot more to worry about than others. In general, the chances of being murdered are higher for men than women, young adults than older people, and blacks than whites.

(Murder is defined by the FBI as the willful and nonnegligent killing of one person by another; suicide, manslaughter by negligence, justifiable homicide in self-defense, and attempted murder are excluded from the FBI tabulations.)

More than three-fourths of all murder victims are males. For both males and females, murder victimization rates vary substantially by age. The chances of being murdered are highest during the mid-to-late twenties. The years between ages five and ten are the safest.

The most striking differences in murder rates are related to race. For the average American, the lifetime chance of being murdered is estimated to be 1 in 157; 0.6 percent of all deaths are due to murder. For white males (of all ages) the odds are 1 in 186; for white girls and women, the risk of being murdered in a lifetime is 1 in 606. But for black (and other nonwhite) females the rate is 1 in 124 (worse than for white males). And for black (and other nonwhite) males, the chance of being murdered soars to 1 in 29. That translates to a projected 3,460 homicide victims for every 100,000 black and other nonwhite males (see the accompanying graph) (Akiyama, 1981: 8–11).

SOURCE: Federal Bureau of Investigation, U.S. Department of Justice, 1982.

Big City Murder Rates, 1981
Number murdered for every 100,000 people

Miami	61	Nashville	17
St. Louis	58	Jacksonville	16
Newark	49	Charlotte	16
Atlanta	43	Oklahoma City	16
Detroit	42	Columbus	16
Cleveland	41	Toledo	15
New Orleans	39	Tulsa	14
Oakland	35	Albuquerque	14
Washington, D.C.	35	Phoenix	12
Birmingham	34	Seattle	12
Dallas	33	Pittsburgh	12
Los Angeles	30	Austin	11
Fort Worth	29	Milwaukee	11
Chicago	29	Honolulu	11
Baltimore	29	Cincinnati	11
New York	26	San Jose	11
Kansas City, Mo.	23	San Diego	11
San Antonio	24	Buffalo	10
Philadelphia	21	Portland	10
Memphis	21	Indianapolis	9
Long Beach	20	Omaha	9
Denver	20	Tucson	8
San Francisco	19	El Paso	8
Louisville	18	Minneapolis	8
Boston	18		

Murder rates vary considerably by locality, as well as by sex, age, and race. In general, the chances of being murdered are higher in cities and lower in suburbs and small towns. Within cities there are great differences in murder rates, as the chart below indicates.

Murder rate by age and race, United States (1978 data)

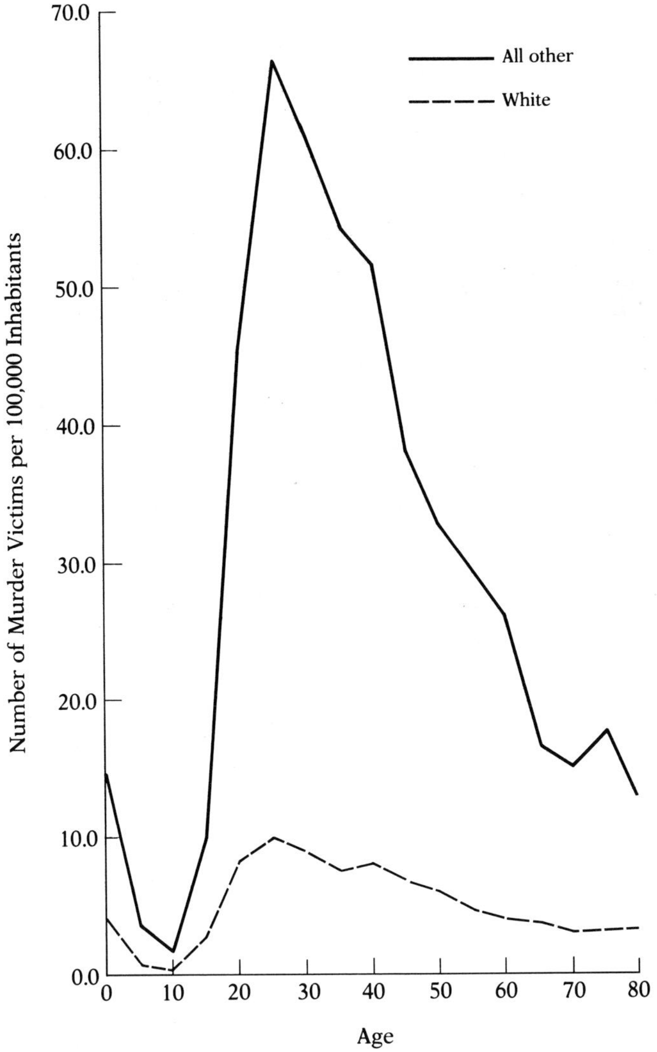

SOURCE: Akiyama, 1981:11.

Businesses: Selling Products and Services to Victims

Businesses have rediscovered victims as an untapped market for goods and services. After suffering through an unpleasant experience, many victims become willing, even eager, consumers and search for products that will protect them from any further harm. Potential victims—everyone else—constitute a far larger market if they can be convinced that the personal security industry can increase their safety. As the advertisements assert, there is, indeed, a product to satisfy every human need and desire.

But the attention paid to the victim's plight by businesses may turn out, like media coverage, to be a mixed blessing. Along with the development of this new personal security market comes the possibility of commercial exploitation. Profiteers can engage in false advertising and fear mongering in order to cash in on the crime problem and capitalize on the legitimate concerns and requirements of vulnerable and sometimes panicky customers.

Of equal significance, the development of a personal and home security industry (which offers services like bodyguards for rent and products ranging from guns to bulletproof clothing to burglar alarms) can impose a commercial and private bias upon efforts to reduce crime. Individuals and small groups equipped with the latest in technological gadgetry may be recruited into the "war on crime," in order to shift responsibility away from the corporate and governmental sources of the problem.

From crime prevention to victimization prevention. The new interest in victims on the part of businesses has contributed to an evolution in crime prevention strategies. The term *crime prevention* refers to efforts taken to forestall or deter offenders before they strike, as opposed to *crime control* measures, which are taken in response to outbreaks of lawlessness.

Formerly, crime prevention strategies centered on government programs designed to get at the social roots of illegal behavior, such as poverty, unemployment, and discrimination. Crime prevention used to conjure up images of campaigns to improve the quality of education in inner city school systems, to provide decent jobs for all those seeking work, and to develop meaningful recreational outlets for idle youth.

But now, the definition of crime prevention has evolved to "the anticipation, recognition, and appraisal of a crime risk, and the initiation of some action to remove or reduce it" (NCPI, 1978). Crime prevention strategies are shifting toward the actions of individuals and small groups rather than large-scale, even national, efforts. Perhaps a better term than *crime prevention* for these preemptive measures is *victimization prevention* (Cohn, Kidder, and Harvey, 1978). Victimization prevention is much more modest in intent than crime prevention. Its goal simply is to discourage or deflect a criminal from a particular target (home, warehouse, car, or person). Like defensive driving, crime prevention hinges on "watching the other guy and anticipating his moves."

A major new focus is on mechanical, or mechanistic, prevention, so named because it seeks to redesign the environment to reduce criminal opportunities, not because the approach necessarily relies on mechanical devices. Methods of mechanical prevention are supposed to reduce crime by increasing the risks of arrest, conviction, and punishment. One strategy is called "crime resistance," or "target hardening." It involves would-be victims (concerned, cautious individuals) in efforts to make the offender's task more difficult (the opposite of facilitating it through carelessness). Two examples of mechanical prevention are installing a burglar alarm in a home or car and wearing bulletproof clothing. The aim in both cases is to deter criminal attack, by making property less vulnerable to theft or a person less subject to harm.

A "valve" theory of crime–shifts predicts that the number of crimes committed will not drop when targets are hardened, but that criminal activity will simply be deflected. If one area of illegal opportunity is "shut off"—for example, protecting bus drivers from robbery by imposing exact fare requirements—criminals will shift their attention to more vulnerable targets—such as cab drivers or storekeepers (NCCPV, 1969). When crime is displaced, the risk of victimization goes down for some but rises for others, assuming that offenders are intent on commiting crimes and that they are flexible in terms of time, place, target, and tactics (Allen, Friday, Roebuck, and Sagarin, 1981).

Whether or not these victimization prevention methods really work, on either an individual or a community-wide level, they lend themselves to commercial exploitation. Many new goods and services are being marketed to direct crime elsewhere.

Cashing in on crime: burglar alarms. In ancient times, cities were surrounded by high walls to ward off invaders. Castles had moats as well as walls to keep intruders out. Guards in watchtowers served as lookouts in fortresses. Today, electronic sensors warn homeowners if prowlers are trying to break in.

Speakers for the home security industry boast that their business is booming and predict that the day is fast approaching when alarm systems will be considered standard equipment for stores, homes, cars, and boats. But at present, only a small percentage of all residences are wired for protection (Hager, 1981). Since there is plenty of potential for growth, some manufacturers are trying to stimulate business by scaring the public with "sales hype"—overstatements similar to media hype. One company advertises its wares through the mail with unnerving messages like "Burglars are looking forward to your vacation as much as you are!"

and "There are no safe neighborhoods . . . but there are safe homes." It says its hardware is "more than a security system, it's a 'Peace of Mind' system" (Shelburne Co., 1982). Its major competitor trades on fear by making a false claim in bold type in full-page newspaper ads that "One Out of Every Four Homes in America Will Be Burglarized This Year" (Vertronix, Corp. in *The New York Times*, 1981). Government figures reveal the actual 1981 burglary rate to have been about 9 percent (Bureau of Justice Statistics, 1983: 3), not the company's inflated prediction of 25 percent.

To clinch sales, alarm company representatives call themselves "security engineers," which is effective as an impression management technique. Depending on the nature of the customer, they can draw upon two different strategies of persuasion: fear accentuation, which is a sophisticated version of high-pressure scare tactics that plays on a former victim's emotions; or the aura-of-protection approach that stresses safety features in a more rational and technical vein (Siegel, 1978).

Installing an alarm (as evidenced by foil tape in widows, and decals) seems to have some value as a deterrent. Would-be trespassers and thieves may be warded off by the warning signs, which admonish that their intended victims are prepared to detect and perhaps help capture them. Such deterrence is shown by statistics compiled by the police in the affluent, relatively safe, yet crime-conscious, suburb of Scarsdale, New York, where over a quarter of the homes are guarded by electronic burglar alarms. From 1976 to 1982, the break-in rate ranged from around 0.5 percent a year to a little more than 2 percent a year for protected homes. During this period, residences without alarms were victimized from two to four times as often ("Alarm Systems," 1982: 26).

But this private solution to the burglary problem can cause hardships for neighbors. They might feel compelled to "keep up with the Joneses" for the sake of self-preservation rather than status seeking. If most nearby residences are protected by alarm systems, a prudent homeowner unwilling to be the only attractively vulnerable target on the block must purchase an alarm system too. The net effect of this "arms race" in security hardware is to deflect predatory street criminals from the well-guarded to the unguarded. To the extent that buying protective devices is more a question of income than consumer priorities, the overall societal impact may be that the affluent will purchase security at the expense of those who can't afford to keep up with them. As alarm sales soar, the burden of victimization will be displaced, falling even more squarely on families that don't have much to lose but who do have a great deal of trouble replacing stolen items.

The most sophisticated (and expensive) systems are creating a headache for the police and the public plus unanticipated risks for their owners. Infrared, photoelectric, microwave, or ultrasonic detectors trigger "silent" alarms rather than ear-piercing sirens. The silent alarm is actually a recorded message that is automatically telephoned to a private guard service or to the nearest police station. The trouble is that 98 percent of the time they are false alarms, according to police records in Los Angeles. The Los Angeles Police Department estimates that 10 percent of all calls for service are investigations of tripped alarms, which waste 200,000 hours of police time annually. In New York City, about 15 percent of all radio-car runs are in response to silent automatic alarms that either malfunctioned or were set off accidentally. In some midtown precincts, more than 30 percent of police manpower is lost checking out false alarms.

To bring the false alarm problem under control, Pasadena, California, requires owners of security systems to obtain permits. Los Angeles has begun to fine "chronic alarm abusers" by charging them for unnecessary police service calls. The New York Police Department lobbied unsuccessfully for years for state legislation that would have imposed higher technical standards on alarm manufacturers. Failing that, in frustration, the department adopted a policy of ignoring the recorded pleas for help from silent alarm systems that have "cried wolf" too many times in the past (Buder, 1981; "L.A. Police," 1982).

What good is an expensive "peace of mind" system that doesn't frighten intruders away, doesn't alert neighbors that a break-in is in progress, and doesn't summon police to the scene to catch the criminal in the act?

Capitalizing on violence: bulletproof clothing. In the Middle Ages, knights wore chain mail suits when they battled their enemies. As weaponry improved, body armor lost its importance. Until recently, only policemen and soldiers on particularly hazardous duty donned cumbersome vests and flak jackets. Then Kevlar was perfected. A lightweight nylon fabric composed of fibers five times stronger than the steel strands in cables, it was developed as a puncture-resistant material for automobile tires. Realizing that it could stop bullets as well as nails, the Du Pont company enthusiastically marketed it as a new version of body armor. Police forces across the country stocked up on Kevlar-lined undershirts and vests. Public officials and political leaders wary of assassins' bullets took to wearing Kevlar clothing. Business executives, storekeepers, and even taxicab drivers snatched up these garments. Now affluent people who are crime conscious as well as fashion conscious can outfit themselves in a smart new line of "high-caliber ballistic apparel." A dozen companies are rushing into production trendy bullet-resistant jumpsuits, safari jackets, parkas, dress shirts, and umbrellas, available in pastel hues. Body armor is marketed as "one answer to the escalating crime rate and rise in terrorism," ideal for "today's active life-styles" because wearers can go where they want in safety (Troup, 1982).

This commercial solution for those who fear that they will come under fire is creating a new problem. Predictably, bulletproof clothing is beginning to show up adorning well-prepared criminals. Some manufacturers make an effort to prevent their product from "getting into the wrong hands," but others indiscriminately accept mail orders, no questions asked.

A debate that bears a striking resemblance to the handgun controversy has broken out. Some members of Congress wanted to pass legislation to license both the sellers and buyers of bullet-resistant clothing, following the firearms model. A similar bill in the New York State Legislature attached an additional proviso: anyone caught committing a serious crime while wearing body armor can be charged with a second felony (just as the use of a gun adds to the severity of an offense). But proponents of citizens' arming themselves against criminals objected that it is unfair to deprive innocent victims of the protection they might need. Their slogan will probably be, "If bulletproof clothing is outlawed, only outlaws will wear bulletproof clothing" (Hinds, 1981; Press and Clausen, 1982).

The invention of body armor has touched off still another round in the domestic arms race. "Super bullets" tipped with Teflon have become available to pierce the so-called "bulletproof" clothing made of Kevlar. Originally developed to improve the penetrating power of police ammunition to enable officers to shoot suspects inside automobiles or behind barricades, these extra deadly bullets now pose a threat to law enforcement agents (and civilians) who thought they had purchased security by buying body armor. A bill designed to disarm criminals by prohibiting the manufacture, importation, and sale of these "cop-killer" bullets (except for police and military use) was introduced in Congress in 1982 and again in 1983. But it faced stiff opposition from the gun lobby, which argued that banning these bullets could lead to further restrictions on the availability of other kinds of ammunition and weapons. Ultimately, the right of citizens to bear arms in self-defense or for sport would be infringed upon, they contended ("Curbs on 'Cop-Killer' Ammunition," 1983).

As new, higher levels of preparedness are achieved both by police forces and by civilians who fear victimization by criminals, disturbing questions arise: Is the net result of the sales of these products a safer, less violent social environment or a potentially more deadly situation, with more severely wounded casualties and a higher body count? Have commercial interests exploited the rediscovery of victims and legitimate concerns about criminal violence?

Social Movements: Taking Up the Victim's Cause

Aside from their misfortune, victims have very little in common. They differ in age, sex, race, class, and other important factors. Despite efforts to organize them, victims of street crime are just too diverse to coalesce into a movement of their own. However, other social movements have discovered that their goals coincide with those of particular groups of victims. The most important contributions to the cause of victims are being made by the women's movement, the law and order movement, and the civil rights and civil liberties movements.

The women's movement. Victims of rape, wife beating, street harassment, sexual harassment at work, and incest have been rediscovered by the feminist movement in the course of its struggle against sexism.

The feminists of the 1800s and early 1900s fought primarily for the rights of women to own property, participate in political affairs, and vote. The contemporary movement began in the late 1960s by challenging the discrimination that women faced in education and employment. By the early 1970s, its focus had grown to incorporate demands by women to control their own bodies. The silence that traditionally shrouded the taboo subjects of abortion and rape (and later wife beating, sexual harassment, and incest) was shattered at consciousness-raising gatherings called "speak-outs," where victims shared their experiences with sympathetic audiences.

The first grass-roots efforts to help crime victims were initiated in 1972, when radical feminists in Berkeley, California, and Washington, D. C., set up rape crisis centers. The idea of providing concrete aid to rape victims spread rapidly. By 1979, over one thousand community projects were in operation. They offered twenty-four-hour hot lines, escorts to accompany victims to hospital emergency rooms and police stations, counseling, and referrals. The staff members, often volunteers who had been victims of sexual assault themselves, acted as advocates to prevent further indignities. Besides furnishing services, the centers engaged in community education programs and in political action to reform the operations of the criminal justice system. A Rape Task Force set up by the National Organization for Women (NOW) helped make rape a significant social issue. In 1976, lobbyists were able to establish a federally funded, research-oriented National Center for the Prevention and Control of Rape within the Department of Health, Education and Welfare (now Health and Human Services). A National Coalition against Sexual Assault improved communication and coordination between rape crisis centers and victim advocates in the continuing struggle to cut the crime rate and improve services for victims (Largen, 1981: 46–52).

By 1977, forty-five states had revised their rape statutes to eliminate certain anti-victim features, especially double standards concerning testimony, evidence, and definitions of appropriate conduct. In some communities, the movement successfully pressured the police department to set up innovative sexual-assault and rape-analysis units, staffed by specially trained officers (Rose, 1977).

The movement to shelter battered women paralleled the pro-victim, anti-rape movement in a number of ways. Both were initiated for the most part by former victims. Both developed a political position that rape and battering are societal and institutional problems rather than personal troubles and instances of individual failings. Both sought to empower victims by confronting established authority, challenging existing procedures, providing peer support and advocacy, and opening up alternative places to go for assistance. The refuges, or "safe houses," for victims of wife beating provided services similar to those offered to rape victims at crisis centers: hot lines, advocates, consciousness-raising groups, counseling, and referrals, plus food and shelter. A federal Office on Domestic Violence coordinated activities, and a National Coalition Against Domestic Violence, begun in 1978, lobbied for new administrative policies and legislation to assist battered women and their children (Capps and Myhre, 1982: 8–13).

Since the shelter movement was not content to let the problem of wife beating remain a "family matter" best handled behind closed doors, it struggled to implement reforms to improve the lot of victims of domestic violence. As with rape, police procedures came under fire and were partly revised. Special training was given in techniques of crisis intervention, and no-arrest policies were ended. Prosecutors were urged to press charges more often if that was what the victims wanted, and judges were encouraged to sentence abusive men to treatment programs and to grant orders of protection more readily to women in danger. Opportunities were broadened for victims to receive counseling; public assistance; legal advice about child custody, separation, divorce, and alimony; job training and placement; and more schooling. Hospital emergency room procedures were reformed as well.

The overall analysis that has guided the women's movement holds that certain male-versus-female offenses (such as rape, wife beating, sexual harassment in the streets and at work, and incest) oppress all women and slow down progress toward equality and liberation. The burden falls most heavily on women with social disadvantages due to economic insecurity, racial discrimination, and separation or divorce. The men at the helm of the criminal justice system have demonstrated that they cannot be counted on to effectively protect or assist victimized women, so victims themselves must be granted power to defend their own interests. Despite the prevalence of a widespread ideology that blames victims of rape, battering, and harassment for their own plight, it is the fundamental institutions on which this social system is built that are the root causes of the crime problems women face. Offenses committed by men against women are reflections of a stubborn and pervasive sexism deeply embedded in the culture (Karmen, 1982). (See box 1-3.)

BOX 1-3 Taking Back the Night

Riddling American popular culture is a perverse preoccupation with stories that accentuate the theme of women as victims. Songs, magazines, television programs, movies, and novels dwell on accounts of women taken captive, bound, gagged, beaten, raped, slashed, mutilated, tortured, and dismembered by psychopaths, motorcycle gangs, monsters, and alien invaders. From cartoons and fairy tales to horror films, plots portray females as weak damsels in distress, passive sex toys, and even willing victims who get what they want or deserve. Pictures of women in humiliating poses assault passersby from newsstands, billboards, and the window displays of fashionable stores.

Angry feminists are finding the relentless barrage of images of women as defenseless victims intolerable. The media blitz of slick, stylized, and glamorized orgies of female degradation and pain has provoked a protest movement. Its goal is to stifle the commercial exploitation of women's suffering, as a step in the struggle to reduce the level of real-life violence directed at women. Its thrust is captured best by the slogan "Take Back the Night," which symbolizes the yearning to regain the freedom to walk about without being stereotyped as "fair game" by males inclined toward sexual harassment and assault. Movement activists are employing a variety of consciousness-raising techniques, including letter-writing campaigns, leafleting, demonstrations, and consumer boycotts. Their pressure tactics have been directed at theater marquees promoting horror movies, record album covers depicting females in pain, pornographic "snuff" films coupling graphic violence with vivid sex, and trend-setting clothing stores featuring "battered chic" styles (where models with bandaged feet and painted-on bruises act disoriented, as if they had just been raped or beaten).

The not-so-subtle messages that are part of a frightening, crippling ideology that infuriates feminists are as follows: that women like to be beaten and enjoy being overpowered and "taken" against their will; that females are handy and appropriate targets for male wrath; that watching women squirm and suffer is entertaining and titillating; and that inflicting mental or physical pain is a legitimate and natural thing for men to do. Activists suspect that in a sexually segregated society males learn about females and about sexuality from pornography and milder forms of sadomasochistic "entertainment." Because women are represented as craving abusive treatment, some males confuse acting violently and being sexually aggressive with courting and expressing romantic interest. The daily exposure of millions of people to anti-female propaganda has not been proven harmless; important new research raises the specter that watching violence against women can contribute to a climate in which too many people are too unmoved about the ordeals of molested children, battered women, and rape victims. The escalating media obsession with sexual violence is interpreted as evidence of the depth of woman-hating and of its acceptability in some quarters. The hate campaign, according to feminist analysis, reflects a growing willingness on the part of some men to resort to force as the ultimate weapon to maintain their increasingly tenuous supremacy over females.

Marchers who want to "Take Back the Night" are dissatisfied with a society in which women have to restrict their activities in order to be reasonably secure. They reject a strategy in which women must rely on men to accompany them as their protectors as a self-defeating one that guarantees continued subordination (see Burgess, 1983; Lederer, 1980).

The law and order movement. For many decades, a movement to restore "law and order" has waged a campaign to win support for a crackdown on crime. In the mid-1960s, law and order advocates added another indictment to their criticisms of the criminal justice system: besides being too "soft" in its handling of criminals, the system was indifferent to the punitive urges of victims. Getting tough with offenders was presented as a way of vindicating victims. Criminal justice procedures were viewed as out of balance, "tilted" in favor of wrongdoers instead of injured parties. The argument that the pendulum had swung too far in the direction of defendants and convicts gained credibility as most people worried more about becoming a victim than about finding themselves falsely accused or unjustly imprisoned (Hook, 1972).

Law and order groups, like Americans for Effective Law Enforcement (founded in 1966) and the National Victims Organization (started in 1981), have been fighting in the political arena to implement their vision of a "victim-oriented" criminal justice system. Fundamentally, it would put more stress on punishment; "permissiveness"—unwarranted leniency—would be rooted out. Imprisonment of offenders would be more certain, swift, and severe. The use of bail, probation, and parole would be restricted. The police, prosecutors, and prison officials would enjoy more power over offenders, and victims would exercise more influence in determining sentences (see Carrington, 1975).

The civil rights and civil liberties movements. For decades, alliances have been forged between civil rights groups—like the National Association for the Advancement of Colored People (NAACP), the NAACP Legal Defense Fund, the Southern Poverty Law Center, the National Conference of Black Lawyers, and the Urban League—and civil liberties groups—such as the American Civil Liberties Union (ACLU), the National Lawyer's Guild, the Center for Constitutional Rights, and the National Coalition Against Repressive Legislation. The main concern of civil rights groups has been the struggle for racial equality in the face of discrimination and intimidation. The central thrust of civil liberties groups has been to preserve and extend constitutional rights and due process guarantees to all, especially those who are poor, powerless, or unpopular.

The greatest achievements of the civil rights movement, as far as crime victims are concerned, have been made in the struggle against racist violence. Civil rights groups have rallied to the defense of victims of terrorist attacks (for example, by the Ku Klux Klan), of police brutality, and of miscarriages of justice (suspected frame-ups such as the trials of the Scottsboro Boys of the 1930s and of the leaders of the Black Panther party during the 1960s and 1970s).

Civil rights groups have always argued that a discriminatory double standard infects the operations of the criminal justice system. Crimes by blacks against whites are treated as high-priority cases, whereas crimes by whites against blacks are largely ignored. The recent rediscovery of "black-on-black" crime shed light on another facet of the discrimination problem: crimes by blacks against blacks were also not taken too seriously; all crimes with black victims seemed to be given low priority by criminal justice officials. Speakers for minority communities and organizations began to address this problem during the 1970s (see "Black on Black Crime," 1979). They pointed out that blacks were victimized more frequently than whites in almost every category of street crime; that fear levels were higher in ghettos than in white neighborhoods; that most blacks who were murdered, raped, robbed, or beaten were attacked by other blacks; that hostility and mistrust due to crime were poisoning the quality of life in black communities and undermining the political solidarity needed for progress; and that rising rates of street crime and arson were destroying housing, driving away jobs, and closing down services.

The brunt of the criticism over unequal treatment under the law has been leveled at the police, accusing them of acting more as an army of occupation in ghetto neighborhoods than as the protector of black (and Hispanic) lives and property. These charges were voiced throughout the riot-scarred 1960s, and they were raised again from 1979 to 1982 with regard to the investigation into the murders of twenty-nine black youths in Atlanta.

Civil liberties groups have been branded as "anti-victim" (Carrington, 1975) and as a "criminal's lobby" by staunch advocates of hard-line policies. Speakers for the conservative law and order movement have contended that liberals and radical leftists in the civil liberties movement show excessive concern for the rights of suspects, defendants, and prisoners at the expense of law-abiding citizens and innocent victims. They have charged that street-wise criminals can "beat the system" by manipulating the rules and using legal technicalities (loopholes) while the police stand by "handcuffed" by restrictions. This supposed imbalance is traced to victories by civil liberties advocates before the U.S. Supreme Court, starting in the 1950s and extending through the early 1970s. These decisions expanded the protections of the Fourth (the *Mapp* decision), Fifth *(Miranda),* Sixth *(Gideon, Escobedo),* and Eighth *(Furman)* Amendments to the U.S. Constitution to state criminal procedures. What the critics of the civil liberties movement fail to appreciate is the contribution these reforms have made toward easing the plight of crime victims. The civil liberties movement has aided victims in two ways: first, by furthering police professionalism; second, by extending guarantees of equal protection of the law to victims who were formerly neglected (Walker, 1982).

Civil liberties victories have stimulated police professionalism in the form of improved hiring procedures, higher qualifications for officers, better training, and closer supervision. As a result, victims are more likely to receive prompt responses, sensitive (nonsexist, nonracist) treatment, and effective service. If they don't, channels have been established for the redress of grievances. The extension of equal-protection guarantees has led to greater access to police and prosecutorial assistance by groups that were previously given second-class service because of their poverty, powerlessness, sex, or race.

Other social movements. In addition to the law and order, feminist, civil rights, and civil liberties movements, important contributions to the rediscovery process have been made by other social movements. They rallied to the defense of particular groups of victims during the 1960s and 1970s and have continued into the 1980s. These include the children's rights, consumer rights, homosexual rights, elderly people's and self-help movements.

The children's rights movement has fought child abuse by defining the limits of permissible punishments of minors by their parents and guardians. The problem of consumer fraud and "rip-offs" has been a major focus of the consumer rights movement. The gay rights movement has pointed up the special vulnerability of homosexuals to robbery, blackmail, violence by bigots, mobster exploitation of commercial services, and police harassment. The senior citizen's movement has succeeded in bringing about the formation of special police units (to combat robbery and confidence games and to teach crime prevention tips), in getting legislation passed that stiffens the penalties for victimizing people over age sixty, and in establishing assistance programs for older victims (for example, round-the-clock locksmith services for burglary victims, escort services for shopping trips, and direct-deposit arrangements with banks for Social Security checks). The special needs of the unusually vulnerable elderly have been the subject of White House conferences, congressional hearings, and many state and local programs and studies (see Boston, 1977; Center, 1980; Goldsmith and Goldsmith, 1976; Hahn, 1976; Hochstedler, 1981).

Groups loosely affiliated with the self-help movement can be credited with some of the most dramatic advances in behalf of crime victims. Drawing on the participatory spirit of the protest movements of the 1960s and the self-improvement themes of the human potential decade of the 1970s, the self-help movement is fed by an impatience with and a distrust of big government, distant bureaucracies, and professional care givers. Self-help groups bring together people who have the same problems. They provide mutual assistance and reliable support networks. Their underlying principles are that the most effective aid can come from people who have been through an experience themselves and that, by accepting the role of helper and providing care, victims are themselves sped along the road to recovery. Members of self-help groups must overcome the stigma of admitting that they are burdened by some problem; crime victims must acknowledge that they have been "bested" by an opponent, injured, harmed, exploited, or perhaps duped. Then they can pursue a course of action that combines taking personal responsiblity for coping with distressing situations in everyday life with political activism to spare others such troubles in the future. Self-help groups have been organized to tackle almost every problem imaginable, such as VOICE (Victims of Incest Can Emerge) (Gartner and Riessman, 1980; Fulman, 1983). Notable achievements have been made by rape victims who set up crisis centers, battered women who established shelters, targets of racist violence who organized self-defense groups, and bereaved parents of murdered, missing, or molested children (see box 1-4).

The Rise of Victimology

The Emergence of a New Focus

While victims were being rediscovered by the law and order movement, criminal justice agencies, civil rights and civil liberties groups, feminists, self-help advocates, the media, and commercial interests, they were also being rediscovered by criminologists. For some time, criminology had been a rapidly expanding field. Criminologists were tackling all aspects of lawlessness—investigating offenders, their methods and motives, the laws directed at them, and the operations of the criminal justice system (police, courts, and prisons). Inevitably, by the process of elimination if nothing else, a small number of criminologists stumbled on victims as a largely ignored group worthy of scientific attention. (See box 1–5.)

Once the term "victimology" was coined to refer to the scientific study of victims, a debate erupted over the boundaries of the field. Some want to restrict the focus to people harmed by illegal acts. Others want to go well beyond the limits of crime in order to embrace victims of accidents, illnesses, natural disasters, and socially harmful policies (such as discrimination, political repression, genocide, and war). (For the pros and cons of these alternative visions of what victimology ought to be, see Friedrichs, 1983; Galaway and Hudson, 1981; Schafer, 1968; Scherer, 1982; Schneider, 1982; Viano, 1976.)

The Scope of Inquiry

Victimology does not have the contending schools of thought that divide criminologists into opposing camps because it lacks well-developed theories. The major split among victimologists centers on a question of emphasis. Some have continued to pursue the original inquiries of the founders of the field by laying bare the many ways in which victims might contribute to their own injuries and losses. Their goal is to prevent

BOX 1-4 Self-Help Groups for Parents of Victimized Children

- *Dealing with Death: "Compassionate Friends" and "Parents of Murdered Children"*

Two self-help groups are meeting the needs of the growing numbers of parents who have lost their children to criminal violence. When a child dies by accident or from illness, distraught parents are beset by many feelings—sadness, disbelief, loneliness, fear, anger, guilt, despair, personal loss. When a child meets sudden violent death at the hands of a molester, robber, lover, playmate, or estranged family member, the grieving process is complicated by the intrusions of the police, prosecutors, judges, juries, and the media, all of whom seek information, evidence, or testimony.

The traditional sources of solace in times of great emotional stress and crisis—doctors, psychotherapists, clergy, family, and close friends—are often ill prepared to give comfort and advice. Self-help organizations now fill this void. Compassionate Friends originated in Coventry, England, in 1969 when some bereaved parents met by coincidence at a hospital. Since 1972, it has set up 150 chapters in the United States and Canada. As it grew, it gave birth to another group, which focuses entirely on the special tribulations of survivors who have to deal with the criminal justice system and media coverage in addition to their own problems. As of 1982, Parents of Murdered Children, a nondenominational support network financed by contributions, had established twenty chapters since its founding in 1978.

The goals of these self-help groups are to offer support and friendship, to improve understanding of the stages in the grieving process, and to share information about criminal justice procedures as they affect survivors of murdered children.

When parents die, survivors lose their past; when children die, survivors lose their future. Recognizing that grief is an expression of love, these groups help their members search for a meaningful life beyond the pain ("Compassionate Friends," 1979: 6; Leerhsen, Abramson, and Prout, 1982: 84).

- *Locating Missing Children: "Child Find" and "Search"*

Every year, approximately 50,000 children across the country are kidnapped by strangers. Only about 5,000 are located and returned to their parents. As many as 5,000 are murdered. The remaining 40,000 simply vanish. Perhaps they are in the clutches of child molesters, "kiddie porn" and prostitution rings, or black market adoption syndicates. Another 100,000 kidnappings are committed not by strangers, but by one divorced or separated parent who wrests custody of a child from the other. Since these abductions turn children into pawns within intrafamily power struggles, it is safe to say that any missing child is a child in danger, as either a "probable runaway" or a "potential victim."

Until recently, distraught parents and relatives had few outlets in which to channel their energies. Then some parents who did not know if their children were dead or alive banded together to form two self-help groups, Child Find, in New Paltz, New York, and Search, in Englewood Cliffs, New Jersey. Both serve as clearinghouses—disseminating reports packed with photos to schools, clinics, social service agencies, and police departments—and as pressure groups—seeking to make the criminal justice system more responsive to their problems.

These self-help organizations criticize local police departments for their inaction and lack of interest. According to searching parents, since so many missing youngsters are runaways, police usually do not act on a report for 24 hours unless there is evidence of foul play or the child is very young. In some cases, because of this policy, when an investigation finally is launched, it is too late. Furthermore, local police departments are reluctant to enlist outside help, reporting less than 15 percent of missing children cases to a nationwide file.

The way the FBI ran its National Crime Information Center (NCIC), a master computerized record-keeping system set up in 1967, also left much to be desired.

Cars, handguns, and stolen silverware could be registered, traced, and recovered more readily than missing children. Provisions were made for storing driver's license and Social Security numbers, which are of little use in tracking down missing children, but the computerized files could not accommodate crucial data concerning identifying scars, blood types, or dental records. Late in 1982, a two-year campaign waged by these self-help groups proved successful. Congress passed a Missing Children's Act, expanding the descriptive data that could be entered into the FBI's NCIC computer and improving the access of parents to this national file (Cohodas, 1982: 2143; "Missing Children: More Hope, Help Needed," 1983; Turbak, 1982).

As parental concern over the nightmare of abduction heightens, thousands of children in more than a dozen states are being fingerprinted voluntarily. Usually, the only copies of the prints are retained by their parents for safekeeping, but in some localities police departments keep sets as well. Civil libertarians have warned that this practice smacks of "big brotherism" and poses a threat to individual privacy should the records ever be used for criminal investigations (to solve burglaries by teenagers, for example). Concerns have also been voiced that mass fingerprinting creates an atmosphere of unfounded fear of kidnapping and paranoia about police intentions among youngsters. Parents of missing children are among the staunchest advocates of the fingerprinting programs ("Fingerprinting of Children Spreading," 1983).

- *Curbing Car Crashes: "Remove Intoxicated Drivers" and "Mothers Against Drunk Drivers"*

Alcohol-impaired drivers cause roughly half of all fatal car crashes. Two self-help groups founded by parents whose children were killed in such accidents have sprung up to try to change these statistics. Remove Intoxicated Drivers (RID) has set up 60 affiliates in 38 states since 1976. RID monitors how seriously local elected officials take the drunk-driving problem and publishes a scorecard noting their votes on legislative reform measures. Its members believe that suspending driving privileges is the most effective deterrent. Mothers Against Drunk Drivers (MADD) has grown to 59 chapters in 29 states in the years since its inception in 1980. Its non-profit services include counseling for victims and survivors. MADD's lobbying has influenced lawmakers in at least five states toward making the punishment for drunk driving more certain and more severe. MADD members have begun to analyze the role of drinking and getting drunk as a rite of passage for teenage boys aspiring to be young men (Lindamood, 1982).

- *Crusading against Sexual Abuse: "Society's League Against Molestation"*

By conservative estimates, one out of every ten children is sexually abused each year, often by a trusted authority figure like a teacher, doctor, camp counselor, or parent. Up to two-thirds of all molestation cases probably never come to light. Children are unusually vulnerable victims, since they can be persuaded to cooperate and then intimidated or embarrassed into keeping the incident secret. That silence can be the source of their most intense emotional suffering, far worse than their physical pain.

An organization called Society's League Against Molestation (SLAM) has lobbied successfully for five state laws that make the crime more severely punishable. SLAM has set up forty-five chapters in California and seven counterparts in other states since it was founded in 1978 by a grandmother of a two-year-old who had been raped, mutilated, and murdered. The group believes that the best way to prevent child molestation is to keep offenders locked away from their prey. It argues that molesters should be sent to prisons rather than to state mental hospitals, where they will be neither cured nor confined for very long. Critics of SLAM's get-tough approach consider pedophilia to be a treatable mental illness, and they predict that imprisoning molesters will only reinforce offenders' drives and ultimately increase the threat they pose to youth when they are released (Salholz et al., 1982).

BOX 1-5 Highlights of the Brief History of Victimology

1941 Hans Von Hentig writes an article about the victim–criminal interaction.
1947 Benjamin Mendelsohn coins the term *victimology* in an article.
1957 The British criminal justice reformer Margery Fry stimulates discussion and debate about how to reimburse victims.
1958 Marvin Wolfgang sheds light on victim-precipitated homicide.
1964 Congress rejects victim compensation legislation but studies the victim's plight for the first time.
1965 California enacts victim compensation legislation and begins keeping records of financial hardships imposed by crime.
1966 The first nationwide victimization survey is carried out.
1968 Stephen Schafer writes the first textbook about victims.
1973 The First International Symposium on Victimology is held in Jerusalem.
1975 The International Study Institute on Victimology is held in Bellagio, Italy. The National Organization for Victim Assistance is founded.
1976 The Second International Symposium on Victimology is held in Boston. *Victimology: An International Journal* begins publication.
1979 The Third International Symposium on Victimology is held in Münster, West Germany. The World Society of Victimology is founded.
1980 The First World Congress on Victimology is held in Washington, D.C.
1981 President Ronald Reagan proclaims April 8–14 Victims Rights Week.
1982 The Second International Study Institute on Victimology is held in Bellagio, Italy. The Fourth International Symposium on Victimology is held in Tokyo.
1983 The President's Task Force on Victims of Crime studies problems and recommends changes in the Constitution and in federal and state laws to guarantee victims' rights.

SOURCE: Galaway and Hudson, 1981; Schneider, 1982.

victimizations in the future by educating potential targets and by learning from other people's mistakes. More recently, a current has developed within victimology that stresses the importance of making victims "whole" again—restoring them to the condition they were in before the crimes took place. These victimologists search for ways of ameliorating physical, emotional, and financial suffering.

Victimology parallels criminology along many dimensions. Criminologists seek out the causes of crime and study the offenders' motives. Victimologists examine the victims' reasons (if any) for placing themselves in risky situations. Offenders are held personally accountable for their lawbreaking, but criminologists explore the possibility that social (cultural), economic, and political forces might contribute to the conditions that generate criminal activity. Similarly, victims might share responsibility with offenders for specific crimes, but larger forces might shape their encounters. Just as criminal behavior can be learned, victims might be taught to play (and accept) their subordinate roles. Criminologists scrutinize the manner in which defendants and convicts are handled by the criminal justice system. Victimologists study how the police, prosecutors, courts, and related agencies handle victims. Criminologists evaluate the effectiveness of treatment and rehabilitation programs intended to transform criminals into law-abiding citizens. Victimologists gauge the efficiency of private and public efforts to reimburse victims for their losses and meet their personal needs. Public opinion about victims (stereotypes, support for various policies, willingness to allocate funds) can be compared to widely held attitudes about criminals. So far, several sets of related questions have captured the attention of most victimologists (Parsonage, 1979). The first set concerns efforts to determine the full extent and true nature of the crime problem, and the varying risks that confront different categories of people.

The following issues, dealing with patterns and trends in victimization, will be examined in chapter 2:

- What are the weaknesses of official crime statistics?
- What are the strengths and weaknesses of victimization surveys?
- According to victimization surveys, who bears the brunt of the burden?
- What differences in risks occur by sex, age, race, and locale?
- What lifestyle factors account for differences in risks?
- What patterns of costs and losses emerge from the data?
- What patterns of injury and resistance emerge?
- What trends are discernible over the ten years of surveys?

Questions examining the controversy over shared responsibility will be covered in chapters 3 and 4:

- What is the meaning of shared responsibility?
- What situations increase vulnerability to criminal attack?
- What acts illustrate facilitation, precipitation, and provocation?
- What is the frequency of shared responsibility?
- What would constitute total innocence and complete guilt?
- What evidence is there for the existence of victim proneness?
- Is victimology inherently wedded to a victim-blaming outlook?
- What is the opposite, victim defending?
- What are the consequences of attempts to fix blame and uncover shared responsibility?
- What are the implications of holding a victim accountable for his or her actions?

A third set of questions asked by victimologists is concerned with the victim's experiences within the criminal justice system.

Chapter 5 deals with conflicts between victims and the police, prosecutors, defense attorneys, judges, and parole boards:

- What are the functions of the criminal justice system, according to various competing theories?
- Whose interests are served by the system?
- What conflicts arise between victims and the police?
- To what extent have conflicts been resolved by police retraining, the use of intermediaries, and the development of crisis centers and similar supplementary services?
- What conflicts arise between victims and prosecutors?
- Can prosecutors serve the interests of the state and their victim clients simultaneously?
- Should victims be allowed to retain private prosecutors?
- To what extent have conflicts been resolved by providing victim–witness assistance programs through the offices of district attorneys?
- What conflicts arise between victims and defense lawyers?
- Must victims be degraded by the adversarial system?
- What conflicts arise between victims and judges?
- Should victims be a party to plea bargaining? Bail determination?
- What role, if any, should victims play in sentencing?
- What is the victim's stake in retribution? Rehabilitation? Deterrence? Incapacitation?

Chapter 6 addresses questions that victimologists ask about the possibility of restitution by the offender to the victim:

- What provisions existed for restitution in antiquity?
- At what points in the criminal justice process can restitution be arranged?
- What experiments in offender restitution have been tried?
- Will restitution lead to reconciliation? Should restitution be reconciliation oriented? Rehabilitation oriented?
- What are the limits of restitution? Which crime victims cannot be repaid or should not be repaid?
- What are the advantages and disadvantages of civil lawsuits?
- What are the prospects for civil suits against third parties indirectly responsible for crimes?

Questions dealing with compensation by the state to the victim are the subject of chapter 7:

- What provisions existed for compensation in antiquity?
- When did interest in compensation revive? Why?
- What were the initial ideological attacks on compensation?
- What rationales justify government aid to crime victims?
- Should compensation be a federal or state obligation?
- What measures will help to contain costs?
- For what losses should compensation be permitted?

- What potential impact will compensation have on the crime rate and on public cooperation with police and prosecutors?
- How can the effectiveness of compensation programs be evaluated?

A final set of questions is concerned with the future of victimology and victim aid. These are examined in chapter 8:

- What are the contradictory trends toward formalism and informalism?
- What are the provisions of a "crime victims' bill of rights"?
- At whose expense will victims' rights be gained, the defendant's or the state's?
- Will victim services be supported by penalties levied on convicts?
- Will victim services be stunted by cutbacks in social spending?
- What victim interests are served by the development of informal alternatives (dispute resolution based on mediation and arbitration) to formal adjudication in criminal or civil court? What formal rights are jeopardized?
- Has the vigilante impulse been contained? Will violence in the name of the victim emerge as another "informal" alternative?

To date, victimologists have been most interested in crimes that are marked by violence (especially sexual abuse) or involve theft and deception. Victimologists have not yet devoted sufficient attention to illegal acts that do not have a single, clearly identifiable person as the injured party. Studies are needed of the victims of acts of omission and neglect, as well as of victimized organizations and entire classes of people (like workers or consumers) that are harmed by violations of law. The human toll exacted by those lawbreakers who are holding public office or representing powerful vested interests has also escaped the scrutiny of most victimologists (Viano, 1983).

Box 1-6 provides a small sampling of the wide variety of studies carried out by victimologists.

The rise of victimology has reversed the historical trend of neglecting victims (which initially inspired the emergence of victimology). In sharp contrast to the indictment of society in general, and the criminal justice system in particular, for ignoring the concerns and interests of victims, some recent developments indicate that professional and public consciousness about the victim's plight has been raised:

- In Chicago, the police use "show and tell me" anatomically detailed rag dolls to facilitate communication between investigators and children who were molested or sexually assaulted but are too young, too scared, or too embarrassed to describe exactly what happened to them ("Police Use Dolls in Child Sex Cases," 1981).
- In Nassau County, New York, the police project full-size color slides

BOX 1-6 What Do Victimologists Do?

- *Testing What Could Trigger a Mugger into Action*

  Pedestrians may signal to prowling criminals by their body language that they are "easy marks."

  Men and women walking down a New York City street were secretly videotaped for several seconds, about the time it takes a criminally inclined person to size up a potential victim. The tapes were then shown to a panel of "experts"—prisoners convicted of assaulting strangers—who sorted out those who looked as if they would be easy to corner from those who might give them a hard time. Individuals who received high "muggability" ratings tended to move along awkwardly, unaware that their nonverbal communication might cause them t rouble (Grayson, in Cloud, 1981).

- *Studying Bias against Victims of White Collar Crime*

  People who have lost money to nonviolent white collar criminals (like swindlers and con artists) often encounter skepticism, suspicion, and contempt when they seek help. This negative treatment leaves them feeling guilty and ashamed. The double standard in handling white collar offenders and their victims—as opposed to the treatment of street criminals and their victims (except rape victims)—has been explained in terms of the higher status of the accused perpetrators, the difficulty of establishing criminal intent in such cases, and a belief that punishment is not the cure for this kind of stealing.

  But another factor is the largely ambivalent attitude toward and negative image of these victims held by the public and by criminal justice officials. A number of aphorisms blame these victims: fraud only befalls those of questionable character; an honest man can't be cheated; people must have larceny in their mind to fall for a con game; and the victims were asking for trouble and got what they deserved. The stereotype of cheated parties is that they disregard the basic rules of sensible conduct regarding financial matters. They don't read contracts before signing and don't demand that guarantees be put in writing before making purchases. Their stupidity, carelessness, or complicity undermines their credibility and saps any enthusiasm to activate the machinery of the criminal justice system in their behalf. A reluctance develops to formally condemn and punish those who harmed them or to validate their claims to be treated as authentic victims worthy of support rather than mere dupes, losers, or suckers who were outsmarted (Walsh and Schram, 1980).

- *Examining How Victims Are Viewed by Pickpockets*

  According to twenty *class cannons* (professional pickpockets) working the streets of Miami, Florida, their preferred *marks* (victims) are tourists who are relaxed, off guard, loaded with money, and lacking in clout with criminal justice

---

and play tapes of suspects' voices to help victims identify their assailants (Van Haintze and Williams, 1983).

- At Colorado State University, a Center for Human Identification provides technical assistance and training for law enforcement agencies in forensic science so that the close friends and relatives of a missing person can find out whether a badly mutilated, decomposed, or burned corpse (of which there are about 20,000 a year) constitutes the

officials. Some pickpockets choose *paps* (elderly men), because their reaction time is lower, but others favor *bates* (middle-aged men), because they tend to carry more valuables. A *moll buzzer*, or *hanger binger* (sneak thief who preys on women), is looked down on in the underworld fraternity as acting without skill or courage.

Interaction with victims is kept to a minimum. Although pickpockets may *trace a mark* (follow an intended victim) for some time, they need just a few seconds to *beat him of his poke* (steal his wallet). This is done quietly and deftly, without a commotion or any jostling. They rarely *make a score* (steal a lot in a single incident). The class cannon *passes* (hands over) *the loot* (wallet, wad of bills) to a member of his *mob* (an accomplice) and swiftly leaves the scene of the crime. Only about one time in a hundred do they get caught by the mark. When the theft is detected, they can usually persuade their victims not to call the police. They give back what they took (maybe more than they stole) and point out that pressing charges can ruin a vacation because of the need to surrender the wallet as evidence and the wasting of time required by court appearances. Cannons show no hatred or contempt for their marks. They rationalize their crimes as impersonal acts directed at targets who can easily afford the losses or who would otherwise be fleeced or swindled by businessmen and other exploitive *legal types* (Inciardi, 1976).

- *Exploring the Bonds between Captives and Their Captors*

Hostages (of terrorists, "skyjackers," kidnappers, bank robbers, rebellious prisoners, and gunmen who go berserk) are used by their captors to exert leverage on a third party—perhaps a family, the police, or some government agency. These victims frequently react to their exploitation in a surprising way. Instead of showing anger and seeking revenge, these pawns, or bargaining chips in a larger drama, may emerge from the siege feeling warmth for, and attachment to, the lawbreakers. Their outrage is directed at the authorities who rescued them, presumably for acting with life-threatening indifference during the protracted negotiations. This surprising emotional realignment has been termed the "Stockholm Syndrome," because it was first noted after a 1973 bank holdup in Sweden.

Several psychological explanations for this "pathological transference" are plausible: the hostages may be identifying with the aggressor; they may be sympathetic to acts of defiance aimed at the establishment; as survivors, they may harbor intense feelings of gratitude toward their keepers for sparing their lives; or as helpless dependents, they may cling to the powerful figures who are endangering them because of a primitive emotional response called "traumatical infantilism." After the ordeal, these terrorized victims need to be welcomed back and reassured that they did nothing wrong during—and right after—their captivity (Fattah, 1979; Ochberg, 1978; Symonds, 1980).

remains of a loved one ("Colorado Center Helps in Victim Identification", 1979).

- In Los Angeles, traumatized children who witnessed the death of their parents receive psychiatric counseling to prevent their suffering from lasting emotional damage. In an estimated 10 percent of the city's one thousand homicides each year, the slaying occurs in the presence of children who "hear that gunshot forever" (Nelson, 1983).

- In Copenhagen, Denmark, an International Rehabilitation and Research Center for Torture Victims has been established with U.N. and government funds. Its aim is not to make victims forget their shattering experiences, which is impossible, but to change the way they remember the events and view themselves. They generally suffer from deep depression, chronic anxiety, severe headaches, sexual dysfunctions, and an inability to concentrate after being subjected to cruel punishments intended to destroy their personalities as well as to extract information. The recovery rate is high because the victims are generally young (between 20 and 45 years old), strong-willed, and share a clear sense of purpose. Torture is routinely employed as a means of interrogation and political repression in about sixty countries (Osnos, 1983).

References

AKIYAMA, YOSHIO. 1981: "Murder Victimization: A Statistical Analysis." *FBI Law Enforcement Bulletin,* 50,3 (March):8–11.

"Alarm Systems Cut Burglary Rate in Scarsdale, N.Y." 1982: *Alarm Signal,* March:26.

ALLEN, HARRY; FRIDAY, PAUL; ROEBUCK, JULIAN; and SAGARIN, EDWARD. 1981: *Crime and Punishment: An Introduction to Criminology.* New York: Free Press.

"Black on Black Crime" (special issue). 1979: *Ebony,* August.

BOSTON, GUY. 1977: *Crime against the Elderly: A Selected Bibliography.* Washington, D.C.: National Criminal Justice Reference Service.

BRIGGS-BUNTING, JANE. 1982: "Behind the Headlines: News Media Victims." In Jacqueline Scherer and Gary Shepherd (Eds.), *Victimization of the Weak: Contemporary Social Reactions,* 80–97. Springfield, Ill.: Charles C Thomas.

BUDER, LEONARD. 1981: "New York Police Moving to Curb False Automatic Burglar Alarms." *The New York Times,* February 12: A1, B6.

BUREAU OF JUSTICE STATISTICS. 1983: *Criminal Victimization in the United States* (technical report). Washington, D.C.: U.S. Department of Justice.

BURGESS, CAROLINE. 1983: "Battered Chic: Fashion's Latest Assault." *Newsreport: Women Against Pornography,* 5,1 (Spring, Summer):9.

CAPPS, MARY, and MYHRE, DONNA. 1982: "Safe Space: A Strategy." *Aegis,* 34 (Spring):8–13.

CARRINGTON, FRANK. 1975: *The Victims.* New Rochelle, N.Y.: Arlington House.

CENTER, LAWRENCE. 1980: "Victim Assistance for the Elderly." *Victimology,* 5,2: 74–390.

CLOUD, BILL. 1981: "Looking at a Victim's Walk." *Newsday,* February 3, Part II:7.

COHN, ELLEN; KIDDER, LOUISE; and HARVEY, JOAN. 1978: "Crime Prevention vs. Victimization Prevention: The Psychology of Two Different Reactions." *Victimology,* 3,3:285–296.

COHODAS, NADINE. 1982: "Committees Vote Out Missing Children's Bills." *Congressional Quarterly Weekly Report,* 40, August 28:2143.

"Colorado Center Helps in Victim Identification." 1979: *Concern for Victims and Witnesses of Crime,* 1,3 (September):5.

"Compassionate Friends Provide Emotional Support." 1979: *Concern for Victims and Witnesses of Crime,* 1,6 (December):6.

"Curbs on 'Cop-Killer' Ammunition Again Proposed in Congress." 1983: *Law Enforcement News,* January 25:3.

FATTAH, EZZAT. 1979: "Some Recent Theoretical Developments in Victimology." *Victimology,* 4,2:198–213.

FEDERAL BUREAU OF INVESTIGATION. 1982: Uniform Crime Reports: *Crime in the United States, 1981.* Washington, D.C.: U.S. Government Printing Office.

"Fingerprinting of Children Spreading." 1983: *The New York Times,* February 23:A12.

FRIEDRICHS, DAVID. 1983: "Victimology: A Consideration of the Radical Critique." *Crime and Delinquency,* 29,2 (April):283–294.

FULMAN, RICKI. 1983: "Incest Victims Find a Voice." *New York Daily News,* April 3:44.

GALAWAY, BURT, and HUDSON, JOE. 1981: *Perspectives on Crime Victims.* St. Louis, Mo.: Mosby.

GALLUP, GEORGE. 1981: *The Gallup Poll.* April 4:8.

GARTNER, ALAN, and RIESSMAN, FRANK. 1980: "Lots of Helping Hands." *The New York Times,* February 19:A22.

GOLDSMITH, JACK, and GOLDSMITH, SHARON. 1976: *Crime and the Elderly: Challenge and Response.* Lexington, Mass.: Heath.

HAGER, STEVEN. 1981: "Do Be Alarmed." *New York Daily News,* July 15:37.

HAHN, PAUL. 1976: *Crimes against the Elderly: A Study in Victimology.* Santa Cruz, Calif.: Davis.

HINDS, MICHAEL. 1981: "One Answer to Violence: Bulletproof Clothing." *The New York Times,* May 16:C21.

HOCHSTEDLER, ELLEN. 1981: *Crime against the Elderly in 26 Cities.* Washington, D.C.: U.S. Department of Justice.

HOOK, SIDNEY. 1972: "The Rights of the Victims: Thoughts on Crime and Compassion." *Encounter,* April:29–35.

INCIARDI, JAMES. 1976: "The Pickpocket and His Victim." *Victimology,* 1,3:446–453.

KARMEN, ANDREW. 1982: "Women as Crime Victims: Problems and Solutions." In Barbara Price and Natalie Sokoloff (Eds.), *The Criminal Justice System and Women,* 185–202. New York: Clark Boardman.

"L.A. Police Imposing Fines for Excessive False Burglar Alarms." 1982: *Law Enforcement News,* January 25:3.

LARGEN, MARY. 1981: "Grassroots Centers and National Task Forces: A Herstory of the Anti-Rape Movement." *Aegis,* 32 (Autumn):46–52.

LEDERER, LAURA. 1980: *Take Back the Night.* New York: Morrow.

LEERHSEN, CHARLES; ABRAMSON, PAMELA; and PROUT, LINDA. 1982: "Parents of Slain Children." *Newsweek,* April 12:84.

LINDAMOOD, JEAN. 1982: "Driving Drunk." *Car and Driver,* November: 68.

McDONALD, WILLIAM. 1977: "The Role of the Victim in America." In Randy Barnett and John Hagel III (Eds.), *Assessing the Criminal: Restitution, Retribution, and the Legal Process,* 295–307. Cambridge, Mass.: Ballinger.

"Missing Children: More Hope, Help Needed." 1983: *NOVA* (National Organization For Victim Assistance) *Newsletter,* 7,3 (March):1,6.

NATIONAL COMMISSION ON THE CAUSES AND PREVENTION OF VIOLENCE (NCCPV). 1969: *Crimes of Violence.* Washington, D.C.: U.S. Government Printing Office.

NATIONAL CRIME PREVENTION INSTITUTE (NCPI). 1978: *Understanding Crime Prevention.* Louisville, Ky.: NCPI Press.

NATIONAL CRIMINAL JUSTICE INFORMATION AND STATISTICS SERVICE (NCJISS). 1978: *Myths and Realities about Crime.* Washington, D.C.: U.S. Department of Justice.

NELSON, BRYCE. 1983: "Counseling Urged for Slain Parents' Children." *The New York Times,* May 4:A19.

OCHBERG, FRANK. 1978: "The Victim of Terrorism: Psychiatric Considerations." *Terrorism, an International Journal,* 1,2:147–167.

"One Out of Every Four Homes in America Will Be Burglarized This Year" (advertisement for Vertronix, Inc.). 1981: *The New York Times,* August 4:A20.

OSNOS, PETER. 1983: "Torture Victims' Haven in Denmark." *Newsday,* July 8:11.

PARSONAGE, WILLIAM. 1979: *Perspectives on Victimology.* Beverly Hills, Calif.: Sage.

"The People's War against Crime." 1981: *U.S. News & World Report,* July 13:53–57.

"Police Use Dolls in Sex Cases." 1981: *The New York Times,* August 16:A32.

PRESS, ARIC, and CLAUSEN, PEGGY. 1982: "Fashion's High Caliber Look." *Newsweek,* May 10:49.

———; COPELAND, JEFF; CONTRERAS, JOE; CAMPER, DIANE; AGREST, SUSAN; NEWHALL, EMILY; MONROE, SYLVESTER; YOUNG, JACOB; and MAITLAND, TERRENCE. 1981: "The Plague of Violent Crime." *Newsweek,* March 23:46–54.

ROSE, VICKI. 1977: "Rape as a Social Problem: A Byproduct of the Feminist Movement." *Social Problems,* 25 (October):75–89.

ROVIN, JEFF. 1982: "Horror in Films Shifting to Gore." *On Cable,* October:11–14.

SALHOLZ, ELOISE; CONTRERAS, JOE; TAYLOR, JOHN; ACHIRON, MARILYN; and YOUNG, JACOB. 1982: "Beware of Child Molesters." *Newsweek,* August 9:43–47.

SCHAFER, STEPHEN. 1968: *The Victim and His Criminal.* New York: Random House.

SCHERER, JACQUELINE. 1982: "An Overview of Victimology." In Jacqueline Scherer and Gary Shepherd (Eds.), *Victimization of the Weak: Contemporary Social Reactions,* 8–30. Springfield, Ill.: Charles C Thomas.

SCHNEIDER, HANS. 1982: "The Present Situation of Victimology in the World." In Hans Schneider (Ed.), *The Victim in International Perspective,* 11–46. New York: Walter DeGruyter.

SIEGEL, GENE. 1978: "Cashing in on Crime: A Study of the Burglar Alarm Business." In John Johnson and Jack Douglas (Eds.), *Crime at the Top: Deviance in Business and the Professions,* 69–89. Philadelphia: Lippincott.

SYMONDS, MARTIN. 1980: "Acute Responses of Victims to Terror." *Evaluation and Change* (special issue): 39–42.

"There Are No Safe Neighborhoods ... But There Are Safe Homes" (flyer). 1982: Owings Mill, Md.: Shelburne Company.

TROUP, STUART. 1982: "Smartly Covered for the Occasion." *Newsday,* March 26:4.

TURBAK, GARY. 1982: "Missing: 100,000 Children a Year." *Kiwanis Magazine* (February):12–20.

VAN HAINTZE, BILL, and WILLIAMS, STEPHEN. 1983: "A Rogue's Gallery with Voices, Too." *Newsday,* July 8:23.

VIANO, EMILIO. 1976: *Victims and Society.* Washington, D.C.: Visage.

———. 1983: "Victimology." *Encyclopedia of Crime and Justice,* 1611–1615. New York: Free Press.

WALKER, SAM. 1982: "What Have Civil Liberties Ever Done for Crime Victims? Plenty!" *ACJS* (Academy of Criminal Justice Sciences) *Today,* October:4–5.

WALSH, MARILYN, and SCHRAM, DONNA. 1980: "The Victim of White Collar Crime: Accuser or Accused." In Gilbert Geis and Ezra Stotland (Eds.), *White Collar Crime,* 32–51. Beverly Hills, Calif.: Sage.

WATERS, HARRY. 1982: "Life According to TV." *Newsweek,* December 6:136–140.

WHITMAN, HOWARD. 1951: *Terror in the Streets.* New York: Dial Press.

WOLCOTT, JAMES. 1982: "Gary Gilmore's Slow Dance on the Killing Ground." *New York,* November 29:68–73.

CHAPTER 2

Victimization as a Burden

Crime in the Streets: The Big Picture

- Every twenty-five minutes of each day, a person is murdered in the United States.
- Every seven minutes, a woman is raped.
- Every fifty-nine seconds, someone is robbed.

These statistics for 1982, collected by the Federal Bureau of Investigation from police departments across the country, paint a chilling portrait of the contemporary crime scene. But another set of statistics, derived from surveys of tens of thousands of people, yields these conclusions:

- Being victimized is a relatively rare experience, especially considering the amount of attention paid to the crime problem and the levels of fear it stimulates.
- Victimization rates are surprisingly stable from year to year.
- Some people face much greater danger than others. In general, victimization poses a larger burden for those who are already saddled with other social disadvantages and problems than for those who lead privileged and comfortable lives.

To bring the "big picture" into focus, the entire range of street crimes will be examined first. Then a close-up investigation of a single kind of crime, robbery, will enrich the analysis.

Statistics are necessary to describe how many crimes are being committed, who is being victimized, and how seriously they are being harmed. But statistics are subject to errors, and they cannot capture in vivid detail how individuals react to the experience of being victimized. Therefore, before looking at numbers that measure people's plight, it is useful to describe in words how they typically react.

Crime as a Burden: Exploring the Victim's Point of View

Traditionally, the impact of crime has been measured in terms of the harm caused to society as a whole by violations of law. With the rediscovery of crime victims, attention shifted to direct losses experienced by victims, their families, and their communities. But the concept of loss emphasizes what is taken away, or what the offender gets away with. The consequences of crime for victims are not limited to financial expenses or even to physical injuries. The psychological damage that lingers is real as well, although such intangible or less visible costs in the form of pain and suffering may defy measurement.

Some victims might not be upset at all. Auto theft is reportedly referred to as the "happy crime" by policemen (Plate, 1975). The owner is relieved of a lemon; the insurance company pays off and then raises rates; and the new- or used-car dealer gets another customer. No one really suffers, according to this economic analysis. Similarly, affluent burglary victims might relish the opportunity to replace objects carted off by thieves with trendy new ones from chic boutiques (especially if insurance coverage pays for the shopping spree). Such a reaction is in keeping with the throwaway mentality of consumer buying habits cultivated by corporations and advertising agencies (Jacob, 1980:18).

But these casual reactions to crime are the exceptions, not the rule. The impact of most crimes on their victims is perceived in an opposite way—as a violation of self and a grim reminder of one's vulnerability and mortality in a hostile world filled with antagonists intent on inflicting harm.

Homes are reflections and extensions of oneself—nests as well as castles. Burglaries strike victims as an invasion, intrusion, or frightening breakdown in security, regardless of how much or how little was spirited away. Robberies involve more than the loss of cherished possessions or hard-earned cash. The victims' sense of independence and autonomy is trampled on as they are forced to surrender and place their fate in the hands of enemies. For wounded victims, not only is the external envelope violated, but a visible reminder lingers of how one can unexpectedly end up helpless and unable to defend possessions and personal integrity.

Rape victims not only are stripped of control over their own bodies but are also "conquered" through an invasion of their inner space, the most sacred and private repository of self (Bard and Sangrey, 1979). After being transformed from a person into an object, one may plunge into a "rape crisis syndrome." An initial acute phase that follows the sexual assault lasts about two or three weeks. It is marked by sleeplessness, nausea, tension headaches, fear, fury, embarrassment, and self-recrimination. A second phase, of longer duration, is a time for personality reorganization. The victims suffer from nightmares, defensive reactions, phobias, strains in their sex lives, and conflicts with men in general (Burgess and Holmstrom, 1974).

Crisis reactions burden survivors of natural disasters, sudden illnesses, serious accidents, and shocking crimes. Such reactions can be normal and appropriate and are not indications of a weak character, emotional immaturity, or mental illness, as previously thought. The severity of the crisis reaction is directly proportional to the degree to which the self was violated.

Three stages can be recognized in crisis reactions: initial disorganization; a period of struggle to restore balance; and, eventually, stability. The first stage lasts from a few hours to a few days. The victims can feel numbed, disabled, shattered, and utterly helpless. During the second phase, the victims recoil from the original shock. They may lose their appetite, have trouble sleeping, and find it difficult to concentrate on their work. Tensions wax and wane, and conflicting emotions bedevil them, until they begin to put the incident into perspective. The final stage is entered as the fear, sadness, self-pity, guilt, and anger subside. For some, weathering a crisis can be a strengthening experience if energies are directed into constructive channels. But others never resolve the problems provoked by the crime, and further disruptions mar their lives (Bard and Sangrey, 1979).

Victimization can therefore be viewed as a burden, not just a loss. Something is left behind as well as taken away. Haunting memories, chilling scenarios, nightmarish images and similar psychological scars are carried about as a crushing mental load. They are oppressive, worrisome, anxiety-provoking, and encumbering to those who bear them. (See box 2-1.)

Victimization can also be conceptualized as a process marked by a

---

BOX 2-1 Which Victims Suffer Most?

Victims of robbery, assault, and burglary are likely to suffer emotionally as well as physically and financially from the aftereffects of the crime. But some take it worse than others. That's the conclusion of a study based on interviews with 274 people conducted by New York City's Victim Services Agency.

On every indicator of degree of suffering, the ones hardest hit were the poorest, rather than the affluent; members of racial and ethnic minorities, rather than the white majority; inner city residents, rather than inhabitants of more desirable communities; and those with limited schooling, rather than the more highly educated. These disadvantaged people experienced more psychological problems (anxiety, nervousness, self-blame, anger, shame, and difficulty sleeping) and more practical problems than the other victims. Their difficulties plagued them for longer periods. They were less likely to get all the help they needed, and the friends and relatives they turned to for assistance found it particularly burdensome to provide aid. The members of the victims' informal support network tended to suffer secondary or indirect victimization, in the form of increased levels of fear and anxiety about their own safety (Friedman, Bischoff, Davis, and Pearson, 1982).

---

series of stages or junctures, each beset by difficult choices or dilemmas. Before the criminal act, the victim must decide whether to embark on a particular course of action and assume risks, or purchase security at the expense of forgoing that activity. Once targeted by the offender, the victim is plunged into a perilous situation in which sudden, irreversible decisions are shaped by personality traits and cultural norms. The victim confronts the issue of whether to give in or put up resistance. In the immediate aftermath of the incident, the victim must decide whether to report the crime and initiate the criminal justice process in order to seek redress and satisfaction, or to accept the outcome as is. Next, the victim must struggle against powerful emotional forces in order to choose which attitudinal and behavioral changes, if any, are the appropriate responses to the injuries and losses that were sustained. The most crucial set of decisions concerns the urge to retaliate in kind. Will the victim interpret the injustice inflicted by the offender as a justification for transforming into an aggressor who becomes adept at using deception, manipulation, or force to subjugate and exploit others? (Fattah, 1981.)

Victimization Surveys: Discovering the Depth of the Problem

Numbers cannot adequately convey the human toll that crime takes. But statistics are useful as indicators of how much suffering might be going on, the kinds of people most frequently burdened by crimes, the extent of their losses and injuries, and the nature of their reactions. Public officials began keeping records about crimes during the 1800s in order to gauge the "moral health" of society. Then, as now, high crime rates were taken as signs of "social pathology"—indications that something was desperately wrong. The criminologists of the time, as they do now, used crime statistics to build and test theories about the kinds of people breaking the law and the reasons for their lawless deeds. But criminologists, and later victimologists, had deep reservations about the accuracy of the official records kept by the police, the courts, and the prisons. The tallies were known to be incomplete and were suspected of being periodically either inflated or deflated by powerful groups intent on proving some point through the manipulation of statistics.

The most important source of facts and figures is the Uniform Crime Report (UCR), published annually by the FBI. It is a compilation of information about crimes and criminals gathered from police departments across the nation. From a victimologist's point of view, it suffers from two serious defects. First of all, very little data about victims is collected and provided. Secondly, many incidents are never reported to the police and, of those that are, some are not interpreted by the authorities as genuine, serious crimes worthy of official tabulation.

Dissatisfaction with official record keeping led criminologists to collect their own data. The first method they used was the "self-report" approach. Small samples of people were promised anonymity if they "confessed" to crimes they had committed. This type of study consistently revealed greater numbers of illegal acts than were indicated by official statistics. It confirmed the hypothesis that a lot of lawbreaking occurred among people who were never investigated, arrested, and convicted, especially members of the middle and upper classes.

After these small self-report studies about criminality were conducted, the next logical step for criminologists was to survey large numbers of people about offenses committed against them, rather than by them. These early "victimization surveys," or simply "victim surveys" (a somewhat misleading label, since most respondents answered that they were not victims recently) provided additional proof of unreported and unrecorded crimes that undercut the accuracy of official statistics.

The first national poll (of ten thousand households) was conducted in 1966 for the President's Commission on Law Enforcement and the Administration of Justice. It uncovered a crime rate that was about twice as high as the official UCR rate because incidents not reported to the authorities were revealed to the interviewers. A nationwide victimization survey has been carried out twice a year since 1972. Called the National Crime Survey (NCS), it was originally funded by the Law Enforcement Assistance Administration (LEAA). Now, the interviews are performed by the U.S. Census Bureau on behalf of the Bureau of Justice Statistics of the Department of Justice.

The National Crime Panel consists of 60,000 households drawn by methods of random selection from a pool of over 80 million U.S. families (including people living alone). This yields approximately 132,000 respondents twelve years old and older who are interviewed in their homes every six months for a total of three years. (Then their participation ends, and other households replace them.) The survey begins with a series of "incident screen" questions like "During the past half-year, was your pocket picked or your purse snatched?" If the answer is yes, a set of follow-up questions is asked to collect the details about the crime. (See figure 2-1.)

When completed, the survey provides data about the number and kinds of offenses committed against the respondents; where and when the incidents occurred; the extent of injuries and losses, if any, suffered by the victims; the characteristics of the offenders, as perceived by their victims; whether the crime was reported to the police and why it was or was not; and the characteristics of the victims in terms of their age, sex, race, income level, education, occupation, and place of residence. The result is a wealth of facts about aspects of the crime problem not found in the UCR.

The survey focuses on four crimes of violence (rape, robbery, and simple and aggravated assault), two kinds of theft against persons (personal larceny with and without contact), and three types of stealing

HOUSEHOLD SCREEN QUESTIONS

38. Now I'd like to ask some questions about crime. They refer only to the last 6 months–

between _______ 1, 19___ and _______, 19___.
During the last 6 months, did anyone break into or somehow illegally get into your (apartment/home), garage, or another building on your property?

☐ Yes–**How many times?** _____
☐ No

39. (Other than the incident(s) just mentioned) Did you find a door jimmied, a lock forced, or any other signs of an ATTEMPTED break in?

☐ Yes–**How many times?** _____
☐ No

40. Was anything at all stolen that is kept outside your home, or happened to be left out, such as a bicycle, a garden hose, or lawn furniture? (other than any incidents already mentioned)

☐ Yes–**How many times?** _____
☐ No

41. Did anyone take something belonging to you or to any member of this household, from a place where you or they were temporarily staying, such as a friend's or relative's home, a hotel or motel, or a vacation home?

☐ Yes – **How many times?** _____
☐ No

42. How many DIFFERENT motor vehicles (cars, trucks, motorcycles, etc.) were owned by you or any other member of this household during the last 6 months?

(117)
0 ☐ None – *SKIP* to 45
1 ☐ 1
2 ☐ 2
3 ☐ 3
4 ☐ 4 or more

43. Did anyone steal, TRY to steal, or use (it/any of them) without permission?

☐ Yes – **How many times?** _____
☐ No

44. Did anyone steal or TRY to steal parts attached to (it/any of them), such as a battery, hubcaps, tape-deck, etc.?

☐ Yes – **How many times?** _____
☐ No

INDIVIDUAL SCREEN QUESTIONS

45. The following questions refer only to things that happened to YOU during the last 6 months –

between ______ 1, 19 __ and ______, 19 __.
Did you have your (pocket picked/purse snatched)?

☐ Yes–**How many times?** _____
☐ No

46. Did anyone take something (else) directly from you by using force, such as by a stickup, mugging or threat?

☐ Yes–**How many times?** _____
☐ No

47. Did anyone TRY to rob you by using force or threatening to harm you? (other than any incidents already mentioned)

☐ Yes–**How many times?** _____
☐ No

48. Did anyone beat you up, attack you or hit you with something, such as a rock or bottle? (other than any incidents already mentioned)

☐ Yes–**How many times?** _____
☐ No

49. Were you knifed, shot at, or attacked with some other weapon by anyone at all? (other than any incidents already mentioned)

☐ Yes–**How many times?** _____
☐ No

50. Did anyone THREATEN to beat you up or THREATEN you with a knife, gun, or some other weapon, NOT including telephone threats? (other than any incidents already mentioned)

☐ Yes–**How many times?** _____
☐ No

51. Did anyone TRY to attack you in some other way? (other than any incidents already mentioned)

☐ Yes–**How many times?** _____
☐ No

52. During the last 6 months, did anyone steal things that belonged to you from inside ANY car or truck, such as packages or clothing?

☐ Yes–**How many times?** _____
☐ No

53. Was anything stolen from you while you were away from home, for instance at work, in a theater or restaurant, or while traveling?

☐ Yes–**How many times?** _____
☐ No

54. (Other than any incidents you've already mentioned) was anything (else) at all stolen from you during the last 6 months?

☐ Yes–**How many times?** _____
☐ No

55. Did you find any evidence that someone ATTEMPTED to steal something that belonged to you? (other than any incidents already mentioned)

☐ Yes– **How many times?** _____
☐ No

56. Did you call the police during the last 6 months to report something that happened to YOU which you thought was a crime? (Do not count any calls made to the police concerning the incidents you have just told me about.)

☐ No – *SKIP* to 57
☐ Yes – What happened?

____
____
____

(118) *

CHECK ITEM D ▶ Look at 56. Was HHLD member 12 + attacked or threatened, or was something stolen or an attempt made to steal something that belonged to him/her?

☐ Yes– **How many times?** _____
☐ No

57. Did anything happen to YOU during the last 6 months which you thought was a crime, but did NOT report to the police? (other than any incidents already mentioned)

☐ No – *SKIP* to *Check Item F*
☐ Yes – What happened?

____
____
____

(119) *

CHECK ITEM E ▶ Look at 57. Was HHLD member 12+ attacked or threatened, or was something stolen or an attempt made to steal something that belonged to him/her?

☐ Yes– **How many times?** _____
☐ No

CHECK ITEM F ▶ Do any of the screen questions contain any entries for "How many times?"

☐ Yes – *Fill Crime Incident Reports.*
☐ No – *Interview next HHLD member*
End interview if last respondent.

Line number

(201)

Screen question number

(202)

Incident number

(203)

Notes

CHECK ITEM A ▶ Has this person lived at this address for 6 months or less? *(If not sure, refer to Item 30, NCS-1.)*

☐ Yes (Item 30 – 6 months or less) – *Read* (A). *Ask 1*

☐ No (Item 30 blank or more than 6 months) – *Read* (A). *SKIP to 2a*

(A) **You said that during the last 6 months –** *(Refer to appropriate screen question for description of crime).*

1. Did (this/the first) incident happen while you were living here or before you moved to this address?

(204) 1 ☐ While living at this address
2 ☐ Before moving to this address

2a. In what month did (this/the first) incident happen? *(Show calendar if necessary. Encourage respondent to give exact month.)*

(205) Month | Year

CHECK ITEM B ▶ **Is this incident report for a series of crimes?**

(206) 1 ☐ Yes – *Ask 2b* (Note: series **must** have 3 or more similar incidents which respondent **can't recall separately.** Reduce entry in screen question if necessary.)
2 ☐ No – *SKIP to 3a*

b. Altogether, how many times did this happen during the last six months?

(207) ________ Number of incidents

c. In what month or months did these incidents take place?
If more than one quarter involved, ask ↓
How many in *(name months)*?

▶*INTERVIEWER: Enter number for each quarter as appropriate. If number falls below 3 or respondent can now recall incidents separately,* ***still fill as a series.*** *If all are out of scope, end incident report.*

Number of incidents per quarter			
Jan., Feb., or March (Qtr. 1)	April, May, or June (Qtr. 2)	July, Aug., or Sept. (Qtr. 3)	Oct., Nov., or Dec. (Qtr. 4)
(208) ____	(209) ____	(210) ____	(211) ____

▶ *INTERVIEWER: If this report is for a* ***series****, read:*
The following questions refer only to the most recent incident.

3a. Was it daylight or dark outside when (this/the most recent) incident happened?

(212) 1 ☐ Light
2 ☐ Dark
3 ☐ Dawn, almost light, dusk, twilight
4 ☐ Don't know – *SKIP to 4a*

b. About what time did (this/the most recent) incident happen?

During day
(213) 1 ☐ After 6 a.m.–12 noon
2 ☐ After 12 noon–6 p.m.
3 ☐ Don't know what time of **day**

At night
4 ☐ After 6 p.m.–12 midnight
5 ☐ After 12 midnight–6 a.m.
6 ☐ Don't know what time of **night**

OR
7 ☐ Don't know whether **day or night**

NOTICE – Your report to the Census Bureau is confidential by law (U.S. Code 42, section 3771). All identifiable information will be used only by persons engaged in and for the purposes of the survey, and may not be disclosed or released to others for any purpose.

FORM **NCS-2**
(1-2-79)

U.S. DEPARTMENT OF COMMERCE
BUREAU OF THE CENSUS
ACTING AS COLLECTING AGENT FOR THE
LAW ENFORCEMENT ASSISTANCE ADMINISTRATION
U.S. DEPARTMENT OF JUSTICE

CRIME INCIDENT REPORT
NATIONAL CRIME SURVEY

4a. Did this incident happen inside the limits of a city, town, village, etc.?

(214) 1 ☐ Outside U.S. – *SKIP to 5*
2 ☐ No – *Ask 4b*
Yes – **What is the name of that city/town/village?**
3 ☐ **Same** city, town, village as **present residence** – *SKIP to 5*
4 ☐ **Different** city, town, village from **present residence.** – *Specify* ↓

(215) ☐☐☐☐☐

If not sure, ask:
b. In what State and county did it occur?

State ____________ County ____________

If not sure, ask:
c. Is this the same State and county as your PRESENT RESIDENCE?

(216) 1 ☐ Yes
2 ☐ No

5. Where did this incident take place?

(217) 1 ☐ At or in **own** dwelling, or own attached garage *(Always mark for break-in or attempted break-in of same)*
2 ☐ At or in **detached** buildings on **own** property, such as detached garage, storage shed, etc. *(Always mark for break-in or attempted break-in of same)*
} *Ask 6a*

3 ☐ At or in vacation home, hotel/motel
4 ☐ Near **own** home; yard, sidewalk, driveway, carport, on street immediately adjacent to own home, apartment hall/storage area/laundry room *(does not include apartment parking lots)*
5 ☐ At, in, or near a friend/relative/neighbor's home, other building on their property, yard, sidewalk, driveway, carport, on street immediately adjacent to their home, apartment hall/storage area/laundry room
6 ☐ On the street *(other than immediately adjacent to own/friend/relative/neighbor's home)*
7 ☐ Inside restaurant, bar, nightclub
8 ☐ Inside other commercial building such as store, bank, gas station
9 ☐ On public transportation or in station *(bus, train, plane, airport, depot, etc.)*
10 ☐ Inside office, factory, or warehouse
11 ☐ Commercial parking lot
12 ☐ Noncommercial parking lot
13 ☐ Apartment parking lot
14 ☐ Inside school building
15 ☐ On school property *(school parking area, play area, school bus, etc.)*
16 ☐ In a park, field, playground other than school
17 ☐ Other – *Specify* ↓
} ***SKIP*** *to Check Item C, page 14*

Notes

FIGURE 2-1. Questionnaire used in the National Crime Survey. (*From* Criminal Victimization in the United States, 1980, *by the Bureau of Justice Statistics. Washington, D.C.: U.S. Department of Justice, 1982: 82–83.*)

TABLE 2-1 National Crime Survey: Definitions and Rates

Crime	*Definition*	*Example*	*Rate per 1,000 people, 1980*
Crimes of violence against persons			
Rape	"Carnal knowledge" through the use of force or threats. Includes attempts; excludes statutory rape of minors.	A woman is assaulted and sexually molested by a stranger. A teenage girl is compelled to have intercourse by her boyfriend who overpowers her.	0.9 overall 0.2 completed 0.7 attempted
Robbery	Completed or attempted theft, directly from a person, of property or cash, by force or threat of force, with or without a weapon.	A man's wallet is taken by a knife-wielding bandit. A stranger grabs a woman and pulls at her gold chain but is scared away by the victim's screams.	7 overall* 2 with injury 4 without injury
Aggravated assault	Attack with a weapon, whether or not the victim is injured. Attack without a weapon that results in serious injury. Includes attempts with weapons.	A man is hit by a chair in a bar and suffers a broken leg. A husband beats his wife unconscious with his fists.	9 overall 3 with injury 6 attempted
Simple assault	Attack without a weapon, resulting in minor injury. Includes attempts.	A boy is pushed to the ground by another youth in a schoolyard quarrel.	16 overall* 5 with injury 12 attempted
Total			33 crimes of violence
Crimes of theft against persons			
Personal larceny with contact	Theft directly from the victim of a purse, wallet, or cash, by stealth but without force or threat of harm. Includes attempts.	A man's wallet is picked; a woman's pocketbook is deftly snatched from her grip.	3 overall 1 purse snatching 2 pocket pickings
Personal larceny without contact	Theft or attempted theft of cash or possessions from any place other than the victim's home or its immediate vicinity.	A bicycle is stolen from a rack; clothing is taken from a parked car.	80 overall
Total			83

Crimes of theft against households

Burglary	Unlawful entry, by force if necessary, of a residence for the purpose of theft. Includes attempts.	A teenager slashes a screen and breaks into a garage to steal tools.	84 overall* 30 forcible entries 37 unlawful entries without force 18 attempted forcible entries
Household larceny	Theft or attempted theft of property or cash from a residence or its immediate vicinity, by a person who is not trespassing.	A maid steals jewels from a drawer; a guest at a party steals the host's rare coin collection.	127 overall 118 completed 9 attempted
Motor vehicle theft	Stealing or taking without authorization any motorized vehicle. Includes attempts.	A driver finds that the ignition of his car was tampered with; a snowmobile is stolen.	17 overall* 11 completed 5 attempted
Total			228

*Sub-categories do not exactly add up to overall rates due to rounding errors.

SOURCE: *Criminal Victimization in the United States, 1980,* by the Bureau of Justice Statistics. Washington, D.C.: U.S. Department of Justice, 1982:23, 96–97.

directed at households (burglary, larceny, and motor vehicle thefts). The fundamental statistic from which others are derived is the rate per 1,000 persons or households per year. (See table 2-1.)

At first, the victimization survey was praised as a major breakthrough by those researchers who distrusted official statistics. But the technique of polling people about the offenses committed against them has not turned out to be the foolproof method for measuring the "actual" crime rate that some victimologists hoped it would be.

Underreporting remains a problem. Communication barriers may inhibit respondents from revealing to interviewers victimizations that were also concealed from the police. "Memory decay" (the inability to recall incidents) also results in an undercount.

Overreporting can arise, as well. The police don't accept all reports of crimes at face value, and pollsters shouldn't either. "Stolen" objects may have been misplaced, and accidentally broken windows may be taken as evidence of an attempted burglary. "Forward telescoping" is the tendency to believe that a crime occurred within the reference period (the previous six months) and should be counted, when actually it was committed long before and ought to be excluded. Noncrimes may be interpreted as illegal acts.

Other more complicated methodological problems undermine the accuracy of victimization surveys. The premise that guides the research endeavor—to find out about the true scope and frequency of crime, ask people if they have been victimized—turns out to be deceptively simple and disturbingly costly. Since being victimized within the previous six months is a relatively rare event, tens of thousands of people must be polled to meet the requirements for statistical soundness. The surveys become very expensive to carry out (Garofalo, 1981; Levine, 1976; Skogan, 1981b). (For additional criticisms of the National Crime Survey, see Lehnen and Skogan, 1981; Reiss, 1981; and Schneider, 1981.)

Interpreting Survey Findings: How Serious Is the Problem?

Since 1981, the findings of the National Crime Survey have been analyzed by using a newly developed statistical indicator called "households touched by crime." The intent is to clarify the big picture of the prevalence and seriousness of street crime in American society. The rationale for treating "households," in addition to individuals, as a unit of analysis is that the effects of crime are not limited to the lives of the immediate victims. Their families suffer, too, sharing their pain, hardships, sense of violation, and fears. Other people living with the victims experience to some degree the injuries, economic losses, inconveniences, and feelings of vulnerability (Bureau of Justice Statistics, 1981).

A household is counted as "touched" by crime if any member at least once during the year is raped, robbed, or assaulted, or sustains a personal larceny with or without contact; or if the unit is victimized by a burglary, household larceny, or motor vehicle theft. For example, a family in which a parent is robbed at gunpoint is considered to have been touched by crime, as is a household in which a child's tricycle is stolen from the front yard.

In 1981, close to twenty-five million American households, about 30 percent of the nation's total, were touched by a crime of violence or theft[1] (Bureau of Justice Statistics, 1982a). Is this figure small or large, a case for alarm or for relief? Does it overstate or understate the problem?

It could be argued that the measurement is flawed, because some important kinds of crime are omitted from consideration. Murder, kidnapping, and arson are not counted because they do not lend themselves to the survey format. (Murder and kidnapping, statistically speaking, are so rare that their inclusion would not change the 30 percent figure by any appreciable amount.) A few common forms of victimization that are not viewed as street crimes are also excluded from the survey: child abuse, neglect, and molestation; vandalism; and consumer fraud by businesses.

But if the new indicator understates the crime problem along certain dimensions, it also overstates it in several ways. The use of the 30 percent figure can be misleadingly ominous, and the interpretation of this number can cause unwarranted anxiety.

President Ronald Reagan, in a speech before Congress introducing his

[1]In 1982, the figure dropped slightly to 29 percent (Rand, 1983).

Criminal Justice Reform Act of 1982, interpreted the 30 percent statistic about the proportion of households touched by crime in the most dire manner possible. In order to convince legislators and the public to accept his controversial law and order proposals, he presented the big picture as negatively and alarmingly as he could: "Last year alone, one out of every three households in the country fell victim to some form of serious crime" ("Text of Reagan Message," 1982:2388). Is this interpretation objective, or does it embody an overstatement of the problem?[2] The whole issue hinges on the meaning of the word *serious.*

"Households touched by crime" is the most inclusive of any crime statistic. It combines, or pools, the experiences of all members. (About a fifth of households are single-person units.) Besides adding together incidents that occurred to several different people, it lumps together (and counts as equal) all sorts of victimization: rapes, severe beatings, and automobile hubcap thefts. This practice of "adding apples and oranges" has been criticized for years when performed by the FBI in the calculation of its "Crime Index." (The index is a huge number, in the millions, summarizing all incidents of the eight index crimes reported to the police in a single year, ranging from murders to attempts to steal a hat from a restaurant coat rack.)

When the NCS index is broken down into its component parts, it turns out that most households that were touched by crime (21 percent out of the 30 percent) were victimized by thefts. (Note that a household is counted as touched, for example, if it experienced two thefts, or three, or a theft and a robbery of one of its members: the average touched household experienced 1.6 incidents in a year.) Are thefts "serious" crimes? In 1980, about 90 percent of all personal larcenies, with and without contact, and of all household larcenies cost victims less than $250 (Bureau of Justice Statistics, 1982c:65).[3] Even if some thefts are "serious," it must be conceded that most are "petty larcenies,"[4] just "minor" crimes, such as the stealing of a battery from a parked car.

The social scientists at the Department of Justice computed a subcategory of crimes of "high concern." A household was counted as touched by a crime of high concern during the year if it had been burglarized at least once or if a family member had been the victim of a crime of violence by a stranger (rape, robbery, aggravated assault, or simple assault). In 1981, nearly 11 percent of all U.S. households experienced a crime of high concern.

[2]Note that the President "rounded off" the 30 percent figure upwards to 33 percent (one-third, or one out of every three).

[3]1980 figures are the latest available in sufficient detail at the time of publication in late 1983.

[4]The FBI's classification of petty larceny (as opposed to grand larceny) was changed from less than $50 to less than $250 to take inflation into account.

The 11 percent figure is a lot less frightening than the original 30 percent, but it still may overstate the extent of the problem. Most of the households touched by crimes of high concern were victimized by burglars (7 percent out of the 11 percent). Once again, the question must be raised, Are all burglaries "serious"? More than two-thirds resulted in losses of less than $250 in 1980 (Bureau of Justice Statistics, 1982c:65). Furthermore, not all the burglaries were successful break-ins; about a fifth were merely "attempted forcible entries," which may have caused some damage to windows, doors, or locks.

The remaining 4 percent of households experienced a violent crime by a stranger. From the victim's point of view, there can be a substantial difference between an attempted and a completed crime that determines the "seriousness" of the act. For example, an attempted sexual assault, terrible though it may be, is obviously not as bad as a completed rape. An attempted robbery will cost the victim less than a completed one, and an attempted assault is less painful than a successful one. Therefore, all the figures for victimization rates need to be corrected, to take into account what percentage was completed and what percentage attempted (including resisted, thwarted, botched, or otherwise aborted), if assessing their "seriousness" is the issue in question.

The percentages of crimes of violence committed by strangers that were completed have been calculated from the victimization surveys conducted from 1973 to 1979 (Bureau of Justice Statistics, 1982b). Rapes were completed 38 percent of the time, robberies 61 percent, aggravated assaults 30 percent, and simple assaults 21 percent. Hence, the 4 percent figure for all households touched by crimes of violence at the hands of strangers may overstate the real degree of harm experienced by the family members.

One final statistic merits closer inspection. Of the assaults, roughly three out of every five were classified as simple rather than aggravated. Simple assaults are attacks without a weapon that result in minor injuries (like bruises, black eyes, cuts, scratches, or swellings) or assorted more substantial wounds requiring a hospital stay of under two days. Although some of these incidents were surely perceived to be "serious" by the participants, others might have been schoolyard shoving matches, barroom scuffles, and similar minor confrontations that might not upset the victims, onlookers, or authorities very much.

In sum, it is very difficult to accurately capture the full scope and depth of interpersonal conflict and exploitation through the use of statistics. One single number may conceal as much as it reveals. The 30 percent figure can be whittled down to less than 4 percent, as the above analysis shows, if certain assumptions are made. It could also be inflated far beyond its present order of magnitude if other assumptions were made or if additional common crimes were included. Statistics must be interpreted as carefully as they are collected and calculated. But frequently they are not used objectively, for scientific purposes, but subjectively, for ulterior purposes.

Victimization Trends: Is There a Crime Wave?

Is the United States in the midst of a crime wave, or have crime rates leveled off? The findings of the National Crime Survey can be assembled to determine whether the rates are climbing steadily, remaining about the same, or dropping. From the early 1960s to the early 1970s, the United States definitely experienced a major crime wave. But whether this breakdown in law and order continued from the early 1970s into the early 1980s is a subject of dispute. (See table 2-2.)

TABLE 2-2 Victimization Rates for Personal and Household Crimes, 1973-1981
Rate per 1,000 people and households

Sector and type of Crime	*1973*	*1974*	*1975*	*1976*	*1977*	*1978*	*1979*	*1980*	*1981*
Personal sector									
Crimes of violence	32.6	33.0	32.8	32.6	33.9	33.7	34.5	33.3	35.3
Rape	1.0	1.0	0.9	0.8	0.9	1.0	1.1	0.9	1.0
Robbery	6.7	7.2	6.8	6.5	6.2	5.9	6.3	6.6	7.4
Assault	24.9	24.8	25.2	25.3	26.8	26.9	27.2	25.8	27.0
Aggravated assault	10.1	10.4	9.6	9.9	10.0	9.7	9.9	9.3	9.6
Simple assault	14.8	14.4	15.6	15.4	16.8	17.2	17.3	16.5	17.3
Crimes of theft	91.1	95.1	96.0	96.1	97.3	96.8	91.9	83.0	85.1
Personal larceny with contact	3.1	3.1	3.1	2.9	2.7	3.1	2.9	3.0	3.3
Personal larceny without contact	88.0	92.0	92.9	93.2	94.6	93.6	89.0	80.0	81.9
Household sector									
Household burglary	91.7	93.1	91.7	88.9	88.5	86.0	84.1	84.3	87.9
Household larceny	107.0	123.8	125.4	124.1	123.3	119.9	133.7	126.5	121.0
Motor vehicle theft	19.1	18.8	19.5	16.5	17.0	17.5	17.5	16.7	17.1

Note: Detail may not add to total shown because of rounding. Estimated population control figures based on the 1980 census were used in calculating the 1980 and 1981 rates. Controls for the 1973–1979 rates were derived from the 1970 census.

SOURCE: Adolfo Paez, 1983, *Criminal Victimization in the United States: 1980–1981 Changes Based on New Estimates;* Bureau of Justice Statistics Technical Report. Washington, D.C.: U.S. Department of Justice.

The data in table 2-2 report the total number of criminal incidents divulged by respondents during the interviews and the computed crime rate for that kind of offense in the given year. (The rate takes into account changes in the number of people and households.) Glancing across the rows, we see no prominent changes over time, either upward or downward. No specific kind of crime is "getting out of hand." No particular crime is "being brought under control," either.

Several types of crime register a slight decline over the years of the National Crime Survey. Burglaries, motor vehicle thefts, and perhaps personal larcenies without contact occurred less often at the end of the 1970s and during the early 1980s than at the start. Two types of crime seem to be on the rise: simple assaults and household larcenies. The most frightening crimes—rape, robbery, and aggravated assault—appear to have hovered at roughly the same levels throughout the period (high levels, compared to their rates two decades ago).

What is striking about the data collected over the years is their relative stability. Crime rates are readily predictable. Knowing the rate from the previous year furnishes an excellent predictor of the rate for the coming year. Such an estimate will be in error by just a few percentage points, plus or minus. Even though each victim and each offender may view their interaction as spontaneous, unconnected, or unanticipated, the sum total of all these events in a year, divided by the number of people or households at risk, is a remarkably constant figure over the short run.

Since there are two respected sets of crime statistics, one from the FBI's UCR (based on citizen reports to the police) and the other from the National Crime Panel (based on interviews with about sixty thousand families a year), for certain crimes one set may show a trend upward while the other indicates stability or a decline over time. Such is the case for rape. The FBI's figures show a steady rise throughout the 1970s and into the 1980s. The NCS data show a dip, then a slight rise, then another dip. Assuming that the NCS is more accurate, the UCR's apparent increase in the rape rate can be explained away in terms of a rise in reporting rates. Perhaps girls and women are notifying the authorities in a greater proportion of cases lately, although National Crime Survey data about reporting rates do not indicate such an increase from 1973 to 1981. See table 5 in chapter 5 for rape reporting rates; see table 2-3 and figures 2-2 and 2-3 below for rape rates according to the two sources.

TABLE 2-3 Rape Rates and Trends, According to Two Different Sources
UCR* vs. NCS* rates†

	1973	*1974*	*1975*	*1976*	*1977*	*1978*	*1979*	*1980*	*1981*
FBI's UCR	.25	.26	.26	.26	.29	.31	.35	.36	.36
NCS	1.0	1.0	0.9	0.8	0.9	1.0	1.1	0.9	1.0

*UCR=Uniform Crime Report; NCS=National Crime Survey.

†Both the FBI's figures and the NCS survey rates are for every 1,000 people (males and females). Hence, rape rates for girls and women, the overwhelmingly more frequent pattern, are approximately twice as high as the FBI and NCS rates.

Comparative Risks: Putting Crime into Perspective

Estimating comparative risks is an important task in the development of the big picture. How does the chance of becoming a crime victim compare with other threats and dangers, such as accidents and illnesses?

In order to make risk assessments, statistical rates have been comput-

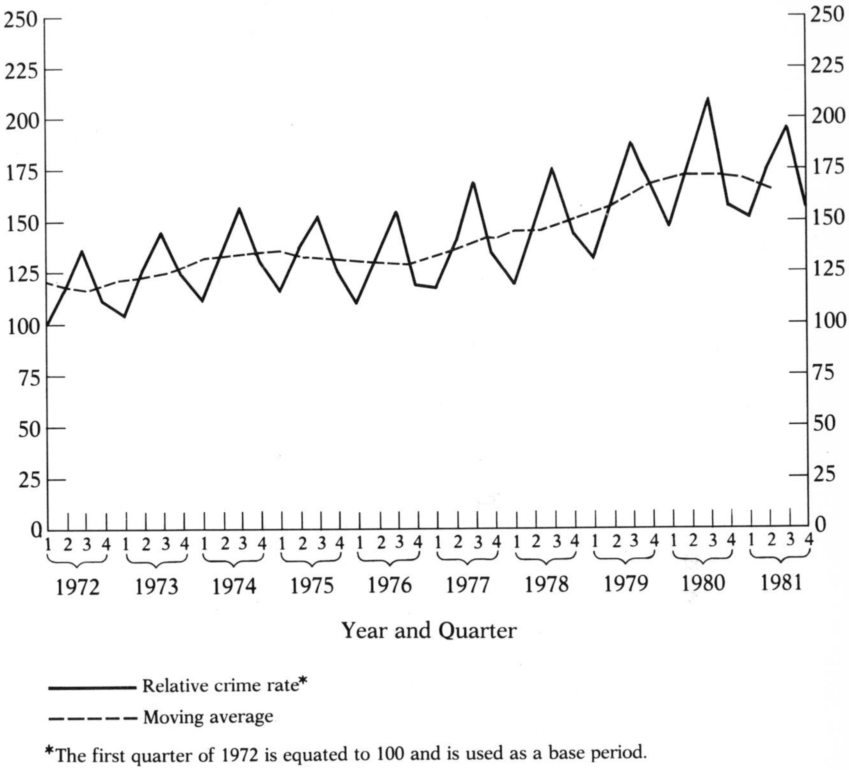

FIGURE 2-2. Trends in rape rates, 1973–1981, according to the FBI's compilation of crimes known to the police. *(From Federal Bureau of Investigation, Uniform Crime Reports:* Crime in the United States, 1981. *Washington, D.C.: U.S. Government Printing Office, 1982:328.)*

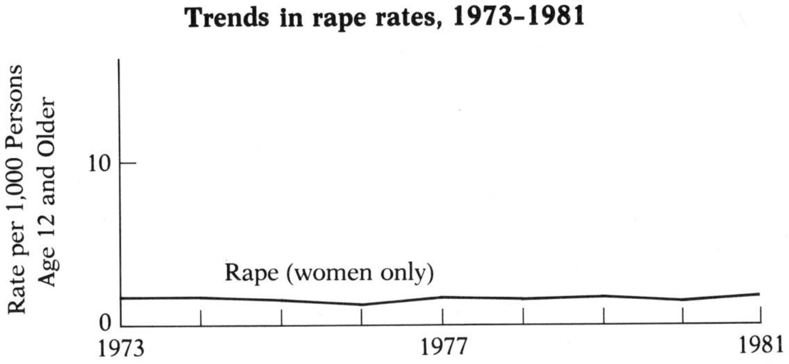

FIGURE 2-3. Trends in rape rates, 1973–1981, according to the National Crime Survey. *(From Adolfo Paez, 1983,* Criminal Victimization in the United States: 1980–1981 Changes Based on New Estimates *(Bureau of Justice Statistics Technical Report). Washington, D.C.: U.S. Department of Justice.)*

ed for various unfortunate happenings. The measurement that can be used for comparison purposes is again households touched by crime, illness, and accidents in a year. By ranking these percentages on a scale, the crime problem can be put into its proper perspective. (See figure 2-4.)

The bar graph reveals that the murder of a family member is the least likely of all tragic life events. Fewer than 1 percent of all households each year suffer the loss of a member to homicide, suicide, or a motor vehicle accident. The flu, pneumonia, and cancer also strike less than one household in a hundred each year. At the other end of the risk spectrum, more than 20 percent of American households experience a theft of their common property or the possessions of one of their members. (As noted in chapter 1, the risk of being murdered varies greatly from group to group, depending on factors like sex, race, and age. Similarly, theft rates vary substantially among groups. This issue of differential risks will be examined after the discussion of comparative risks.)

Comparing risks, the graph shows that an average household is in greater danger of being burglarized than of being damaged by fire. Heart disease, although rare in any given year, poses more of a threat than rape, which is an even more unusual occurence. A family member is twice as likely to be hurt in an automobile accident (between 4 and 5 percent of all households experience a car crash with injury each year) than to be physically wounded by an assailant (aggravated assault occurs roughly half as often, striking about 2 percent of all households) (Bureau of Justice Statistics, 1982a).

These data can put fears and concerns about unwanted events into proper perspective. For example, homeowners should be more concerned about the adequacy of their insurance coverage for burglary than for fire. (The statistics reveal nothing about the severity of the burglary incidents or the fires. Some burglaries were merely attempted break-ins; some fires were small kitchen blazes.) More dramatically, a study of comparative risks leads to the conclusion that the public ought to be more worried about injuries from automobile accidents than from street criminals. Yet campaigns to improve highway safety, remove drunken drivers from the road, and add crash protection devices like air bags to vehicles attract much less attention and arouse much less passion than campaigns to make the streets safer by cracking down on criminals.

Differential Risks: Who Bears the Burden?

The burden of victimization falls unevenly, hitting certain groups of people much harder than others. Or, to put it somewhat more bluntly, particular kinds of people face great dangers, whereas other kinds have little to fear.

Looking only at personal crimes of violence and theft (rather than household crimes), significantly different group victimization rates emerge. In 1980, men were victimized more than women (except for

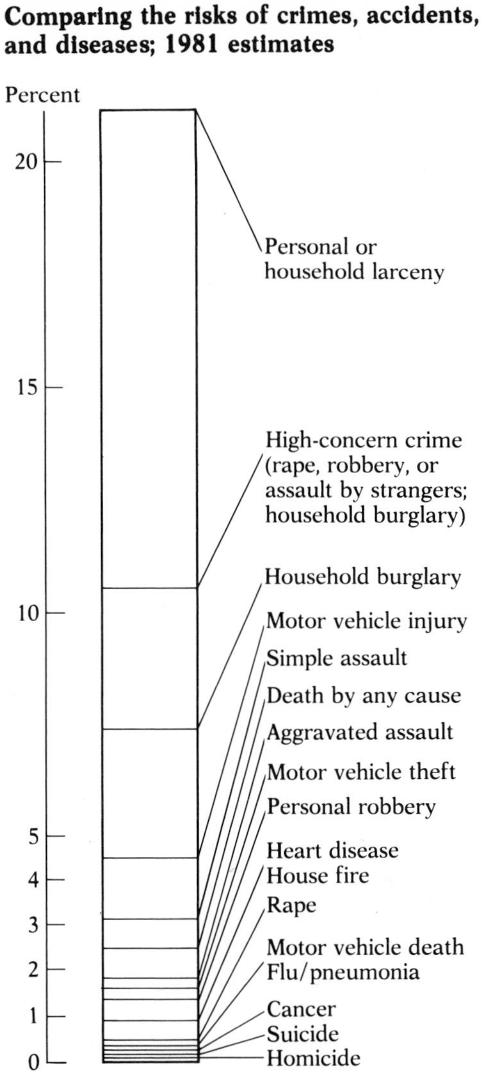

FIGURE 2-4. Percentage of households touched by crime and other negative life events in a year. *(From* Households Touched by Crime, 1981, *by the Bureau of Justice Statistics. Washington, D.C.: U.S. Department of Justice, 1982a:3.)*

cases of rape and purse snatching, of course). Younger people, especially teenagers and adults in their early twenties, were the targets of criminal attack much more often than older people, particularly the aged (except for pocket pickings and purse snatchings). Divorced or separated people and those who had never married experienced far greater troubles than married couples or widowed individuals. Black and Hispanic people suffered more incidents than whites of European ancestry (except for personal larcenies). Higher-income persons were burdened much less often by violence but more often by thefts than lower-income people. City dwellers faced higher risks than their suburban or rural counterparts (Bureau of Justice Statistics, 1982c:4). (See figure 2-5.)

Differential Reporting: Why Call the Cops?

In order for an event to be entered into the records as a crime known to the police, it must survive a series of tests. First, the act must be discovered or detected by a victim, witness, or police officer. Second, it must be recognized or interpreted as an instance of lawbreaking. (For example, a demand for a student's lunch money—"or else"—may or may not be defined as a robbery.) Third, the incident must be reported to the authorities. Fourth, the police must not redefine it as a trivial, noncriminal event unworthy of their attention. Fifth, the police must commit themselves to take action, at least to the extent of filling out an official report and filing it in the appropriate manner. Those incidents that make it through the first two steps but fail to pass one of the last three steps constitute unreported and unrecorded crimes. The first three steps involve what might be termed the "social reaction" to crime, and the last two are the "official reaction." Victimization surveys shed light for the first time on aspects of the social reaction—why some people report crimes and others don't and which kinds of crimes are reported most faithfully (Sparks, Genn, and Dodd, 1977).

When deciding whether to call the police, a victim probably performs a rough cost-benefit analysis. Possible costs include time, money, pride, and future safety. A victim might believe that it would be futile to notify the police, because they wouldn't respond or would be unwilling or unable to help out. (For example, a victim might have no idea who hit him over the head and fled with his wallet.) A person might be reluctant to become a complainant because it would mean formal involvement with the criminal justice system (at the police station, looking at mug shots or viewing lineups; and in court, appearing and testifying as a key witness for the prosecution). Such obligations can lead to further losses of time and money. A victim's pride might also be at stake. In the process of recounting the details of the crime, the victim's own illegal, immoral, or embarrassing conduct might be exposed. (For example, a person seeking to buy illicit drugs might have been held up by someone posing as a dealer.) Getting the alleged perpetrator into trouble might lead to serious reprisals, so victims of intimidation must suffer in silence. Finally, victims might not approve of the anticipated outcome of the criminal justice process, which could be either too severe (against a neighbor's son, for example) or too lenient. For any of these reasons, they do not set the process in motion by calling the police.

The benefits victims might derive from turning over their problems to

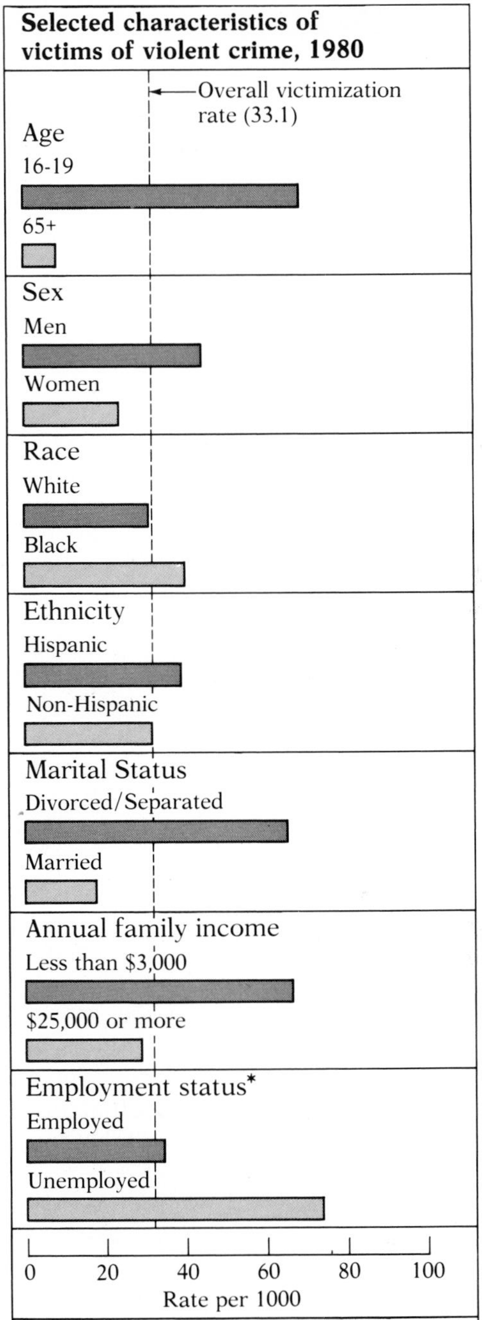

Note: The differences between rates within categories are statistically significant. Rate differences between categories may or may not be significant.
*Limited to persons age 16 and over.

FIGURE 2-5. Selected characteristics of victims of violent crime, 1980. *(From* Criminal Victimization in the United States, 1980, *by the Bureau of Justice Statistics. Washington, D.C.: U.S. Department of Justice, 1982:4.)*

the proper authorities include satisfaction from revenge, restored pride, and financial reimbursement. If, by reporting and cooperating, the victims can help the police to arrest the suspect, and the prosecution to convict the person, then the victims might gain peace of mind from knowing that the criminal is being punished. They might also feel proud that they had fulfilled a civic duty by aiding in the apprehension, prosecution and conviction of a troublemaker. The victims might also be repaid for their efforts. The police could recover stolen goods, or the court could order the convict to make restitution to them. By reporting the crime, the victims might become eligible for reimbursement from an insurance company or for compensation from a state fund if they were seriously hurt (Sparks, Genn, and Dodd, 1977).

The NCS victimization surveys reveal that the proportion of incidents perceived as crimes by victims and reported to the police varies substantially by the type of crime and the type of victim. The crimes that are reported most completely are those involving injury or considerable financial loss. Minor crimes against property and attempted crimes against property are usually not reported to the police. Serious crimes of violence like rape, robbery, and aggravated assault are reported about half the time.

In 1980, successful auto thefts were reported at a higher rate than any other street crime. These victims were probably concerned about recovering their car, collecting insurance reimbursement, and avoiding any liability for an accident involving the stolen vehicle. Break-ins were also well reported, again presumably because of hopes of recovering stolen property and collecting burglary insurance reimbursements. (See figure 2-6.)

The age, sex, and social class (but not ethnicity or race) of the victim turned out to be important factors in whether the crime was reported to the police. Variations by age were the most substantial. Teenagers were the most reluctant of all age groups to notify the authorities. Men were slightly less inclined to call the police than women. Lower-income people were less likely to complain about crimes against their property than higher-income ones. The most common reasons for nonreporting offered by all kinds of victims were that the offenses were not important enough to merit official action and that the police could do nothing for the victims even if they were notified. Inconvenience to the victim and fear of offender reprisal were not significant causes of nonreporting (Bureau of Justice Statistics, 1982c: 16–17). (See table 2-4 and figure 2-7.)

Focus on Robbery: Theft with Violence

Looking at the big picture was a worthwhile first step, because impressions were gained about how crimes of all kinds burden victims of all types in a number of ways. Now, a more in-depth investigation of one

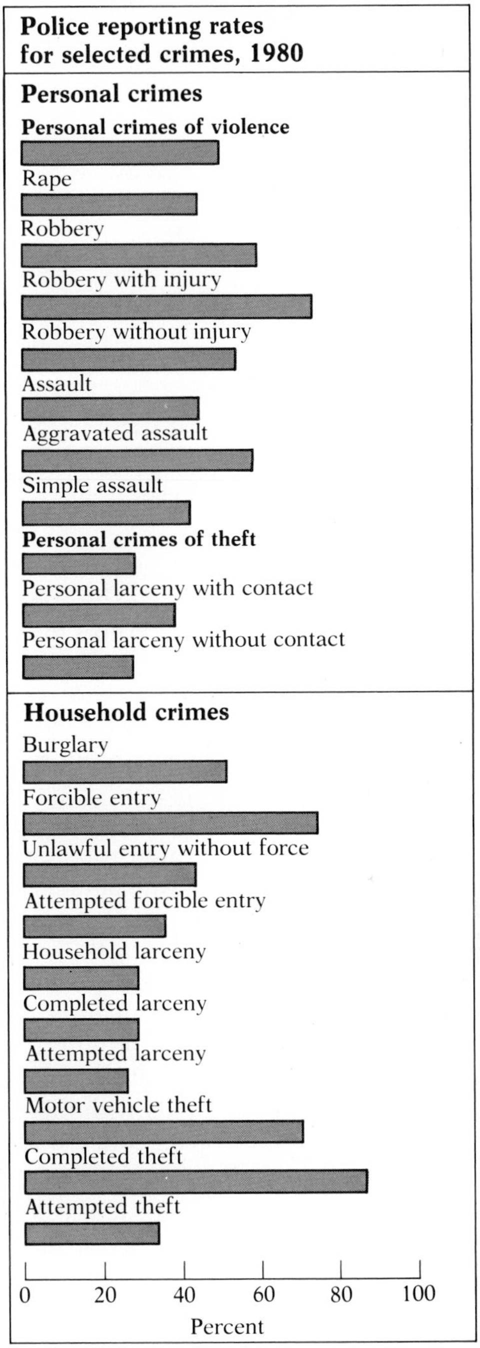

FIGURE 2-6. Rates of reporting specific crimes, 1980. *(From* Criminal Victimization in the United States, 1980, *by the Bureau of Justice Statistics. Washington, D.C.: U.S. Department of Justice, 1982:16.)*

TABLE 2-4 Reporting Rates by Groups

Characteristics of victims	*Percentage reporting crimes of violence*	*Percentage reporting thefts*
By age		
12–19	36%	13%
20–34	49%	30%
65 and over	55%	38%
By sex		
Males	44%	27%
Females	52%	27%
By race and ethnicity		
White	47%	27%
Black	52%	27%
Hispanic	50%	27%

SOURCE: *Criminal Victimization in the United States, 1980,* by the Bureau of Justice Statistics. Washington, D.C.: U.S. Department of Justice, 1982:72–73.

offense—robbery—will underscore how the burden of victimization falls more heavily on some than others. The questions that will be addressed are: Who faces the greatest risks? Who is most likely to put up resistance? Who is most often wounded? Who suffers the most, financially? Who is most inclined to call the police?

Robbers are among the most feared and hated of all street criminals. Their offense combines stealing with extortion or outright violence, so it carries some of the stiffest prison sentences permissible under law. Historically, bandits were considered much more interesting than their victims. Their exploits were often romanticized. The highwaymen of Robin Hood's band; the pirates who plundered ships laden with treasure; the frontier outlaws who ambushed stagecoaches and trains; and the gangsters who stuck up banks during the Great Depression—all were the subjects of stories and songs sympathetic to, or at least understanding of, their dramatic deeds. But now the glitter has largely faded, and in its place is the image of the mugger or gunman as a vicious thug, a cruel predator, and an exploiter of weakness whose random violence casts a shadow over everyday life. Along with this decline in the popularity of robbers has come an upsurge in concern for their victims.

The Interaction between Robber and Victim

All victim–offender interactions can be described in terms of a set of roles. The roles can be considered complementary, since each party has a "part" to play. Offenders generally play the part of the initiator and aggressor. The victims are usually passive, at least at the start. But the persons targeted by the offender can refuse to play their assigned part, reject the "script," and overturn the scenario imposed on them. The victims might even gain the upper hand, switch roles, and break off the interaction or end it in a way dreaded by the offenders. (Most criminal incidents do not proceed according to the offenders' plan—attempts outnumber successful completions.)

A successful, or completed, robbery involves a face-to-face confronta-

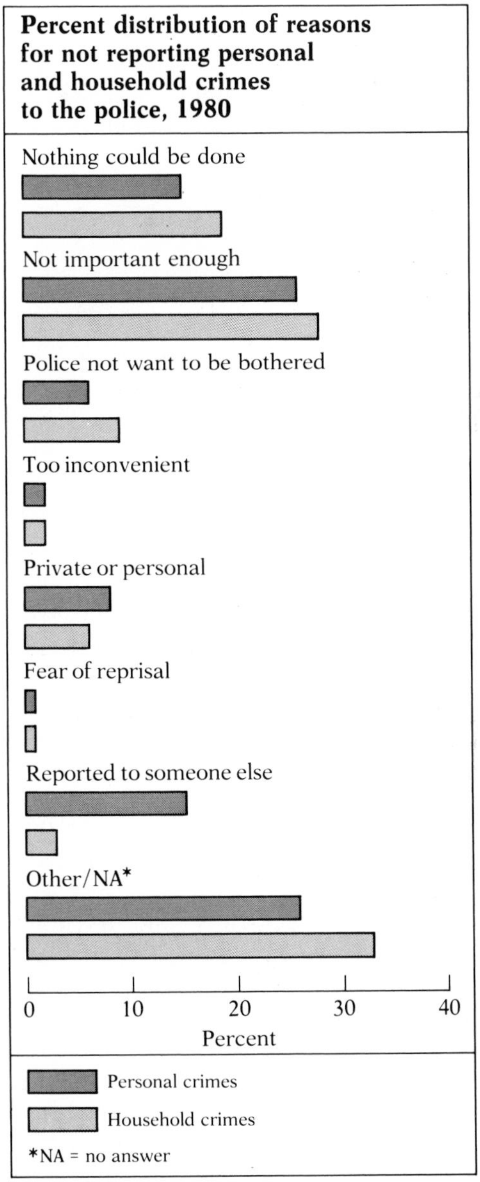

FIGURE 2-7. Reasons for not reporting crimes to the police, 1980. (*From* Criminal Victimization in the United States, 1980, *by the Bureau of Justice Statistics. Washington, D.C.: U.S. Department of Justice, 1982:17.)*

tion in which the perpetrators take something of value from the victims against their will either by force or by threatening violence. The law considers armed robberies more serious than unarmed ("strong-arm") ones ("muggings" or "yokings"). Successful robbers, whether armed or unarmed, must be skilled at what has been termed "target manipulation" or "victim management" (Letkemann, 1973).

When analyzed as a transaction based on "instrumental coercion" (applying force to accomplish a goal), a typical robbery proceeds through five stages, or phases: planning; establishing "co-presence"; developing "co-orientation"; transfering valuables; and leaving (Best and Luckenbill, 1982).

During the planning stage, the offenders make preparations such as choosing accomplices, weapons, sites, and getaway routes. The robbers also pick out a victim or victims. The potential target should have certain desirable characteristics: valuable possessions; vulnerability to attack; relative powerlessness to resist; and isolation from potential protectors. Strangers are preferred, because they will have greater difficulty in identifying the offenders.

During the second phase of the interaction, the offenders establish co-presence by moving into striking range. The robbers try not to arouse the victims' suspicion or to provoke either unmanageable opposition or fright and flight. Some offenders rely on speed and stealth to rush up to unwitting victims. Others employ deceit to trick the victims into letting down their guard.

When the transaction enters the third stage, the victim–offender relationship changes from a routine, tranquil encounter into a conflict situation. The robbers announce their intentions to dominate the relationship and exploit the victims. They give orders and demand compliance. They instruct the targets to surrender their valuables. The victims either acquiesce or contest the robbers' bid to take charge, depending on their assessment of the robbers' punitive resources (ability to inflict injury). Robbers who fail to develop co-orientation (secure cooperation) by threats may resort to violence to subdue, incapacitate, or intimidate their intended victims.

If the robbers successfully gain and maintain the upper hand, the interaction moves into the fourth phase. The victims are searched, and their valuables are seized. But the interaction is terminated prematurely (from the offenders' point of view) if the victims put up stubborn resistance, have no valuables, are unexpectedly rescued by an intruder (from the robbers' viewpoint), or escape the exploiters' clutches.

The fifth and final stage is marked by the robbers' attempts to break off the relationship at a time and under conditions of their choosing. As they prepare to leave the scene, they may inflict additional wounds upon the victims in order to prevent interference with the getaway. Or, they may direct additional threats at the victims about the dangers of pursuing them or reporting the crime to the authorities (Best and Luckenbill, 1982:166–170).

Being Targeted

For every 1,000 people of all kinds within the United States who were at least twelve years old in 1980, about 7 were robbed that year. (Roughly 0.7 percent—that is, seven-tenths of 1 percent of the teenage and adult population—was confronted by a mugger or armed bandit within the year.) In relative terms, this is a tiny proportion. An overwhelming 99.3 percent of the at-risk public went about its business unmolested. Most people don't know and won't meet a person who was robbed within the previous year. However, the ranks of robbery victims might appear quite large in absolute terms. Over a million people were robbed in 1980, according to projections from the National Crime Panel sample. Estimates of the probability of being robbed during an entire lifetime, given current rates, approach 50 percent (Skogan and Maxfield, 1981). The prospect of every other person's becoming a robbery victim, over a lifetime, might sound like a dire prediction of grim things to come.

But all the above statistics are limited in value, because victimization surveys confirm the suspicion that robbery rates vary considerably from one group to another. The odds a person faces depend on which categories he or she falls into. The important variables are age, ethnicity/race, sex, marital status, family income level, and area of residence.

The robbery rate for adolescents and young adults is several times higher than that for the elderly. Blacks are robbed more than twice as often—and Hispanics twice as often—as whites. Males are mugged and held up more than twice as frequently as females. Married men and women have comparatively low rates, whereas single men and women, especially divorced or separated people, face much greater risks. Unemployed persons are more than twice as likely to be robbed as those with jobs. The risks of being robbed go down as family income goes up. City residents, particularly in central districts of the nation's biggest metropolitan areas, are robbed more than seven times as often as those who dwell in small towns and country settings. (See table 2-5.)

Although the robbery rate for elderly women (many are widows) is the lowest of any group, these victims have received special attention because there are teenage boys who specialize in preying on them. The juvenile offenders rob and assault the elderly in lobbies and doorways of buildings ("push-ins") out of public view. Police decoys, posing as easy marks, have trapped such robbers by flashing money in front of them. If they take the bait and accost the undercover officer dressed as an elderly person, then the back-up team from the senior citizen robbery unit closes in and arrests the suspect while the crime is in progress (Morello, 1982).

TABLE 2-5 Robbery Rates, by Groups

Characteristics of victims	*Robbery rate (number of victims for every 1,000 people of this type, age 12 and over)*
All types of people	7
By age	
12–19	10
20–24	11
65 and over	4
By race and ethnicity	
Whites	6
Blacks	14
Hispanics	12
By sex	
Males	9
Females	4
By marital status and sex	
Married women	3
Married men	5
Widowed women	3
Widowed men	11
Never-married women	5
Never-married men	16
Divorced or separated women	12
Divorced or separated men	16
By employment status	
Have a job	6
Unemployed	13
By family income levels	
Less than $3,000	14
$3,000–$7,499	11
$7,500–$9,999	7
$10,000–$14,999	6
$15,000–$24,999	5
$25,000 or more	5
By place of residence	
Within the central city, 1,000,000 or more population	22
Within the central city, 500,000–999,999 population	13
Suburbs of metropolitan areas	5
Small towns and rural areas	3

SOURCE: *Criminal Victimization in the United States, 1980,* by the Bureau of Justice Statistics. Washington, D.C.: U.S. Department of Justice, 1982:23–35.

Resisting Robbers

Most victims surveyed in 1980 resisted the advances of robbers to some degree. Roughly six out of ten victims made the robbers' tasks more difficult to carry out. About four out of ten were successful in their efforts to thwart the robbers' aims. (The completion rate was 61 percent; 39 percent of the incidents were classified as attempted robberies, because the offender tried but failed to take something of value away from the victim.) From the victim's standpoint, however, a bungled attempt is not necessarily an unqualified victory. Some resisting victims are physically injured during the confrontation, and valuable property (a camera, for example) may be damaged or destroyed.

A number of resistance strategies were tried by victims and recorded by the survey interviewers. The most common forms of resistance were fighting back physically, either with bare hands or with a weapon (other than a gun or knife); acting nonviolently but trying to escape; and screaming to frighten the offender away and attract help from bystanders. Very few victims drew their own knife or gun to ward off the attacker. Men were more likely than women to fight the robber, and women were more likely than men to call for assistance.

Different types of people resisted to greater or lesser degrees. Younger victims put up more resistance than older victims. Whites resisted a little more frequently than blacks. If the robber was not a stranger, the victim was more likely to resist. Women tended to resist more often than men. (See table 2-6.)

To some extent, whether a victim resisted, and to what degree, depended on what weapon, if any, the robber brandished. Slightly more than half of all robberies in 1980 were by unarmed bandits. When robbers were armed, the weapons they chose most often were knives and guns. Robbers with guns successfully completed 80 percent of their crimes, compared with an overall completion rate of 61 percent.

The relationship between resistance and injury is more complex, in part because the robbers' weapons represent a third factor. The statistics from victimization surveys are subject to different interpretations. In general, the data show that a victim up against a robber with a gun was less likely to resist and also was less likely to get hurt. During a strongarm robbery, or when the offender wielded a brick or bottle, the victim was more likely to wind up injured. Either the victims in such situations were more prone to resist than victims facing a knife or gun, or the robbers at the outset were more inclined to inflict a wound to prove to the victims that they "meant business." Overall, victims took self-protective measures more often in incidents in which they were injured. What cannot be determined from the tables is whether they first resisted and then were injured, or first were injured and then began to resist.

According to some recent studies by behavioral scientists, the victim of an armed robber is most likely to avoid injury if he or she is deferential and quickly surrenders valuables. When confronted by an unarmed assailant, the victim is most likely to escape harm and prevent losses by offering nonforceful resistance, such as yelling for help or running away ("Psychologists Advise on Street Criminals," 1983).

Becoming a Casualty: Physical Injuries and Financial Losses

Robbers may hurt their victims for a number of reasons. They may inflict a wound initially to intimidate the target into submission. They may become violent during the holdup as a reaction to any perceived resistance, noncooperation, or stalling. Offenders may relish taking advantage of a helpless person or may seize the opportunity to show off to accomplices. Injuring victims may be a sign of anger, disappointment in the haul, scorn, contempt, sadism, fear, or loss of self-control. But it may also be instrumental. Wounding the victims can render them incapable of later identifying the robbers, pursuing them, or even calling for help. Violent outbursts at the end of the interaction may be intended to shock, stun, or preoccupy the victims, their associates, and any bystanders, so that they will hesitate to call the police.

Despite all these possible motives for harming victims, robbers usually don't inflict injuries. The 1980 survey showed that about one-third of all robbery victims were physically assaulted. Most of their wounds were minor injuries such as bruises, cuts, scratches, and swellings. Only about a fifth of the injured victims—and about one-fourteenth of all robbery

TABLE 2-6 Making it Harder for Robbers

Part A: Resistance by Groups, 1980

Characteristics of victims	*Percentage of victims who resisted*
All types of people	63%
By age	
12–19	66%
20–34	66%
65 and over	54%
By race	
Whites	64%
Blacks	59%
By prior relationship	
Complete stranger	59%
Not a stranger	80%
By sex	
Males	60%
Females	67%
By seriousness	
Injured victims	70%
Uninjured victims	59%

Part B: Methods of Resistance

Self-protective measures used by victim	*Percentage of all resisting victims using this measure*
Used or brandished a gun or knife	3%
Used other weapon or physical force	24%
Tried to get help or frighten offender away by shouting	27%
Threatened or reasoned with offender	16%
Resisted nonviolently or tried to escape	24%
Other methods	6%

SOURCE: *Criminal Victimization in the United States, 1980,* by the Bureau of Justice Statistics. Washington, D.C.: U.S. Department of Justice, 1982:58–59.

victims—were seriously hurt: shot, stabbed, knocked unconscious, bones broken.

The chance of being injured varied from group to group. Older persons were more likely to be hurt than teenage victims. Lower-income people suffered more wounds than higher-income ones. Victims confronted by robbers they recognized were more likely to be injured than those accosted by strangers. Males and females, and whites and blacks, were wounded at roughly the same rate, one out of three. (See table 2-7.)

In 1980, only about one robbery victim in ten needed hospital care. Of those who were injured, the medical attention provided in the emer-

TABLE 2-7 Getting Hurt by Robbers

Part A: Proportions Wounded, 1980

Characteristics of victims	*Percentage of victims physically injured*
All types of people	34%
By age	
12–19	25%
20–34	35%
65 and over	37%
By family income levels	
Less than $3,000	40%
$3,000–$7,499	37%
$10,000–$14,999	33%
$25,000 or more	31%
By prior relationship	
Complete stranger	32%
Not a stranger	44%
By sex	
Males	32%
Females	39%
By race	
Whites	36%
Blacks	31%

Part B: Nature of Wounds

Type of injury	*Percentage of victims injured (by robbers who were strangers, 1973–79)*
Minor injuries	
Bruises, cuts, scratches, swellings	26%
Serious injuries	
Knife or bullet wounds	2%
Broken bones, teeth	2%
Internal injuries, knocked unconsious	3%
All injuries	33%

SOURCE: Part A: From *Criminal Victimization in the United States,* 1980, by the Bureau of Justice Statistics. Washington, D.C.: U.S. Department of Justice, 1982:60.
Part B: *Violent Crime by Strangers,* by the Bureau of Justice Statistics. Washington, D.C.: U.S. Department of Justice, 1982:3.

gency room was usually sufficient. About three out of every one hundred victims had to be hospitalized for a day or more.

Fewer than one victim in ten incurred any medical expenses from the assaults that accompanied the thefts. Fewer than three of every one hundred victims in 1980 accumulated doctor and hospital bills exceeding $250.

About one victim in seven missed work because of injuries sustained during the crime. Most (77 percent) were out for less than a week.

Surprisingly, as many as three out of ten victims in 1980 suffered no tangible economic loss from the completed or attempted robbery. Eight out of ten lost property worth less than $250. Most (nearly 75 percent) were not able to recover any of the dollar value of what was taken or damaged. For those who did get at least something back, the most likely source of recovery was police seizure of stolen goods or cash, not insurance reimbursement. (Few victims had coverage for robbery losses; most policies protect against burglary, arson, vandalism, and auto theft, but not muggings and stick-ups.) Whites were substantially more likely to recoup some of their losses than blacks (Bureau of Justice Statistics, 1982c:60–70).

Reporting Robberies

Reporting rates varied by age, sex, and physical condition in the aftermath of the robbery. Older people were more likely to notify the authorities than teenagers. Females were more inclined to call the police than males. Injured victims reported robberies more readily than uninjured ones. Hispanics were less likely than blacks or whites to call the cops. Whether the offender was a complete stranger was a minor factor. (See table 2-8, Part A.)

The reasons why victims didn't report robberies were explored during the survey interview. The most frequent rationales were that the incident was not important enough to warrant police attention (presumably because the robber's haul was small and violence had only been *threatened*); that the victims felt that nothing could be accomplished, because they were unable to describe the offender or furnish proof that a crime had taken place; and that in their opinion the offense was a private or personal matter that shouldn't involve outsiders and would be bothersome to the police. (A catchall category of assorted reasons actually represented the highest percentage of cases.) (See table 2-8, Part B.)

Explaining the Patterns: Vulnerability and Risks

What factors explain why the burden of victimization falls more heavily on certain people than others? What is it—if anything—that catches the attention of criminals? Which behaviors and activities heighten risks, and which ones reduce the odds of being harmed?

TABLE 2-8 Turning Robbers In

Part A: Rate of Reporting by Groups

Characteristics of victims	*Percentage who reported the crime to the police*
All robbery victims	57%
By age	
12–19	46%
20–34	55%
65 and over	61%
By sex	
Males	53%
Females	64%
By seriousness	
Injured victims	70%
Uninjured victims	50%
By race and ethnicity	
Whites	58%
Blacks	54%
Hispanics	43%
By prior relationship	
Complete stranger	56%
Not a stranger	60%

Part B: Reasons for Not Reporting Robberies

Rationale	*Percentage of nonreported incidents*
Not important enough	11%
Nothing could be done, lack of proof	14%
Private, personal matter	12%
Police would not want to be bothered	10%
Reported to someone else	5%
Fear of reprisal	6%
Too inconvenient and time-consuming	5%
Other reasons, or no reasons given	38%

SOURCE: *Criminal Victimization in the United States, 1980,* by the Bureau of Justice Statistics. Washington, D.C.: U.S. Department of Justice, 1982:71–75.

Vulnerability to crime is always a matter of degree. The statistics from victimization surveys confirm the long-held suspicion that particular kinds of people are more vulnerable to exploitation and injury than others. But victimologists cannot agree among themselves exactly what characteristics victims have in common that make them relatively more susceptible than nonvictims. Inasmuch as patterns clearly emerged from the data, victimization is definitely not a random process, striking people just by chance. When victims ask, "Why me?" victimologists suggest that the answer may be more than simply "plain bad luck."

The Determinants of Vulnerability

Someday, it will be possible to compute a vulnerability index to predict the possibility of a given individual's becoming a casualty of a specific type of crime (Galaway and Hudson, 1981). The calculation would take into account characteristics like sex, age, race, income, occupation, marital status, and locality, since these factors have proven to be correlated with victimization rates. In the meantime, there can be only informed speculation about what traits are relatively advantageous or disadvantageous in terms of susceptibility to criminal attack.

Personal attributes might play a part in determining vulnerability. The mentally retarded, newly arrived immigrants, uneducated people, and inexperienced people would appear to be unusually exploitable by criminals employing deception and fraud. Con men swindle the greedy, heartbroken, and lonesome with legendary ease. Physically handicapped people, the elderly and frail, the very young, and perhaps females in general are thought to be more assailable by violent offenders. A varied collection of psychological, biological, and social conditions may set whole categories of people apart as peculiarly vulnerable (Von Hentig, 1941).

Situational factors might play a part as well. People are more susceptible at certain times, periods, or phases than at others. For example, tourists are a notoriously vulnerable group. Offenders prey on them with impunity, knowing that because of considerations of money, time, or both, few tourists will be willing and able to return to the jurisdiction of the crime to take part in the criminal justice process, even if their assailants are caught red-handed by the police. A tourist's average length of stay of a few days to a few weeks is invariably too brief to see a case through to its conclusion. As a result, charges against defendants are usually dropped or drastically reduced because of the absence of a key witness or the complainant (victim). For instance, Waikiki Beach in Honolulu, Hawaii, was a haven for muggers and rapists until an apprehensive tourist industry, convinced that crime was hurting business, began to fund a victim–witness return project. Free transportation back to the island, free accommodations, and child care are furnished to victims who press charges and testify at trials. Government officials even intercede with employers back home to assure them of the importance of the return visit. As a result, an umbrella of protection is extended to tourists who otherwise suffer high temporary, situational vulnerability. Conviction rates are rising, and crime rates are dropping ("Hawaii Return-Witness Program," 1982).

The vulnerability of a person or group depends on an attractiveness factor and an opportunity variable (Sparks, 1981:774). Anyone or anything can be of interest to offenders, but certain targets are surely more appealing than others (high-priced sports cars as opposed to beat-up jalopies, for example). In order for offenders to close in on targets that attract them, they must seize opportunities that present themselves. Extremely vulnerable people and property are unfortunately "at the right time and the right place" from the criminal's frame of reference.

Certain lifestyles expose people and their possessions to threats and dangers more than others. The highway accident rate is much higher for new, young, male drivers than for older and more experienced motorists. Automobile insurance premiums reflect this disparity. Similarly, the life expectancy of women is longer than that of men, and life insurance premiums mirror this divergence. The explanations for both these differences in rates between groups center on dissimilarities in lifestyles. The lifestyle–exposure hypothesis seems to be the most reasonable explanation for variations in victimization rates by age, sex, race, class, marital status, and locality as well (Hindelang, Gottfredson, and Garofalo, 1978).

The sociological expression *lifestyle* refers to the daily, routine activities and special events a person engages in on a predictable basis. It embraces how one spends time and money and the social roles (like housewife, worker, commuter, or student) one plays. Differences in lifestyle lead to differences in exposure to risks. In the long run, exposure is the key determinant of victimization rates. (In the short run, anything can happen.) People who regularly find themselves in dangerous situations are the most likely candidates to join the ranks of crime victims.

The data published in the UCR from police files and the information about incidents gathered directly from victims concerning where and when crimes take place confirm everyday, common-sense impressions. Public places like streets, parks, and mass transit stations are the favored sites for acts of theft and violence committed by strangers. After dark is when offenders prefer to operate. Frequenting public places at night increases one's odds of winding up as a crime statistic. Associating with the type of people who tend to commit most street crimes also jeopardizes one's health and financial well-being. The more that people insulate themselves from known offenders and those who statistically resemble offenders, the safer they will be. The more convenient, inviting, and vulnerable people appear to be, the greater is the danger that they will attract offenders.

The lifestyle–exposure model asserts that vulnerability is a function of coming into contact with motivated offenders and of being viewed as a suitable target. In sharp contrast with most theories about the causes of criminal incidents, the willingness to commit an illegal act on the part of the offender is assumed, as a given. The question is not, Why is a person criminally inclined? The focus is instead, Under what situations is this inclination most likely to be restrained—or unleashed? That is, under what conditions are would-be offenders most able to translate their criminal impulses into actions? Restricting opportunities, rather than curbing desires, takes on primary importance (Gottfredson, 1981).

Reducing Risks: How Safe Is Safe Enough?

Life is marred by all sorts of unanticipated and undesirable consequences. When social scientists estimate risks, they are predicting how many people will suffer from unwanted events.

The statistical concepts underlying risk estimates can be difficult to grasp and fathom. Only three distinct probabilities can be readily understood: "0," which signifies that an event cannot occur (is impossible); "1," which means that an event will surely occur (must happen); and "0.5," which indicates a "toss-up," or "50–50" chance, as in hoping for "heads" when flipping a coin. But risks that are 0.1 (1 in 10), or 0.01 (1 in 100), or 0.007 (7 in 1,000) are harder to gauge or evaluate. If the odds of something happening are one in a million, statisticians would advise people not to worry about it (or not to count on it, if it is a desirable event). But when 7 people in every 1,000 are robbed each year, should the risk of robbery be taken into account when planning one's daily schedule? How much preparation, fear, and anxiety would be rational in the face of these odds? What sacrifices would be appropriate, in terms of forgoing necessary or welcomed activities (like taking evening classes or walking through the park on a warm spring night)? At what point does it become foolhardy to disregard the risks and to ignore precautions (like buying an expensive bicycle lock or purchasing crime insurance)?

The proper balance between safety and risk is ultimately a personal decision and yet a matter of public debate. In general, more protection can be secured by greater expenditure. Dangers can be reduced if individuals and groups are willing to pay the price. Any demand for absolute safety (zero risk) is irrational, in statistical terms. Probabilities can be reduced but never entirely eliminated. How safe is safe enough, is strictly a value judgment. At some point, it is reasonable to declare the odds an "acceptable risk" (Lynn, 1981). When performing a risk–benefit analysis, a point of diminishing returns may be discovered. Additional efforts to increase safety are largely futile and wasteful (for example, adding more locks to a front door). Risk–benefit analyses seem scientifically sound and precise, but on close inspection they hinge on questionable assumptions and debatable value judgments. How much is a human life worth, in monetary terms? Can the pain and suffering of a crime victim be converted by some formula into dollars and cents?

Victimologists and criminologists have coined terms to describe the ways in which people try to reduce the risks they face. These risk reduction activities, seen by the participants as "crime prevention" measures (or, more precisely, victimization prevention, as noted earlier, since offenders are deflected more than dissuaded), become incorporated into lifestyles.

Avoidance strategies (Furstenberg, 1972) are actions people take to limit their personal exposure to dangerous persons and frightening situations (such as staying home at night, barring strangers from one's home, or ignoring passersby who attempt to engage in conversations on deserted streets). *Risk management tactics* (Skogan and Maxfield, 1981) minimize the chances of being harmed when exposure is unavoidable. Examples include walking with others rather than traveling alone, or carrying a weapon rather than going about unarmed. *Crime prevention through environmental design* (abbreviated as CPTED) stresses the importance of creating "defensible space" (Newman, 1972) by "hardening targets" (improving locks, erecting fences) and maintaining surveillance (watching, guarding). Risk reduction actions are categorized as *individual* or *collective* (when arranged in concert with others) (Conklin, 1975) or, similarly, as either *private-minded* or *public-minded* (Schneider and Schneider, 1978).

Risk reduction strategies do work to a degree that is plainly observable but not readily quantifiable. The best example concerns the relatively low victimization rates experienced by women as compared with men, and by the elderly as opposed to other age groups. Women and elderly people are presumed to be highly vulnerable to predatory street criminals. The apparent paradox can be explained by noting that women and the elderly incorporate risk reduction strategies into their lifestyles on a routine basis, to the point that the self-imposed restrictions become second nature to the participants and to observers. For example, it seems normal to find young men out late at night drinking in taverns; it appears unusual to encounter unescorted women or elderly people in such settings at those hours.

The relatively high rates for assault, robbery, and rape that burden divorced, separated, and unmarried women as compared with married women can also best be understood as a function of lifestyle. Married women are better able to abide by risk reduction prescriptions. Their daily routines, social companions, leisure activities, and family-centered obligations are less likely to expose them to danger than the lifestyles of women without husbands (except for widows, who tend to be elderly and follow elderly lifestyles) (Skogan, 1981a).

Contradictory messages permeate American culture on the subject of risk taking. On the one hand, the entrepreneurial ideology extols risk taking and generously rewards those enterprises that survive hardships and thrive in a highly competitive environment. Culture heroes are invariably risk takers who defy overwhelming odds: pioneers, explorers, captains of industry, private detectives, secret agents, soldiers of fortune, high-stakes gamblers, and other adventurers. On the other hand, middle-class values counsel prudence in the face of risks. Conscientious, responsible people plan, build, invest, and save in order to be prepared for adversity, illness, old age, accidents, or devastating victimizations. Safety, peace of mind, and protection can be purchased to ensure against unforeseen dangers and unavoidable tragedies. Mastery of events and control over nature are the hallmarks of scientific achievement. Technological progress is recognized as the reduction of uncertainty and the attainment of reliable, predictable performance. Autonomy (personal independence) and security are highly desired goals. Underlying all these aspirations and accomplishments is the notion of reducing or practically eliminating risks.

The ambivalent attitudes towards risks in American culture are mirrored by ambivalent responses to victimizations. Victims are risk takers who have lost or failed in their gambits. Their suffering evokes sympathy, but it also stimulates criticism about what, if anything, within their lifestyle might be altered to avoid further trouble in the future. This line of inquiry leads to a close inspection of the specific acts that immediately preceded the crime, as well as the general routines that define lifestyles. As the victim–offender interaction is reconstructed and scrutinized, exactly how the victim behaved—what he or she said or did—becomes the focus of attention. The keen interest many victimologists have shown toward victim actions that increase rather than reduce risks is the subject of the next chapter.

References

BARD, MORTON, and SANGREY, DAWN. 1979: *The Crime Victim's Book.* New York: Basic.

BEST, JOEL, and LUCKENBILL, DAVID. 1982: *Organizing Deviance.* Englewood Cliffs, N.J.: Prentice-Hall.

BUREAU OF JUSTICE STATISTICS. 1981: *The Prevalence of Crime.* Washington, D.C.: U.S. Department of Justice.

———. 1982a: *Households Touched by Crime, 1981.* Washington, D.C.: U.S. Department of Justice.

———. 1982b: *Violent Crime by Strangers.* Washington, D.C.: U.S. Department of Justice.

———. 1982c: *Criminal Victimization in the United States, 1980.* Washington, D.C.: U.S. Department of Justice.

BURGESS, ANN, and HOLMSTROM, LINDA. 1974: "Rape Trauma Syndrome." *American Journal of Nursing,* 131:981–986.

CONKLIN, JOHN. 1975: *The Impact of Crime.* New York: Macmillan.

FATTAH, EZZAT. 1981: "Becoming a Victim: The Victimization Experience and Its Aftermath." *Victimology,* 6:1:29–47.

FEDERAL BUREAU OF INVESTIGATION. 1983: Uniform Crime Report: *Crime in the United States, 1982.* Washington, D.C.: U.S. Government Printing Office.

FRIEDMAN, LUCY; BISCHOFF, HELEN; DAVIS, ROBERT; and PEARSON, ANN. 1982: *Victims and Helpers: Reactions to Crime.* New York: Victim Services Agency.

FURSTENBERG, FRANK. 1972: "Fear of Crime and Its Effect on Citizen Behavior." In Albert Biderman (Ed.), *Crime and Justice,* 52–65. New York: Justice Institute.

GALAWAY, BURT, and HUDSON, JOE. 1981: *Perspectives on Crime Victims.* St. Louis, Mo.: Mosby.

GAROFALO, JAMES. 1981: "Victimization Surveys: An Overview." In Burt Galaway and Joe Hudson (Eds.), *Perspectives on Crime Victims,* 98–103. St. Louis, Mo.: Mosby.

GOTTFREDSON, MICHAEL. 1981: "On the Etiology of Criminal Victimization." *Journal of Criminal Law and Criminology,* 72, 2:714–726.

"Hawaii Return-Witness Program Turns Tide against Crime." 1982: *Criminal Justice Newsletter,* 13,11 (June 7): 1.

HINDELANG, MICHAEL; GOTTFREDSON, MICHAEL; and GAROFALO, JAMES. 1978: *Victims of Personal Crime: An Empirical Foundation for a Theory of Personal Victimization.* Cambridge, Mass.: Ballinger.

JACOB, HERBERT. 1980: *Crime and Justice in Urban America.* Englewood Cliffs, N.J.: Prentice-Hall.

LEHNEN, ROBERT, and SKOGAN, WESLEY. 1981: *The National Crime Survey: Working Papers—Volume I: Current and Historical Perspectives.* Washington, D.C.: U.S. Department of Justice.

LETKEMANN, PETER. 1973: *Crime as Work.* Englewood Cliffs, N.J.: Prentice-Hall.

LEVINE, JAMES. 1976: "The Potential for Crime Overreporting in Criminal Victimization Surveys." *Criminology,* 14:307–331.

LYNN, WALTER. 1981: "What Scientists Really Mean by 'Acceptable Risk.'" *U.S. News & World Report,* 90 (March 30):60.

MORELLO, F. 1982: *Juvenile Crimes against the Elderly.* Springfield, Ill.: Charles C Thomas.

NEWMAN, OSCAR. 1972: *Defensible Space: People and Design in the Violent City.* London: Architectural Press.

PAEZ, ADOLFO. 1983: *Criminal Victimization in the United States: 1980–81 Changes Based on New Estimates* (Bureau of Justice Statistics Technical Report). Washington, D.C.: U.S. Department of Justice.

PLATE, THOMAS. 1975: *Crime Pays: An Inside Look at Burglars, Car Thieves, Loan Sharks, Hit Men, Fences, and other Professionals in Crime.* New York: Simon & Schuster.

"Psychologists Advise on Street Criminals." 1983: *The New York Times,* August 16:C1.

RAND, MICHAEL. 1983: *Households Touched by Crime, 1982* (Bureau of Justice Statistics Bulletin). Washington, D.C.: U.S. Department of Justice.

REISS, ALBERT, Jr. 1981: "Towards a Revitalization of Theory and Research on Victimization by Crime." *Journal of Criminal Law And Criminology,* 72,2: 704–713.

SCHNEIDER, ANNE. 1981: "Methodological Problems in Victim Surveys and Their Implications for Research in Victimology." *Journal of Criminal Law and Criminology,* 72,2:818–830.

——— and SCHNEIDER, PETER. 1978: *Private and Public-Minded Citizen Responses to a Neighborhood Crime Prevention Strategy.* Eugene, Ore.: Institute of Policy Analysis.

SKOGAN, WESLEY. 1981a: "Assessing the Behavioral Context of Victimization." *Journal of Criminal Law and Criminology,* 72,2:727–742.

———. 1981b: *Issues in the Measurement of Victimization.* Washington, D.C.: U.S. Department of Justice.

———, and MAXFIELD, MICHAEL. 1981: *Coping with Crime: Individual and Neighborhood Reactions.* Beverly Hills, Calif.: Sage.

SPARKS, RICHARD. 1981: "Multiple Victimization: Evidence, Theory, and Future Research." *Journal of Criminal Law and Criminology,* 72,2:762–778.

———; GENN, HAZEL; and DODD, DAVID. 1977: *Surveying Victims.* New York: Wiley.

"Text of Reagan Message on Crime Legislation." 1982: *Congressional Quarterly Weekly Report,* September 25:2388.

VON HENTIG, HANS. 1941: "Remarks on the Interaction of Perpetrator and Victim." *Journal of Criminal Law, Criminology and Police Science,* 31:303–309.

CHAPTER 3

The Victim's Role in Crime

The Possibility of Shared Responsibility

- A teenager props his shiny new ten-speed bicycle against a wall and enters a pizzeria to play video games. When he emerges, his prized possession is gone.
- Late at night, a stranger pays for his drink at a neighborhood tavern with a $100 bill. The bartender slowly counts out his change twice, just to be sure. When the stranger leaves, two men follow him, push him into a deserted alley, and rob him of $98.
- An unemployed steelworker gets drunk at a bar and proclaims that he can lick any man in the place. He picks a fight with a patron and is beaten up.
- A crowd of unruly high school students barge onto a bus. The driver orders them to "shut up" or he'll "kick them off the bus." They assault him and steal his wallet (see McDonald, 1970).
- Two rival street gangs square off in a deserted playground and hurl insults at each other. One gang's members pull out knives. Seeing that they are outnumbered, the other gang's members draw handguns and shoot down their foes.

Orthodox criminology has consistently ignored the role that victims might play in the consummation of crimes. Victimologists have pledged to correct this imbalance by examining any and all situations in which the people who were harmed played some identifiable part in their own downfall. Victimologists have departed from the traditional offender-oriented explanations of crime (which assume that the problem lies within the lawbreaker) and have raised the possibility of shared responsibility. As a substitute for a preoccupation with the offenders' motives and actions, victimologists have suggested that criminal incidents be viewed as the results of a process of interaction between (at least) two parties. The goal has been to explain why a particular offender harmed a particular victim at a particular time and place. What has emerged is a dynamic model, which takes into account initiatives and responses, actions and reactions, motives and intentions. The terms coined by the pioneers in victimology which capture the enthusiasm for examining interactions include the "duet frame of reference" (Von Hentig, 1941), the "penal couple" (Mendelsohn, 1956) and the "doer-sufferer relationship" (Ellenberger, 1955). These situational explanations represent an improvement over earlier, static, one-sided, perpetrator-centered accounts (Fattah, 1979).

A fundamental theme (albeit a controversial one) within criminology concerns the differences, if any, between offenders and law-abiding people. Criminologists ask, "What distinguishes the offender from the nonoffender?" In a similar vein, victimologists ask, "What distinguishes the victim from the nonvictim? Do victims think or act any differently from nonvictims?"

Once the question is posed, the possibility of shared responsibility is raised. Victimologists have borrowed the terminology of the legal system, traditionally used to describe criminals' behaviors, to apply to the motives and actions of victims as well. The words *responsibility, culpability, guilt,* and *blame* crop up routinely in studies based on the dynamic, situational, interaction process model. In the broadest sense, the concept of shared responsibility implies that the victims—as well as the offenders—did something "wrong." The victims acted carelessly, foolishly, or even provocatively. Instead of minimizing the risks they faced, the victims heightened them. The incidents in which they were harmed were partly of their own making. The unfortunate events were perhaps preventable. To some degree, in instances of shared responsibility, the victims are also at fault.

Victimologists have generally welcomed inquiries into the role of the victim in the generation of criminal incidents, and they have shown enthusiasm for the concept of shared responsibility as a guiding theme inspiring research. The earliest empirical studies of the interaction between offenders and victims, and the first theoretical speculations about victim risks, centered on shared responsibility. Some statements that demonstrate a spirit of encouragement for scrutinizing the victim's behavior in search of evidence of shared responsibility appear in box 3-1.

BOX 3-1 *Expressions of Support for Inquiries into the Victim's Role*

- A real mutuality frequently can be observed in the connection between the perpetrator and the victim, the killer and the killed, the duper and the duped. The victim in many instances leads the evil-doer into temptation. The predator is, by varying means, prevailed upon to advance against the prey (Von Hentig, 1941:303).
- In a sense, the victim shapes and molds the criminal. Although the final outcome may appear to be one-sided, the victim and criminal profoundly work upon each other, right up until the last moment in the drama. Ultimately, the victim can assume the role of determinant in the event (Von Hentig, 1948:384).
- Criminologists should give as much attention to "victimogenesis" as to "criminogenesis." Every person should know exactly to what dangers he is exposed because of his occupation, social class, and psychological constitution (Ellenberger, 1955).
- The distinction between criminal and victim, which used to be considered clear cut as black and white, can become vague and blurred in individual cases. The longer and the more deeply the actions of the persons involved are scrutinized, the more difficult it occasionally will be to decide who is to blame for the tragic outcome (Mannheim, 1965:672).
- In some cases, the victim initiates the interaction, and sends out signals that the receiver (doer) decodes, triggering or generating criminal behavior in the doer (Reckless, 1967:142).
- Probation and parole officers must understand victim–offender relationships. The personality of the victim, as a cause of the offense, is oftentimes more pertinent than that of the offender (Schultz, 1968:135).
- Responsibility for one's conduct is a changing concept, and its interpretation is a true mirror of the social, cultural, and political conditions of a given era. . . . Notions of criminal responsibility most often indicate the nature of societal inter-relationships and the ideology of the ruling group in the power structure. Many crimes don't just happen to be committed—the victim's negligence, precipitative actions, or provocations can contribute to the genesis of crime. . . . The victim's functional responsibility is to do nothing that will provoke others to injure him, and to actively seek to prevent criminals from harming him (Schafer, 1968:4; 144; 152).
- Scholars have begun to see the victim not just as a passive object, as the innocent point of impact of crime on society, but as sometimes playing an active role and possibly contributing to some degree to his own victimization. During the last 30 years, there has been considerable debate, speculation, and research into the victim's role, the criminal–victim relationship, the concept of responsibility, and behaviors that could be considered provocative. Thus, the study of crime has taken on a more realistic and more complete outlook (Viano, 1976:1).
- There is much to be learned about victimization patterns and the factors that influence them. Associated with the question of relative risk is the more specific

question (of considerable importance) of victim participation, since crime is an interactional process (Parsonage, 1979:10).

- In short, becoming a victim is a process, just as there is a process of becoming a criminal (McCaghy, 1980:54).

Calls for Inquiries into the Victim's Role in Specific Crimes

- *Murder:* In many crimes, especially criminal homicide which usually involves intense personal interaction, the victim is often a major contributor to the lawless act. . . . Except in cases in which the victim is an innocent bystander and is killed in lieu of an intended victim, or in cases in which a pure accident is involved, the victim may be one of the major precipitating causes of his own demise (Wolfgang, 1958:245; 264).
- *Rape:* The offender should not be viewed as the sole "cause" and reason for the offense, and the "virtuous" rape victim is not always the innocent and passive party. The role played by the victim and its contribution to the perpetration of the offense becomes one of the main interests of the emerging discipline of victimology. Furthermore, if penal justice is to be fair it must be attentive to these problems of degrees of victim responsibility for her own victimization (Amir, 1971:275–276).
- *Thefts:* Careless people set up temptation–opportunity situations when they carry their money or leave their valuables in a manner which virtually invites theft by pocket picking, burglary, or robbery. Carelessness in handling cash is so persistently a part of everyday living that it must be deemed almost a national habit. . . . Because victim behavior today is conducive to criminality, it will be necessary to develop mass educational programs aimed at changing that behavior (Fooner, 1971:313; 315).
- Victims cause crime in the sense that they set up the opportunity for the crime to be committed. By changing the behavior of the victim and potential victim, the crime rate can be reduced. Holders of fire insurance policies must meet fire safety standards, so why not require holders of theft insurance to meet security standards (Jeffrey, 1971:208–209)?
- *Burglary:* In the same way that criminologists compare offenders with non-offenders to understand why a person commits a crime, we examined how the burglary victim and non-victim differ in an attempt to understand the extent to which a victim vicariously contributes to or precipitates a break-in (Waller and Okihiro, 1978:5).
- *Auto theft:* Unlike most personal property, which is preserved behind fences and walls, cars are constantly moved from one exposed location to another; and since autos contain their own means of locomotion, potential victims are particularly responsible for varying the degree of theft risk by where they park and by the occasions they provide for starting the engine. The role of the victim is especially consequential for this crime; many cases of auto theft appear to be essentially a matter of opportunity. They are victim facilitated (McCaghy, Giordano, and Henson, 1977: 369).

Repeat Victims: Repeated Mistakes?

The strongest cases to prove that some victims share responsibility with offenders for crimes involve repeat victims.[1] Victims who suffer over and over again are probably doing something "wrong." By studying their mistakes, victimologists can uncover their problem behaviors and ultimately correct them.

It seems reasonable to hypothesize that there are such victims who repeatedly share responsibility. The obvious analogy is with repeat offenders (also called recidivists or career criminals) who break the law regularly. Another analogy is with accident-prone people. Just as some people repeatedly injure themselves, others might repeatedly expose themselves to great risks, which occasionally result in encounters with criminals.

It has been difficult, however, to gather evidence to support the hypothesis. In most victimization surveys, respondents report that none of the incidents being surveyed happened to them during the period covered; a small number confide that they experienced a single such incident; and successively smaller groups report having suffered two, three, or more victimizations during the period in question. Since victimization of any kind is relatively rare, and repeat victims are even harder to locate, no study as yet has determined just why these people were unusually vulnerable, especially attractive to offenders, or peculiarly exposed to danger (Sparks, 1981).

A tentative conclusion about victim-prone people, drawn from a complex statistical analysis of victimization survey data, is that repeat victims are more likely to experience the same type of loss or injury twice (for example, to suffer two burglaries within the period) than to experience two different kinds of crime—for example, first a burglary, then a robbery (Reiss, 1980). But the nature of their problem remains a mystery. If their repeated suffering is considered to be a series of nonrandom events—that is, they become embroiled in more trouble than might be expected by chance alone—then exactly what are they doing "wrong"? How do they somehow share responsibility, to some degree, with the offenders?

Several explanations have been advanced to account for "victim-

[1]The literature of victimology has also referred to repeat victims as "multiple victims." This has led to some confusion because that term is also used in two other ways: in cases in which there is more than one victim in a specific incident, and cases in which a single victim suffers more than one type of harm during the same incident (for example, a woman is assaulted, raped, and robbed). Further problems of usage arise because there is no consensus over definitions. Is a person a repeat victim if he is robbed once in 1956 and again in 1983? Is a person a repeat victim if her home is burglarized one year and vandalized the next? Someone who is robbed two separate times by two different persons during the same six-month period is certainly a repeat victim. But whether the other examples describe repeat victims depends on the definitions the researcher chooses (Sparks, 1981).

proneness." The possibility of "born victims," with an inherited predisposition toward being harmed, has been the subject of some speculation (see Von Hentig, 1948). The desire to suffer might be a basic element in the personality structure of some repeat victims if they are masochistic, according to psychological interpretations (see Ellenberger, 1955). An alternative to such biological and psychological approaches, with their assumptions about inherent tendencies or unconscious desires, is provided by the social/cultural perspective. Victim-prone people have acquired certain attitudes and habits that make them more vulnerable to criminal attack (see McDonald, 1970). The images of the country boy (sucker) and the city slicker (con man) exemplify two extremes—one a victim-prone person unaware of risks and unprepared to guard his interests until it is too late, the other schooled in the art of deception and experienced in the ways of hustlers.

If victim-proneness needs to be explained, then its opposite (awkward phrases such as victimization avoidance, evasion, minimization might be applied) does too. People learn how to reduce risks from experts: other victims, the police, ex-offenders, and safety consultants. Victimization prevention tips have evolved, from tidbits in the "Crimestopper's Notebook" of the Dick Tracy comic strip to entire books with titles such as "How to Protect Yourself from . . .," "How to Defend against . . .," and "How to Be Safe and Secure . . .". The field of crime prevention and security management is dedicated to the education of potential targets so that they will no longer be victim-prone.

Victim Facilitation, Precipitation, and Provocation

A number of concepts have been derived from the broad theme of shared responsibility. The notions of victim facilitation, precipitation, and provocation have been defined to describe the specific, identifiable, blameworthy actions taken by certain victims immediately before the commission of the crimes. Unfortunately, these three terms have been used somewhat loosely and inconsistently by criminologists and victimologists, to the point that important distinctions have been blurred or buried. They all refer to the degree of shared responsibility.

Victim Facilitation

Facilitation is a term that ought to be reserved for those situations in which victims unknowingly, carelessly, negligently, foolishly, and unwillingly make it easier for the criminal to commit and consummate the crime. Facilitating victims inadvertently assist the offender and therefore share a minor amount of blame. They increase the dangers they face and open themselves up to trouble by their own thoughtless actions. If it is assumed that the criminal who chooses them as targets was looking for someone to victimize, then victim facilitation is not in any sense a root cause of crime. Facilitation is more like a catalyst in a chemical reaction, which, given the right ingredients and conditions, speeds up the interaction. Facilitating victims attract criminally inclined people to them and thereby influence the distribution of crime.

Auto theft and burglary are the crimes cited by victimologists most often in discussions of the problem of facilitation. A motorist who carelessly leaves the keys dangling in the car's ignition is considered guilty of facilitation if a juvenile joyrider impulsively hops behind the wheel and drives off. Similarly, a residential burglary is considered victim facilitated if force is not used to enter the premises because a homeowner or apartment dweller left the door unlocked or a window wide open.

Data from the National Crime Survey revealed some details about victim-facilitated burglaries. During a three-year period in the mid-1970s, roughly nine million unlawful entries through unlocked doors and windows were committed across the United States, resulting in losses totalling more than a billion dollars. Only about two out of every five of these no-force entries were reported to the police. Younger people were found to be more lax about security than older people; higher-income households were entered without force more frequently than lower-income dwellings; renters were more careless than owners; central city households were burglarized more often than suburban or rural ones; and whites appeared to be more negligent about locking doors and windows than blacks. No-force entries were found to be more common than break-ins. But these easily preventable losses were generally smaller, indicating the greater participation of amateur thieves acting spontaneously, seizing the opportunities provided by victims who made their tasks easier (NCJISS, 1979:1–30). (See Waller and Okihiro, 1978, for an analysis of the victim's role in burglaries in Canada.)

Victim Provocation and Precipitation

Whereas facilitation is usually raised as a possibility in crimes of theft, charges about precipitation and provocation are directed at victims of violent crimes, such as murder and rape. The first in-depth investigation of victim precipitation (Wolfgang, 1958) centered on homicides committed in Philadelphia from 1948 to 1952. Although its specific findings concern events that occurred more than three decades ago, its influence on current thinking about criminals and victims remains strong.

Victim precipitation was the label applied to those cases in which the person who was killed had been the first to use force—to brandish and use a weapon, to strike a blow during an argument, or to resort to physical violence to settle a dispute. Often, the victim and the offender had a prior relationship; perhaps they had quarreled previously. Situations that incited people to violence included infidelity by a mate or lover, failure to pay a debt, drinking bouts, confrontations over insults, and the utterance of "fighting words." Some typical cases drawn from police reports would be:

- A husband threatened to kill his wife. He attacked her with a knife. In the ensuing struggle, he fell on his own weapon and bled to death.
- The person who ended up the victim was the one who had started a barroom brawl. His friends tried to break up the fight, but he persisted. Finally the tide turned, and the aggressor was knocked down; he hit his head on the floor and died from his injuries.
- A man demanded money that he believed was owed to him. Incensed by the accusations, the victim maintained that he had repaid the debt and advanced on the creditor, wielding a knife. The creditor pulled out a gun and shot him.

(An armed robber killed in a shoot-out with the police would be classified as an offender, not a victim. His demise was not a murder but an act of justifiable homicide on the part of the police, provided that they used deadly force appropriately, according to state law and departmental ordinances.)

These victim-precipitated cases differ in a number of statistically significant ways from other homicides in which the slain people in no way brought about their own demise—according to police reconstructions of the events leading up to the killings. Nearly all the precipitative victims were men, whereas a sizable minority of totally innocent victims were women. Conversely, few women committed homicide, but of those that did, a substantial proportion were provoked by the violence of the men they slew. Victim-precipitated killings were carried out by offenders wielding knives or other sharp instruments in more than half the cases, whereas other homicides were due to stabbings in only a third of the cases. Alcohol was used before most killings, especially victim-precipitated ones. It turned out that in precipitated homicides, more often than in the killings of totally innocent people, the victim was the one who had been doing the drinking, rather than the offender. Examinations of the victims' past police records revealed that in cases of precipitation the victim was more likely to have had a prior run-in with the law than in cases of no precipitation. Over a third of the precipitative victims had a history of committing at least one violent offense against some person, as opposed to only a fifth of the blameless victims. Most of the homicides in Philadelphia were committed by blacks against blacks; an even higher four out of every five precipitative victims were black.

About one murder out of every four in that city during those years was apparently victim precipitated. This finding—that a considerable proportion of slain people were partly responsible for their fate—has provided a basis for a pervasive tendency within victimology and criminology to view some victims in a rather harsh light—as troublemakers not deserving of much compassion or support.

The conclusion in the Philadelphia homicide study was that in a quarter of the cases, the popular stereotypes surrounding victims and offenders were incorrect. The images of victims as weak and passive people shrinking from a confrontation, and of offenders as strong, brutal, and aggressive people hunting down their prey, departed from reality. In many of the victim-precipitated homicides, the characteristics of the victims closely resembled those of the offenders. In some cases, two potential offenders clashed, and chance alone determined which one would be designated the loser—and therefore the victim—in their encounter (Wolfgang, 1958).

It is possible that some of these precipitative victims actually wanted to die (Wolfgang, 1959). Their rash actions and foolhardy initiatives could be interpreted as attempts to commit suicide, as if they had a death wish but could not quite carry it through without help (Reckless, 1967). Victim-precipitated homicide is indeed tantamount to suicide if the victim's outright dares and subliminal invitations are interpreted within this framework (Mueller, in Edelhertz and Geis, 1974). The term *subintentional death* can be applied to all situations in which victims play a contributory role in their own demise, either by exercising poor judgment, by taking excessive risks, or by pursuing a self-destructive lifestyle (Allen, 1980).

This type of speculation, based on unverifiable interpretations of possible motives, is clearly unsympathetic to dead victims who allegedly manipulated others to kill them. But this line of thought does raise intriguing questions about whether some people want to suffer and be punished and consciously or unconsciously enter into risky situations or engineer tragic events that ultimately harm them. This charge is leveled most commonly at people who are victimized repeatedly. In the case of homicide victims, the argument rests on a record of several "near misses" that preceded the final dramatic violent outbursts that cost the victims their lives.

An equally plausible explanation, which is not psychologically based, is that these precipitative victims didn't want to die. They thought they would emerge from the battles as winners, not losers. They didn't welcome their fate. What might be misinterpreted as their death wish was really their adherence to a "subculture of violence" (Curtis, 1974; Wolfgang and Ferracuti, 1967). This willingness to resort to physical combat and to escalate arguments into deadly confrontations is thought to be most prevalent among young men in urban slums. However, the approval of the use of force as a method of solving problems characterizes world politics as well as street-corner life.

The Frequency of Shared Responsibility in Violent Crimes

The issue of the victim's role in cases of street crime was of interest to the National Commission on the Causes and Prevention of Violence (NCCPV). As its name suggests, the blue-ribbon commission was searching for the roots of the crime problem and for practical remedies. If large numbers of victims were found to be partly at fault for what happened to them, then changing the behavior of potential victims—the general public—would be a promising crime prevention strategy.

Social scientists working for the commission analyzed a 10 percent sample of all reports contained in police files in seventeen cities. For each type of crime, a definition of "victim precipitation" was derived from previous studies by criminologists and victimologists. Every case in the sample was reviewed, and if there was enough detailed information, a judgment was made about whether the victim had shared responsibility with the offender for the crime. Five crimes of violence were examined: criminal homicide (first- and second-degree murder and voluntary or non-negligent manslaughter); aggravated assault (with the intent to kill or at least inflict severe bodily injury by shooting, stabbing, poisoning, and so on); forcible rape (including attempted rape); and both unarmed and armed robbery (taking anything of value from a person, either through intimidation or by force). The percentages of cases that could be described as "victim precipitated" were calculated and compared with the findings of earlier studies (see table 3-1).

When the definitions of victim precipitation were applied to the data collected by the commission from police reports, these conclusions were drawn: instances of victim complicity were not uncommon in cases of homicide and aggravated assault; victim precipitation was less frequent but still empirically noteworthy for robbery; and the issue of shared responsibility was least relevant as a contributing factor in rapes (Curtis, 1974:594–595).

Complete Innocence and Full Responsibility

Up to this point, the degree of responsibility a victim might share with an offender has ranged from facilitation through precipitation to provocation. But the spectrum of responsibility extends further in each direction, from complete innocence to full responsibility.

Complete Innocence

Completely innocent victims will be defined as crime-conscious people who tried not to be victimized. They did what they could, within reason, to avoid trouble. (After the fact, it can always be argued they did not do

TABLE 3-1 Estimates of the Relative Frequency of Victim Precipitation

Type of violent crime	*Definition of victim precipitation*	*Frequency*	*Source*
Criminal homicide	Whenever the murder victim was the first to use physical force against the subsequent slayer	26% Philadelphia 22% 17 cities* 38% Chicago	Wolfgang (1958) NCCPV (1969)† Voss and Hepburn (1968)
Aggravated assault	Whenever the victim was the first to use either physical force or insinuating language and gestures against the subsequent attacker	14% 17 cities	NCCPV (1969)
Forcible rape	Whenever a situation ended in forced intercourse where a female first agreed to sexual relations, or clearly invited them verbally and through gestures, but then retracted before the act	19% Philadelphia 4% 17 cities	Amir (1967) NCCPV (1969)
Armed robbery	Whenever temptation–opportunity situations arose where the victim clearly had not acted with reasonable self-protective behavior in handling money, jewelry, or other valuables	11% 17 cities 11% Philadelphia	NCCPV (1969) Normandeau (1968)
Unarmed robbery	Same as for armed robbery	6% 17 cities	NCCPV (1969)

*The rates reported are for cases cleared (solved) by arrest in the 17 cities. The figures differ for cases not cleared by arrest.
†National Commission on the Causes and Prevention of Violence

enough.) In cases of property crimes, these victims took steps to safeguard their possessions in anticipation of the possibility of burglary, larceny, or some other form of theft. They cannot be faulted for negligence, or even passive indifference. They actively sought ways to make the criminals' tasks more difficult in order to deter them. (In the language of crime prevention, they "hardened the target.") In cases of crimes of violence, they did nothing to attract assailants and resisted the criminals' advances.

Resistance can be defined as the behavior of persons, selected as targets by offenders, that is intended to forestall the consummation of the criminal act or to minimize the harm (suffering or loss). Resistance can be any action by the potential victim during a confrontation that might interfere with the criminal's plans or escape. Such conduct can range from active, physical retaliation—matching force with force—to calling for help, to passive noncooperation with the offender's demands. The impact of acts of resistance can vary from total success to total failure. Resisting victims who are successful thwart the offenders; although their overt victory might mask internal injuries in the form of new phobias, heightened fears, and increased inhibitions. Totally unsuccessful resisters lose the battle; the offenders end up doing just what they had intended to do. "Fighting victims" (Von Hentig, 1948) may sustain more serious injuries than ones who acquiesce, if their resistance infuriates the offenders. The victims' perception of the criminals' strength (physical prowess, in crimes of violence; political and economic clout, in other crimes) is probably a major factor determining the degree of resistance the victims put up. Until recently, the study of which types of victim resist, why they do, and how successful they are, had been neglected (Claster and David, 1976).

Full Responsibility

If resistance by the victim is taken as an indication of complete innocence, then complicity becomes the basis for recognizing shared responsibility. Logically, a victim can be entirely guilty only when there is no offender at all. The spectrum of responsibility runs from "fighting" all the way across to "faking." Victims who bear total responsibility for what happened are by definition really not victims at all. They are offenders posing as victims for some ulterior motive.

In cases of property crimes, phony victims are usually seeking reimbursement from private insurance policies, or government aid, for imaginary losses. They file false claims (and thereby break the law) in order to come out ahead rather than "break even."

Fake victims may have motives other than financial gain. Some people may claim to be victims in order to cover up what really occurred. For example, a husband who gambled away his paycheck may tell his wife and the police that he was robbed.

The most dramatic and controversial cases of nonvictimization concern false charges of rape. Some victimologists argue that false accusations pose a serious problem for law enforcement. They cite a long list of possible motives, ranging from revenge, blackmail, and jealousy to attempts to account for cases of venereal disease or unwanted pregnancy. Unconscious desires are also said to be behind many baseless charges (MacDonald, 1971:202–225).

According to FBI statistics (published for the last time in 1976) derived from police reports throughout the nation, about one out of every five complaints of forcible rape was determined to be "unfounded." However, this category is not synonymous with "false accusations." Some of the cases were deemed legally weak by the police, but that doesn't mean they were "imaginary." Social workers at a hospital and a police sex crime unit have reported a false-complaint rate of only 1 or 2 percent in recent years. Yet the criminal justice system operates as if false cries of rape constituted the rule and not the exception, and as if many victims were entirely responsible for their plight (Bode, 1978:24).

The skepticism routinely directed at women who report rapes can be attributed to the domination of the criminal justice system by men and the subordination of women within society. But the hostile questions that some rape victims are subjected to could be due to the lingering effects of several well-publicized cases in which false accusations were lodged against innocent men. The most notorious of these involved the "Scottsboro Boys." The miscarriage of justice was so blatant that it led to a Supreme Court decision (*Powell* v. *Alabama*, 1932) which established the right of all people accused of serious crimes to be represented by competent counsel (see Carter, 1969).

The history of the Old South, with its courtroom travesties and lynch mob violence, demonstrates how false accusations about rapes can be exploited for political gain. The cry of rape was a deliberate invention of white men who made accusations against black men and then compelled white women to echo the charges. The alleged suffering of these simulating victims was seized upon to intensify the repression of black people. Historians suspect that nothing remotely resembling forcible sexual attack occurred in the overwhelming majority of cases in which black males were convicted and either imprisoned, executed, or simply handed over to vigilante groups to be tortured and put to death (Sagarin, 1975).

Typologies of Shared Responsibility

Previous Efforts

A number of victimologists have devised typologies to illustrate the degree of shared responsibility, if any, that victims bear in particular crimes. A typology is a classification scheme that aids in the understanding of what a group of people has in common and how it differs from other groups. All the typologies parcel out responsibility along a continuum marked by a number of boundaries. But the typologies do not have similar end points or intermediate categories. (See table 3-2.) The nomenclature used to describe the varying degrees of responsibility was usually self-explanatory, but the examples picked to illustrate the groupings often lacked clarity. None of these typologies has stood the test of time, in that few other victimologists have found the categories very useful and the criteria unambiguous. Each, however, represents a contribution toward sorting out how and why a victim might share responsibility with an offender for a crime.

TABLE 3-2 Degrees of Shared Responsibility

Victimologist	*Types of victims (or encounters)*
Mendelsohn (1956)	(1) completely innocent, (2) having minor guilt, (3) as guilty as offender, (4) more guilty than offender, (5) most guilty—fully responsible, (6) simulating or imagining
Fattah (1967)	(1) nonparticipating, (2) latent—predisposed, (3) provocative, (4) participating, (5) false
Lamborn (1968)	(1) initiation, (2) facilitation, (3) provocation, (4) perpetration, (5) cooperation, (6) instigation
Schafer (1977)	(1) unrelated, (2) biologically weak, (3) socially weak, (4) political, (5) precipitative, (6) provocative, (7) self-victimizing
Sheley (1979)	(1) active offender–passive victim, (2) active offender–semi-active victim, (3) active offender–active victim, (4) semi-passive offender–active victim, (5) passive offender–active victim

A Typology of Auto Theft Victims

Instead of illustrating a typology by citing different kinds of crimes, as all previous researchers have done, it might be useful to develop a typology of different kinds of victims of a single crime. Such a typology follows for the crime of auto theft. Six categories of victims are defined, ranging from totally innocent through various degrees of shared responsibility to completely guilty (see table 3-3).

Conscientiously resisting victims are totally innocent of any responsibility for the theft of their car. These unwilling victims tried to protect their auto by scrupulously following the crime prevention tips suggested by security specialists. They did all they could to minimize their risks and reduce their vehicle's vulnerability to attack by purchasing anti-theft devices. Yet their resistance proved futile, and they were preyed on by professional thieves who knew how to disarm or circumvent the most sophisticated alarm systems and anti-crime hardware.

Conventionally cautious victims routinely used the anti-theft features provided as standard equipment. They took the precautions of removing all valuables from sight, rolling up the car's windows, locking its doors, and pocketing the keys. Even though they did all they were supposed to do, experienced thieves with the proper tools had no trouble stealing their car. They did nothing "wrong," but since they did not attempt to make their car more theft resistant, they might be faulted and be considered only largely—rather than totally—innocent.

Carelessly facilitating victims set the stage for crimes of opportunity. In many cases they were victimized by inexperienced thieves and teenage

TABLE 3-3 Types of Victims of Auto Theft

Type of victim	*Conscientiously resisting*	*Conventionally cautious*	*Carelessly facilitating*	*Precipitative initiators*	*Provocative conspirators*	*Fabricating simulators*
Degree of responsibility	*Totally innocent*	*Largely innocent*	*Partly innocent*	*Substantially responsible*	*Largely responsible*	*Fully responsible*
Actions of victim	Takes special pre-cautions	Takes conven-tional measures	Facilitates theft through negligence	Precipitates theft by leaving car exposed and vulnerable	Provokes theft by arrange-ments with criminals	Fabricates theft of nonexistent car
Motiva-tions of victim	Seeks to minimize risks	Concerned about risks	Indifferent to risks	Wants car to be stolen	Determined to have car stolen	Seeks to make it look as if car were stolen
Financial outcome after theft	Loses money	Loses money	Loses money	Gains money from victimization	Gains money from victimization	Makes large profit from alleged vic-timization
Approxi-mate pro-portion of all victims, currently	← 55% →		← 20% →	← 25% →		
Legal status	Actual victims ← →			Criminals posing as victims, in order to ← → Commit insurance fraud		
Extent of attention	Overlooked ← →		Object of ← → public education campaigns, sometimes scapegoated	Object of investigations ← → and new legislation		

From "Auto Theft: Beyond Victim Blaming," by Andrew Karmen. *Victimology*, 5, 2 (1980):164.

joyriders. They made the criminals' tasks easier by failing to use the standard crime prevention methods available to them. They left their car doors unlocked or the windows rolled down, and they left their keys inside. They can be considered partly responsible precisely because they acted irresponsibly. Their thoughtless, negligent acts and indifferent attitudes were significant contributing factors to their own losses. However, they were unintentional, unwilling, inadvertent victims.

Precipitative initiators were knowing and willing victims who intentionally singled out their car for trouble. They wanted their car to be stolen because they had a "gas guzzler" or "lemon." They coldly calculated that they would be better off financially if they received the "blue book" value as reimbursement from the insurance company than if they kept their car or tried to sell it. So they took steps that went beyond carelessness. They deliberately left their car unlocked, with the keys dangling inside it, parked invitingly in a high-crime area. By maximizing the vulnerability of their auto, they incited would-be thieves to steal it. But the relationships between the precipitating victims and the criminals were impersonal; they never met despite the symbiosis between them. These substantially responsible victims, if challenged or investigated, could conceal their motives and contend that they were merely negligent motorists with innocent intentions who had accidentally left their keys in the car.

Provocative conspirators are largely responsible victims. They contributed so much to the genesis of the crime that without their instigation the act would not have taken place. These victims are not really victims, but accomplices of thieves. These victims are actually criminals, part of a conspiracy to commit insurance fraud. If the deal was arranged at their initiative—if they offered money to amateurs or professionals to dispose of their unwanted vehicle—then they are more guilty than the direct offenders. These criminals posing as victims arranged to have their car "splashed" (driven off a bridge into deep water), "squished" (compacted, crushed, and then shredded beyond recognition), or "torched" (set on fire) in order to collect insurance reimbursement. Largely responsible victims have the same motives as substantially responsible victims. But the provocative conspirators leave nothing to chance; they know—and often pay—the criminals who victimize them.

Fully responsible victims are not victims at all. They make false claims in order to defraud insurance companies. They insured a nonexistent vehicle—a "paper car," or "phantom car"— and then reported it stolen to the authorities so they could collect money. They simulated being a victim and fabricated the entire episode for their own dishonest purposes.

Rough estimates can be derived of the relative proportions of several combinations of these six types of auto theft victims. Currently, carelessness (key facilitation) accounts for 20 percent or less of all thefts. Police and insurance sources report that 25 percent of all thefts, at most, are due to the actions of motorists who want their car to be stolen. The remaining 55 percent of stolen vehicles are taken from conscientiously resisting and conventionally cautious motorists (Karmen, 1980).

The Importance of Fixing Responsibility

The question of whether—or to what degree—the victim shares responsibility with the criminal for a violation of the law is a crucial one. A number of important decisions that affect the fate of the criminal, the plight of the victim, and the perception of the crime problem by the public hinge on determinations of victim responsibility. Whether the victim facilitated, precipitated, or provoked the offender is taken into account by policemen, prosecutors, juries, judges, compensation boards, insurance examiners, politicians, and crime control strategists. Victim responsibility arises as an issue at many stages in the criminal justice process; in applications for compensation; in demands for restitution and compensatory damages; in complaints about how crime victims are treated by family, friends, and strangers at home, in hospital emergency rooms, in court, and in the newspapers; and in the development of crime prevention programs and criminological theories.

At every juncture in the operation of the criminal justice system, judgments must be made about the degree of responsibility—if any—the victim shares with the offender. The police confront this issue first. For example, when called to the scene of a barroom brawl, officers have to decide whether to arrest one or more of the participants and what charges to lodge if arrests are made. Perhaps the loser is declared the victim, and the combatant still on his feet is taken into custody for assault.

When a district attorney reviews the charge brought by the police against a defendant, he or she must decide if a crime was actually committed and if the complainant was indeed an innocent victim. When some degree of blame can be attributed to the victim, this aggrieved party's credibility is impaired. The district attorney may decide that the accused person would probably be viewed (by a jury and a judge) as less culpable and less deserving of punishment, and therefore that the person has less chance of being convicted. Since relatively few cases are ever brought to trial, district attorneys tend to engage in plea bargaining (accepting a guilty plea to a lesser charge) when allegations would be tough to prove in court. Cases with a blameworthy victim who is an unconvincing witness are often screened out, and indictments against the defendant are dropped. A study of files in the District of Columbia during the early 1970s revealed that evidence of victim provocation halved the chances that a case would be prosecuted (Williams, 1978).

Killings defined as justifiable homicides (perhaps due to extreme provocation by the deceased persons) are not prosecuted. Different jurisdictions use varying standards to define what constitutes provocation and justification. A study of Houston's murders turned up a figure of 12 percent deemed justifiable, whereas in Chicago only 3 percent of all killings were considered justifiable. It appears that the definition of justification is broader in Texas than in Illinois (Block, 1981).

In cases where provocation does not constitute sufficient grounds for justifiable homicide, it might serve as an extenuating circumstance. Evidence of victim provocation can force the district attorney to put the defendant on trial for manslaughter rather than murder. In a homicide or assault case, the defendant can assert that he or she acted in self-defense, contending that the victim threatened to attack or actually struck the first blow, causing the defendant, as a reasonable person, to be fearful of serious bodily injury or death. In order for the charges to be reduced or for the defendant to be acquitted on the grounds of justifiable self-defense, the victim's provocation must have been "adequate." In most states, that means that the defendant's violent responses to the victim's provocations must have occurred during the heat of passion, before there had been a reasonable opportunity for intense emotions to cool (Williams, 1978; Wolfgang, 1958).

At the conclusion of criminal trials, judges sentence convicted felons with the victims' shared responsibility in mind as a potential mitigating factor that would permit a prison term or a fine to be reduced. In those jurisdictions where restitution by offenders to victims is permitted or even mandated (see chapter 6), the culpability of victims can be a cause for reducing the amount of repayment that criminals must undertake. In a similar manner, the judge or the jury in civil court is likely to consider victims' actions when it decides on monetary damages from defendants for the loss, pain, and suffering they allegedly caused. (See chapter 6 for a discussion of civil lawsuits against offenders.) Parallel considerations arise when victims of violent crimes apply to a criminal injury compensation board for money to cover their unreimbursed losses. If the board at a hearing determines that the victims bear some of the responsibility for their own injuries, it will reduce the amount of its award or may disallow their claims entirely in extreme cases of shared guilt and provocation. (See chapter 7 for an examination of victim compensation programs.)

In some minor disturbances that erupt after considerable interactions between two mutually hostile parties, the designations "offender" and "victim" simply do not apply. In these cases of shared responsibility, in which the question of guilt or innocence is so difficult to unravel, adjudication under the adversary system may not be appropriate. Neighborhood justice centers have been set up to handle cases in which both parties are clearly at fault for what happened. These disputes are settled through mediation and arbitration. Compromise solutions offer the greatest hope for reconciliation, since both parties are to some degree "right" as well as "wrong" (see chapter 8).

Widely held beliefs and stereotypes about the question of shared responsibility profoundly shape public policies towards crime and its victims. Popular images and public opinion concerning unworthy, undeserving victims as opposed to bona fide, innocent victims can influence the priorities of the criminal justice and social service systems. For example, throughout the 1970s, feminist groups raised the public's consciousness about the plight of women who were sexually harassed at work, beaten by their mates at home, or raped by strangers or acquaintances. As a result, public opinion shifted from callousness to a new consensus that such victims are deserving of help. Support groups, shelters for battered women, and rape crisis centers have been established by victim advocates. Administrators of criminal justice agencies

BOX 3-2 *Prof Calls for Crackdown on Crime Victims*

There is so much talk about crime in the streets and the rights of the criminal that little attention is being paid to the victims of crime. But there is a current of opinion that our courts are being too soft on the victims, and many of them are going unpunished for allowing a crime to be committed against them.

One man who feels strongly about this is Prof. Heinrich Applebaum, a criminologist who feels that unless the police start cracking down on the victims of criminal acts, the crime rate in this country will continue to rise.

"The people who are responsible for crime in this country are the victims. If they didn't allow themselves to be robbed, the problem of crime in this country would be solved," Applebaum said.

"That makes sense, Professor. Why do you think the courts are soft on victims of crimes?"

"We're living in a permissive society and anything goes," Applebaum replied. "Victims of crimes don't seem to be concerned about the consequences of their acts. They walk down a street after dark, or they display jewelry in their store window, or they have their cash registers right out where everyone can see them. They seem to think that they can do this in the United States and get away with it."

"You speak as if all the legal machinery in this country was weighted in favor of the victim, instead of the person who committed the crime."

"It is," Applebaum said. "While everyone is worried about the victim, the poor criminal is dragged down to the police station, booked and arraigned, and if he's lucky he'll be let out on bail. He may lose his job if his boss hears about it and there is even a chance that if he has a police record, it may prejudice the judge when he's sentenced."

"I guess in this country people always feel sorrier for the victim than they do for the person who committed the crime."

"You can say that again. Do you know that in some states they are even compensating victims of crimes?"

"It's hard to believe," I said.

"Well, it's true. The do-gooders and the bleeding hearts all feel that victims of crimes are misunderstood, and if they were treated better, they would stop being victims. But the statistics don't bear this out. The easier you are on the victim, the higher the crime rate becomes."

"What is the solution, Professor?"

"I say throw the book at anybody who's been robbed. They knew what they were getting into when they decided to be robbed, and they should pay the penalty for it. Once a person has been a victim of crime and realizes he can't get away with it, the chances of his becoming a victim again will be slim."

"Why do people want to become victims of crime, Professor?"

"Who knows? They're probably looking for thrills. Boredom plays a part, but I would think the biggest factor is that victims think they can still walk around the streets of their cities and get away with it. Once they learn they can't, you'll see a big drop in crime statistics."

"You make a lot of sense, Professor. Do you believe the American people are ready to listen to you?"

"They'd better be, because the criminal element is getting pretty fed up with all the permissive coddling of victims that is going on in this country."

SOURCE: From "Victim Precipitation," by Art Buchwald. Copyright © *The Washington Post,* February 4, 1969. Reprinted by permission.

have been pressured to develop new remedies for harassment victims, more effective orders of protection for battered wives, and more sensitive police interviewing techniques for rape complainants.

A careful study of patterns in the behavior of crime victims in cases where shared responsibility is suspected can yield useful insights for the development of strategies for "crime prevention" (a better term is *risk reduction*). By discovering what it was that the victims did "wrong" that brought them to the attention of prowling criminals, crime prevention researchers can compile "dos and don'ts" and other tips to teach past and potential victims to act differently and thereby reduce the risks they face of being singled out for trouble in the future. Intense public education campaigns have been launched to warn about the "mistakes" made by burglary, robbery, rape and auto theft victims, among others. (If taken to extremes, the calls for a crackdown on victim misbehavior are humorous. See box 3-2.)

References

ALLEN, N. 1980: *Homicide: Perspectives on Prevention.* New York: Human Sciences Press.

AMIR, MENACHEM. 1967: "Victim Precipitated Forcible Rape." *Journal of Criminal Law, Criminology, and Police Science.* 58:493–502.

——. 1971: *Patterns in Forcible Rape.* Chicago: University of Chicago Press.

BLOCK, RICHARD. 1981: "Victim–Offender Dynamics in Violent Crime." *Journal of Criminal Law and Criminology,* 72:743–761.

BODE, JANET. 1978: *Fighting Back.* New York: Macmillan.

BUCHWALD, ART. 1969: "Victim Precipitation." *Washington Post,* February 4.

CARTER, DAN. 1969: *Scottsboro: A Tragedy of the American South.* Baton Rouge, La.: Louisiana State University Press.

CLASTER, DANIEL, and DAVID, DEBORAH. 1976: "The Resisting Victim: Extending the Concept of Victim Responsibility." *Victimology,* 1:109–117.

CURTIS, LYNN. 1974: "Victim Precipitation and Violent Crime." *Social Problems,* 21:594–605.

EDELHERTZ, HERBERT, and GEIS, GILBERT. 1974: *Public Compensation to Victims of Crime.* New York: Praeger.

ELLENBERGER, HENRI. 1955: "Psychological Relationships between the Criminal and His Victim." *Archives of Criminal Psychodynamics,* 2:257–290.

FATTAH, EZZAT. 1967: "Towards a Criminological Classification of Victims." *International Criminal Police Review,* 209:162–169.

——. 1979: "Some Recent Theoretical Developments in Victimology." *Victimology,* 4,2:198–213.

FOONER, MICHAEL. 1971: "Money and Economic Factors in Crime and Delinquency." *Criminology,* 8,4 (February):311–320.

JEFFREY, C. RAY. 1971: *Crime Prevention through Environmental Design.* Beverly Hills, Calif.: Sage.

KARMEN, ANDREW. 1980: "Auto Theft: Beyond Victim Blaming." *Victimology,* 5,2:161–174.

LAMBORN, LEROY. 1968: "Toward a Victim Orientation in Criminal Theory." *Rutgers Law Review,* 22:733–768.

MacDONALD, JOHN. 1971: *Rape: Offenders and Victims.* Springfield, Ill.: Charles C Thomas.

MANNHEIM, HERMANN. 1965: *Comparative Criminology.* Boston: Houghton Mifflin.

McCAGHY, CHARLES, GIORDANO, PEGGY, and HENSON, TRUDY. 1980: *Crime in American Society.* New York: Macmillan.

———. 1977: "Auto Theft: Offenders and Offense Characteristics." *Criminology,* 15 (November):367–385.

McDONALD, WILLIAM. 1970. *The Victim: A Social Psychological Study of Criminal Victimization* (unpublished doctoral dissertation). Ann Arbor, Mich.: University Microfilms.

MENDELSOHN, BERNARD. 1956: "The Victimology." Études Internationales de Psycho-Sociologie Criminelle (July):23–26.

NATIONAL COMMISSION ON THE CAUSES AND PREVENTION OF VIOLENCE (NCCPV). 1969: *The Offender and His Victim* (staff report by Donald Mulvihill, Lynn Curtis, and Melvin Tumin). Washington, D.C.: U.S. Government Printing Office.

NATIONAL CRIMINAL JUSTICE INFORMATION AND STATISTICS SERVICE (NCJISS). 1979: *The Cost of Negligence: Losses from Preventable Household Burglaries.* Washington, D.C.: U.S. Government Printing Office.

NORMANDEAU, ANDRE. 1968: "Patterns in Robbery." *Criminologica* (November): 2–15.

PARSONAGE, WILLIAM. 1979: *Perspectives on Victimology.* Beverly Hills, Calif.: Sage.

RECKLESS, WALTER. 1967: *The Crime Problem.* New York: Appleton, Century, Crofts.

REISS, ALBERT, Jr. 1980: "Victim Proneness in Repeat Victimization by Type of Crime." In Stephen Fineberg and Albert Reiss, Jr. (Eds.), *Indicators of Crime and Criminal Justice: Quantitative Studies,* 41–54. Washington, D.C.: U.S. Department of Justice.

SAGARIN, EDWARD. 1975: "Forcible Rape and the Problem of the Rights of the Accused." *Intellect,* 103 (May–June):515–520.

SCHAFER, STEPHEN. 1968: *The Victim and His Criminal.* New York: Random House.

———. 1977: *Victimology: The Victim and His Criminal.* Reston, Va.: Reston Publishing.

SCHULTZ, LEROY. 1968: "The Victim–Offender Relationship." *Crime and Delinquency,* 14:135–141.

SHELEY, JOSEPH. 1979: *Understanding Crime: Concepts, Issues, Decisions.* Belmont, Calif.: Wadsworth.

SPARKS, RICHARD. 1981: "Multiple Victimization: Evidence, Theory, and Future Research." *Journal of Criminal Law and Criminology,* 72,2:762–778.

VIANO, EMILIO. 1976: *Victims and Society.* Washington, D.C.: Visage.

VON HENTIG, HANS. 1941: "Remarks on the Interaction of Perpetrator and Victim." *Journal of Criminal Law, Criminology, and Police Science,* 31 (March–April): 303–309.

———. 1948: *The Criminal and His Victim: Studies in the Sociobiology of Crime.* New Haven, Conn.: Yale University Press.

VOSS, HAROLD, and HEPBURN, JOHN. 1968: "Patterns in Criminal Homicide in Chicago." *Journal of Criminal Law, Criminology, and Police Science,* 59:499–508.

WALLER, IRVIN, and OKIHIRO, NORMAN. 1978: *Burglary: The Victim and the Public.* Toronto: University of Toronto Press.

WILLIAMS, GERRY. 1978: Address to the National Workshop on Auto Theft Prevention (pp. 67–71 in the Compendium of Proceedings). Albany: N.Y. Senate Committee on Transportation.

WOLFGANG, MARVIN. 1958: *Patterns in Criminal Homicide.* Philadelphia: University of Pennsylvania Press.

———. 1959: "Suicide by Means of Victim Precipitated Homicide." *Journal of Clinical and Experimental Psychopathology and Quarterly Review of Psychiatry and Neurology,* 20:335–349.

———, and FERRACUTI, FRANCO. 1967: *The Subculture of Violence: Towards an Integrated Theory in Criminology.* London: Tavistock.

CHAPTER 4

Victim Blaming versus Victim Defending

The Developing Controversy over Shared Responsibility

- A man pulls into his driveway, turns off his car's engine, and enters his home. A teenager walks by and spots the car's keys dangling in the ignition switch. He hops behind the wheel and drives off. Was the motorist partly responsible for the crime because he made the thief's task easier? Is victim facilitation a major factor in the auto theft problem?
- A young woman tries to thumb a ride home from a local beach on a hot summer's day. A young man in a sports car picks up the hitchhiker and interprets her appreciation as a sign of sexual interest. He drives to a deserted parking lot and makes sexual advances. She resists but he assumes her protests are just feigned. When he tries to pin her down, she bolts from the car and runs screaming along the road. Did she contribute to the attempted rape by miscommunication? Is victim precipitation a major reason for sexual assaults?
- An appliance store in a ghetto neighborhood lures customers with deceptive ads. Its salesmen use high-pressure tactics to persuade poor people to buy costly items on "lay-away" plans. If they fall behind in their installment payments, the items are repossessed or their wages are garnished by order of civil court judges. If the items are defective, the store's policy is "no refunds, no exchanges." One night, the store's windows are smashed and it is looted. Did the shady business practices incite neighborhood residents to retaliate? Is victim provocation an explanation for the looting that accompanies inner city disturbances?

Because social scientists strive for objectivity when examining other people's thoughts and actions, the questions of bias, subjectivity, and partisanship arise repeatedly in victimology and criminology. Criminologists frequently challenge each other's commitment to neutrality. They argue among themselves over whether a particular theoretical perspective is biased, perhaps in favor of the legal system and the interests it protects, or whether some criminologists are too "sympathetic" toward delinquents or too "punitive" toward criminals.

One major issue that confronts victimologists, introduced in the previous chapter, involves shared responsibility. When, and to what degree, should the burden of responsibility be placed on the victims of crime? The problem of bias emerges because it is difficult to examine the situation of crime victims from a standpoint free of values. Laws have been broken, losses incurred, and injuries inflicted. Judgments about right and wrong conduct, appropriate and inappropriate actions, and desirable and undesirable behaviors pervade the law, the criminal justice system, criminology, and victimology.

Attempts to achieve an objective understanding of the process of victimization are influenced by biases from various sources. In the first place, victimologists as individuals have their personal beliefs about what is fair and unfair and about how people ought to treat one another. In addition, victimology, as a fledgling offspring of criminology, already has strong currents swirling through it, some of them pro-victim, others condemnatory. Finally, the overall social cllimate within which everyone —criminals, victims, victimologists—operates has its shifting moods and changing themes, sometimes hopeful, periodically cynical, with reformist impulses and conservative backlashes. The outcome is that ideological explanations develop that consciously (or even unconsciously) reflect interests, preferences, and priorities.

The process of fixing responsibility for crime unavoidably rests on judgments that are subject to question and attack. These judgments are based on values, ethics, prejudices, loyalties, and allegiances. Much of the crime that plagues everyday life grows out of conflicts between people and groups that have allies and enemies. Long-standing disputes and smoldering struggles that erupt into acts of violence and destruction have caused polarizations within society. Lines have been drawn and sides chosen. When crimes are committed as part of the conflict between family members, neighbors, schoolmates, or co-workers, determinations of responsibility can be made with a considerable degree of objectivity by outsiders and other disinterested parties. But when the criminality arises from conflicts between members of different races, sexes, or social classes, employers and their employees, merchants and their customers, landlords and their tenants, officers and soldiers (superiors and subordinates in general), or "haves and have-nots," it is much more difficult to assign responsibility in a scientific, neutral manner. Such issues tend to be approached ideologically. Prejudgment, with empathy for one side and hostility toward the other, is likely.

Research and theorizing about shared responsibility span the entire short history of victimology. As victimologists have pushed back the frontiers of ignorance about shared responsibility by elaborating the concepts of facilitation, precipitation, provocation, proneness, vulnerability, and accountability, a more complete—but also a more controversial—picture of crime-producing conditions and situations has taken shape. Victimology has enriched criminology, but it has also stimulated further schisms. Starting in the 1970s, a countercurrent formed within victimology in reaction to the enthusiasm over inquiries into shared responsibility. Some criminologists and victimologists began to express concern over the implications of studies into mutual interactions and reciprocal influences. Those who raised doubts and voiced dissent might be taken as loosely constituting a different school of thought. Just as criminology, with a much longer, richer, and stormier history, has recognizable orientations and camps (for example, labeling theory, conflict models, and functionalist paradigms), so too does victimology have its rifts and factions.

Victim Blaming and Victim Defending

Arguments that the victims of crime might share responsibility with the offenders for what happened can be characterized as examples of *victim blaming*. Victim blaming finds facilitation, precipitation, and provocation to be valid descriptions of what some people do "wrong" that gets them into trouble. Arguments that question the soundness and usefulness of notions of shared responsibility can be termed examples of "victim defending." Victim defending denies that certain victims are partly at fault for the crimes committed against them.

Victim Blaming

Victim blaming casts doubt on the legal categories of "offender" and "victim" as sometimes misleading descriptions of who did what to whom. Applying such wrong–right, bad–good, guilty–innocent labels to real people in actual situations often results in gross simplifications and even distortions of the truth of what happened, according to this view.

Victimologists have observed that the offender and the victim are sometimes "partners in crime." A degree of mutuality, symbiosis, or reciprocity may exist between them (Von Hentig, 1948). In such cases it is justifiable to investigate the past police record, possible motives, reputation, and actions of the victim as well as the offender (Schultz, 1968).

A doctrine of "personal accountability" underlies victim blaming. Just as criminals are condemned for their lawbreaking and punished, so too victims must answer for their behavior before and during an incident. In the aftermath of the event, victims can be given credit for minimizing the harm they experienced or can be faulted for errors in judgment that (in retrospect) only made things worse. Such assessments of praise or blame are grounded in the belief that people exercise some substantial degree of control over the course of events in their lives. They may not be totally in command, but they are not powerless or helpless either.

A basic tenet of victim blaming (Ryan, 1971) is that there is something "wrong" with the victim (as well as with the offender). Victim blaming presumes differences that distinguish victims from nonvictims. Victims are said to hold different attitudes and to behave differently from the unafflicted majority. These differences are thought to be the source of the victims' problems. If victims want to avoid further misery, they must change how they think and act.

If getting into trouble is partly the victim's fault, then escaping harm is also the victim's responsibility. Just as cautious motorists should study the techniques of "defensive driving" to minimize the risks of getting involved in an accident, crime-conscious people are obliged to review their lifestyle to do what they can, within reason, to increase their personal safety from criminal attack. By following the advice of experts about how to avoid vicitimization, would-be victims might be able to deter would-be offenders or divert their attention elsewhere.

Victim blaming as a psychological process. Victim blaming might result from a fervent belief in a "just world"—a place where people get what they deserve and deserve what they get. Bad things happen only to evil characters; good people are rewarded for following the rules. Hence, if someone is harmed by a criminal, he or she must have done something wrong to deserve such a fate. People who believe that the real world is a just world don't want to find fault with victims if they can help it. They would prefer to blame other people or conditions. But when put on the spot with other explanations foreclosed, they will blame victims, if only for the sake of their own peace of mind. It is too disconcerting and threatening to imagine a world governed by random events. The realization that senseless, brutal acts might be inflicted on anyone at any time is unnerving. The belief that victims did something neglectful, mistaken, or provocative that brought about their misfortune is comforting. It dispels feelings of helplessness and extreme vulnerability to be reassured that crime doesn't strike good people who act properly (Lerner, 1965; Symonds, 1975).

Some of the most virulent victim-blaming arguments are made by people who profess to have the victim's best interests in mind. Social workers, ministers, doctors, teachers, and others in the helping professions are among the first to blame those who suffer from social problems like poverty, bad housing, ill health, unemployment, and inadequate education for bringing about their own downfall. By finding fault with victims' attitudes and actions, victim blamers are able to reconcile their own self-interest with their humanitarian impulses. They do not want to criticize a social system that they believe is sound. And they do not want to abandon their commitment to alleviating suffering. Without realizing why, victim blamers feel comfortable with an ideology that stresses that it is the victim, not society's institutions (organized ways of accomplishing tasks), that must change if trouble is to be avoided in the future (Ryan, 1971).

Victim blaming as the offender's view. The offender's view of victims plays a key role in the selection of targets and in the infliction of pain. The question is often asked, "How can offenders be so devoid of feelings of empathy and pity for their victims?" Evidently, they have undergone a process of desensitization that reduces or even eliminates the guilt, shame, remorse, pangs of conscience, and moral inhibitions that would otherwise constrain and beset them. Victim blaming appears to be a central feature of the desensitizing process. By derogating and denigrating the victim, juvenile delinquents or adult criminals can picture their harmful acts as justifiable and their choice of an object for injury as legitimate. Acts of stark cruelty and savagery become possible when the victim is viewed as worthless, as less than human, as an appropriate target for venting hostility and aggression, or as an outcast deserving of mistreatment (Fattah, 1976, 1979).

Juvenile delinquents frequently stereotype their intended victims as having negative traits in order to neutralize any sense of guilt. They try to dismiss their victims as mere abstractions (like the public or the school system), maintain that the victims were consenting and willing, or argue that the victims were "asking for it and got what they deserved." The personal worth of victims is often devalued (they are thieves themselves), or their loss is denied (it was borrowed, not stolen). In extreme cases, offenders picture the suffering inflicted on victims as an act of retaliatory justice that ought to be applauded (Schwendinger and Schwendinger, 1967; Sykes and Matza, 1957).

Victim Defending

Victimology, despite its aspirations toward objectivity, may harbor an unavoidable victim-blaming strain within it. To some extent, it is inevitable that an in-depth investigation of the behavior of victims before, during, and after a crime will turn up instances of rash decisions, foolish mistakes, errors in judgment, and inexcusable carelessness that in hindsight so clearly shaped the final outcome of a criminal–victim interaction.

More sophisticated inquiries into the patterns and trends running through hundreds or thousands of encounters and confrontations are sure to reveal examples of what the victims did (or failed to do) that contributed to their own losses and suffering.

To counter this way of thinking, victim defending dismisses the explanatory value of notions about shared responsibility and derides victim blaming as warped reasoning. Victim defending denies that victims differ significantly from nonvictims and that victims are their own "worst enemies." It argues that crime victims need understanding and support, not inquisitions, condemnation, and neglect.

The critics of victim blaming have generally identified themselves as champions of the underdogs in society, especially of those who are victimized by street criminals and then blamed for bringing about their own downfall. The attack on the possibility of shared responsibility has centered on the fuzzy concept of victim precipitation in particular. Some of the sharpest challenges and denunciations appear in box 4-1.

Two strategies within victim defending can be recognized. The first is *criminal blaming.* It resents any attempt by offenders to shift the burden of full responsibility off their backs and onto victims' shoulders. Victim defending coupled with criminal blaming rests on the doctrine of personal accountability for misbehavior, but it limits accountability to the perpetrators alone.

The second kind of victim defending is not predicated on criminal blaming, but rather on *system* blaming. According to the tenets of system blaming, neither the offender nor the victim is the real culprit; both, to varying degrees, are "victims." The roots of the crime problem are to be found in the basic institutions on which the social system is built. (See Balkan, Berger, and Schmidt, 1980; and Franklin, 1978.)

Victim Facilitation and Auto Theft: Is It the Careless Who Wind Up Carless?

More than a million cars are stolen in the United States each year (about 1 out of every 140 on the road). But the problem of car stealing is nothing new. As long ago as 1919, the Dyer Act was passed by Congress because rings of thieves were crossing state borders to evade local police forces. And ever since the first cars were marketed with the message that owning one was a sign of manhood, teenage boys have been seizing opportunities to go joyriding.

Since the dawn of the automobile age at the start of the century, criminals have received most of the blame for the theft problem. Studies of joyriders and commercial thieves, their motives and their methods, have led to strident calls for stronger enforcement and stiffer penalties.

BOX 4-1 Criticisms of Shared Responsibility

- The concept of victim precipitation has become confused because it has been operationalized in too many different, often incompatible ways. As a result, it has lost much of its usefulness as an empirical and explanatory tool (Silverman, 1974:99).
- The study of victim precipitation is the least exact of the sociological approaches; it is part a priori guesswork and part "armchair detective fun and games" because the interpretation rests in the final analysis on a set of arbitrary standards (Brownmiller, 1975:353).
- A tendency of investigators to assign responsibility for criminal acts to the victims' behavior reinforces similar beliefs and rationalizations held by most criminals themselves. . . . Scientific skepticism should be maintained regarding the concept of victim participation, especially for crimes of sudden, unexpected violence where the offender is a stranger to the victim (Symonds, 1975:22).
- Victims of crime, long ignored but now the object of special scholarly attention, had better temper their enthusiasm because they may be more maligned than lauded, and their plight may not receive sympathetic understanding. Some victimologists have departed from the humanitarian, helping orientation of the founders of the field and have turned victimology into the art of blaming the victim. If the impression of a "legitimate victim" is created, then part of the burden of guilt is relieved from the perpetrator, and some crimes, like rape for example, can emerge as without either victims or offenders (Weis and Borges, 1973:230–231).
- Victim precipitation explanations are plagued by the fallacy of circular reasoning about the cause of the crime, suffer from over-simplified stimulus–response models of human interaction, ignore incongruent facts that don't fit the theory, and inadequately explore the victim's intentions (Franklin and Franklin, 1976:134).
- An analytical framework must be found that salvages the positive contributions of the concept of victim precipitation, while avoiding its flaws—its tendency to consider a victim's provocations as both a necessary and sufficient condition for an offense to occur; its portrayal of some offenders as unrealistically passive; and its questionable moral and legal implications about who is the guilty party (Sheley, 1979:126–127).
- Crime victimization is a neglected social problem in part because victim precipitation studies typically fail to articulate the distress of the victims and instead suggest that some may be to blame for their own plight. The inferences often drawn from these studies—that some individuals can steer clear of trouble by avoiding certain situations—suffer from the "post hoc ergo propter hoc" fallacy of treating the victims' behavior as both necessary and sufficient to cause the crime (Teevan, 1979:7).
- To accept precipitation and provocation as legitimate excuses for attenuating responsibility for violent crime is false, illogical, psychologically harmful to victims, and socially irresponsible. . . . Victim-blaming has been injected into the literature on crime by well-meaning but offender-oriented professionals. It becomes the basis and excuse for the indifference shown to supposedly "undeserving" victims (Reiff, 1979:12,14).
- The eager acceptance of arguments about victim responsibility by scholars and the public alike is undeserved; these accounts of why the crime occurred often lack empirical verification, can lead to cruel insensitivity to the suffering of the victim, and tend to exonerate or even justify the acts of the offenders, especially rapists (Anderson and Renzetti, 1980:325).

Blaming the Victim for Facilitating the Crime

In the case of auto theft, the criminal blamers have tended to be victim blamers, too. Besides devising ways to deter would-be thieves through threats of punishment, they have pioneered strategies of influencing the behavior of potential victims through educational campaigns. For several decades, victim blamers have castigated drivers and car owners for carelessly making the car thieves' task easier. This "motorist blaming," which pictures victim facilitation as a central feature of the auto theft problem, emanates from executives at the pinnacles of automobile manufacturing, the insurance business, and law enforcement, as box 4-2 shows.

Auto theft may be the only crime for which there is an organized victim-blaming lobby. Committees composed of representatives of the automakers, insurance companies, and law enforcement agencies, along with other civic groups and business interests, have sponsored "Lock It and Pocket the Key" campaigns around the United States since the early 1960s. These drives have sought to curb car thefts by reducing victim facilitation.

The contribution of victim facilitation to the auto theft rate has usually been measured as the percentage of recovered stolen cars in which there was evidence that the thief had used the owner's keys. Although this methodology has its problems, surveys based on it show a trend that casts doubt on the continued importance of negligence as a factor. At one time, when the public was less concerned about crime, facilitation may have contributed to a very substantial degree to the joyriding problem. But teenage amateurs no longer account for most of the car stealing. Professionals, often working for commercial rings—which in turn may be affiliated with organized crime syndicates—now represent the greater threat to car owners. Surveys confirm that, as time rolls by, key facilitation is declining in significance. (See table 4-1.)

Defending the Victim from Outmoded Charges

Victim blamers portray the typical victim of car theft as a careless motorist, but the picture has changed in recent years, as the data in table 4-1 indicate. Victim blamers also charge that the typical driver is negligent about taking precautions, but the available survey data on this subject again fail to substantiate their contention. Only a few studies have been conducted about how often motorists leave their parked cars with the windows open and keys inside. (Leaving the car unlocked varies according to the time of day, the place, and the weather.) Three surveys conducted by the police and insurance companies have come up with a negligence rate that ranges from .5 percent to as much as 6 percent for different times and places (see Karmen, 1979). Even taking the higher figure, only six out of every one hundred car owners walk away from a parked vehicle and leave the keys behind. The other ninety-four out of

BOX 4-2 *Examples of "Motorist Blaming"*

Source *Affiliation* *Date*	*Statement*
George Henderson Criminologist 1924	Careless owners of automobiles have their cars standing on the street with their engines running, with the magneto key in the locks or entirely unlocked on avenues of the city or in unprotected garages. And in so doing they make life a picnic for the car thief . . . . Nine tenths of the loss by theft of automobiles is due to the carelessness of the owner (pp. 36; 38).
James Bulger Publicity director Chicago Motor Club 1933	Motorists must be made to realize that they have a responsibility. . . . [They] should make it difficult for a thief to steal a car (p. 810).
Jerome Hall Law professor 1935	Accommodating owners leave doors unlocked, windows open, keys in the switch, and sometimes leave the motor running, all conveniently arranged for automobile thieves who specialize in these easy pickings (p. 269).
August Vollmer Police chief Berkeley, California 1936	No intelligent person would put from $1,000 to $5,000 in good money in the street and expect to find it there an hour later, yet that is exactly what a large number of people do when they leave an automobile in the street without locking it. Even more, not only are they leaving money at the curb but they are also putting four wheels under it to make it easier for the thief to take it (p. 65).
Henry Clement Judge 1946	There must surely be some way to educate Mr. Average careless driver—you and me—to prevent us from stealing our own car (p. 24).

one hundred are properly cautious. If only a few drivers out of a hundred act carelessly, then continuing victim "education" campaigns to "Lock It and Pocket the Key" have little potential for making substantial inroads into the auto theft problem. Most motorists are crime conscious most of the time already.

Victim defending in the case of auto theft means arguing that the bulk of victims did nothing wrong. The theft of their cars was not victim facilitated in any way. These victims don't have bad attitudes (negligence) and don't act incorrectly (carelessly). Their problems are due to

William Davis National Automobile Theft Bureau 1954	What is it about the American public that makes them so disrespectful of their own property as it applies to automobiles? . . . To us the greatest single cause of the theft of these cars is public indifference and irresponsibility (in U.S. Senate, 1954, pp. 383; 385).
J. Edgar Hoover FBI director 1966	Yet through all this practical, emotional and monetary attachment to the automobile, there emerges convincing evidence that it is one of the motorist's most carelessly neglected possessions (p. 23621).
John Roche President General Motors Corporation 1967	Carelessness by car owners is a major factor in car theft, and a strong educational effort will be required to alert the public to the dangers of theft (p. 7594).
John Damian Vehicle regulations manager Ford Motor Company 1968	Until we can get drivers to stop handing over their cars to thieves, all anti-theft activities are practically useless (in Raskin, 1968:435).
Donald Wolfslayer Assistant chief engineer for security Chrysler Corporation 1975	All the security you put in a car is not going to do a darned bit of good if people are careless. People have to learn to take better care of their autos (in "Offenders Get Wrists Slapped," 1975: 2).
Travelers Insurance Company 1977	Will your car be next? It needn't be. Not if you follow these simple precautions. . . . If you're careless about these tips you may wind up carless (pp. 1–2).
Ira Lipman Security industry executive 1982	If people would simply quit leaving their keys in their cars, they would eliminate half of all auto thefts (p. 78).

the inadequacy of the standard security equipment (and even some of the optional anti-theft hardware).

The stereotype of the absent-minded victim is deeply rooted in the literature of auto theft. The overstatements by victim blamers have created an inaccurate image of car stealing as a typically victim-facilitated crime when it is not any longer. The dwindling of joyriding and the growth of professional, commercial, and organized auto theft undercuts the very foundation of victim blaming. As the careless practice of leaving keys in cars fades into insignificance, motorists are being criticized for

TABLE 4-1 Estimates of the Extent of Victim Facilitation in Auto Thefts

Year of study	*Percentage of thefts that were victim facilitated*	*Methodological notes*
1941–1945	85% to 93% of cars had "keys available"	Plainfield, N.J.
1954	40% of cars had keys in them or unlocked ignitions*	Estimates from insurance companies
1960	60% to 70% had keys or unlocked ignitions	National figures
1962	42% had keys or unlocked ignitions	National survey of recovered vehicles by FBI
1966	11% had keys; 22% had unlocked ignitions	Milwaukee
1966	42% had keys; 17% had unlocked ignitions	Estimates of apprehended auto thieves
1966	12% had keys or unlocked ignitions	Recovered vehicles, Chicago
1967	45% to 50% had keys or unlocked ignitions	Police estimate, national figures
1968	About 50% had keys or unlocked ignitions	Los Angeles
1974	14% to 17% had keys	National survey of recovered vehicles by FBI
1978	20% had keys; 20% more had keys hidden in car, found by thieves	New York state
1978	13% to 14% had keys	Recovered vehicles, minimum estimate, national figures
1978	15% had keys	Recovered vehicles, insurance claims, Michigan

*In 1970, a federal standard promulgated by the National Highway Transportation Safety Administration went into effect. Vehicle design was changed so that removing the key automatically locked the ignition. Unlocked ignitions could no longer pose a problem on post-1970 models.

SOURCE: "Victim Facilitation: The Case of Auto Theft," by Andrew Karmen. *Victimology*, 1979, p. 364. Citations for each survey listed in this table appear in this article.

parking in isolated or dimly lit areas and for not purchasing optional anti-theft devices at their own (considerable) expense. Yet, motorist blaming about leaving keys behind continues unabated. Perhaps victim blaming has become a diversionary tactic, even a form of scapegoating. The most virulent victim blaming, when traced back to its sources, emanates from automobile industry speakers, insurance company representatives, and top law enforcement officials. Who or what are they protecting? Certainly, they are not apologists for the lawbreakers—the joyriding juveniles who they insist should not be "coddled" and the professional criminals whom they are trying to put out of business. It appears that these attacks on motorists who make their cars easier to steal are intended to draw attention away from the automobile manufacturers who design and sell cars that are easily stolen! Considerable evidence exists to substantiate the charge that vehicle security, like safety, has always been assigned a low priority by the Detroit automakers and their foreign counterparts (see Karmen, 1981).

Victim Precipitation and Rape: Was It Somehow Her Fault?

A paradox surrounds the crime of rape. The severe penalties for committing the offense (455 men were executed in the United States between 1930 and 1968; in 1976 the Supreme Court struck down capital punishment for rape; now life imprisonment is the maximum sentence in most states) indicate that it is one of the most terrible and strictly forbidden of acts. Yet rape remains the subject of jokes, and its victims are routinely stigmatized, as they have been throughout history.

The clash between victim blaming and victim defending is particularly sharp in the case of rape. If auto theft provided a clear example of a crime for which there is a well-organized and well-financed victim-blaming vested-interest group, then rape is the best example of a crime for which there is a militant, vocal, victim-defending movement.

The threat of rape burdens all women, although certain categories of females face greater dangers than others (see box 4-3). A controversy erupts over the question of whether rapes are acts of uncontainable sexual passion that might be victim precipitated, or acts of brutality, inspired by woman-hating themes interwoven throughout the fabric of a sexist society, that claim innocent victims.

A great deal is at stake in the battle for public support between victim blamers and victim defenders. The problem of rape forces a choice between two very different solutions. Who or what has to change—the way women behave in the company of men, or the way social and cultural institutions treat women?

Victim-Blaming Viewpoints

When a woman complains to the authorities that she has been raped, she is often met with disbelief. The skepticism (sometimes outright hostility) is based on suspicions regarding her plea to be treated as a bona fide crime victim. Perhaps the entire charge is a fabrication (no sexual intercourse was attempted or completed); maybe intercourse did take place, but she consented to it (and later decided to accuse her partner of compelling her to accede to his demands); or she was indeed raped but in good faith has identified the wrong man as the culprit. These are not the issues, however, that fuel the debate over whether there is such a thing as victim precipitation.

Victim blamers contend that some of the females who are raped share

BOX 4-3 Who Gets Raped?

Although it is true that any female could be singled out by a rapist for attack, certain categories of girls and women are sexually assaulted more often than others. Since crime rates generally vary only a few percentage points from one year to the next, they can be used for predictions. The rape rates of the recent past provide a basis for forecasting rape risks in the near future.

Occasionally, accounts of tragic attacks on infants or elderly grandmothers make the news. But statistics from victimization surveys over the years show that the highest risks are faced by those females who are young, not married, and poor (Bureau of Justice Statistics, 1982).

Groups	*Rape rates (number of victims for every 1,000 females of this type, age 12 and over), 1980*
All types of females	*1.6 per 1,000*
Completed	*.4*
Attempted	*1.2*
By age	
12–15	1*
16–19	5
20–24	4
25–34	2
35–49	1
50–64	0*
65 or older	0*
By race	
Whites	2
Blacks	2
By marital status	
Never married	3
Divorced and separated	4
Widowed	0*
Married	1
By family income	
Less than $3,000	3
$3,000–$7,499	2
$7,500–$9,999	1
$10,000–$14,999	1
$15,000–$24,499	0*
$25,000 or more	1

*Not enough cases to produce a statistically reliable estimate.

SOURCE: *Criminal Victimization in the United States, 1980,* by the Bureau of Justice Statistics. Washington, D.C.: U.S. Department of Justice, 1982:22–29.

responsibility with the male offenders for the crimes. Their selection by rapists was no accident or quirk of fate. They did something "wrong" that contributed to their "downfall." These girls and women who are partly at fault differ in their attitudes and actions from other females who have not been victimized.

The controversial charge is that a significant proportion of rapes are victim precipitated, although accusations of facilitation and even provocation are leveled as well. Girls and women who are considered guilty of victim precipitation are blamed for singling themselves out for trouble through their own reckless and rash acts. They are said to have tempted fate by attracting would-be offenders, and they are condemned for showing poor judgment and for failing to heed warnings (MacDonald, 1971:79). Because of their interactions with the offenders as the incidents unfolded, these victims are held responsible for any breakdown of communication, for the arousal of uncontrollable passions in males, or for triggering any criminal inclinations that already existed in them.

The most widely cited (and most criticized) study of victim precipitation in rape was based on data drawn from the files of the Philadelphia police dealing with cases in 1958 and 1960 (Amir, 1971). Victim precipitation was defined as having occurred whenever a female's behavior was interpreted by a teenage boy or man either as a direct invitation to engage in sexual relations that was later retracted (she agreed and then changed her mind, according to him), or as a sign that she would be available if he persisted in his demands (she was saying "no" but meant "yes," in his opinion). Included in this working definition of victim precipitation were acts of commission—like agreeing to a drink or accepting a ride with a stranger, or using what could be taken as indecent language or gestures—as well as acts of omission—like failing to object strongly enough to suggestions and overtures charged with sexuality. The offender's interpretation of the victim's intentions was considered to be the crucial element in recognizing a case of victim precipitation. Even if the offender was mistaken in his beliefs about the victim, his perceptions led to actions, and that is what mattered. In the police files, the indicators of victim precipitation were statements by the offender, witnesses, or detectives that "she behaved provocatively," "she acted seductively," "she was irresponsible and endangered herself," or "she had a bad reputation in the neighborhood." Using these criteria, 195 of 646 forcible rapes were deemed to be victim precipitated. The typical victim, statistically speaking, was a black woman raped by a black man who was known to her as a friend, neighbor, relative, or acquaintance. Comparing victim-precipitated rapes with nonprecipitated rapes, it was found that consuming alcohol was more likely to be a factor, that the victim was more likely to have had a "bad reputation," and that the offender was more inclined to sexually humiliate his victim. A higher percentage of precipitating victims than innocent victims were white females; a higher percentage were teenage girls; and a higher percentage first encountered their assailants at bars or parties (Amir, 1971:493–502).

From the victim-blaming perspective, some women precipitate rapes by their activities and their personalities (see Dean and deBruyn-Kops, 1982:57–59). These women did not understand or chose to ignore the risks involved in certain situations, such as going to bars unescorted or accepting lifts home with men they hardly knew. They were unaware, naive, or gullible in their dealings with men. They wore clothing or used language that men stereotyped as signaling sexual availability. They ignored the dangers that might arise if they were suddenly confronted with a weapon or were overpowered by the influence of alcohol or some other drug. Perhaps they were fatalistic about the risk of rape as the price of being "free" to come and go as they pleased, and to do the same things men do.

Personality traits traditionally defined as "feminine" may also unwittingly attract rapists who "size up" potential victims by the "vibes" they emit. Women who are particularly vulnerable to "confidence rapes," which involve deceit and betrayal, as opposed to "blitz rapes," which are ambush attacks, have a personality that combines good manners with a lack of assertiveness. They have been taught to be polite, to try not to hurt other people's feelings, to help those in distress, and to avoid making a scene. As a consequence, they are susceptible to men who are extremely aggressive at parties, to sexual psychopaths who pose as repairmen, or to deceptive strangers who, for example, "must desperately" use their home telephone. Such women are especially defenseless when they are depressed, worried, or lonely. Since it will appear that they entered into risky situations of their own accord, convictions of the rapists in court will be difficult.

Victim blamers have developed various explanations to account for the complicity of those rape victims who are not totally innocent, chosen at random, or entirely "virtuous."

One victim-blaming line of thought centers on the alleged psychological makeup of the female personality. Passivity and masochism (enjoyment of suffering) are said to be universal characteristics. The result is a common yearning, often expressed in fantasies, to be roughly handled, dominated, and violently possessed, despite any outward protestations to the contrary. As a result of this secret desire, precipitative victims might actually set the stage for their own rapes, either consciously or unconsciously. Some victim blamers go so far as to suggest that certain females are so deeply masochistic that rape may actually be a pleasurable event or a "liberating" experience for them.

Another victim-blaming line of reasoning built on the assumption of psychopathology proposes that some women fear being raped to such a degree that they take unnecessary risks and expose themselves to great dangers in order to precipitate an incident and "get it over with"—a so-called "riddance rape"—to relieve intense anxiety about what the experience is like (see Amir, 1971:254).

The reckless behavior of teenage girls is explained as a form of "acting out." These adolescents, especially if they come from poverty-stricken homes and rejecting parents, are said to be seeking protection, attention, love, intimacy, and status through precocious sexuality. As a result, they get involved with older male casual acquaintances and find themselves in situations in which they are forcefully exploited (Amir, 1971:255).

Two sets of consequences follow from an acceptance of victim-blaming arguments: if a female shares responsibility for the "tragic misunderstanding," it lessens the male's guilt; and if precipitation is a common occurrence, then girls and women must be "educated" to act more cautiously to avoid the company of potential rapists and to avoid miscommunication.

If the victim is partly to blame, then it is not entirely the offender's fault. The legal principle involved is that the female "assumed the risk" of attack when she voluntarily participated in the events leading up to the rape, like hitching a ride or agreeing to drink liquor. Even though the male remains legally responsible, her contributory behavior can provide the basis for granting the benefit of the doubt to the offender. The impact of this line of reasoning can influence every stage of the criminal justice system's handling of a case of victim-precipitated rape.

If, after a thorough interrogation of the complainant to determine her background, reputation, actions, and possible motives, the police believe that she contributed to her own victimization, the charges may be determined to be "unfounded" and the investigation closed. If police do make an arrest, the prosecutor may decide that the case is "unwinnable" for lack of compelling evidence that she was violated against her will and resisted to her utmost, and will drop the charges. If the case is brought to trial, jurors may exercise their discretion in interpreting the facts, and they may find the assailant guilty of a lesser charge than forcible rape (assault, for example). If the defendant is convicted, the judge may hand down a lenient sentence in view of the mitigating circumstances—her alleged precipitation, provocation, instigation, or misleading seductiveness ("implied consent").

The other major consequence of accepting the victim-blaming point of view is to shift the burden of preventing rape from males, the police, or any other responsible parties to the potential victims themselves. Girls and women are told that it is their obligation to review their lifestyle and to do what they can to minimize risks and maximize their safety. They are held personally accountable for their own security and are urged to follow crime prevention tips developed by experts in the field of police work. Those who fail to heed the advice, who neglect to take precautions, and who don't draw lessons from the past misfortunes of others are told that they have themselves to blame if they precipitate a rape.

Just as the threat of punishment is intended to make would-be rapists think twice before breaking the law, the public humiliation of victim blaming is meant to compel potential victims to think twice before acting rashly. Since it is so difficult to control the actions of offenders, victim blamers seek to reduce the incidence of rape by influencing the behavior of girls and women—whom they associate with, what they say in conver-

BOX 4-4 *Who Are the Victim Blamers?*

The controversy over attributing fault in rape cases has generated many assertions about who the victim blamers are. It seems plausible that men would be more likely to adopt a victim-blaming stance than women and that feminists would be less likely to criticize rape victims than policemen. But attitudinal research has not verified these predictions. The findings of polls and experiments are inconclusive and sometimes contradictory. For example:

- In one study, males, more often than females, considered rape victims responsible for precipitating the crime (Thornton, Robbins, and Johnson, 1981).
- In another study, however, policemen, other men, and feminists did not differ significantly from one another in the average degree of fault that they assigned to rape victims. Women not considered feminists were significantly more likely than any other group to attribute blame to rape victims (Ellison, 1976).
- In a large survey, white women were more likely than white men to place some of the blame for rapes on the victims. Black and Hispanic men were more likely to find fault with rape victims than black and Hispanic women (Williams, 1979).

Many different interpretations of these findings are possible. Methodological issues, like the way questions were phrased and the manner in which subjects were chosen, might explain some of the discrepancies. But the overall conclusion must be that social attitudes are complex, in constant flux, and difficult to characterize. Commonsense notions and plausible hypotheses must be tested scientifically by gathering evidence of their truth or falsity.

---

sations, where they go, and how they appear (particularly what clothing styles they wear). Females must learn how to communicate clearly, how to signal their true intentions, and how to avoid teasing or taunting males.

In sum, victim blamers believe that to avoid responsibility for rape, potential targets must maintain constant vigilance; reckless lifestyles that are courting disaster must be changed before it is too late (see box 4-4).

Victim-Defending Arguments

The views of victim blamers, rooted in cultural traditions about the proper roles that males and females should play, have recently become very controversial. Victim defenders, drawn originally from the ranks of activists in the women's movement, have challenged these interpretations of the causes of certain rapes and developed explanations of their own.

Victim defenders insist that most rapes are not victim precipitated in any way. Further, they question the entire notion of precipitation as applied to the crime of rape. As a result, they condemn victim blamers for inflicting a "second wound" by unfairly scapegoating the injured party for situations beyond her ability to control.

Victim defenders embrace new ideas about equality of the sexes, personal dignity, individual autonomy, and self-determination. They don't ask for special treatment for rape victims—just equal rights. They argue that for centuries rape victims have been singled out for discriminatory handling by the men running the criminal justice system. Women who came forward and contended that they had been "wronged" never received the "chivalrous" treatment promised to them. Instead, they were branded as a "prosecutrix" for pressing charges and stigmatized as "fallen," "marred," "spoiled," "impure," or "unchaste" for reputedly collaborating in the series of events that had led to their "downfall."

Victim defenders have questioned the validity of the concept of victim precipitation, which was originally developed to describe the blameworthy, violent initiatives taken by people killed during fights. Interpretations of certain rapes as victim precipitated have been dismissed as ex post facto conclusions that fail to take into account the victim's version of the incident (LeGrande, 1973:925); a personification and embodiment of rape mythology cleverly stated in academic–scientific terms (Weis and Borges, 1973:112); and an academic endorsement of the rapist's point of view that provides an excuse for blaming the victim (Clark and Lewis, 1978).

There is no such thing as justifiable rape in the sense that there is justifiable homicide (Amir, 1971:266). Therefore, the meaning of victim precipitation in rape cannot be parallel to its meaning in murder cases. Rape victims rarely take aggressive physical initiatives against the rapist before his assault. The only way to make headway with the concept of precipitation in rape is to consider the crime primarily as a sexual encounter rather than a brutal act of aggresion. Only then can real or presumed sexual advances by the victim be deemed precipitative. If rape is viewed as a violent assault expressed through sexual degradation, then it is difficult to argue that the victim set the process in motion. In victim-precipitated homicides, the offender acts defensively after the victim has begun to use physical force. In victim-precipitated rapes, the male acts offensively after the female makes sexual overtures, or what he perceives as invitations to engage in sex. In homicides, violence begets violence. In rapes, misinterpreted signals beget violence. The two classes of stimuli are not equivalent, in terms of socially approved responses. Acts of physical force can be recognized without much debate. But there is little consensus over what constitutes a sexual overture. For these reasons, the value of victim precipitation as an explanatory tool in understanding why specific males attacked particular females is undermined. Since the victim's behavior can be subjected to a wide range of interpretations, whose perceptions should be accepted when determining precipitation—the police's, the jury's, the researcher's, the victim's, or the offender's? (See Chappell, Geis, and Geis, 1977; McCaghy, 1980; Silverman, 1974).

At the heart of the victim defenders' critique of prevailing misunderstandings about rape is a rejection of what are considered to be widespread "myths" about rapists and their victims. (See Brownmiller, 1975; Schwendinger and Schwendinger, 1974; and Dean and deBruyn-Kops, 1982, for lists of misconceptions and realities about rape.)

The primary myth is that rapes are outpourings of sexual desire. According to victim defenders, most sexual assaults are just that—assaults involving sexual acts symbolizing domination, conquest, subjugation, humiliation, and contempt. Consequently, it is also a mistake to believe that it is the woman's fault because a man cannot control himself once he is aroused. Men can control their sexual appetites, although in court the assailant may be portrayed by his lawyer as the innocent victim of an evil seductive woman who recklessly stirred up his passions. By normalizing rape as an act of lust, the burden of responsibility is shifted from the male to the female.

Similarly, the belief that women invite rape by their actions or appearance is undermined by the recognition of rape as an assault. Females may desire men's interest, but they do not want to be terrorized into submission. The notion that "nice girls" are not raped dates back to the days when "good girls" were always chaperoned and never strayed far from home, especially at night. The callous assertion that rape is not a serious crime, because engaging in sexual relations is normal and healthy, overlooks the potentially devastating reactions to the violation of a woman's personhood by an aggressive act of sexual objectification imposed against her will. The fatalistic conclusion that there is nothing a woman can do to prevent rape, that a woman who resists will be seriously injured, and that a woman who submits will not be hurt are also unfounded, since in particular situations the outcome of the aggression remains an open question (see box 4-5).

A final myth is that the accusation is easily made, and although hard to prove, is even more difficult to defend against by an innocent man. This often-quoted outlook, attributed to the jurist Sir Matthew Hale in 1630, contradicts reality. Only a fraction of all rapes are reported, and only a small percentage of rape trials end in convictions. The major reasons for not reporting the crime, or for later deciding not to press charges, are fear of retaliation; fear of police, hospital, and court procedures; fears by teenagers of parental wrath; fear of not being believed; feelings of embarrassment; feelings of self-blame; concern for the reaction of a jealous boyfriend or husband directed at the victim or the assailant; and a lack of faith in the criminal justice system (Belden, 1979).

Victim defenders argue that even the well-intentioned advice of genuinely concerned victim blamers who want to prevent future tragedies is ideologically tainted. A woman who abides by the long (and growing) list of recommended self-protection measures ends up resembling the "hysterical old maid armed with a hatpin and an umbrella who looks under the bed each night before retiring." Long a laughable stereotype of prudery, she is now a model of prudence (Brownmiller, 1975:398). Following crime prevention tips means forgoing many of the small pleasures and privileges in life that men are accustomed to (like taking a walk at night). Warding off would-be rapists requires women to engage in an extraordinary amount of pretense and deception (like claiming that a

BOX 4-5 Resisting Rapists

How the victim reacts can profoundly influence the outcome of a rape attack. Her behavior—either submission or resistance—affects the attacker's decisions about whether to try to complete the act and how much force is needed to subdue her. Her actions also determine the seriousness of the charges he will face if caught. Some victims are blamed for not resisting fiercely enough.

The results of a survey (of over 30,000 victims in twenty-six cities assaulted by strangers during the mid-1970s) confirm that the majority of girls and women did something to defend themselves during the confrontations. When victims resisted, only 20 percent of the rapes were completed. When victims did not try any self-protective measures, 67 percent of the rapes were completed. The most common steps taken by the victims were to scream for help to scare the offender away and attract attention (48 percent of the cases) and to fight back physically (45 percent). Smaller percentages of victims tried to run away (29 percent), or threaten, argue with, or reason with the attacker (22 percent). Some victims tried several strategies.

The victims who resisted improved their chances of thwarting the rapists' aims of completing the act, but they also increased their risks of suffering additional injuries. One-third of the nonresisting victims were wounded besides being sexually assaulted, whereas two-thirds of the victims who used self-defense measures were physically hurt—bruised, cut, scratched, even stabbed or shot.

Rape victims—and those who would advise them how to behave when confronted—face a dilemma. Resistance may foil a rape but may also more seriously endanger the victim. Studies assessing the relative effectiveness of various self-protection measures have produced mixed findings, so the question of how to react to a rapist has no clear-cut answer as yet (McDermott, 1979:29–42).

The apparent acquiescence of some victims can be explained readily. The primary reaction of nearly all rape victims is to fear for their lives, according to interviews conducted at a hospital emergency room (Burgess and Holmstrom, 1974). Faced with the prospect of death or at least severe physical injury, many conclude that their only way out is to "strike a bargain" or an "understanding" with the attacker and trade submission for survival (to exchange sexual violation for some sort of pledge that they won't be killed, savagely beaten, or cruelly disfigured). Those who don't take this gamble and apparently acquiesce anyway might simply be immobilized by terror, shock, and disbelief. There is, of course, no guarantee that compliance will minimize physical injury. The rapists do not have to keep any promises (Brownmiller, 1975). A study of sex offenders incarcerated in a mental hospital revealed that the overwhelming majority of rapists wanted their victims to give in without a fight and agree to do anything, but a minority of them actually preferred that the victim plead, scream, or tell them off (Chappell and James, 1976).

Whether or not resistance is the best strategy under all circumstances, until recently all state laws required it. Rape was the only crime of violence in which the victim was expected to resist "within reason" and to prove later that her eventual submission had not been tacit consent.

---

boyfriend, husband, or father is nearby). Seeking the protection of men to fend off the unwanted advances of other men undermines the efforts of women to develop their own strengths and networks of support. Even worse, it can result in a false sense of security with sometimes tragic results (see box 4-6).

BOX 4-6 *When "Nice Guys" Won't Take "No!" for an Answer*

Although the term *rape* at first conjures up the image of a knife-wielding stranger leaping from the shadows, in more than a quarter of all reported sexual assaults the victim knows the offender. It is suspected that the overwhelming majority of unreported rapes are committed by casual acquaintances, bosses, co-workers, neighbors, friends, relatives, and dates.

"Date rapes"—or, more inclusively, "acquaintance rapes"—that are brought to the attention of the authorities usually go unpunished. Police investigations determine the charges to be "unfounded," or district attorneys consider the cases "unprosecutable." Even the victims may begin to doubt that they were really raped, although they were "forced to consent" to have intercourse. Typically, they blame themselves for what happened and feel guilty and ashamed as well as abused and violated.

Various commonsense precautions can be taken to avoid the risks of being attacked by a stranger. But there is really no way to protect against rape by an acquaintance or date who suddenly transforms himself from Dr. Jekyll to Mr. Hyde (Mithers, 1980).

Like spouse abuse and incest, acquaintance rape represents a violation of trust. For that reason, the more intimately the victim knew the attacker before the crime, the more likely it is that she will suffer lingering psychological problems afterward. Acquaintance-rape victims are more likely to be blamed than those sexually assaulted by strangers, perhaps because other people find it doubly disturbing to live with the knowledge not only that all women are potential targets but also that potential rapists are men they know (Bart, 1979).

Statistics about acquaintance rape, which is the kind of incident most likely to be categorized as somehow victim precipitated, are available from victimization surveys. The extent of the problem is probably grossly underestimated from the following data, since acquaintance rapes are suspected to be reported much less often than stranger rapes. (The survey defines a stranger as someone not known by the victim, or known only by sight. Everyone else can be considered an acquaintance.)

Comparing rapes with other violent crimes, the statistics show that strangers are responsible for a higher percentage of robberies than they are of rapes. Acquaintances pose a greater threat in aggravated assaults than in rapes (probably because of the high rate of family violence).

The possibility of acquaintance rape is never negligible, and it grows to substantial proportions for certain age, race, marital, and income categories.

Feminists have sought to combat rape by raising the level of public awareness about these acts of "terrorism" waged by some men. Asserting that "the personal is political," activists in the women's movement have stressed that private troubles need to be seen as aspects of larger social problems besetting millions of other people. Collective solutions hold out greater promise in the long run than a reliance on personal strategies of risk reduction. To force the criminal justice system to assign rape cases a higher priority and to alleviate the plight of rape victims, women's groups have politicized the issues in a number of conventional and unconventional ways: through speakouts at which rape victims came forward and shared their experiences; at rallies in support of women who had killed

Percentage of Rapes Committed by Strangers and by Acquaintances, 1980

Type of crime	*Percentage by strangers*	*Percentage by acquaintances*
All crimes of violence	64%	36%
Rape	72%	28%
Robbery	83%	17%
Aggravated assault	65%	35%
Victim's age		
All ages	72%	28%
12–15	56%*	44%
16–19	66%	34%
20–24	76%	24%
25–34	73%	27%
35–49	82%	18%
50 or older	——%*	——%*
Victim's race		
White	72%	28%
Black	79%	21%
Victim's marital status		
Never married	73%	27%
Separated or divorced	60%	40%
Married	94%	6%
Widowed	46%*	54%*
Victim's family income		
Less than $3,000	66%	34%
$3,000–$7,499	70%	30%
$7,500–$9,999	73%*	27%*
$10,000–$14,999	77%	23%
$15,000–$24,999	65%	35%
$25,000 or more	87%	13%

*Not enough cases to produce a statistically reliable estimate

SOURCE: *Criminal Victimization in the United States, 1980,* by the Bureau of Justice Statistics. Washington, D.C.: U.S. Department of Justice, 1982:45–46.

rapists in self-defense; through resolutions at conferences; during marches to "take back the night" (to be able to walk around without harassment or attack); at picket lines to discourage movie goers from attending films glorifying violence against women; and through lobbying campaigns for changes in criminal justice practices and laws.

The anti-rape movement of the 1970s that was launched by victim defenders has won many victories (Rose, 1977).

A major achievement on the community level has been the establishment of rape crisis centers. Victims are offered counseling and the services of a volunteer advocate who will accompany them as their complaints are processed by the medical, police, and court agencies. In some communities, the anti-rape movement has successfully pressured the police to set up special sexual assault and rape-analysis units, staffed in part by policewomen. Self-defense classes have also sprung up.

In the legislative arena, rape laws have been revised in some states to rid them of their traditional notions of appropriate female conduct, blatant double standards based on the victims' gender, and views of females as the property of males. Victim defenders have criticized the corroboration requirements (for additional witnesses), which cast suspicion on the complainant's motives, and the rules permitting exploration of the victims' sexual history (in order to build a case that if she consented in the past, she may have consented during the incident in question). On the federal level, women's groups convinced Congress in 1975 to establish a Center for the Prevention and Control of Rape (under the auspices of the National Institute of Mental Health), which conducts research into the causes of the crime and ways of treating its victims.

Among the consequences of accepting victim-defending arguments have been procedural changes that might increase the conviction rate of rapists and ease the suffering of their victims. Yet institutionalized biases remain within the male-run criminal justice system. Since the disagreements between victim blamers and victim defenders are far from resolved, more conflict and further changes are sure to come.

What are really at stake in the debate between victim blamers and victim defenders are issues much larger than just acquittal or conviction of accused rapists, or the complainants' innocence versus precipitation. Victim blamers are not trying to excuse criminals, but rather to get sexist social institutions and cultural themes "off the hook." Victim defenders are not trying merely to "nail" rapists but are seeking sweeping changes that will benefit all women, not only rape victims. They are challenging the anti-female biases found within rigid sex roles, prevailing definitions of masculinity and femininity, existing criminal laws and criminal justice practices, and popular culture (Hills, 1981).

Victim Provocation and a Looting Spree: Why Were the Stores Sacked?

Most of the theory, research, and discussions about criminal victimizations are person centered. Yet victims can be organizations (governmental agencies, schools, businesses) as well as real people. Many nonviolent crimes (like embezzlement, shoplifting, and fraud) and acts of criminal violence (such as vandalism and robbery) can be directed at entities as easily as at private individuals. Organizations can be offenders as well as victims, and they can be repeat offenders as easily as repeat victims. The study of organizations as victims has received very little attention by victimologists, in part because of formidable methodological problems that arise in data-gathering efforts; but adding analyses of organizations as victims would advance the development of victimological theories (Reiss, 1981).

The urban uprisings (ghetto rebellions or, to use the condemnatory term, "riots") of the 1960s provide many cases for study of street crime (vandalism, arson, burglary, and massive looting) directed at impersonal targets (stores and businesses) rather than specific individuals. The continuing outbursts of community anger, as in Miami in 1980 and again in 1982, underscore the relevance of examining the conflicts within neighborhoods between people and commercial establishments (which erupt, along with other antagonisms, such as tensions between residents and the police, during "civil disturbances"). As in all criminal incidents, victim-blaming and victim-defending perspectives offer competing explanations and intepretations of what happened, why, and who or what was at fault.

One sultry evening in July 1977, lightning struck some power lines during a thunderstorm and the lights went out in New York City. The blackout triggered an upheaval in the balance of power within poor neighborhoods. What followed was a "night of terror" for some but "Christmas in July" for others. By the time darkness had given way to daylight and police control had been reestablished, merchandise was missing from 2,000 stores in the metropolitan area's black and Hispanic ghettos, and over 3,000 looters were jammed into sweltering local jails.

As the communications capital of the world revived, the mass media became preoccupied with the glaring social problems and the illuminating lessons highlighted by the blackout looting. Most major newspapers and magazines carried editorials on the subject, and many syndicated columnists commented on the event. In general, the formula that ran through most of the editorials and columns was to blame the criminals and defend the victims.

Criminal Blaming in the Media

The predominantly black and Hispanic young men who were arrested were sharply condemned in print by various authors as "ruffians," "pariahs," "the scum of the city," "litter of the streets," "debris," "parasites," and "riffraff." They were described as "idle, menacing, and strutting," and as being "poor and unemployable," and "on welfare and food stamps for doing nothing." Some writers went further in their denunciations of the looters, depicting them as less than human in various ways. The people who took part in the looting spree were branded as "animals with no human guilt pangs," "animals and scum," "a new creature, like the Loch Ness monster," "a multiheaded beast," "piranhas," "young sharks," "urban insects," "an unstoppable swarm," "scavenging and travelling in packs," "prowling," "roachlike," and "swarming like driver ants." Perhaps the most blatantly offensive racist epithet to appear in print in a mass-circulation publication was "welfare mommas lumbering about like overfed heifers." A handful of commentators condemned the use of these animal metaphors and stressed that such imagery has been used historically to dismiss genuine economic, political, or social grievances. (See Karmen, 1978, for citations for these quotes.)

Victim Defending in the Media

Most of the authors of editorials and columns made little or no attempt to bridge the gulfs of race or class that separated them from the participants in order to try to understand the reasons for the outbreak of lawlessness from the standpoint of the perpetrators. But the majority of commentators made every effort to empathize with the victims of the looting spree. Their close identification with the victims took several forms. The plight of the victims was consistently described in personalized terms, through anecdotes about particular merchants and businessmen, even though a substantial proportion of the looted stores were owned by corporations and franchise chains. The victimized businesses were portrayed in very favorable terms that made it seem as if they were totally innocent and had done nothing to bring about the tidal wave of destruction that swept their goods away. The proprietors (of all races and nationalities) were presented as "hard working," "courageous," "envied because they were successful," "leading productive lives," "striving and loved," "providers of jobs to those willing to work," "deserving of more community and customer support," and "believers in the American dream of capitalist free enterprise." These "victims of unfairness" endured "heart-breaking losses," and "they lost their entire life's work and savings." They were "decent people" who were "incapable of cheating anyone" (for citations, see Karmen, 1978).

The Case for Victim Blaming

Most articles did not address the issue of what the ghetto businesses might have done or not done to seal their fate. Just a few authors raised the possibility that the victims might have been partly or even fully responsible for their own misfortunes. Yet journalists in those same publications who interviewed men, women, and youths in the streets in the blackout's aftermath turned up indications of what might have motivated many of the participants. Neighborhood residents viewing the gutted stores contended that certain businesses had deserved to be looted because they cheated their customers all the time, charging high prices for junk. Community leaders confided that the looting had expressed the hatred and resentment of poor people striking back against businesses that drained financial resources out of the area.

Shortly after the event, pollsters asked a nationwide sample of people from all walks of life whether they thought the blackout looters had seized the opportunity to "get even" with ghetto businesses. Despite the media coverage, which had largely avoided this interpretation, as many as a quarter of the whites and a third of the blacks accepted this explanation as plausible. A larger proportion of the general public than of the print media opinion shapers was willing to consider the possibility of shared responsibility.

Although the event took place in 1977, nearly everyone overlooked the wealth of social science data compiled during the 1960s about the strained relationship between ghetto businesses and their customers. Surveys and other studies revealed that significant numbers in minority-group communities viewed the local small businesses as petty exploiters. To almost no one's great surprise, it was documented that the poor pay more—for less. Marginal businesses operating in a hostile environment and with many disadvantages (high rent, little or no insurance, low volume, slow turnover, considerable shoplifting and robbery losses, high interest rates, poor credit risks) were largely compelled by economic forces to take unfair advantage of their customers in order to survive financially in competition with huge downtown enterprises. Hence, ghetto merchants typically used deceptive advertising (like "bait-and-switch" come-ons) and easy credit schemes (lay-away plans) to lure customers into the stores, where they were sold inferior goods (seconds and defective merchandise misrepresented as "in perfect condition") at inflated prices. The strategy of many businesses was to maintain their customers in constant debt via the installment plan. Questionable pressure tactics, as well as legal actions to repossess goods and garnish wages, were applied when the overextended buyers fell hopelessly behind in their payments.

How Much Heat, How Much Light?

The tone of the media coverage of New York's blackout looting was unusually emotional and subjective. The event generated a great deal of heat, but how much light was shed on its root causes and on what was at stake?

The motive of the victim defenders was to exonerate the sacked stores of any charges of shared responsibility for their losses to the angry crowds. Victim defenders argued that the criminals were entirely at fault and deserved the harshest punishments for their lawless acts. They campaigned for emergency government loans and for private donations to help ruined merchants who were uninsured or underinsured to replenish their stocks and reopen their businesses.

The motive of the few victim blamers among the media commentators was not to justify the looting but rather to focus attention on its underlying causes—the hardships of ghetto life. Their purpose in blaming the victims was to argue not that they had deserved to suffer but that they were obliged to change their exploitive ways if they wanted to be spared during future uprisings.

There was not much of a debate between victim blamers and victim defenders in the aftermath of the blackout looting spree. One point of view, the victim-defending perspective, dominated media coverage. Few articles were written from an opposing standpoint, even though the case for victim blaming rested on a firm foundation of social science research findings. The consensus in the media was that the victim defenders were correct: the thieves were entirely at fault; the ghetto businesses had done nothing wrong to provoke their wrath. The public, according to opinion polls, basically agreed. But was that the reality of the situation?

Beyond Victim Blaming and Victim Defending

A review of the three cases presented above uncovers some misleading impressions and some strengths and weaknesses of victim blaming and victim defending.

Contrary to the characterizations of some victimologists, victim blaming is not inherently an exercise in scapegoating or an example of twisted logic and callousness. It all depends on which crime is the focus of attention, who the victims are, and why some people are blaming them. Similarly, victim defending is not invariably a "noble" enterprise in behalf of underdogs.

To blame a teenage girl who has been raped by a gang of bikers surely smacks of scapegoating. But the victim is not always weaker and defenseless. To criticize the businesses that were looted during the blackout is to assign some of the blame to the relatively more powerful parties (commercial enterprises vis-a-vis shoppers). To defend the looted businesses from charges that they provoked their customers is to side with vested interests in their attempts to preserve a favorable public image.

Hence, victim blamers are not necessarily liberal or conservative, rich or poor, young or old, male or female, or black or white. Victim defenders are at other times victim blamers; individuals do not line up consistently on one side or the other. Everyone blames certain victims and defends others, when the full scope of criminals and victims is taken into account.

The strengths of victim-blaming and victim-defending outlooks lie in their willingness to address actual events, specific criminal acts, and real cases. In the course of their dialogues and debates, victim blamers and victim defenders examine the details of who did and said what to whom. Victim-blaming and victim-defending arguments bridge the gap between theoretical propositions and abstractions, on the one hand, and how people genuinely think and act, on the other. In dissecting how particular crimes unfolded, victim blamers and victim defenders pay attention to detailed exchanges and interactions that otherwise are overlooked.

The great weaknesses of both victim blaming and victim defending arise from the limitations of such "nearsighted" investigations. Victim blamers and victim defenders get so caught up (or bogged down) in the particularities of each case that they tend to ignore the larger social forces and conditions that shape the ideas and behaviors of both criminals and victims.

This tendency to parcel out blame between only two parties, the criminal and the victim, is reinforced by the way the criminal justice system operates. It deals almost entirely with conflicts between particular individuals. Rarely are more abstract forces or conditions considered to be "parties to the crime" and to be partly at fault for what happened.

In the case of auto theft, for example, victim-blaming and victim-defending arguments revolve entirely around the actions of motorists and thieves. What is excluded from the analysis is perhaps more important to an understanding of the crime than what is included—how sophisticated commercial thievery has become; how lucrative the market for stolen cars and stolen parts is and how economically rational stealing is; how inadequate the standard security provided by manufacturers is; how the practices of insurance companies provide incentives for thieves to steal cars and parts; and how the operations of salvage yards facilitate the thieves' tasks (Karmen, 1980).

In cases of rape, victim blamers and victim defenders focus too narrowly on female victims and male attackers. What tend to be overlooked are prevailing cultural definitions of femininity and masculinity and their role in preparing girls to become victims and boys to become aggressors. The possibility that the roots of rape lie in the economic, social, and political inequality of the sexes is likely to get lost when the horizons of the analysis are limited to the offender–victim interaction.

In reconstructing the events leading up to New York City's blackout looting, any preoccupation with what is "wrong" with ghetto residents or ghetto businesses will turn out to be misleading. The forces that create ghettos and heap misery on ghetto residents must be taken into account in order to understand the tensions that were building before the lights went out. Similarly, the larger economic climate fashioned by big businesses (like banks, department stores, and insurance companies), within which the smaller, marginal ghetto businesses try to survive financially, must be understood so that the inflammatory practices of the victimized stores are not viewed in a vacuum, but are seen as part of a larger picture of consumer fraud and the exploitation of the poor.

Victimology complements criminology by drawing attention to the other party in the drama. But if it is to make a major contribution to understanding human behavior, victimology must transcend any tendencies to limit attention to just the criminal and the victim.

References

AMIR, MENACHEM. 1971: *Patterns in Forcible Rape.* Chicago: University of Chicago Press.

ANDERSON, MARGARET, and RENZETTI, CHRISTINE. 1980: "Rape Crisis Counseling and the Culture of Individualism." *Contemporary Crises,* 4,3(July):323–341.

BALKAN, SHEILA; BERGER, RONALD; and SCHMIDT, JANET. 1980: *Crime and Deviance in America: A Critical Approach.* Belmont, Calif.: Wadsworth.

BART, PAULINE. 1979: "Rape as a Paradigm of Sexism in Society—Victimization and Its Discontents." *Women's Studies International Quarterly,* 2,5:1–11.

BELDEN, LINDA. 1979: "Why Women Do Not Report Sexual Assault." *Aegis,* September:38–42.

BROWNMILLER, SUSAN. 1975: *Against Our Will.* New York: Simon & Schuster.

BULGER, JAMES. 1933: "Automobile Thefts." *Journal of Criminal Law, Criminology, and Police Science,* 23:806–810.

BUREAU OF JUSTICE STATISTICS. 1982: *Criminal Victimization in the United States, 1980.* Washington, D.C.: U.S. Department of Justice.

BURGESS, ANN, and HOLMSTROM, LYNDA. 1974: "Rape Trauma Syndrome." *American Journal of Nursing,* 131:981–986.

CHAPPELL, DUNCAN; GEIS, ROBLEY; and GEIS, GILBERT. 1977: *Forcible Rape: The Crime, the Victim, and the Offender.* New York: Columbia University Press.

———, and JAMES, JENNIFER. 1976: "Victim Selection and Apprehension from the Rapist's Perspective: A Preliminary Investigation." Paper presented at the Second International Symposium on Victimology, Boston, September 8.

CLARK, LORENNE, and LEWIS, DEBORAH. 1978: *Rape: The Price of Coercive Sexuality.* Toronto: Women's Press.

CLEMENT, HENRY. 1946: "Stealing Your Own Car." *FBI Law Enforcement Bulletin,* April:21–34.

DEAN, CHARLES, and deBRUYN-KOPS, MARY. 1982: *The Crime and the Consequences of Rape.* Springfield, Ill.: Charles C Thomas.

ELLISON, KATHERINE. 1976: *The "Just World" in the "Real World": Attributions about Crime as a Function of Group Membership, Victim Precipitation and Injury.* Ann Arbor, Mich.: University Microfilms.

FATTAH, EZZAT. 1976: "The Use of the Victim as an Agent of Self-Legitimation: Toward a Dynamic Explanation of Criminal Behavior." In Emilio Viano (Ed.), *Victims and Society,* 105–129. Washington, D.C.: Visage.

———. 1979: "Some Recent Theoretical Developments in Victimology." *Victimology,* 4,2:198–213.

FRANKLIN, BRUCE. 1978: *The Victim as Criminal and Artist: Literature from the American Prison.* New York: Oxford University Press.

FRANKLIN, CLYDE, and FRANKLIN, ALICE. 1976: "Victimology Revisited." *Criminology,* 14,1:125–136.

HALL, JEROME. 1935: *Theft, Law, and Society.* Boston: Little, Brown.

HENDERSON, GEORGE. 1924: *Keys to Crookdom.* New York: Appleton.

HILLS, STUART. 1981: *Demystifying Deviance.* Englewood Cliffs, N.J.: Prentice-Hall.

HOOVER, JOHN EDGAR. 1966: "The Car Theft Problem: How You Can Help Beat It." *Congressional Record*—Senate, September 22:23621.

KARMEN, ANDREW. 1981: "Auto Theft and Corporate Irresponsibility." *Contemporary Crises,* 5:63–81.
——. 1980: "Auto Theft: Beyond Victim Blaming." *Victimology,* 5,2:161–174.
——. 1979: "Victim Facilitation: The Case of Auto Theft." *Victimology,* 4,4: 361–370.
——. 1978: "How Much Heat, How Much Light?: Coverage of New York City's Blackout and Looting in the Print Media." In Charles Winick (Ed.), *Deviance and the Mass Media,* 179–202. Beverly Hills, Calif.: Sage.
LeGRANDE, CAMILLE. 1973: "Rape and Rape Laws: Sexism in Society and Law." *California Law Review,* 61:919–941.
LERNER, MICHAEL. 1965: "Evaluation of Performance as a Function of Performer's Reward and Attractiveness." *Journal of Personality and Social Psychology,* 1:355–360.
LIPMAN, IRA. 1982: "Ways to Protect Yourself from Burglars, Muggers." *U.S. News & World Report,* December 13:77–78.
MacDONALD, JOHN. 1971: *Rape: Offenders and Victims.* Springfield, Ill.: Charles C Thomas.
McCAGHY, CHARLES. 1980: *Crime in American Society.* New York: Macmillan.
McDERMOTT, JOAN. 1979: Rape Victimization in 26 American Cities. Washington, D.C.: U.S. Government Printing Office.
MITHERS, CAROL. 1980: "Date Rape: When 'Nice Guys' Won't Take 'No!' for an Answer." *Mademoiselle,* November:210–211; 269.
"Offenders Get Wrists Slapped; Car Thefts Total Million a Year." 1975: *Salem* (Mass.) *News,* October 2:2.
RASKIN, LEE. 1968: "A Heist a Minute." *Nation,* April 7:434–436.
REIFF, ROBERT. 1979: *The Invisible Victim.* New York: Basic Books.
REISS, ALBERT, Jr. 1981: "Foreword: Towards a Revitalization of Theory and Research on Victimization by Crime." *Journal of Criminal Law and Criminology,* 72,2:704–713.
ROCHE, JOHN. 1967: "Statement to Senate." *Congressional Record*—Senate. March 22:7594.
ROSE, VICKI. 1977: "Rape as a Social Problem: A By-Product of the Feminist Movement." *Social Problems,* 25:75–89.
RYAN, WILLIAM. 1971: *Blaming the Victim.* New York: Vintage.
SCHULTZ, LEROY. 1968: "The Victim–Offender Relationship." *Crime and Delinquency,* 14:135–141.
SCHWENDINGER, HERMAN, and SCHWENDINGER, JULIA. 1967: "Delinquent Stereotypes of Probable Victims." In Malcolm Klein (Ed.), *Juvenile Gangs in Context,* 92–105. Englewood Cliffs, N.J.: Prentice-Hall.
——. 1974: "Rape Myths in Legal, Theoretical, and Everyday Practice." *Crime and Social Justice,* 1:18–26.
SHELEY, JOSEPH. 1979: *Understanding Crime: Concepts, Issues, Decisions.* Belmont, Calif.: Wadsworth.
SILVERMAN, ROBERT. 1974: "Victim Precipitation: An Examination of the Concept." In Israel Drapkin and Emilio Viano (Eds.), *Victimology: A New Focus,* 99–10. Lexington, Mass.: Heath.
SYKES, GRESHAM, and MATZA, DAVID. 1957: "Techniques of Neutralization: A Theory of Delinquency." *American Sociological Review,* 22:664–670.
SYMONDS, MARTIN. 1975: "Victims of Violence: Psychological Effects and Aftereffects." American Journal of Psychoanalysis, 35,1:19–26.
TEEVAN, JAMES, Jr. 1979: "Crime Victimization as a Neglected Social Problem." *Sociological Symposium.* 25:6–22.

THORNTON, B.; ROBBINS, M.; and JOHNSON, J. 1981: "Social Perception of the Rape Victim's Culpability: The Influence of Respondents' Personal–Environmental Causal Attribution Tendencies." *Human Relations,* 34,3:225–237.

TRAVELERS INSURANCE COMPANY. 1977: "Your Car's a Steal in More Ways Than One." Hartford, Conn.: Author.

U.S. SENATE, COMMITTEE ON THE JUDICIARY, SUBCOMMITTEE TO INVESTIGATE JUVENILE DELINQUENCY. 1954: *Hearings,* 83rd Congress, 2nd session, January 15. Washington, D.C.: U.S. Government Printing Office.

VOLLMER, AUGUST, and PARKER, ALFRED. 1936: *The Police and Modern Society.* San Francisco: University of California Press.

VON HENTIG, HANS. 1948: *The Criminal and His Victim: Studies in The Sociobiology of Crime.* New Haven, Conn.: Yale University Press.

WEIS, KURT, and BORGES, SANDRA. 1973: "Victimology and Rape: The Case of the Legitimate Victim." *Issues in Criminology,* 8,2:71–115.

WILLIAMS, JOYCE. 1979: "Sex Role Stereotypes, Women's Liberation, and Rape: A Cross Cultural Analysis of Attitudes." *Sociological Symposium,* 25:61–97.

CHAPTER 5

The Victim versus the Criminal Justice System

What Can the System Do for the Victim?

The criminal justice system is a branch of government that comes under scathing attack from all quarters. Conservatives, liberals, and radicals; feminists; law and order advocates; civil rights activists; and civil libertarians: all find fault with its rules and operations. Even its officials join the chorus of critics calling for change.

- If there is one word that describes how the criminal justice system treats victims of crimes and witnesses to crimes, it is "badly." (James Reilly, director of the Victim/Witness Assistance Project of the National District Attorney's Association [1981:8])
- Crimes that terrorize take many forms, from aggravated assault to petty thievery. But one crime goes largely unnoticed. It is a crime against which there is no protection. It is committed daily across our nation. It is the painful, wrongful insensitivity of the criminal justice system toward those who are the victims of crime. . . . The callousness with which the system again victimizes those who have already suffered at the hands of an assailant is tragic. (Senator John Heinz, sponsor of the Omnibus Victims Protection Act passed by Congress [1982:A19])
- Without the cooperation of victims and witnesses in reporting and testifying about crime, it is impossible in a free society to hold criminals accountable. When victims come forward to provide this vital service, however, they find little protection. They discover instead that they will be treated as appendages of a system appallingly out of balance. They

> learn that somewhere along the way the system has lost track of the simple truth that it is supposed to be fair and to protect those who obey the law while punishing those who break it. Somewhere along the way, the system began to serve lawyers and judges and defendants, treating the victim with institutionalized disinterest . . . . The neglect of crime victims is a national disgrace. (Lois Herrington, chairperson of the President's Task Force on Victims of Crime [President's Task Force, 1982:vi–vii])

The consensus among experts is that the criminal justice system does not measure up to expectations. It fails to deliver what it promises. It does not meet the needs and wants of victims as its "clients," or as "consumers" of its services.

Suppose a person is a victim of a robbery (or a rape, assault, or burglary). What could and should the system do?

The police could rush to the victim's aid and provide whatever physical and psychological first aid that might be needed. They could catch the culprit and speedily return stolen goods to the rightful owner. The prosecutor could indict the suspect and press for a swift trial. Alongside the legal proceedings, the prosecutor as a lawyer could attend to the victim's economic interests. Upon conviction of the offender, the prosecutor could see to it that the victim's views were fully aired. The judge could hand down a sentence that would satisfy the victim that indeed justice had been done.

But this scenario is rarely played out. More often than not, victims find themselves embroiled in conflicts with the police, prosecutors, defense attorneys, judges, and parole boards.[1]

Of all street crime victims, women who have been raped suffer most from the shortcomings of the criminal justice system. Their plight will be highlighted in order to dramatize the nature of the conflict between victims and officials, to illustrate the philosophical and political issues that arise in calls for reform, and to demonstrate that progress is possible.

The following account is reprinted from the report of the President's Task Force on Victims of Crime (1982:3–11). It pinpoints all the difficulties that can arise as one woman's ordeal is processed as just another case winding its way through the system. (See box 5-1.)

Punishment, Treatment, or Restitution?

Most of the deliberations of criminal justice officials concern punishment: who, why, when, where, how much. Yet punishment is a contro-

[1]The analysis that follows pertains solely to the operations of the adult criminal justice system. The juvenile justice system follows different procedures and presents a separate set of problems for crime victims. Juvenile offenders (under age eighteen) account for about a fifth of all arrestees for violent crimes, and nearly half of all those taken into custody for committing property crimes.

Box 5-1 The System, from a Victim's Point of View

The Crime

You are a 50-year-old woman living alone. You are asleep one night when suddenly you awaken to find a man standing over you with a knife at your throat. As you start to scream, he beats and cuts you. He then rapes you. While you watch helplessly, he searches the house, taking your jewelry, other valuables, and money. He smashes furniture and windows in a display of senseless violence. His rampage ended, he rips out the telephone line, threatens you again, and disappears into the night.

At least, you have survived. Terrified, you rush to the first lighted house on the block. While you wait for the police, you pray that your attacker was bluffing when he said he'd return if you called them. Finally, what you expect to be help arrives.

The police ask questions, take notes, dust for fingerprints, make photographs. When you tell them you were raped, they take you to the hospital. Bleeding from cuts, your front teeth knocked out, bruised and in pain, you are told that your wounds are superficial, that rape itself is not considered an injury. Awaiting treatment, you sit alone for hours, suffering the stares of curious passersby. You feel dirty, bruised, disheveled, and abandoned. When your turn comes for examination, the intern seems irritated because he has been called out to treat you. While he treats you, he says that he hates to get involved in rape cases because he doesn't like going to court. He asks if you "knew the man you had sex with."

The nurse says she wouldn't be out alone at this time of night. It seems pointless to explain that the attacker broke into your house and had a knife. An officer says you must go through this process, then the hospital sends you a bill for the examination that the investigators insisted upon. They give you a box filled with test tubes and swabs and envelopes and tell you to hold onto it. They'll run some tests if they ever catch your rapist.

Finally, you get home somehow, in a cab you paid for and wearing a hospital gown because they took your clothes as evidence. Everything that the attacker touched seems soiled. You're afraid to be in your house alone. The one place where you were always safe, at home, is sanctuary no longer. You are afraid to remain, yet terrified to leave your home unprotected.

You didn't realize when you gave the police your name and address that it would be given to the press and to the defendant through the police reports. Your friends call to say they saw this information in the paper, your picture on television. You haven't yet absorbed what's happened to you when you get calls from insurance companies and firms that sell security devices. But these calls pale in comparison to the threats that come from the defendant and his friends.

You're astonished to discover that your attacker has been arrested, yet while in custody he has free and unmonitored access to a phone. He can threaten you from jail. The judge orders him not to annoy you, but when the phone calls are brought to his attention, the judge does nothing.

At least you can be assured that the man who attacked you is in custody, or so you think. No one tells you when he is released on his promise to come to court. No one ever asks you if you've been threatened. The judge is never told that the defendant said he'd kill you if you told or that he'd get even if he went to jail. Horrified, you ask how he got out after what he did. You're told the judge can't consider whether he'll be dangerous, only whether he'll come back to court. He's been accused and convicted before, but he always came to court; so he must be released.

You learn only by accident that he's at large; this discovery comes when you turn a corner and confront him. He knows where you live. He's been there. Besides, your name and address were in the paper and in the reports he's seen. Now nowhere is safe. He watches you from across the street; he follows you on the bus. Will he come back in the night? What do you do? Give up your home? Lose your job? Assume a different name? Get your mail at the post office? Carry a weapon? Even if you wanted to, could you afford to do these things?

You try to return to normal. You don't want to talk about what happened, so you decide not to tell your co-workers about the attack. A few days go by and the police unexpectedly come to your place of work. They show their badges to the receptionist and ask to see you. They want you to look at some photographs, but they don't explain that to your co-workers. You try to explain later that you're the victim, not the accused.

The phone rings and the police want you to come to a line-up. It may be 1:00 A.M. or in the middle of your work day, but you have to go; the suspect and his lawyer are waiting. It will not be the last time you are forced to conform your life to their convenience. You appear at the police station and the line-up begins. The suspect's lawyer sits next to you, but he does not watch the stage; he stares at you. It will not be the last time you must endure his scrutiny.

Charges Are Pressed against a Defendant

You have lived through the crime and made it through the initial investigation. They've caught the man who harmed you, and he's been charged with armed burglary, robbery, and rape. Now he'll be tried. Now you expect justice.

You receive a subpoena for a preliminary hearing. No one tells you what it will involve, how long it will take, or how you should prepare. You assume that this is the only time you will have to appear. But you are only beginning your initiation in a system that will grind away at you for months, disrupt your life, affect your emotional stability, and certainly cost you money; it may cost you your job, and, for the duration, will prevent you from putting the crime behind you and reconstructing your life.

Before the hearing, a defense investigator comes to talk to you. When he contacts you, he says he's "investigating your case," and that he "works for the county." You assume, as he intends you to, that he's from the police or the prosecutor's office. Only after you give him a statement do you discover that he works for the man who attacked you.

This same investigator may visit your neighbors and co-workers, asking questions about you. He discusses the case with them, always giving the defendant's side. Suddenly, some of the people who know you seem to be taking a different view of what happened to you and why.

It's the day of the hearing. You've never been to court before, never spoken in public. You're very nervous. You rush to arrive at 8 A.M. to talk to a prosecutor you've never met. You wait in a hallway with a number of other witnesses. It's now 8:45. Court starts at 9:00. No one has spoken to you. Finally, a man sticks his head out a door, calls out your name, and asks, "Are you the one who was raped?" You're aware of the stares as you stand and suddenly realize that this is the prosecutor, the person you expect will represent your interests.

You only speak to the prosecutor for a few minutes. You ask to read the statement you gave to the police but he says there isn't time. He asks you some questions that make you wonder if he's read it himself. He asks you other questions that make you wonder if he believes it.

The prosecutor tells you to sit on the bench outside the courtroom. Suddenly you see the man who raped you coming down the hall. No one has told you he would be here. He's with three friends. He points you out. They all laugh and jostle you a little as they pass. The defendant and two friends enter the courtroom; one friend sits on the bench across from you and stares. Suddenly, you feel abandoned, alone, afraid. Is this what it's like to come to court and seek justice?

You sit on that bench for an hour, then two. You don't see the prosecutor, he has disappeared into the courtroom. Finally, at noon he comes out and says, "Oh, you're still here? We continued that case to next month."

You repeat this process many times before you actually testify at the preliminary hearing. Each time you go to court, you hire a babysitter or take leave from work, pay for parking, wait for hours, and finally are told to go home. No one ever asks if the new dates are convenient to you. You miss vacations and medical appointments. You use up sick leave and vacation days to make your court appearances. Your employer is losing his patience. Every time you are gone his business is disrupted. But you are fortunate. If you were new at your job, or worked part-time, or didn't have an understanding boss, you could lose your job. Many victims do.

The preliminary hearing was an event for which you were completely unprepared. You learn later that the defense is often harder on a victim at the preliminary hearing than during the trial. In trial, the defense attorney cannot risk alienating the jury. At this hearing, there is only the judge—and he certainly doesn't seem concerned about you. One of the first questions you are asked is where you live. You finally moved after your attack; you've seen the defendant and his friends, and you're terrified of having them know where you now live. When you explain that you'd be happy to give your old address, the judge says he'll dismiss the case or hold you in contempt of court if you don't answer the question. The prosecutor says nothing. During your testimony, you are also compelled to say where you work, how you get there, and what your schedule is.

Hours later you are released from the stand after reliving your attack in public, in intimate detail. You have been made to feel completely powerless. As you sat facing a smirking defendant and as you described his threats, you were accused of lying and inviting the "encounter." You have cried in front of these uncaring strangers. As you leave no one thanks you. When you get back to work they ask what took you so long.

You are stunned when you later learn that the defendant also raped five others; one victim was an 8-year-old girl. During her testimony she was asked to describe her attacker's anatomy. Spectators laughed when she said she did not understand the words being used. When she was asked to draw a picture of her attacker's genitalia the girl fled from the courtroom and ran sobbing to her mother, who had been subpoenaed by the defense and had to wait outside. The youngster was forced to sit alone and recount, as you did, each minute of the attack. You know how difficult it was for you to speak of these things; you cannot imagine how it was for a child.

Now the case is scheduled for trial. Again there are delays. When you call and ask to speak with the prosecutor, you are told the case has been reassigned. You tell your story in detail to five different prosecutors before the case is tried. Months go by and no one tells you what's happening. Periodically you are subpoenaed to appear. You leave your work, wait, and are finally told to go home.

Continuances are granted because the courts are filled, one of the lawyers is on another case, the judge has a meeting to attend or an early tennis match. You can't understand why they couldn't have discovered these problems before you came to court. When you ask if the next date could be set a week later so you can attend a family gathering out of state, you are told that the defendant has the right to a speedy trial. You stay home from the reunion and the case is continued.

The defense attorney continues to call. Will you change your story? Don't you want to drop the charges?

Time passes and you hear nothing. Your property is not returned. You learn that there are dozens of defense motions that can be filed before the trial. If denied, many of them can be appealed. Each motion, each court date means a new possibility for delay. If the defendant is out of custody and fails to come to court, nothing can happen until he is reapprehended. If he is successful in avoiding recapture, the case may be so compromised by months or years of delay that a successful prosecution is impossible. For as long as the case drags on, your life is on hold. You don't want to start a new assignment at work or move to a new city because you know that at any time the round of court appearances may begin again. The wounds of your attack will never heal as long as you know that you will be asked to relive those horrible moments.

No one tells you anything about the progress of the case. You want to be involved, consulted, and informed, but prosecutors often plea bargain without consulting victims. You're afraid someone will let the defendant plead guilty to a lesser charge and be sentenced to probation. You meet another victim at court who tells you that she and her family were kidnapped and her children molested. Even though the prosecutor assured her that he would not accept a plea bargain, after talking with the attorneys in his chambers, the judge allowed the defendant to plead as charged with the promise of a much-reduced sentence. You hope that this won't happen in your case.

The Trial

Finally the day of trial arrives. It is 18 months since you were attacked. You've been trying for a week to prepare yourself. It is painful to dredge up the terror again, but you know that the outcome depends on you; the prosecutor has told you that the way you behave will make or break the case. You can't get too angry on the stand because then the jury might not like you. You can't break down and sob because then you will appear too emotional, possibly unstable. In addition to the tremendous pressure of having to relive the horrible details of the crime, you're expected to be an actress as well.

You go to court. The continuances are over; the jury has been selected. You sit in a waiting room with the defendant's family and friends. Again you feel threatened, vulnerable, and alone.

You expect the trial to be a search for the truth; you find that it is a performance orchestrated by lawyers and the judge, with the jury hearing only half the facts. The defendant was found with your watch in his pocket. The judge has suppressed this evidence because the officer who arrested him didn't have a warrant.

Your character is an open subject of discussion and innuendo. The defense is allowed to question you on incidents going back to your childhood. The jury is never told that the defendant has two prior convictions for the same offense and has been to prison three times for other crimes. You sought help from a counselor to deal with the shattering effect of this crime on your life. You told him about your intimate fears and feelings. Now he has been called by the defense and his notes and records have been subpoenaed.

You are on the stand for hours. The defense does its best to make you appear a liar, a seductress, or both. You know you cannot relax for a moment. Don't answer unless you understand the question. Don't be embarrassed when everyone seems angry because you do not understand. Think ahead. Be responsive. Don't volunteer. Don't get tired.

Finally you are finished with this part of the nightmare. You would like to sit and listen to the rest of the trial but you cannot. You're a witness and must wait outside. The jury will decide the outcome of one of the major events of your life. You cannot hear the testimony that will guide their judgment.

The verdict is guilty. You now look to the judge to impose a just sentence.

The Sentence

You expect the sentence to reflect how terrible the crime was. You ask the prosecutor how this decision is reached, and are told that once a defendant is convicted he is interviewed at length by a probation officer. He gives his side of the story, which may be blatantly false in light of the proven facts. A report that delves into his upbringing, family relationships, education, physical and mental health, and employment and conviction history is prepared. The officer will often speak to the defendant's relatives and friends. Some judges will send the defendant to a facility where a complete psychiatric and sociological work-up is prepared. You're amazed that no one will ever ask you about the crime, or the effect it has had on you and your family. You took the defendant's blows, heard his threats, listened to him brag that he'd "beat the rap" or "con the judge." No one ever hears of these things. They never give you a chance to tell them.

At sentencing, the judge hears from the defendant, his lawyer, his mother, his minister, his friends. You learn by chance what day the hearing is. When you do attend, the defense attorney says you're vengeful and it's apparent that you overreacted to being raped and robbed because you chose to come and see the sentencing. You ask permission to address the judge and are told that you are not allowed to do so.

The judge sentences your attacker to three years in prison, less than one year for every hour he kept you in pain and terror. That seems very lenient to you. Only later do you discover that he'll probably serve less than half of his actual sentence in prison because of good-time and work-time credits that are given to him immediately. The man who broke into your home, threatened to slit your throat with a knife, and raped, beat, and robbed you will be out of custody in less than 18 months. You are not told when he will actually be released, and you are not allowed to attend the parole release hearing anyway.

SOURCE: Adapted from the report of the President's Task Force on Victims of Crime, 1982:3–11.

---

versial practice. People have always punished one another, but they have never agreed over their reasons for subjecting others to pain and suffering.

Punishment is usually justified on utilitarian grounds as a necessary evil. It is argued that punishing wrongdoers curbs future criminality in a number of ways. The offender who experiences unpleasant consequences learns a lesson and is deterred from breaking the law again. Making an example of a convicted criminal serves as a warning to deter other would-be offenders contemplating the same act. Imprisoning criminals has been defended as a method of incapacitating dangerous predators so that they can't prey on innocent victims, as well as a way of containing people who need compulsory treatment in order to be rehabilitated.

Punishment also has been justified on nonutilitarian grounds, as a morally sound practice regardless of any value it has in deterring, rehabilitating, or incapacitating criminals. According to the theory of punishment as retribution, offenders must be made to suffer because notions of justice and fairness require them to experience pain commensurate with the suffering they caused. From biblical times onward, a belief in *lex talonis*—retaliation in kind, symbolized by the phrase "an eye for an eye. . ."—has had a grip on the thought of scholars and lay persons alike. From this perspective, people who harm someone must get their just deserts. Retribution by society in behalf of its own interests, as well as the victim's, evens the score, rights a wrong, and restores balance to the moral order. The severity of the punitive response should be in proportion to the gravity of the offense. (See box 5-2, pp. 136-137.)

The quest for retribution and vengeance has shaped history. It becomes incorporated into the customs and consciousness of entire groups, classes, and nations, and it expresses itself in prejudice, feuds, and wars. Revenge fantasies can sustain people and even give purpose and direction to their lives. However, the thirst for revenge can destroy victims as well, by depriving them of their humanity and driving them mad. Even when fulfilled, revenge fantasies are rarely as satisfying as had been imagined. Yet it is entirely human for victims to feel a sense of rage, even murderous rage, toward those who have abused them. In the hours and days following a crime, it is psychologically useful and cathartic for victims to dream of inflicting pain on offenders. But a chronic preoccupation with vengeance must be avoided. Otherwise, the victimization experience becomes needlessly and endlessly prolonged. Vengeful victims never break free of the pernicious influence of their victimizers. Survivors learn that the best revenge is to transcend the offender's grip, put the experience behind them, and lead a fulfilling life (Halleck, 1980).

Despite the current popularity of punishment as an antidote to crime, the punitive approach has always been subjected to devastating criticisms (see Menninger, 1968; Prison Research, 1976; Wright, 1973). Utilitarian opponents have documented how ineffective and even counterproductive punishment can be. Humanists have condemned punishment as a tool of domination and oppression, used to terrorize people into submission.

There are victims who do not look to the criminal justice system to quench their thirst for revenge. They want the professionals and experts to help the offenders become decent, law-abiding citizens, especially if they are not strangers but relatives, neighbors, classmates, or colleagues. Such rehabilitation of criminals might require one or more of the following therapies and treatments: counseling, intense psychiatric care, additional schooling, job training and placement, detoxification from addictive drugs, removal from intolerable home or neighborhood situations, or medical and dental attention. Despite the temporary ascendancy of a pessimistic, "nothing-works" disenchantment with the ideal of rehabilitation (see Martinson, 1974), "helping" offenders remains as much a part of the system's mission as "hurting" them. Rehabilitation is a long-term strategy that serves the interests of both offenders and society. Incapacitation is a short-term strategy that merely buys time and promotes a false sense of security. Victims who overcome their initial emotional outrage over what offenders did to them might become equally infuriated over imprisonment that backfires and drives offenders to new heights of antisocial conduct, or over inept efforts to rehabilitate inmates.

Among those victims who want more than just revenge from punishment are those who seek the system's help to recover their losses. Full reimbursement is a necessary prerequisite for total recovery. Restitution collected from offenders can be the mechanism to restore these victims to the financial condition they were in before the crimes occurred. Criminals will pay back their victims only with the assistance, guidance, and supervision of officials and agencies.

Whether they desire that something be done to the offender (punishment), for the offender (treatment), or for themselves (restitution), victims want the criminal justice system to react effectively to violations of law. What they don't want is inaction, lack of interest, neglect, abuse, or manipulation.

Victims versus the Police

Police officers are the first representatives of the criminal justice system victims encounter. The conflict between victims and the police can erupt over several issues: the slowness of police responses to a call for help, a reluctance by the police to believe the victim's account of what happened, an inability to apprehend a suspect and to recover stolen property, an unwillingness to make an arrest, and an insensitivity on the part of some officers toward victims at a time of great vulnerability.

The Complainants' Complaint: Dropped and Unsolved Cases

To crime victims, police officers ought to be on-the-spot problem solvers. To police officers, crime victims should be accurate reporters. These differing expectations can cause a falling out between potential allies.

Victims want the police to spring into action immediately. But dispatchers manning the "911" emergency phone lines might evaluate the urgency of the calls for assistance as not warranting the immediate attention that victims desire.

Victims would like the police to accept their version of what transpired without question. They forget that they are only "presumptive" victims until the police establish whether laws were broken and innocent parties harmed. As the cost, range, and depth of services to victims increase, the process of screening people claiming to have suffered at the hands of criminals takes on added importance. A variety of incentives can motivate people to pose as victims and to falsify injuries and losses. As a result, the police cannot take victims' claims at face value. After an investigation, a crime report or complaint may be declared "unfounded," and won't be counted. Or the seriousness of an incident may be reevaluated, a process that can be termed "defounding" (Lundman, 1980). (For example, what was originally reported as a burglary—a felony—may on further investigation be reclassified as merely a case of breaking and entering or criminal trespass—both misdemeanors.) By defounding and unfounding complaints, police departments lower the crime rate and raise their solution rate. Victims can feel repudiated by such decisions. (See box 5-3, p. 138.)

Statistics revealing "unfounding rates" are rarely made public. From the mid-1960s to the mid-1970s, the FBI published the percentage of rape complaints that had been declared unfounded by local police across the country after a preliminary investigation. The figures provided in the Uniform Crime Reports were nearly one-fifth of all rape complaints (20 percent in 1966; 18 percent in 1968; 15 percent in 1973; and 19 percent in 1976, the last year for which data were printed) (FBI, 1966:11; 1968:12; 1973:15; 1976:16). A study of a California police force turned up an unfounding rate of 32 percent for burglary reports and 8 percent for robbery complaints (Skolnick, 1966:173). In each complaint that is declared unfounded, either the police are correct and the complainant is falsely claiming to be a victim, or the police are mistaken and a legitimate plea for help is being disregarded, perhaps because of some ulterior motive on the part of the detectives who investigated the case.

In Chicago, an investigative report by a local television station that charged that the police department was disregarding complaints in order to keep crime statistics down became an issue in a mayoralty campaign and led to an internal audit. It was discovered that for more than twenty years, detectives were too quick to clear up cases by dismissing the victims' accounts as unfounded. The reason for the detectives' insensitivity to the victims' problems was their perception that they would receive higher ratings if they closed more cases (unfounding was easier than making arrests). About 21 percent of all complaints about major offenses were dropped as unfounded in Chicago, whereas the average rate for other cities was between 1 percent and 2 percent, according to the FBI. The police department auditors suspected that as many as 40 percent of the rape, robbery, burglary, and theft reports classified as unfounded really did take place as the victims claimed. The kinds of cases that were prime candidates for official disbelief involved victims who knew their assailants, were difficult to contact, or did not lose much money ("Chicago Police Found to Dismiss Cases Erroneously," 1983; "Burying Crime in Chicago," 1983).

When their reports about incidents are taken seriously, victims expect action in the form of arrests. The percentage of cases "cleared by arrest" (solved, as far as the police are concerned, although the suspects taken into custody may not ultimately be convicted of the crimes originally lodged against them) is a widely available statistic. It is usually interpreted as a measure of police efficiency. Well-run departments have clearance rates that are higher than the national average. Looking at clearance rates as solution rates, this same statistic can indicate the proportion of victims who are satisfactorily served by their local police force. That is, the police are able to accomplish all that can be asked of them: suspects are taken into custody and are charged with the crimes reported by victims. (See table 5-1.)

TABLE 5-1 U.S. Clearance Rates, by Type of Crime, and Year

				Year			
Type of Crime	*1953*	*1958*	*1963*	*1968*	*1973*	*1978*	*1982*
Murder	93%	94%	91%	86%	79%	76%	74%
Rape	78%	73%	69%	55%	51%	50%	51%
Aggravated assault	75%	79%	76%	66%	63%	62%	60%
Robbery	36%	43%	39%	27%	27%	26%	25%
Burglary	27%	30%	27%	19%	18%	16%	15%
Larceny	20%	20%	20%	18%	19%	20%	19%
Auto theft*	26%	27%	26%	19%	16%	15%	14%

*Since the 1970s, this category of the Uniform Crime Report has included the theft of all motorized vehicles, including trucks, vans, motorcycles, and so on.

SOURCE: *Crime in the United States,* by the Federal Bureau of Investigation. Washington, D.C.: U.S. Government Printing Office, 1954, 1959, 1964, 1969, 1974, 1979, 1983.

The statistics in table 5-1 present the average clearance rates for police departments across the country for the FBI's index crimes. The data show that clearance rates are reasonably high for crimes against people (murder, rape, aggravated assault, and robbery). With the exception of murder (which receives the highest priority and occupies the attention of the best detectives on the homicide squad), the victims of these crimes are usually able to furnish valuable clues and leads to the police. Because robbers often don disguises to hide their identity, victims are less able to describe these strangers, and the clearance rate is substantially lower than for rape or assault. Victims are generally unable to provide any useful information in crimes against their property (burglary, larceny, and auto theft), so the clearance rates for these offenses are uniformly low. The data indicate that the ability of victims to supply detectives with clues and leads is the single most important factor in solving cases (Lundman, 1980). The overall trend is downward. As the years pass, the proportion of cases solved for any of the index crimes is dropping. Growing numbers of victims are disappointed with the outcomes of their cases. The police are less able to solve crimes today than in the past, and thus are less able to satisfy the victims' basic demand for service.

Box 5-2 How Much Punishment Is Enough?

Victims, and people speaking in their behalf, frequently charge that the criminal justice system doesn't punish offenders severely enough. The uproar over "unwarranted leniency," "permissiveness," and the "coddling of criminals" is predicated on a flawed assumption: that some consensus exists within the general public and among legislators over how much time a convict should serve for committing a particular type of crime. The profound disagreements that divide people over the issue of whether there should be a death penalty are well known. Usually overlooked, however, are the dramatic differences in penalties from state to state for lesser crimes than murder. It is impossible to conclude with any degree of objectivity that a particular offender "got off too lightly" when the maximum sentences differ so sharply from one jurisdiction to another. Victims might feel cheated that the offenders convicted of harming them didn't stay in prison long enough, but no formula or equation exists to translate the gravity of an offense into the "proper" length of sentence. For example, simple assault is a misdemeanor in all states. But in Illinois, the maximum jail sentence for this offense is just one month, while in Pennsylvania the maximum penalty is twenty-four times as severe. Similarly, burglary is a felony in all states. But the maximum prison sentences range from four years in California to as many as twenty in Texas. Rapists might not be imprisoned for more than twenty years in Texas while such felons in California might spend the rest of their lives behind bars (Katz, 1980:66–67). (See table below.)

How Much Punishment Is Too Much?

The penalities for crimes in the United States are among the most severe in the world. Yet stiff penalties do not automatically protect victims from harm. Sometimes harsh penalties have unanticipated consequences that endanger victims.

During the 1970s many state legislatures rewrote their sex crime statutes

Arrests are never automatic. Police officers exercise a great deal of personal and departmental discretion in deciding whom to take into custody and book and whom to let go. The factors that influence these decisions include pressures from colleagues and superiors, the individual predilections of officers, the nature of the offense and offenders, and the relationship of the victim to the suspect. Victims can become angry when police officers don't arrest persons they have accused of committing crimes.

Victims intent on having suspects arrested can bypass reluctant police officers and make citizen's arrests. Most states permit private citizens who act in good faith to take suspects into custody. But victims who take such direct action subject themselves to great risks. They may encounter resistance and physical danger, and they are vulnerable to civil lawsuits for false arrest and false imprisonment (Hall, 1975).

Besides catching the criminals, victims would like the police to recover stolen property. Just as the clearance rates indicate the percentage of cases in which victims receive optimum service in terms of arrests, recovery rates show the percentage of cases in which victims get back

Maximum Prison Sentences for Crimes

State	*Assault (Misdemeanor)*	*Burglary (Felony)*	*Rape (Felony)*
California	6 months	4 years	life
Florida	2 months	5 years	30 years
Illinois	1 month	20 years	life
Michigan	12 months	15 years	life
New York	12 months	25 years	25 years
Ohio	6 months	15 years	25 years
Pennsylvania	24 months	10 years	20 years
Texas	12 months	20 years	20 years

SOURCE: Adapted from *The Justice Imperative: An Introduction to Criminal Justice,* by Lewis Katz. Cincinnati, Ohio: Anderson, 1980:66–67.

because of the lobbying efforts of the pro-victim movement against rape. In most places, the changes included increased penalties and mandatory minimum sentences (specifying the number of years that must be served in prison before parole eligibility). In 1977, the Supreme Court ruled in *Coker* v. *Georgia* that the death penalty was grossly disproportionate to the offense. But life sentences, and severe sentences like ninety-nine years, were ruled constitutional.

Now lawyers, prosecutors, judges, and victim advocates are beginning to question whether the new "get-tough" policy will work out as intended—as a deterrent to would-be rapists. Two fears are surfacing. The first is that rapists who think about getting caught will kill their victims when they are through with them. Murder charges might not be any heavier than rape charges; with the victim disposed of, the chances of being caught are reduced. The second concern is that juries will become reluctant to reach guilty verdicts. Citizens have a tendency to find "reasonable doubts" when the penalties hanging over the defendant's head are so severe (UPI, 1982).

lost valuables with the help of the police. Recovery rates can be roughly estimated from data published in victimization surveys. By subtracting from 100 percent the proportion of victims who recover nothing and the proportion who receive only reimbursement from insurance companies, the remainder represents the proportion who either get stolen property back by their own efforts (for example, they know where to find a purse that was snatched, emptied, and then discarded) or who get back items seized from offenders by the police. The estimated police recovery rates computed in table 5-2 below reveal that in this aspect of police work, as in solving cases by arrests, most victims will be disappointed with the outcome of their case. Only victims of motor vehicle theft are likely to ever get back part or all of what was stolen from them. (See table 5-2.)

The "Second Injury": A Type of Police Brutality

The police have many admirers and staunch supporters. They also have severe critics. Civil libertarians concerned about constitutional rights point out tendencies in some police officers to be disrespectful of citizens

BOX 5-3 Lie Detector Tests for Rape Complainants

One reason that rapes are badly underreported is that women anticipate and dread the psychologically painful interrogation administered by police, prosecutors, and defense attorneys. The prospect of submitting to a lie detector test looms as an added indignity that serves as a deterrent to coming forward and pressing charges. There is no other crime in which the motives of the complainants as an entire group are so automatically suspect. But some police departments and prosecutors' offices consider arrests for rape so potentially damaging to defendants that they routinely administer polygraph tests to complainants. In some jurisdictions, more than half the women who report that they were raped "fail" the test. "Most women just crawl home after flunking, they're so humiliated," observed an advocate for rape victims.

Women's groups have gone to court to try to get the practice discontinued. What makes polygraph testing so controversial is the device's highly questionable accuracy in distinguishing fact from fiction. Test results that confirm the victim's version of the events can't be used as evidence in court. Requiring the defendant to take a lie detector test would violate his constitutional rights. So the purpose of the test is solely to check the victim's credibility. If she fails, there is the remote possibility that she could be charged with giving false information to an officer of the law. More frightening is the chance that the man she accuses can sue her for monetary damages in civil court for malicious prosecution for making an unsubstantiated charge ("Polygraphs and Other Perils," 1979). The President's Task Force (1982) recommended that practices that reflect routine distrust of complainants, like polygraph testing for rape victims, be stopped.

---

and to use unnecessary force against certain types of people. Crime victims voice complaints about another kind of police "brutality." Expecting the police to comfort them, they sometimes find that officers unwittingly make them feel worse.

After the first injury (the suffering brought about by the criminal), victims are particularly susceptible to a "second injury." These mental wounds can be delivered by care providers, like emergency room personnel; intimates, like family members and close friends; and law enforcement officials, like policemen and prosecutors. Since policemen are usually the first to arrive at the scene of a crime, the way they react to people in distress has a crucial impact on the victims' rate of recovery.

In the aftermath of a street crime, victims are likely to feel powerless, disoriented, and infuriated. Fear, guilt, depression, and fantasies of revenge engulf them. Authority figures such as police officers are expected to nurture and comfort the injured parties to help restore a sense of equilibrium and dispel any lingering feelings of helplessness. But if officers act callously and prolong suffering needlessly, victims feel let down, rejected, and betrayed by those counted on for support (Symonds, 1980).

Studies of police work suggest that what victims are reacting to is the protective coating of emotional detachment that officers develop to shield themselves from the unnerving impact of the human misery they

TABLE 5-2 Estimated Police Recovery Rates, 1980

Type of crime	*Percentage of victims who recover some or all of stolen goods*
All personal crimes	12%
Robbery	14
Personal larcenies	12
All household crimes	15
Burglary	12
Larceny	12
Motor vehicle theft	65

SOURCE: *Criminal Victimization in the United States, 1980,* by the Bureau of Justice Statistics, 1982, p. 66–67. Washington, D.C.: U.S. Department of Justice.

routinely encounter. To avoid "burnout," police officers (like others in "helping" professions) inhibit their impulses to get deeply involved in the cases they investigate. The paramilitary nature of police organizations and the bureaucratic imperatives of specialization and standardization reinforce the inclinations of the officer to approach personal tragedies in an impersonal manner. In addition, the "macho" norms of police subculture—with its emphasis on toughness, camaraderie, suspicion of outsiders, inside jokes, graveyard humor, and profound cynicism—put pressure on police officers to act businesslike when dealing with potentially upsetting situations (Ahrens, Stein, and Young, 1980).

If individual officers appear particularly jaded to the suffering that surrounds them, it might be that they fear "contamination" (Symonds, 1975). People who regularly come into close contact with the casualties of natural and social disasters tend to isolate and ostracize these victims as if they had a contagious disease. Such distancing is a defense mechanism to preserve the helper's faith that ultimately justice prevails: misfortunes happen only to those who somehow deserve them.

Special Training, Special Squads: Professionalizing Police Work

Whether victims expect too much or receive too little, their grievances against the police lead to a "community relations" problem. Administrators of the system have proposed police professionalism as the solution. It involves upgrading the caliber of academy recruits, applying psychological tests to weed out potentially brutal or corrupt members of the force, devising regulations and procedures to cover every kind of anticipated emergency, monitoring on-the-job performance, and adding special training and specialized squads to handle problems that were addressed unsatisfactorily in the past.

Some departments have initiated training programs to prepare at least a portion of their officers to act differently when they deal with victims with acute needs. To supplement their good intentions, the police are taught how to administer "psychological first aid" (Symonds, 1980) to people in distress. They are instructed to respond swiftly, listen attentively, show concern, and refrain from challenging the victims' version of events or judging the wisdom of their reactions while the crime was in progress. Officers are told not to show skepticism because a rape victim is not badly bruised or bleeding, a child did not report a molestation immediately, an elderly person has trouble communicating, or a blind person offers to assist the prosecution. At the conclusion of the training sessions, the officers are informed that responsiveness to victims carries a high priority within the department and has become a criterion for evaluating performance and a consideration for promotion (President's Task Force, 1982).

In many departments special squads have been set up to more effectively administer aid to victims and catch offenders. A senior citizen task force helps elderly victims of muggings, purse snatchings, and swindles. A sex-crime investigation unit responds to rapes and molestations without making the complainants feel as if they are the guilty parties. A trained team of officers intervenes in domestic disputes without adding insults to the injuries of battered women.

Police officers have a legal obligation to inform suspects of their rights. Although victims do not enjoy comparable guarantees under the Constitution, officers have a duty to inform them of their rights and responsibilities as well. They need to be told about required court appearances, opportunities to recover stolen property, and sources of financial aid and psychological assistance. In particular, the victims need to know the name and badge number of the officer or detective handling their case, where he or she can be reached, the case identification number, and whether any suspect has been apprehended (President's Task Force, 1982).

In response to community pressures, some police departments have grudgingly undertaken another course of action to improve the quality of services offered to victims with special needs. The departments have hired some women and members of racial minorities under affirmative action plans (often court ordered). It is assumed that much of the insensitivity of police officers who deliver second wounds arises from their inability to identify or empathize with particular victims due to barriers of sex, race, class, age, or lifestyle. Women and minority officers may have greater rapport with victims like themselves, and they may be able to alert the white men on the force to any offensive behavior of which they were not aware.

Crisis Centers and Shelters: Independent Solutions

The other major reaction to the shortcomings of police officers has been to do the tasks the police refuse to do or cannot do well.

Emergency aid programs furnish advocates who look after the victims' interests. Staff members are trained in the techniques of stress management (handling tensions so that they don't spiral out of control) and crisis intervention (resolving intolerable situations to restore victims to the level at which they functioned before disaster struck). Counseling and advocacy programs can work with the police in three different ways (Ahrens, Stein, and Young, 1980). Under the interagency cooperation model, advocates receive the names of potential clients from the police. Under the collaboration model, advocates spring into action as soon as officers at the scene radio for them. A comprehensive model combines the follow-up services of the cooperation model with the on-the-spot aid of the collaboration model.

During the early 1970s, women in the anti-rape movement began to aid victims in a very tangible way. They set up crisis centers (also known as distress or relief centers) to provide practical services and to offer emotional support. By the early 1980s, over 200 programs were functioning, sometimes in cooperation with hospitals, the visiting nurses' association, criminal justice agencies, or local feminist organizations (Dean and deBruyn-Kops, 1982). (See box 5-4.)

BOX 5-4 Women Helping Women

Rape/Sexual Assault Care Center, Des Moines, Iowa

Designated as an "Exemplary Project" by the LEAA in 1976, it enlarged its operations in 1980 to serve victims of all types of violent crime (National Institute of Justice, 1982). The center's activities include:

- a twenty-four-hour telephone hot line
- providing advocates to accompany victims to medical examinations and to interviews with the police and prosecutors
- peer counseling within a support group of other victims
- referrals to other community agencies that provide aid
- in-service training for medical and criminal justice professionals to sensitize them to victims' needs
- outreach efforts to educate the public about the realities of violent crimes, especially sex crimes

Transition House for Battered Women, Cambridge, Massachusetts

Transition House was established in the Boston area in 1976 to provide a safe and supportive environment for women (and their children) who have fled their violent mates (Warrior, 1977). Its self-help and advocacy activities include:

- shelter, emergency transportation, food, clothing
- peer counseling within a support group of other victims
- legal counseling for separation, divorce, child custody, alimony, and orders of protection
- job counseling, job placement, and educational counseling
- referrals to other community agencies that provide aid
- outreach efforts to inform the public about the problems of battered women

---

The existence of a crisis center in a community can have a favorable impact on criminal justice operations. In Baton Rouge, Louisiana, reporting rates increased and arrest rates climbed from 38 percent to 69 percent after the Stop Rape Crisis Center opened its doors and effectively reached out to victims. The improvement in conviction rates, which jumped from a mere 3 percent of all cases brought to trial to 88 percent, was even more impressive (Whitcomb, Day, and Studen, 1979:35).

The first rape crisis centers in North America and Europe were offshoots of the feminist movement. Their staffs of volunteers—many of them former victims—shared a common commitment to care for and work in behalf of women in crisis; to reform rape laws to the advantage of complainants; and to improve the treatment provided by hospitals, police departments, and prosecutors' offices. The founders of these centers incorporated into their operations many of the themes embodied in rights and protest movements. From the feminist movement came the conviction that rape was primarily a women's issue, best understood and more effectively dealt with by women than by male authorities. A distrust of remote bureaucracies and of control by professionals who claim to know what is best for their clients was derived from the youthful counterculture of the 1960s, which spawned "crash pads" (emergency shelters), "drop-in" centers (for counseling and advocacy), and free clinics (for drug-related health crises) in "hippie" neighborhoods. The New Left's emphasis on egalitarianism, voluntarism, and collective action led to grass-roots, community-based projects stressing self-help and peer support, and to symbolic confrontations with the power structure (demonstrations at trials, police stations, and hospitals).

With the passage of time, however, rifts developed within many rape crisis centers. More pragmatic and less ideological staffers challenged the fundamental principles of these nonprofit, nonbureaucratic, nonhierarchical, nonprofessional, nongovernmental organizations. They pressed for a more service-oriented approach that would avoid radical critiques, improve chances for funding, increase referrals from hospitals and police departments, and cooperate more closely with prosecutors. To the founders of the centers, such changes represented a co-optation by the establishment and a retreat from the original mission (see Amir and Amir, 1979).

Even though the majority of rape crisis centers and battered women's shelters are intended to restore harmonious relations between police departments and disgruntled victims, many officers reportedly resent their staffs (O'Reilly, 1980). The opposition of the rank and file takes the form of noncooperation. This resistance and obstructionism can arise for a number of reasons: supervisors might fail to notify patrolmen about the program's services, goals, and responsibilities; indifference at headquarters might torpedo any enthusiasm for collaboration at the precinct level; cooperation might generate more paperwork for police officers, even though it relieves them of other unpleasant duties; and victim advocates might be resented as intruders, "bleeding hearts," "do-gooders," perhaps "cop haters," or even troublemakers looking to uncover scandals and abuses.

Yet crisis intervention services can benefit law enforcement agencies as much as they do crime victims. Emergency aid personnel can take on tasks that waste police time and upset officers. For example, in Pima County, Arizona (Tucson), the victim–witness field team also handles suicide attempts, homeless people, drug overdoses, mentally deranged people, accident victims, and death notification responsibilities, to the great relief of the local police and at a great saving to the local budget (Bolin, 1980).

Victims versus Prosecutors

The District Attorney's Office: A Public Law Firm?

Prosecutors are the chief law enforcement officials within their jurisdictions. As government attorneys, they represent the interests of the community (municipality, county, state, or the entire nation). Yet they describe their office as a public law firm for aggrieved parties directly harmed by offenders. Victims find themselves in conflict with prosecutors over a number of issues in which the interests of the government diverge from their needs and wants. Specifically, victims may oppose the decisions of prosecutors about the training of the police, the return of stolen property, protection from intimidation by the offender, information regarding the status of the case and the whereabouts of the offender, the dropping or dismissing of charges, notification about court appearances and scheduling changes, and opportunities to express their views and defend their interests.

Prosecutors are responsible for overseeing police training. They are partly to blame when insensitive officers deliver a "second wound" to victims, and they deserve some of the credit when departments improve their performance in handling victims in crisis. Prosecutors are also responsible for returning recovered property to the rightful owners. When a criminal steals a possession, victims should not have to battle the justice system to get the item back or have to wait for months or years until it is released. Some items have special significance as evidence, whether seized from the defendant, found at the scene of the crime, or taken from the victim (for example, tattered clothing from a raped woman). These items must be entered as exhibits at trials. But other items could be presented to judges and juries just as effectively in the form of photographs (this is now a routine practice in shoplifting cases; stores get the items back quickly so they can be sold). Prosecutors have the authority to set policies that require the return of recovered property as expeditiously as possible. Once the defense attorney has inspected the item (if it is not an issue in the case), the police should notify the victim that property was recovered, where it is stored, when it can be claimed, and what documents are needed to prove ownership. The speedy return of recovered items is cost effective, because it relieves the government of the expense of storing possessions in a police warehouse or court clerk's office (President's Task Force, 1982).

Offenders Intimidating Victims: The Need for Protection

The conflicts between offenders and victims that erupt in the streets can continue long after the criminal incidents have ended. Offenders may try to intimidate victims (and witnesses to the crime) from cooperating with the authorities. Victims of intimidation can conclude that the criminal justice system has failed to protect them—again. The primary responsibility for safeguarding a victim's health and possessions falls to the prosecutor handling the case. As with the return of stolen property, close coordination with the police is needed.

The actual extent of the intimidation problem is not known. Contradictory findings about how often it happens have emerged from different studies. Measuring intimidation incidents is a difficult task, in part because successfully intimidated victims (and witnesses) are afraid to talk. Only unconvincing threats are reported—and occasionally acted on by the police and prosecutors. Yet if intimidation occurs routinely, the effectiveness of the criminal justice process as a guarantor of public safety and order is seriously undermined.

According to victimization surveys, just 1 percent of nonreporting interviewees concede that "fear of reprisal" stopped them from informing the police. As might be expected, the number of intimidated victims is higher for crimes of violence (especially rape) than for property crimes. (See table 5-3.)

Yet intimidation is suspected to be the number-one cause of victim-witness noncooperation, in the opinion of a sample of police officers, prosecutors, and judges. However, victims contacted by the same researchers attributed their disenchantment with the system to trial delays rather than offender threats (Docksai, 1979:52). In New York City, the Victim Services Agency found that about 13 percent of a sample of approximately one thousand victims confided that attempts to intimidate them had occurred. The most common form was verbal threats during a face-to-face confrontation. Some victims suffered losses from vandalized property, but fewer than 1 percent were actually assaulted. The intimidation came from offenders out on bail and also from their families and friends. The incidents occurred in police stations and courthouses, as well as in the neighborhoods and homes of the victims. But the

TABLE 5-3 Intimidation Rates

Type of crime	*Main reason for not reporting a crime during 1980* *Fear of reprisal*	*Other reasons*
All personal crimes	1%	99%
Crimes of violence	5%	95%
Rape	12%	88%
Robbery with injury	10%	90%
Robbery without injury	4%	96%
Aggravated assault	6%	94%
Simple assault	3%	97%
Crimes of theft	0.3%	99.7%
Personal larceny		
With contact	3%	97%
Without contact	0%	100%
All household crimes	0.5%	99.5%

SOURCE: *Criminal Victimization in the United States, 1980,* by the Bureau of Justice Statistics, 1982, p. 75. Washington, D.C.: U.S. Department of Justice.

intimidation attempts did not affect the willingness of victims to cooperate with prosecutors, and they did not influence conviction rates to any statistically significant extent (Fried, 1982).

(The intimidation problem goes beyond the direct threats made by offenders against victims. Would-be complainants may experience strong pressures from their own families and friends not to come forward and tell the police what happened. Subjected to this kind of "cultural intimidation" by their community, they are forced to either settle the score privately or let the matter rest. Another type of intimidation arises from perceptions rather than overt acts. Victims may be haunted by visions of what offenders might do, even though no specific threats have been made. The thought of exploitative media exposure can also be chilling. Finally, intimidation can be directed against defense lawyers, defendants, and reluctant witnesses in the form of harassment by the authorities, especially in well-publicized and controversial cases. One-sided formulations of the intimidation problem imply that it is improper for anyone other than law enforcement agents to contact witnesses and victims. But defense attorneys must be allowed to, since a person accused of a crime has a constitutional right to confront the accusers and put on a vigorous defense against the charges lodged by witnesses (including the victim) for the prosecution [ABA Committee on Victims, 1979].)

Much of the intimidation problem can be traced to officials who have shirked their responsibilities to victims. Police officers con victims into cooperating by making empty promises of added protection, knowing full well that their precincts don't have the resources to provide special attention. Prosecutors allow cases to collapse when key witnesses and complainants fail to appear after being subpoenaed, perhaps due to intimidation, because attrition lightens their workload. Judges fail to act for the same reason—intimidation leads to nonappearance and ultimately dismissals, which alleviate caseloads (American Bar Association, 1979).

Reducing victim-witness intimidation. After holding hearings on the subject of intimidation, a committee of the American Bar Association (1979) issued these recommendations:

New Legislation

In all states, it should be a misdemeanor to knowingly and maliciously prevent or try to dissuade a victim or witness from reporting a crime, seeking the arrest of a suspect, and cooperating with the prosecution. In all states, it should be a felony to threaten a victim or witnesses that force and violence will be used against them or their property, or any third person of concern to them, whether or not the threats are carried out, and whether or not the intimidation succeeds or fails.

Responsibilities of the Police

Police departments in major urban areas should establish victim/witness protection squads, staffed by specially trained officers who are on-call 24 hours a day, to provide telephone hot-line service, emergency relocation capabilities, personal protection, increased patrols, transportation, and investigation of threats.

Responsibilities of Prosecutors

Prosecutors should insist that as a condition of bail the defendant must not intimidate a witness or the victim. Prosecutors should refer cases in which intimidation is anticipated to local police victim/witness protection squads, and should urge continued attention after cases are resolved if retaliation against cooperative victims and witnesses is feared. Prosecutors should press for speedy trials in such cases, and should guard against any careless and unnecessary leaks of information concerning the whereabouts of victims and witnesses afterward.

Responsibilities of Judges

Judges should issue court orders to defendants not to communicate with victims or witnesses except through their attorneys. Clear evidence of intimidation ought to furnish the grounds for a contempt of court citation, the revocation of pretrial release, the forfeiture of bail and incarceration in jail. When victims and witnesses fail to appear as scheduled in court, judges should investigate the reasons for their non-cooperation, if possible. If intimidation is suspected, the judge might grant a continuance rather than permit charges against the defendant to be dropped. To prevent last-minute intimidation, courthouses should have separate waiting rooms, one for prosecution witnesses and victims and another for defendants on bail, their families and friends, and defense witnesses.

According to the President's Task Force (1982), prosecutors ought to pursue to the fullest extent of the law defendants who harass, threaten, injure, or otherwise retaliate against victims or witnesses. When they don't take intimidation seriously, one of the victim's worst fears is confirmed—namely, that the criminal justice system can't furnish protection, and that the only way to escape reprisal is to stop cooperating with it. Anonymous calls in the middle of the night or acts of vandalism are difficult to trace. But, if left unattended, these incidents convey to victims the message that they are on their own, and they signify to offenders that intimidation is worth a try: it may have the desired effect, and it carries little risk of additional penalties.

Adrift within the System: Assistance Is Necessary

Prosecutors can handle victims' cases as neglectfully as government-provided defense lawyers handle defendants' cases. Both sets of attorneys keep their clients in the dark wherever staggering workloads demand assembly-line treatment.

The most frequently voiced complaint concerns impersonality. Victims feel mistreated, as if they were merely pieces of physical evidence temporarily placed on exhibit to sway juries. They are interrogated, badgered, summoned, threatened with contempt of court for noncooperation, dismissed, and perhaps later recalled without explanation or consultation. Then, after the state is through with them, whether their case was won or lost, they are cast adrift to fend for themselves (American Bar Association, 1980:2). Those who react angrily to such manipulation by the state exert the only leverage left to them. They discontinue their participation in the process and cut their losses of additional time, money, and pride by dropping out.

As a consequence of the neglectful and impersonal handling of their cases, victims and their supporters have been demanding a right to know about their opportunities and obligations. They thirst for progress reports about the current status of the case (for example, whether a suspect is in custody), explanations about the duties of complainants and witnesses, notifications about required court appearances, assurances that their presence is really necessary at hearings and trials, and knowledge about how the criminal justice process works. Furthermore, victims want to know about their chances to exert leverage at various points (bail hearings, pretrial plea negotiations, sentencing hearings, and parole board meetings) in their quest for revenge, restitution, or offender rehabilitation.

The difficulties, inconveniences, and frustrations faced by victims serving as witnesses for the prosecution have been known for decades (McDonald, 1976:28). The National Commission on Law Observance and Enforcement commented in 1931 that the administration of justice was suffering because of the economic burdens imposed on citizens who participated in trials. The American Bar Association noted in 1938 that witness fees were deplorably low, courthouse accommodations were inadequate, intimidation went unchecked, and witness time was often wasted. Its report argued that the state had an obligation to ease the sacrifice of witnesses as much as possible. Similar conclusions and recommendations were issued in 1967 by the President's Commission on Law Enforcement and the Administration of Justice, and in 1973 by the National Advisory Commission on Criminal Justice Standards and Goals. In 1974 the National District Attorneys Association surveyed the extent of the problem facing victims and witnesses who wanted to cooperate with the authorities but encountered obstacles (see box 5-5).

BOX 5-5 Prosecutors' Neglect of Victims as Clients

A survey conducted in Alameda County, California, documented what was up until that time merely an impression: the fact that crime victims were also victimized by an inadequate and indifferent criminal justice system (Lynch, 1976:172–173). The study found that:

- Almost 12 percent of those surveyed were never notified that an arrest had been made in their case.
- Almost 30 percent of all victims never got their property back, even though it had been recovered and used as evidence.
- Almost 61 percent of injured victims who were eligible for compensation for unreimbursed losses under a state program were never informed of their right to file a claim.
- Almost 13 percent of the victims (and witnesses) were never notified to appear for an interview or to attend a court session.
- About 45 percent reported that no one had explained to them what their court appearance would entail.
- Almost 27 percent of all witnesses (including victims) called to court were not subsequently asked to testify.
- Almost 78 percent lost pay to come to court.
- About 95 percent received no witness fees for their court appearance.
- About 42 percent were never notified of the outcome of the case.

From the prosecutorial standpoint, these sources of friction and frustration have undermined good working relationships between victims and the government. Confusion about scheduled court appearances and last-minute cancellations are wasteful financially, as well. Witness fees and police overtime are paid out, yet nothing is gained in return. Unnecessary and inconvenient trips to the courthouse make victims and witnesses feel reluctant to return. Then, the taxpayers' money spent on police and prosecutorial services is lost because charges must be dismissed if complainants or key witnesses do not appear. Winning is what counts within the adversary system, but the government cannot be victorious (and prosecutors cannot accumulate an impressive conviction rate) if victims fail to show up. To overcome this public-relations problem and to minimize wasteful expenditures, programs have been devised to restore citizen cooperation and community support.

Most of the funding for victim–witness assistance programs (VWAPs) was initially provided by the Law Enforcement Assistance Administration to the National District Attorneys Association. The first experiments were located in prosecutors' offices in California, Illinois, Utah, Colorado, Kentucky, Louisiana, Pennsylvania, and New York during the mid-1970s. There were more than one hundred federally funded units by 1977. At the end of the decade as many as four hundred VWAPs were in operation, but by 1982 only two hundred remained, because of budget cuts (Geis, 1983; Gest and Davidson, 1982; "NDAA Strengthening Commitment," 1981; Schneider and Schneider, 1981).

The development of VWAPs had several aims; to reverse the tide of noncooperation by minimizing the losses of time and money of victims and witnesses; to provide incentives for cooperation by furnishing convenience services and modest reimbursements (like maps of the facilities and car fare); to strengthen victims by referring them to social service agencies and counseling, if needed, so that they could serve as effective witnesses; to satisfy their demands for participation by keeping them informed about the criminal justice process and the progress of their case; and to allay their fears of reprisal by responding to attempts at intimidation (Geis, 1983; Schneider and Schneider, 1981). (The kinds of support, notification services, convenience services, limited advocacy, and extra protection offered by VWAPs are described in box 5-6.)

The programs offering assistance, referrals, notification, and convenience services implemented on an experimental basis were supposed to provide incentives to lure reluctant victims and witnesses back into the system. Preliminary evaluations of the impact of VWAPs have yielded mixed results. Support services may improve police–community and prosecutor–community relations. An attitude poll (Harris, 1981) showed that victims who received help from programs in New York State were more satisfied with the way the police and prosecutors had handled their case than those who were entirely on their own. Records kept by a witness information service in Peoria, Illinois, indicated that victims and witnesses receiving help were more likely to appear when summoned than those who had not been aided (National Institute of Justice, 1982). However, an evaluation of a comprehensive assistance program in Brooklyn revealed no statistically significant improvement in appearance rates. Similarly, a model program in Milwaukee was unable to make an appreciable dent in the high rate of dismissals due to witness problems (Rosenblum and Blew, 1979).

Whether or not VWAPs have the desired effect of improving cooperation by victims and witnesses, these programs can be beneficial to prosecutors. The notification services can save unnecessary costs in the form of police overtime and witness fees. Trial assistants (assistant dis-

BOX 5-6 *Inducements to Victims to Serve as Witnesses*

A federally funded victim assistance program was set up within the District Attorney's Office in Multnomah County, Portland, Oregon, in 1975 (Rosenblum and Blew, 1979). Most of its clients are victims of assaults, purse snatchings and robberies. It helps people by:

- providing information about how the criminal justice system works and about the responsibilities of complainants as witnesses
- providing information about the victim's case and monitoring its status as it winds its way through the system, from arrest to arraignment, plea, trial, sentencing, and parole board hearing
- speeding up the return of recovered stolen property by photographing it, unless it must be examined by a jury
- making court appearances more convenient by furnishing transportation, child care, and comfortable reception lounges to wait in
- injecting the victim's feelings into the presentencing report and soliciting victim reactions to plea bargains
- referring victims to social service agencies for emergency food, shelter, money, medical and dental services, welfare, Social Security benefits, legal advice, state compensation for unreimbursed losses, and child care
- counseling victims in crisis, immediately after the crime and at the time of grand jury and trial appearances
- notifying the district attorney of attempts at intimidation

trict attorneys) waste less of their own time, as do judges, juries, bailiffs, stenographers, and other courtroom personnel, when cases are managed more efficiently. Employers benefit from notification systems that cut down needless employee absenteeism. The financial costs to the prosecutor's office for all the services it furnishes are minimized by the use of volunteers such as students, retirees, and members of women's groups (Reilly, 1981).

The development of victim–witness assistance programs raises some constitutional and ethical questions. To deny services to a victim whose cooperation is not needed (or whose pursuit of the case is actively discouraged by the prosecutor's office) would be unfair but not illegal, since the aid is granted as a privilege rather than as a right. To deny similar services (free parking, child care, last-minute phone calls canceling a scheduled appearance) to witnesses for the defense would violate notions of fairness within the adversary system. As long as the defendant is presumed innocent unless proven guilty, even-handed treatment of all witnesses should prevail. Too close a rapport between a victim and VWAP personnel can cause another problem: the victim's testimony can be "coached" or "rehearsed" to the extent that it departs from the original statements and covers up contradictions in order to make the most convincing case against the accused person.

To staunch advocates of the victim's cause, the most objectionable aspect of VWAPs is that they do not address the fundamental grievance of many victims—their apparent powerlessness to influence the course of events within the criminal justice process. Instead of empowering victims, or at least giving them a voice, VWAPs furnish services as a substitute for direct participation (in bail hearings, plea negotiations, sentencing, and parole decisions).

Dismissed Cases, Dropped Charges, Disturbing Deals

Crime victims, police officers, and prosecutors are all on the same side within the adversary system. Yet their alliance, based in theory on a common commitment to convict people guilty of crimes, often unravels. The police can feel rebuffed when the district attorney decides not to prosecute a case they have prepared. The victim can feel abandoned when the district attorney dismisses or reduces charges against a person arrested as the offender. To the victim, a dropped charge or count or a decision not to prosecute at all means that satisfaction is denied—whether the victim was looking for maximum punishment as revenge, compulsory treatment of the offender, or eligibility for court-ordered restitution. To the prosecutor, these decisions that infuriate some victims are unavoidable. It's impossible for a prosecutor to fulfill the legal mandate to enforce all laws and seek the conviction of all lawbreakers.

In evaluating the cases brought before them, prosecutors weigh many factors: What are the chances of conviction rather than acquittal? Is the effort worth the state's limited resources? Would indictment, prosecution, and conviction have deterrent value or serve some other worthwhile social purpose? Would pressing or dropping charges touch off protests from powerful groups? And would a victory in this case substantially advance a prosecutor's career?

In assessing the strength of any given case, the prosecutor takes into account the quality of the evidence; the credibility and cooperativeness of the victim and witnesses who may be called to testify in court; the credentials of the defense attorney; the nature of the offense and the background of the defendant; the value of the defendant as a possible informant or star witness against other criminals; and the degree to which the particulars of the case fit into formulas for routinely disposing of such incidents (Sheley, 1979).

At least one-third, and up to one-half or more, of all cases prepared against suspects by the police are screened out by prosecutors in high-crime urban jurisdictions. The process can be compared to filtration. The end product is a homogeneous mass of cases that embody predetermined victim–offender relationships and patterns (Shelden, 1982).

A number of factors explain why such high percentages of cases are dropped or reduced in severity at the prosecutorial level. Limited resources dictate priorities; some types of cases and crime are deemed trivial and not worth the state's time and money. Also, police arrests are based on a much lower standard of proof—probable cause—than that required to secure a conviction—guilt beyond a reasonable doubt. In some jurisdictions, the police devote much more effort to case preparation than in others. Just because a case is cleared (by the arrest of a suspect) doesn't mean that it is ready for presentation to a grand jury for indictment. (See box 5-7.)

BOX 5-7 Prosecuting Rapists

It is widely assumed that rape victims are reluctant to press charges because a trial will become an inquisition into their sex life. But a study of prosecutorial records discovered that rape victims tended to be *more* determined to pursue their cases to conclusion than victims of other serious crimes, such as robbery, felonious assault, and burglary. In many of these cases, problems arose because of the prosecutor's doubts about the victim's credibility rather than the victim's unwillingness to cooperate with the prosecution (Kristen Williams, 1978).

Prosecutors are the ones who are reluctant to pursue rape cases. A study of 1,200 rape complaints in Seattle, Detroit, New Orleans, Kansas City, and Phoenix uncovered a consensus among prosecutors that bringing a rape case to trial is not good for one's career because conviction rates are so low. An aggregate of sixty-five prosecutors had tried an average of only 4.5 rape cases each in their entire careers and had secured only 2.5 convictions.

The study closely analyzed 635 rape complaints in Seattle and Kansas City. Criminal cases were prepared by the police against a total of 167 defendants. In only forty-five of those cases were charges of rape or attempted rape pressed by prosecutors. Just thirty-two felony cases were resolved. Ten defendants were convicted (found guilty or pleaded guilty) of rape or attempted rape, and another ten were convicted for lesser offenses. Overall, less than 2 percent of all complaints led to a conviction on the most serious felony charges (LeGrand, Reich, and Chappell, 1977).

In general, the chances for conviction are maximized when victims report the assaults promptly, provide evidence of force or at least coercion, and refute any accusations of shared responsibility (Dean and deBruyn-Kops, 1982).

As many as nine out of ten cases in high-crime areas are resolved by a "plea bargain" rather than a trial. The expression refers to a situation in which the defendant agrees to make a confession of guilt in return for some concession—the dropping of certain other charges or counts or a less painful punishment, like a suspended sentence, probation, or imprisonment for an agreed-on number of years which is less than the maximum permitted by law.

Although the expression *plea bargain* implies that defendants who "cop a plea" invariably get a break or good deal that permits them to escape the punishment they deserve, this impression is sometimes erroneous. Police officials and prosecutors routinely engage in "bedsheeting" and "overcharging" in anticipation of the negotiations that will follow. Bedsheeting refers to the prosecutorial practice of charging a defendant with every applicable crime committed during a single incident. For example, an armed intruder captured in someone's home can be held accountable for criminal trespass, breaking and entering, burglary, grand larceny, and carrying a concealed weapon, in addition to the most serious charge of robbery. Overcharging means filing a criminal indictment for an offense that is more serious than the available evidence can support—for example, charging someone with attempted murder after a fistfight. The point is that many of these charges could not be proven in court, but defendants and their lawyers might be too cautious to gamble and call the prosecutor's bluff. For these reasons and others, in the majority of cases accused persons who plead guilty in return for "concessions" receive substantially the same penalties that they probably would have received if convicted after a trial (Beall, 1980; Katz, 1980:124; Rhodes, 1978). Nevertheless, most victims are convinced that criminals are getting away with something when they accept plea bargains. Consequently, victims and their advocates are increasingly demanding an end to negotiated pleas (although studies of jurisdictions where plea bargaining has been "abolished" reveal that greater discretion is exercised at earlier or later stages of the criminal justice process). If all defendants exercised their constitutional right to a trial by jury and to appeals of convictions on procedural grounds, the courts would be overwhelmed and paralyzed. Some victims who are convinced that it is unrealistic to do away with deals and inducements want to play a role in the negotiations that resolve their cases.

Victims and their advocates justify their demand for empowerment by emphasizing that they were directly involved in the criminal incidents and were personally harmed. But defense attorneys, prosecutors, and judges make dire predictions about what would happen if victims (and police officers and defendants as well) joined them at pretrial conferences. These insiders contend that emotional and potentially violent confrontations between victims and offenders would ensue; that candid discussions necessary to foster settlements would be inhibited by the presence of outsiders; that both victims and defendants would misconstrue the role of the judge and accuse him or her of improper conduct; and that the dignity of the judge would be diminished by open involvement in negotiations in front of outsiders (Heinz and Kerstetter, 1979). Prosecutors, in particular, feel threatened by the inclusion of victims—whom they supposedly represent, in addition to the state—at such meetings. They object because victims might try to use the administrative machinery as an instrument of personal revenge and might put forward unreasonable demands for the imposition of maximum penalties. Deals would fall through, and risky and costly trials would be necessitated (McDonald, 1976).

The law does not provide victims with any formal mechanisms to challenge the decisions of these attorneys who act in their name as well as in behalf of "the people." But victims who want offenders prosecuted—whether out of a desire for revenge, a concern for rehabilitation, or a wish for financial restitution—can in several states exercise a "do it yourself" option. Just as a citizen's arrest can be made to circumvent police inaction, a private prosecutor can be hired to get around the government attorney's inaction. In 1955, at least twenty-eight states permitted private prosecution in accord with English common-law traditions. But today, only a few states—most notably, North Carolina—allow victims to be represented by private attorneys as well as government attorneys in criminal proceedings. Public prosecutors resent and resist any additional outside help. They contend that private prosecutors advocate the victim's desires at the expense of the public interest by pressing for costly trials on the most serious charges imaginable, while spurning any negotiated agreements for guilty pleas on lesser charges (McDonald, 1976; Sigler, 1979; Ziegenhagen, 1977).

Another course of action has been proposed by advocates of the victim's cause who also want to minimize friction with the prosecutor's office. The alternative to private prosecution is to make government attorneys represent their clients' wishes more faithfully. This entails conceding to victims a larger and more direct role in the criminal justice proceedings.

According to this new point of view, prosecutors have an obligation to bring to the attention of the court (the judge) the needs and wants of victims at bail hearings, scheduling conferences, plea bargain negotiations, dismissals, and sentencing appearances. Specifically, victims should have a chance to air any fears of reprisal when bail is set and to report any attempts to intimidate them. When cases are postponed, the victim's availability and convenience should be taken into account along with the schedules of the other participants. When charges are dropped or cases are dismissed, victims should at least be informed and at most be allowed to question the decisions. Most dramatically, after conviction, either through a plea bargain or a trial, victims should be allowed to inform the judge of the full effect of the crime on them and their family. The appropriate vehicle would be a "victim-impact statement" as part of the written presentencing report prepared by the probation department. The logic of this concession is that two lives, the offender's and the victim's, are profoundly shaped by the judge's sentence. The court cannot make an informed decision on an appropriate sentence if it hears from only one side: the defense. When the judge hears from defendants and their lawyers, families, friends, and other character witnesses, notions of fairness dictate that those who have borne the brunt of the defendants' crime be allowed to speak in their own behalf before the sentence is handed down.

Victims view the sentence as a barometer of the seriousness of the crime and as an evaluation of the harm done to them. Although prosecutors can present the victims' case, they cannot fully describe the victims' plight, because they were not directly affected by the crime. It is as unfair to require victims to depend entirely on a prosecutor to speak for them as it would be to insist that defendants rely solely on their counsel to speak for them before the judge imposes a sentence (President's Task Force, 1982). Critics of this proposal to permit victims to make a statement before the judge hands down a sentence argue that this direct participation places improper pressures on the judge. It tilts the balance of the scales of justice toward harsh punishment and undermines the professional objectivity of judges by injecting inflammatory emotional considerations into the proceedings.

Legal scholars have justified the exclusion of victims from sentencing decisions on several grounds. If the purpose of sentencing offenders is to rehabilitate them, then the type and length of treatment should be determined by experts, not victims. If the goal of punishment is to deter potential criminals, then sentences must be swift, sure, and predictable, not subject to victim modification. If the purpose of sentencing is social retribution, then the lawbreakers must receive their just deserts; the punishment must fit the crime rather than the desired of victims (McDonald, 1979).

Victims versus Defense Attorneys

Victims and defense lawyers are natural enemies within the adversary system of criminal justice. Lawyers for the accused act as counselors, advising clients about their best interests, the risks they face, and the options they can exercise. In addition, such attorneys, whether hired privately for a fee or provided free to indigents, advocate their client's cause. They seek the best "deal" the prosecutor will agree to in plea negotiations. During a trial before a judge or jury, they pit themselves against the prosecutors (assistant district attorneys in routine cases) and try to cast doubt on the government's version of events. In so doing, they draw on all their skills and training to undermine the victim's cause.

Abusing Continuances to Wear Victims Down

If their clients are free on bail, defense lawyers may stall proceedings as much as possible to "buy time on the streets." They typically achieve this objective by instructing defendants to plead not guilty at the arraignment and by pretending that they are preparing for a trial. They then create scheduling difficulties and ask for postponements to prepare the defense. This serves an additional purpose. As the delays mount and unnecessary court appearances accumulate, the victims (or crucial witnesses) may lose patience with the system and enthusiasm for seeing the case through to resolution. If the victims or key witnesses give up in disgust and fail to appear in court as required (or forget crucial details, move away, or die in the interim), the strategy succeeds. At that point, the defense attorneys assert that they are ready to proceed and move for a dismissal of all charges (Reiff, 1979). (Prosecutors also manipulate the continuance provisions for their own ends. If defendants are in jail rather than out on bail, government attorneys may stall to keep them behind bars longer and to pressure them to accept unfavorable plea bargains. In the process, the defendants' right to a speedy trial is violated.)

Postponements prolong and intensify the plight of victims. Victims must be allowed to put their upsetting experiences behind them as swiftly as possible. They should not have to repeatedly bear the burdens of arranging for child care, missing work, canceling vacations, and breaking appointments only to discover (usually at the last moment) that their case has been rescheduled. Prosecutors should oppose requests from the defense for postponements unless they are necessary for legitimate investigatory probes or to accommodate the time limitations of victims. Judges must not grant continuances to ease an assistant district attorney's workload; to cater to his desire to avoid pursuing a difficult case; or to play into a defense lawyer's strategy to wait until a victim or witness is tired of the delays, is unavailable, or has forgotten important details. The healing process for victims of violence, and sexual assault in particular, cannot be completed until the case is resolved (President's Task Force, 1982).

Discrediting Victims on the Stand

If they can't wear victims down through stalling tactics, defense attorneys will try to discredit them (and other prosecution witnesses) on the stand during the trial so the jury won't give much weight to their testimony.

Under the adversary system, each side puts forward its own best case and assails the version of events presented by the opposition. Cross-examination is the art of exposing the weaknesses of witnesses. The intent is to impeach their credibility by trapping them into revealing any hidden motives, lapses of memory, unsavory character traits, embarrassing indiscretions, prejudices, incompetencies, or dishonest inclinations.

Under the Sixth Amendment to the U.S. Constitution, a defendant has the right to confront accusers. Since the burden of proof falls on the prosecution, and the accused is innocent unless proven guilty, the accuser must be presumed mistaken until his or her credibility is established beyond a reasonable doubt. When the accuser is a police officer (the credibility of police testimony is the subject of much debate) or an expert witness, the defense lawyer enters into battle against a formidable, professional foe. But when the full brunt of the defense's counterattack is directed at impeaching the credibility of the victim, the potential for adding insult to injury reaches disturbing proportions. At its best, the confrontation in the courtroom puts the victim-as-eyewitness to the test. At its worst, the victim is set up as a target, isolated and vulnerable, unprotected by the prosecutor and subjected to relentless attack by the defense attorney, to be injured again when made to look like either a liar or a fool. (See box 5-8, p. 159.)

Defense attorneys sometimes clash with victims over access to files maintained by counselors. Now that rape crisis centers, shelters for battered women, and victim–witness assistance programs provide counseling services, lawyers for defendants have begun to subpoena the records of these interviews in order to prepare their attacks on the complainant's credibility. In most states, the privilege of confidentiality covers only sessions held with psychologists and psychiatrists. But many counselors are social workers, nurses, or former victims. Without the protection of confidentiality, victims can feel betrayed when notes about their fantasies, reactions, feelings, and personal history—which they assumed would remain private—are publicly scrutinized in court. Since current statutes shield only the intimate revelations made to licensed professionals by those who can afford private treatment, legislation is needed to ensure that designated victim-counseling sessons are legally privileged and not subject to defense discovery or subpoena. If a guarantee of confidentiality is not extended to crisis counseling, its effectiveness will decline, and some victims who need this kind of help will be reluctant to seek it (President's Task Force, 1982).

Some of the information used to undermine the credibility of complainants while they are on the stand may have been obtained illegally, or at least in violation of professional ethics. Assistants working for the defense attorney may hide their real identity while legitimately interviewing the victim by saying that they are working for the county (technically they might be, if they are employed by the Public Defender's Office) or that they are "investigators" (but without specifying for which side). Victims divulge information in the belief that the interviewers are gathering evidence to be used against, rather than in behalf of, the accused. Such deceptive conduct is improper (President's Task Force, 1982). (On the other hand, the substantial investigatory resources of the prosecution, which can draw on the police, massive files, crime laboratories, expert witnesses, and taxpayers' funds, usually dwarf the time, talents, and money of Legal Aid lawyers, public defenders, and nearly all private attorneys. For this reason, among others, the burden of proof rests with the government.)

Victims versus Judges

Judges are supposed to play the role of referee within the adversary system. Defendants often consider them as partisans representing the state and favoring the prosecution. Victims frequently see judges as guardians of the rights of criminals rather than protectors of the innocent. Angry victims who have been mistreated by the offender, the police, the prosecutor, and the defense attorney expect that the judge will finally accord them the justice they seek. But conflicts between victims and judges can erupt over bail, scheduling, and sentencing.

Bitterness over Bail: Change the Criteria?

Police officers often resent bail as a repudiation of their hard work to apprehend offenders. To them, releasing a defendant on bail symbolizes turning a dangerous criminal loose. Victims can also be outraged by judges' decisions to grant bail if they are convinced that the defendants are indeed the culprits.

The Eighth Amendment of the Bill of Rights prohibits the setting of excessive bail. Whether it establishes being bailed out as an affirmative right is a subject of scholarly debate and considerable public concern. State and federal courts routinely deny bail to defendants accused of crimes that could carry the death penalty. In noncapital cases, bail can be denied to jailed suspects who have a history of flight to avoid prosecution or who have tried to interfere with the administration of justice (by intimidating a witness or a juror, for example). Otherwise, defendants are given a chance to raise money or post bond to guarantee that they will show up for their trial. The amount of bail is usually determined by the judge and is set according to the nature of the offense and the record of the offender. The prosecutor can recommend a figure. Making bail is a major problem for defendants who are poor and have no prosperous friends or relatives. Across the nation, houses of detention are crammed with people unable to raise a few hundred dollars to purchase their freedom until their case is resolved.

On the other side, many criminal justice professionals, politicians, and victim advocates believe that bail laws need to be revised to make pretrial release more difficult to achieve. They argue that an additional factor, the threat posed by the defendant to the community, be taken into account when setting bail. The U.S. Congress, the American Bar Association, the National Conference of Commissioners on Uniform State Laws, the Attorney General's Task Force on Violent Crime, and the President's Task Force on Victims of Crime have all raised this issue. They have contended that existing practices respect the defendant's rights to procedural safeguards but ignore the victim's need for protection from intimidation and further harm and the community's desire for safety (President's Task Force, 1982).

BOX 5-8 Limiting Cross-Examination in Rape Trials

Rape trials pit the complainant's right to dignified treatment with regard to private sexual matters against the defendant's right to a fair chance to clear himself of very serious charges.

The difference between sexual intercourse and rape rests on the issue of consent. The prosecution must prove beyond a reasonable doubt that the complainant was violated against her will. The defense attorney must persuade the jury that the complainant might have been a willing partner (assuming that it is not a question of mistaken identity).

To counteract the charges leveled by the complainant against the accused in her testimony, the defense lawyer will try to establish during cross-examination that she had sexual relations with the defendant, or with other boys or men, in the past. By introducing evidence of prior sexual behavior, the defense hopes to undermine her assertions that she was forced to engage in sex.

Victim advocates who want to reform rape laws argue that the existing rules unfairly burden complainants. Complainants and the men in their lives have a right to privacy about intimate sexual matters. Rules that permit the defense to cross-examine the complainant with only few restraints allow the trial about the defendant's guilt or innocence to evolve into an exposé of the complainant's morality and sexual history. Countercharges by the defendant about the complainant's alleged complicity in the act are publicly humiliating and discourage other rape victims from coming forward to cooperate with the police and the prosecution. Judges and juries, swayed by double standards for sexual behavior, may acquit guilty men.

Civil libertarians concede most of these points but insist that relevant evidence cannot automatically be ruled inadmissible in court. Cross-examination is routinely upsetting to witnesses, including complainants in rape cases. But if defense attorneys were not allowed to ask embarrassing questions of prosecution witnesses, then the right of the defendant to confront his accusers and to try to refute their charges would lose its meaning. The complainant's concern for protection from public humiliation must be weighed against the public humiliation experienced by the defendant who is arrested and put on trial. Since the question of guilt or innocence might hinge on the distinction between consent and resistance, the rules of evidence must permit the conduct of the complainant to be scrutinized. Even though guilty people might escape punishment, falsely accused men will be spared the injustice of undeserved punishment as long as the burden of proof remains on the prosecution (Herman, 1976).

In 1978, Congress passed legislation to protect the privacy of complainants in rape trials. Since rape cases are usually tried in state courts, the real impact of the legislation was to spur states to reform their evidentiary proceedings and limit the kinds of question asked of complainants.

The new law prohibited the introduction of testimony that is mere opinion or concerns the general sexual reputation of the complainant. The reform legislation also restricted the use of direct evidence about any alleged past sexual relationships to specific types of situations. Before any such testimony is presented in public and to the jury, it must first be ruled admissible by the judge at a private meeting in his chambers ("Rape Victim Privacy," 1978).

Civil liberties groups denounce these proposals to limit bail as attempts to bring about "preventive detention." Such pretrial imprisonment may enhance the security of victims and the community only if the defendants are actually the perpetrators of the crimes, and only if it is assumed that their past record of offenses provides a sound basis for predicting further criminal behavior on their part in the immediate future. Otherwise, preventive detention represents a gross violation of the fundamental tenet of the American criminal justice system—that a person is innocent unless proven guilty. Without bail, an accused person immediately undergoes punishment. Ironically, the living conditions in jails and houses of detention are usually far worse than in prisons. Defendants awaiting trial are treated more harshly by the authorities than are convicts.

Frustration with Schedules and Exclusions: Include Victims?

The criminal justice process is rarely swift. Many delays are unavoidable. The determination of guilt or innocence should not be rushed, although unnecessary postponements could jeopardize a defendant's right to a speedy trial. What aggravates some victims is inefficient courtroom management by judges. Judges bear some responsibility for court congestion if they do not use time effectively. Some courts convene in mid-morning and recess in mid-afternoon. Such practices should not be allowed to become the norm simply to accommodate judges' schedules and conveniences. Judges must begin proceedings on time and must require those who appear before them to be punctual and well prepared (President's Task Force, 1982).

More upsetting than the slow pace of the proceedings is the practice of excluding victims and their families from the courtroom. Judges do this if victims or family members will be called as witnesses, in order to prevent them from being influenced by their observations of the trial. But this practice means that the parties most directly affected by the outcome cannot watch the decision-making process. Testifying can be a traumatic experience, especially for children, relatives of murder victims, or people who have been subjected to violence and terrifying ordeals. The absence of family members in the courtroom makes the task even more harrowing. For these reasons, judges might make an exception to the general rule about barring witnesses, and permit victims and their families to attend trials from start to finish (President's Task Force, 1982).

Dissatisfaction with Sentences: Make Restitution Mandatory?

After a defendant is convicted—either by an admission of guilt as part of a plea bargain, or by the verdict of a jury (or a judge) after a trial—it is the judge's responsibility to pronounce sentence. Judges exercise a great deal of discretion in the sentences they impose, in large part because most states' laws provide for a wide range of penalties. The substantial variations from judge to judge in the severity of the punishments meted out in comparable cases is termed "sentence disparity." These differences trouble civil libertarians, because the disparities might reflect a general consensus among judges to deal harshly with disadvantaged persons and mildly with more privileged offenders. The disparities anger convicts as unjustifiable arbitrariness on the part of judges. To activists in the law and order movement, the disparities are taken as evidence that some judges are "too soft on crime." Their solution is to press for new legislation restricting the discretionary authority of judges by narrowing their sentencing options (for example, by prohibiting probation and requiring that a mandatory minimum prison sentence be served before a convict is eligible for parole).

Although some victims are most concerned that offenders be punished for their misdeeds, others place a high priority on receiving restitution. These victims are disappointed that judges rarely impose restitution obligations on offenders, and they are critical of prosecutors for not routinely demanding that offenders pay back their victims as part of a plea bargain or a recommended sentence (Forer, 1980).

In the vast majority of cases, it is the victim and not the offender who eventually shoulders the burden of paying for the crime. Civil law embraces the concept of personal accountability for one's conduct and the allied notion that a person who causes damages must bear the financial consequences. Victims and their supporters want to guarantee that criminal law incorporates the same principles. As a result, they have sought mandatory restitution legislation. The President's Task Force (1982:79) recommended that the judge's sentence should include restitution for expenses arising from bodily harm or property loss, unless there are compelling reasons (which must be stated for the record) to waive this requirement. The court could accept responsibility for enforcing restitution orders. That would involve progress reports about whether offenders are meeting their obligations, and a commitment to extend the term of probation or parole until full repayment has been achieved. In 1982, Congress made restitution mandatory for federal crimes as part of a pro-victim legislative package.

Court Monitoring: Should Citizens Police Judges?

Victims and concerned citizens who are dissatisfied with the routine operations of the police and of prisons have few opportunities to observe the daily functioning of these components of the criminal justice system. But they have nearly unlimited occasions to observe the handling of cases in court. The right of the public and the press to attend criminal trials is guaranteed under the First and Fourteenth Amendments. Television coverage of court proceedings has been authorized in some jurisdictions. The only cases regularly closed to the public are those heard in juvenile court, in order to avoid excessively stigmatizing young offenders. On rare occasions, cases in which victims of sex crimes might suffer extreme embarrassment are closed to outsiders (Alper and Nichols, 1981).

Critics of criminal justice procedures have engaged in "court-monitoring" projects in order to expose and eventually eliminate judicial practices that they find objectionable. Civil liberties groups have monitored cases to document how disadvantaged defendants were treated in either an arbitrary or a discriminatory fashion. Radical political groups have filled courtrooms with their supporters to try to ensure that their members received fair trials (Sternberg, 1971). Conservative groups have mobilized court watchers to keep track of the decision-making patterns of judges. Volunteers observe dispositions and keep "box scores" that are publicized at election time. Their intent is to pressure judges to set higher bail figures, accept plea bargains only if they are unfavorable to defendants, and hand down stiffer sentences to convicts. Law and order groups view such changes as being in the best interests of victims. On occasion, feminists in the anti-rape movement have followed the same approach of turning out in large numbers during a trial to see if the offender gets the kind of sentence they believe he deserves (see box 5-9).

Packing the courtroom is a highly controversial tactic, since in the not-too-distant past intense community pressures from outraged citizens caused miscarriages of justice. Defendants were "railroaded," subjected to "kangaroo courts," and then "legally lynched" when prosecutors, juries, and judges abandoned the fact-finding process and caved in to pressures imposed by angry mobs, inflammatory media coverage, and demands from elites.

Victims versus Parole Boards

The majority of convicts who leave prison each year are placed on parole, although the actual proportions vary substantially from state to state, from very few to almost all. Parole is conditional liberty before the judge's sentence has expired; a parolee's obedience to rules and restrictions is supervised by a parole officer. The rationales for permitting parole are that an offender can make a smoother transition from prison life to civilian life with the guidance of a parole department, and that corrections authorities can better manage prisoners as long as the possibility of early release looms as an incentive for good behavior. A parole board decides whether to let an offender out based on evidence (reports from the corrections department) that the inmate has made progress toward rehabilitation and will no longer pursue a criminal lifestyle. Also taken into account are the needs of the prison system for cell space to house new arrivals. Less dangerous prisoners are released to make room for more dangerous ones.

BOX 5-9 Judging Judges

A study based on interviews with thirty-eight judges in Philadelphia in the early 1970s revealed that their attitudes toward rape victims departed from the impartiality that is usually assumed. The judges were sympathetic to "genuine" victims and hostile to the offenders in cases of blitz rapes (for example, when an intruder breaks into a woman's bedroom at night). But judges considered other cases as indicative of "consensual intercourse" (if a conversation preceded the attack, for instance) and their disdain for the complainant was indicated by the mocking terms they coined to describe these situations: "friendly rape," "felonious gallantry," "assault with failure to please," and "breach of contract." The judges also suspected some cases embodied "female vindictiveness" (for example, when the woman cried rape in order to get a man in trouble); here, they were unsympathetic to the complainants and lenient toward the defendants. The judges generally were very concerned about shielding victims from the frightening aspects of testifying in court, but they lacked compassion for minority group victims (Bohmer, 1974).

In 1977, a judge in Madison, Wisconsin, lost his job because of his decision and his remarks in a rape case. He provoked a storm of protest when he permitted a fifteen-year-old boy who had raped a classmate in a high school stairwell to continue to live at home under court supervision. He based his ruling on his belief that the teenager had been reacting "normally" to the climate of "sexual permissiveness" in contemporary society and to the provocative clothing worn by women. The judge's views were considered examples of "unbelievable callousness" and "blatant sexism" by the leader of the local chapter of the National Organization for Women (NOW). Feminists and their supporters gathered enough signatures to recall the judge and force him to run for reelection before his six-year term had expired. He lost his seat on the bench to a female attorney ("Judge's Ruling," 1977; "Judge Defeated," 1977).

After the case received national coverage from the media, the Harris polling organization surveyed public opinion about the issues that had been raised. A majority of respondents disapproved of the judge's sentence and his reasoning and approved of the recall vote to unseat him (Williams and Holmes, 1981).

The election of judges is an important democratic mechanism that permits victims and concerned groups to hold judges accountable for their actions. However, most elections for judicial offices fail to achieve their stated purposes. The vast majority of voters are poorly informed about the merits of the candidates. Running for election provides an incentive for incumbents and challengers to make promises and render decisions that are popular but legally incorrect and socially irresponsible (National Advisory Commission, 1973).

Decision Making Behind Closed Doors: Impose Accountability?

Prisoner support groups have rejected the image of parole as a form of "benevolence" or a privilege earned through self-improvement. They criticize the parole system as a way of extending the length of time an ex-offender is under government control; as a source of anxiety and uncertainty to prisoners; and as a device to prolong punishment. These groups call for the abolition of the practice of parole, and they suggest that definite sentences of shorter duration replace long indeterminate prison terms (Shelden, 1982). Law and order groups have also demanded an end to the parole system, but their perception is that it functions as a device for letting dangerous criminals out prematurely. They want parole ended and replaced with definite sentences of longer duration (President's Task Force, 1982).

Victims can come into conflict with parole boards over several matters. Boards don't notify victims about hearings and don't permit them or their representatives to attend and to argue either against early release or for restitution as a condition of parole. Furthermore, victims are not warned that offenders are being let out. Therefore, they are unable to take precautions or, at the very least, prepare themselves mentally for the possibility of a face-to-face encounter. Besides demanding a role in parole board decision making, victim advocates have also called for ways of punishing parole board members for acts of gross negligence that enable ex-inmates to commit new atrocities. Such accountability could take the form of dismissing board members or suing them for monetary damages arising from the crimes of parolees (President's Task Force, 1982).

And Justice for All?

The Fourteenth Amendment to the Constitution promises "equal protection of the law" for all citizens. The standard interpretation of this pledge is that federal and state criminal justice systems ought to regard factors like social class, race, nationality, religion, and sex as irrelevant to the administration of the law. The traditional concern of criminologists and political activists about this important principle of equal protection has centered on how suspects, defendants, and convicts who are poor or members of a minority group are subjected to discriminatory treatment. But the equally significant problem of discrimination against certain kinds of victims has escaped notice until recently.

It is often said that the United States is a country "ruled by laws, not men." The maxim implies that the principles of due process and equal protection limit the otherwise arbitrary powers of criminal justice officials. Due process means procedural regularity, and equal protection requires that all people be treated similarly. Yet enough discretion remains at each step in the criminal justice process to generate predictably unequal outcomes. Different groups of people—both criminals and victims—tend to receive different treatment at the hands of criminal justice officials. Of course, those who exercise discretion can explain and defend their policies. Their justifications range from pragmatic considerations about time and money to philosophical rationales about the true meaning of justice. But regardless of their explanations, their actions reveal double standards or, more accurately (since more than two factors are involved), "differential handling."

Discovering "Second-Class" Complainants

Criminologists have documented the discrepancy between official dogma and actual practices. Race and class are supposed to be extraneous factors, but in reality they turn out to be major predictors of how officials respond to offenders. The handicaps imposed by the social system on lawbreakers who are from the "wrong" race or classes show up as difficulties in making bail, in obtaining effective counsel, in receiving favorable psychiatric dispositions, and in mounting an adequate legal defense (Blumberg, 1967). As a result of these disadvantages, and others, for the same criminal act, poor offenders are more likely than affluent ones to be arrested; and if arrested, more likely to be indicted and prosecuted; and if prosecuted, more likely to be convicted; and if convicted, more likely to be sentenced to prison, and for longer terms (see Reiman, 1979). Similarly, blacks are more likely than whites who break the same law to be arrested, prosecuted, convicted, and imprisoned, and they are less likely to be granted suspended sentences, probation, parole, pardons, or commutations (see Sutherland and Cressey, 1974).

Piecing together scattered research findings about how different *victims* are treated yields a comparable picture for them. Certain victims are more likely to be neglected or abused as "second-class" complainants by these same agencies and officials. How a case is handled is determined by who the victim is as well as who the offender is (in addition to the particular circumstances of the crime). (See box 5-10.)

It should come as no surprise that many of the social disadvantages that hold people back in other aspects of everyday life also impede their ability to receive fair treatment as crime victims. The same discretionary powers that result in "overzealous" law enforcement in some neighborhoods contribute to "underzealous" enforcement in other neighborhoods. For example, conduct that would provoke vigorous actions in affluent communities might be ignored or belittled by authorities presiding over ghetto areas. An unofficial "forty-stitch" rule reportedly prevails in poor sections of Brooklyn that are populated by minorities. An assailant hauled into court need not face charges of felonious assault unless the combined injuries to the victim exceed forty stitches. A similar symptom of official discrimination that denies equal protection to all is revealed by the expression "There is no such thing as rape in slums and ghettos" (Katz, 1980). A seemingly pragmatic prosecutorial screening criterion can also subvert the intent of justice for all. The policy in many jurisdictions of not investigating and not pressing charges in minor burglaries (ones that result in losses of less than a certain amount) in effect means that criminals have a license to ransack the homes of the poor without penalty.

Apparently, the claims of victims from discriminated-against groups are not perceived as being entirely legitimate or compelling by the men at the helm of the criminal justice system. The credibility of the calls for

BOX 5-10 Which Victims Get Better Services?

Arrests:

A suspect is more likely to be taken into custody if the victims:

- request that the police make an arrest in a deferential, nonantagonistic manner (Black, 1968)
- convince the police officer that they were not involved in any illegal activity themselves before the incident (La Fave, 1965)
- prove to the officer that they are not a friend, relative, or neighbor of the suspect (Black, 1968; Giacinti, 1973; Goldstein, 1960; La Fave, 1965; Reiss, 1971)

Prosecutions:

Charges are more likely to be lodged against the defendant if the victims:

- are middle aged or elderly, white, and employed (Myers and Hagan, 1979)
- have high status in the community ("Prosecutorial Discretion," 1969)
- are women, and the offender is a male stranger (Myers, 1977)
- are women without a reputation for promiscuity (Newman, 1966)
- are not known to be homosexual (Newman, 1966)
- are not alcoholics or drug addicts (Williams, 1976)
- have no prior arrest record (Williams, 1976)
- can establish that they weren't engaged in misconduct themselves at the time of the crime (Miller, 1970; Neubauer, 1974; Williams, 1976)
- can prove that they didn't provoke the offender (Neubauer, 1974; Newman, 1966; Williams, 1976)
- can show that it wasn't a "private matter" between themselves and a relative, lover, friend, or acquaintance (McIntyre, 1968; Williams, 1976)

help from disadvantaged victims is eroded by a belief that these same people are offenders in other incidents. These stereotypical responses by the authorities poison relations between the two camps. From bitter experience, victims drawn from out-groups, the lower strata, and marginal lifestyles anticipate that their requests for intervention will be greeted with suspicion or even hostility. They expect perfunctory treatment at best. As a consequence, they turn to the criminal justice system only under the most desperate circumstances (Ziegenhagen, 1977).

With these observations in mind, the under-reporting of criminal incidents by victims can be interpreted to some degree as a result of alienation. Victims do not inform the authorities for many reasons; some are personal and would persist even if the criminal justice system were run more efficiently. But other reasons directly reflect the inadequacies of the system as the victims perceive them—the inability of the police to solve most cases and to recover most stolen property; the possibility of a second wound at the hands of the authorities; the frustrations of appearing as a witness for the prosecution; and the unsatisfactory resolutions of cases (whether the victims seek revenge, restitution, or rehabilitation of

- and the offender are not both black, and the incident is not viewed as "conforming to neighborhood subcultural norms" (McIntyre, 1968; Miller, 1970; Myers and Hagan, 1979; Newman, 1966)

Convictions:

A judge or a jury is more likely to find the defendant guilty if the victims:

- are employed in a high-status job (Myers, 1977)
- are perceived as being young and helpless (Myers, 1977)
- appear "reputable," with no prior arrest record (Kalven and Zeisel, 1966; Newman, 1966)
- had no prior illegal relationship with the defendant (Newman, 1966)
- in no way are thought to have provoked the offender (Kalven and Zeisel, 1966; Newman, 1966; Wolfgang, 1958)
- are white, and the defendants are black (Allredge, 1942; Bensing and Schroeder, 1960; Garfinkel, 1949; Johnson, 1941)
- and the offenders are not both black and are not viewed as acting in conformity to subcultural norms (McIntyre, 1968; Miller, 1970; Myers and Hagan, 1979; Newman, 1966)

Punishments:

A judge will hand down a stiffer sentence to a defendant if the victims:

- are employed in a high-status occupation (Myers, 1977)
- did not know the offender (Myers, 1977)
- were injured and didn't provoke the attack (Dawson, 1969; Neubauer, 1974)
- are white and the offenders are black (Green, 1964; Southern Regional Council, 1969; Wolfgang and Riedel, 1973)

the offenders). The administrators of the agencies within the system have acknowledged its shortcomings. For at least a decade, substantial amounts of resources have been directed toward research and demonstration projects to better serve victims. Yet the reporting rates (which symbolize a willingness to activate the criminal justice machinery) have not improved substantially. The stability of reporting rates indicates the stubbornness of the underlying problems. More than half of the victims of violent episodes and nearly three quarters of larceny victims are not turning toward a system that allegedly has been set up to serve them. (See table 5-4.)

Whose Interests Does the Criminal Justice System Serve?

The discovery of the many sources of conflict between victims and the agencies and officials designated to help them raises a crucial question: "Just whose interests are primarily served by the current operations of this system?" Answering this question is not merely an academic exer-

TABLE 5-4 Reporting Rates over the Years, According to the National Crime Surveys

	Percentage of incidents reported to survey interviewers that were also reported to the police								
	Years								
Type of crime	*1973*	*1974*	*1975*	*1976*	*1977*	*1978*	*1979*	*1980*	*1981*
Crimes of violence	46%	47%	47%	49%	46%	44%	45%	47%	47%
Rape	49%	52%	56%	53%	58%	49%	51%	41%	56%
Robbery	53%	54%	53%	53%	55%	51%	56%	57%	56%
Personal larcenies	22%	25%	26%	27%	25%	25%	24%	27%	27%
Household burglaries	47%	48%	49%	48%	49%	47%	48%	51%	51%

SOURCE: *Criminal Victimization in the U.S.: 1980–1981 Changes Based on New Estimates.* A Bureau Of Justice Statistics Technical Report, by Adolfo Paez, 1983, p. 3. Washington, D.C.: U.S. Department of Justice.

cise. How victims view themselves, the demands they make as clients of the criminal justice system, and the reforms they work for politically, all hang in the balance.

Does the System Serve Victims?

The traditional or official answer is that the justice system primarily serves the interests of "the people," or "society," and weak, disadvantaged groups in particular (Van den Haag, 1975). In a democratic society, all branches of government are supposed to be responsive to the will of the law-abiding majority.

The police are granted authority to maintain order, guarantee public safety, and protect the lives and property of the innocent. The prosecutorial offices should act as public law firms, with victims as their clients. Correctional officials are charged with the responsibility of supervising and rehabilitating dangerous criminals so that the streets might be safer.

The criminal justice system ought to place a high priority on satisfying the needs of victims, according to two rationales. The first argues on humanitarian grounds that crime victims, like people suffering from natural disasters (floods, tornadoes, fires) and economic dislocations (such as widespread unemployment) need assistance if their predicament is so great that they can't cope with it by themselves. If such help is not forthcoming, the restoration of victims as productive members of society is delayed. The second rationale asserts that the criminal justice system is obliged to intervene in behalf of the innocent, the injured, and the exploited and to serve as their forum for airing grievances against people and entities that have allegedly harmed them, because there is a social contract that binds members of society together. When rules are violated and losses inflicted, the government must intervene to restore order and harmony.

Assuming that the criminal justice system is designed to serve victims but doesn't satisfy their needs and wants very well today, then it simply needs some adjustment. There is no basis for any long-term conflict between victims and officials over how the system is administered.

Does the System Serve Its Own Bureaucratic Components?

Students of bureaucracy have noted that agencies primarily look after their own interests. Official actions are usually self-serving. Police administrators are most concerned about what is good for their department and profession. Prosecutors worry about their own futures and the well-being of their branch of government. Corrections departments are preoccupied with maintaining order within prisons and with making their jobs tolerable.

Like all bureaucracies, criminal justice agencies are subject to goal displacement. The men at the top may substitute unofficial goals, like minimizing strain and maximizing personal and group rewards, for the officially proclaimed goals of serving the public interest and aiding victims. Goal displacement occurs most readily in situations where decision makers exercise great discretion without fear that their hidden agenda will be detected and that they will be punished. Criminal justice officials are subjected to strong pressures to depart from their stated purposes and dispose of cases in ways that hide their mistakes, lighten their workload, and curry political favors (McDonald, 1979).

Criminal justice professionals have little incentive to act in conformity with the wishes and needs of victims, since they are not directly accountable to them, either legally or organizationally. Official priorities are to achieve high levels of productivity and to maintain smooth coordination with other components of the system. Victims are viewed as a resource to be drawn on, as needed, in the pursuit of organizational objectives that are usually only incidental to the satisfaction of the interests of the individual victims (Ziegenhagen, 1977). In everyday operations, whenever minor inconveniences to insiders (prosecutors, judges, defense attorneys) have to be balanced against major inconveniences to outsiders (defendants, victims, witnesses, jurors), insider interests will prevail (Ash, 1972).

If criminal justice agencies and officials act in ways that primarily serve their own interests at the expense of victims, then there is a basis for continuous conflict between the various contending parties. Any victories won by victims must come at the expense of the privileges and benefits currently enjoyed by the police, prosecutors, judges, and parole boards. Any empowerment of victims could threaten the discretion enjoyed by officials concerned mostly with looking after their own interests. Procedural reforms, like granting victims a greater role in setting bail, negotiating plea bargains, fixing sentences, or determining who gets paroled, are subject to co-optation (attempts to return power relationships to their earlier configuration).

Does the System Serve the Wealthy and Powerful?

The criminal justice system is a potent arm of the state. The question of whose interests are served by the system cannot be answered apart from the larger query "Whose interests does the government protect?"

A radical, critical view is that the state serves the interests of the wealthy and powerful more faithfully than those of any other groups, coalitions, or movements. In particular, the criminal justice system operates in ways that strengthen the control of giant corporations and rich people over other classes and constituencies in society.

The policies of the men at the summits of the criminal justice machinery help to foster an ideology that buttresses acceptance of the status quo and undermines support for movements seeking greater social, political, and economic equality. The strategy of top officials is to convince people that the system is shackled by misguided rules that compel them to neglect deserving victims but "coddle" undeserving criminals. This ploy works remarkably well in one respect: it deflects the discontent of "decent, hard-working, law-abiding taxpayers" away from the wealthy and powerful above them (who, it can be argued, are responsible for the social problems that beset American society) and redirects (misdirects) anger and frustration toward troublemakers below them. The formula that top criminal justice officials follow is simple enough: concentrate public concern and resources on predatory street crime, committed primarily by the destitute and desperate; at the same time, divert attention away from the reckless lawlessness of those at the top. The system's ineffectiveness makes more sense if it is presumed that the policies of the police, courts, and prisons are designed to fail (to reduce street crime) rather than succeed. Such failure is actually a successful accomplishment of the system's mission—to maintain a visible, frightening "criminal class" recruited from the ranks of marginal sectors of the population and then "schooled" and "hardened" in juvenile institutions and prisons (Reiman, 1979). If crime victims grow bitter and hostile due to unsatisfied needs, then the system has fulfilled its purpose. It has set individual against individual, social stratum against stratum, generation against generation, females against males, often race against race. People and groups who ought to be united find themselves divided. They are furious with one another, rather than with the conditions that generate street crime.

The criminal justice system might serve the wealthy and powerful in an additional way. It is "their" system to use against their opponents. The rules that pertain to street crimes and criminals also govern the handling of dissidents. Laws concerning searches for evidence, bail, trial procedures, prison conditions, and the unleashing of police power are applicable to political enemies as well as to "common criminals." The inadequacies of the criminal justice system in its fight against street crime provoke public alarm and disgust. In reaction, appeals are issued to strengthen the forces of law and order in the "war on crime." But as part of a package deal, the control of the government over its people is tightened at the same time. Crime fighting can become intertwined with political repression. In the name of convicting more criminals to satisfy more victims and to make the streets safer, vital due-process guarantees and civil liberties may be weakened or even nullified. Under the guise of cracking down on street crime, the wealthy and powerful can prosecute and imprison those who challenge their right to rule American society.

If the radical, critical view is correct, then it is understandable why most victims find themselves neglected or abused by the criminal justice system. The service it provides them as clients or consumers is unsatisfactory because it is not designed to operate for their benefit and is not chiefly accountable to them. It serves other masters.

References

AHRENS, JAMES; STEIN, JOHN; and YOUNG, MARLENE. 1980: *Law Enforcement and Victim Services.* Washington, D.C.: Aurora Associates.

ALLREDGE, E.P. 1942: "Why the South Leads the Nation in Murder and Manslaughter." *Quarterly Review,* 2:123–134.

ALPER, BENEDICT, and NICHOLS, LAWRENCE. 1981: *Beyond the Courtroom.* Lexington, Mass.: Lexington Books.

AMERICAN BAR ASSOCIATION COMMITTEE ON VICTIMS. 1979: *Reducing Victim/Witness Intimidation: A Package.* Washington, D.C.: ABA.

—— 1980: *Bar Leadership on Victim/Witness Assistance: A Criminal Justice Manual for State and Local Bar Associations.* Washington, D.C.: ABA.

AMIR, MENACHEM, and AMIR, DELILA. 1979: "Rape Crisis Centers: An Arena for Ideological Conflicts." *Victimology,* 4, 2:247–257.

ASH, MICHAEL. 1972: "On Witnesses: A Radical Critique of Criminal Court Procedures." *Notre Dame Lawyer,* 48 (December):386–425.

BEALL, GEORGE. 1980: "Negotiating the Disposition of Criminal Charges." *Trial,* October:10–13.

BENSING, ROBERT; and SCHROEDER, OLIVER. 1960: *Homicide in an Urban Community.* Springfield, Ill.: Charles C Thomas.

BLACK, DONALD. 1968: *Police Encounters and Social Organization.* Unpublished Ph.D. dissertation, University of Michigan.

BLUMBERG, ABRAHAM. 1967: *Criminal Justice.* Chicago: Quadrangle.

BOHMER, CAROL. 1974: "Judicial Attitudes toward Rape Victims." *Judicature,* 57 (February): 303–307.

BOLIN, DAVID. 1980: "The Pima County Victim/Witness Program: Analyzing Its Successes." *Evaluation and Change,* 7,1:120–126.

BUREAU OF JUSTICE STATISTICS. 1982: *Criminal Victimization in the United States, 1980.* Washington, D.C.: U.S. Government Printing Office.

"Burying Crime in Chicago." 1983: *Newsweek,* May 16:63.

"Chicago Police Found to Dismiss Cases Erroneously." 1983: *The New York Times,* May 2:A20.

DAWSON, ROBERT. 1969: *Sentencing: The Decision as to Type, Length, and Conditions of Sentence.* Boston: Little, Brown.

DEAN, CHARLES, and deBRUYN-KOPS, MARY. 1982: *The Crime and the Consequences of Rape.* Springfield, Ill.: Charles C Thomas.

DOCKSAI, MARY. 1979: "Victim/Witness Intimidation: What It Means." *Trial,* August:51–54.

FEDERAL BUREAU OF INVESTIGATION (FBI). 1953–: *Crime in the United States* (Uniform Crime Reports). Washington, D.C.: U.S. Government Printing Office. Selected years.

FORER, LOIS. 1980: *Criminals and Victims.* New York: Norton.

FRIED, JOSEPH. 1982: "Intimidation of Witnesses Called Widespread." *The New York Times,* May 2:51.

GARFINKLE, HAROLD. 1949: "Research Note on Inter- and Intra-Racial Homicides." *Social Forces,* 27(May):370–381.

GEIS, GILBERT. 1983: "Victim and Witness Assistance Programs." *Encyclopedia of Crime and Justice,* 1600–1604. New York: Free Press.

GEST, TED, and DAVIDSON, JOANNE. 1982: "Easing the Pain for Crime Victims." *U.S. News & World Report,* June 21:45.

GIACINTI, THOMAS. 1973: *Forcible Rape: The Offender and His Victim.* Unpublished master's thesis, Southern Illinois University.

GOLDSTEIN, JOSEPH. 1960: "Police Discretion Not to Invoke the Criminal Process." *Yale Law Journal,* 69(March):543–594.

GREEN, EDWARD. 1964: "Inter- and Intra-Racial Crime Relative to Sentencing." *Journal of Criminal Law, Criminology, and Police Science,* 55(September): 348–358.

HALL, DONALD. 1975: "The Role of the Victim in the Prosecution and Disposition of a Criminal Case." *Vanderbilt Law Review,* 28,5:932–985.

HALLECK, SEYMOUR. 1980: "Vengeance and Victimization." *Victimology,* 5,2: 99–109.

HARRIS, LOUIS. 1981: *A Pilot Survey of Crime Victims in New York State.* New York: Louis Harris.

HEINZ, ANNE, and KERSTETTER, WAYNE. 1979: "Pretrial Settlement Conference: Evaluation of a Reform in Plea Bargaining." *Law and Society Review,* 13,2:349–366.

HEINZ, JOHN. 1982: "On Justice to Victims." *The New York Times,* July 7:A19.

HERMAN, LAWRENCE. 1976: "What's Wrong with the Rape Reform Laws?" *Civil Liberties Review,* 3,5:60–73.

HERRINGTON, LOIS. 1982: "Statement of the Chairman." In the *Final Report* of the President's Task Force on Victims of Crime, vi–viii. Washington, D.C.: U.S. Government Printing Office.

JOHNSON, GUY. 1941: "The Negro and Crime." *Annals of the American Academy of Political and Social Science,* 217:93–104.

"Judge Defeated after Remarks in Rape Case." 1977: *Crime Control Digest,* September 12:7.

"Judge's Ruling on Teen Rapist Brings Storm of Protests." 1977: *Crime Control Digest,* May 30:7.

KALVEN, HARRY, and ZEISEL, HANS. 1966: *The American Jury.* Boston: Little, Brown.

KATZ, LEWIS. 1980: *The Justice Imperative: An Introduction to Criminal Justice.* Cincinnati: Anderson.

LA FAVE, WAYNE. 1965: *Arrest: The Decision to Take a Suspect into Custody.* Boston: Little, Brown.

LeGRAND, CAMILLE; REICH, JAY; and CHAPPELL, DUNCAN. 1977: *Forcible Rape: An Analysis of Legal Issues.* Washington, D.C.: U.S. Department of Justice.

LUNDMAN, RICHARD. 1980: *Police and Policing: An Introduction.* New York: Holt, Rinehart & Winston.

LYNCH, RICHARD. 1976: "Improving the Treatment of Victims: Some Guides for Action." In William McDonald (Ed.), *Criminal Justice and the Victim,* 165–176. Beverly Hills, Calif.: Sage.

MARTINSON, ROBERT. 1974: "What Works—Questions and Answers about Prison Reform." *Public Interest,* 35(Spring):22–54.

McDONALD, WILLIAM. 1976: "Criminal Justice and the Victim." In William McDonald (Ed.), *Criminal Justice and the Victim,*" 17–56. Beverly Hills, Calif.: Sage.

——— 1979: "The Prosecutor's Domain." In William McDonald (Ed.), *The Prosecutor,* 15–52. Beverly Hills, Calif.: Sage.

McINTYRE, DONALD. 1968: "A Study of Judicial Dominance of the Charging Decision." *Journal of Criminal Law, Criminology, and Police Science,* 59 (December): 463–490.

MENNINGER, KARL. 1968: *The Crime of Punishment.* New York: Viking.

MILLER, FRANK. 1970: *Prosecution: The Decision to Charge a Suspect with a Crime.* Boston: Little, Brown.

MYERS, MARTHA. 1977: *The Effects of Victim Characteristics on the Prosecution, Conviction, and Sentencing of Criminal Defendants.* Ann Arbor, Mich.: University Microfilms.

———, and HAGAN, JOHN. 1979: "Private and Public Trouble: Prosecutors and the Allocation of Court Resources." *Social Problems,* 26,4:439–451.

NATIONAL ADVISORY COMMISSION ON CRIMINAL JUSTICE STANDARDS AND GOALS. 1973: *The Courts.* Washington, D.C.: U.S. Government Printing Office.

NATIONAL INSTITUTE OF JUSTICE. 1982: *Exemplary Projects: Focus for 1982—Projects to Combat Violent Crime.* Washington, D.C.: U.S. Department of Justice.

"NDAA Strengthening Commitment to Victims." 1981: *Victim/Witness Support Center News,* 1, 2:3–4. Washington, D.C.: Aurora Associates.

NEUBAUER, DAVID. 1974: *Criminal Justice in Middle America.* Morristown, N.J.: General Learning Press.

NEWMAN, DONALD. 1966: *Conviction: The Determination of Guilt or Innocence without Trial.* Boston: Little, Brown.

O'REILLY, HARRY. 1980: "Victim–Witness Services: The Police Perspective." In Emilio Viano (Ed.), *Victim/Witness Programs: Human Services of the 1980s,* 14–35. Washington, D.C.: Visage.

PAEZ, ADOLFO. 1983: *Criminal Victimization in the U.S.: 1980–1981 Changes Based on New Estimates.* A Bureau of Justice Statistics Technical Report. Washington, D.C.: U.S. Department of Justice.

"Polygraphs and Other Perils." 1979: *Aegis,* July–August:10–11.

PRESIDENT'S TASK FORCE ON VICTIMS OF CRIME. 1982: *Final Report.* Washington, D.C.: U.S. Government Printing Office.

PRISON RESEARCH AND ACTION PROJECT. 1976: *Instead of Prisons.* Geneseo, N.Y.: Author.

"Prosecutorial Discretion in the Initiation of Criminal Complaints." 1969: *Southern California Law Review,* 42(Spring):519–545.

"Rape Victim Privacy." 1978: *Congressional Quarterly Almanac,* 34:196.

REIFF, ROBERT. 1979: *The Invisible Victim.* New York: Basic.

REILLY, JAMES. 1981: "Victim/Witness Services in Prosecutors' Offices." *Prosecutor,* October:8–11.

REIMAN, JEFFREY. 1979: *The Rich Get Richer and the Poor Get Prison: Ideology, Class, and Criminal Justice.* New York: Wiley.

REISS, ALBERT, Jr. 1971: *The Police and the Public.* New Haven, Conn.: Yale University Press.

RHODES, WILLIAM. 1978: *Plea Bargaining: Who Gains? Who Loses?* PROMIS Research Project No. 14. Washington, D.C.: Institute for Law and Social Research.

ROSENBLUM, ROBERT, and BLEW, CAROL. 1979: *Victim/Witness Assistance.* Washington, D.C.: U.S. Government Printing Office.

SCHNEIDER, ANNE, and SCHNEIDER, PETER. 1981: "Victim Assistance Programs." In Burt Galaway and Joe Hudson (Eds.), *Perspectives on Crime Victims,* 364–373. St. Louis, Mo: Mosby.

SHELDEN, RANDALL. 1982: *Criminal Justice in America: A Sociological Approach.* Boston: Little, Brown.

SHELEY, JOSEPH. 1979: *Understanding Crime.* Belmont, Calif.: Wadsworth.

SIGLER, JAY. 1979: "The Prosecutor: A Comparative Functional Analysis." In William McDonald (Ed.), *The Prosecutor,* 53–74. Beverly Hills, Calif.: Sage.

SKOLNICK, JEROME. 1966: *Justice without Trial: Law Enforcement in a Democratic Society.* New York: Wiley.

SOUTHERN REGIONAL COUNCIL. 1969: *Race Makes the Difference: An Analysis of Sentence Disparity among Black and White Offenders in Southern Prisons.* Atlanta: Author.

STERNBERG, DAVID. 1971: "The New Radical–Criminal Trials: A Step toward a Class-for-Itself in the American Proletariat?" *Science and Society,* Fall:274–301.

SUTHERLAND, EDWIN, and CRESSEY, DONALD. 1974: *Criminology* (9th edition). Philadelphia: Lippincott.

SYMONDS, MARTIN. 1975: "Victims of Violence: Psychological Effects and After-Effects. *American Journal of Psychoanalysis,* 35:19–26.

—— 1980: "The 'Second Injury' to Victims." *Evaluation and Change,* 7,1: 36–38.

UNITED PRESS INTERNATIONAL. 1982: "Are Rape Laws too Tough?: Lawyers Fear Killing of Victims to Avoid Witnesses." *The New York Daily News,* December: 1:4.

VAN DEN HAAG, ERNEST. 1975: *Punishing Criminals.* New York: Basic.

WARRIOR, BETSY. 1977: "Transition House Shelters Battered Women." *Sister Courage* (Boston), February:12.

WHITCOMB, DEBRA; DAY, DEBRA; and STUDEN, LAURA. 1979: *Stop Rape Crisis Center, Baton Rouge, Louisiana: An Exemplary Project.* Washington, D.C.: U.S. Department of Justice.

WILLIAMS, JOYCE, and HOLMES, KAREN. 1981: *The Second Assault: Rape and Public Attitudes.* Westport, Conn.: Greenwood Press.

WILLIAMS, KRISTEN. 1976: "The Effects of Victim Characteristics on the Disposition of Violent Crimes." In William McDonald (Ed.), *Criminal Justice and the Victim,* 177–214. Beverly Hills, Calif.: Sage.

—— 1978: *The Effects of Victim Characteristics on Judicial Decisions.* PROMIS Research Project Report. Washington, D.C.: Institute for Law and Social Research.

WOLFGANG, MARVIN. 1958: *Patterns in Criminal Homicide.* Philadelphia: University of Pennsylvania Press.

——, and RIEDEL, MARC. 1973: "Race, Judicial Discretion, and the Death Penalty." *Annals of the Academy of Political and Social Science,* 407(May): 119–133.

WRIGHT, ERIK. 1973: *The Politics of Punishment.* New York: Harper & Row.

ZIEGENHAGEN, EDUARD. 1977: *Victims, Crime, and Social Control.* New York: Praeger.

CHAPTER 6

Restitution by the Offender to the Victim

Back to Basics?

- A teenager convicted of purse snatching is ordered to serve as his victim's escort and errand boy for one year. Every weekend he must accompany the elderly widow to the supermarket and carry her packages home.
- A dentist convicted of vehicular manslaughter for killing a motorcyclist while driving drunk is required to fix the teeth of poor patients at his own expense for two years.
- A heroin addict is caught breaking into the trunk of a parked car. A job is found for him by the court. He must pay the victim 10 percent of his paycheck until his debt is worked off.

These kinds of "alternative," "creative," or "constructive" sentences herald a renewed interest in restitution to crime victims.

As they finish serving their time behind bars, convicts are told that they have paid their debt to society. But their victims often wonder, "How about the debt owed to me?" It seems that the criminal justice system shows concern for the state, society, and itself at the expense of the immediate victims' needs and rights. Using victims merely as complainants to initiate criminal proceedings and as witnesses to secure convictions, the system limits their "satisfaction" to retribution. Those who want monetary satisfaction are steered away from criminal court to civil court.

Advocates of restitution—and there are many—argue that it's time to get back to basics. Victims shouldn't be neglected by a system ostensibly set up to look after their interests. Criminal acts are more than symbolic assaults against abstractions like the social order or public safety; real flesh-and-blood people suffer losses. Offenders shouldn't be prosecuted solely on behalf of the state or "the people." Justice demands that victims be "made whole again"—restored to their condition before the crime occurred. Convicts must right wrongs, make amends, and repair what they've damaged. Their sentences ought to fit their crimes. When restitution is restored to its rightful place, criminals will routinely repay their victims, removing the profit from crime.

Restitution refers to the responsibility that offenders bear to their victims. Compensation refers to the financial obligations of governmental agencies to reimburse suffering citizens, or of third parties like insurance companies to indemnify their customers. Restitution and compensation are alternative methods of repaying losses.

Restitution occurs whenever authorized officials of the criminal justice system impose sanctions that require offenders to either return stolen goods to their owners, hand over equivalent amounts of money to cover out-of-pocket expenses, or provide services to those they have harmed. Four combinations of restitution arrangements are possible: payments by the offender to the actual victim, perhaps through an intermediary (the most common); earnings shared with some community agency or group serving as a substitute victim (rather than a fine collected by the government); personal services performed by the offender to benefit the victim (an uncommon outcome); and labor donated by the offender for the good of the community (frequently ordered) (Galaway, 1977).

Full restitution through sustained effort is preferred over payments by offenders from their savings or from their ill-gotten gains. Partial restitution is often the only realistic goal. "Symbolic restitution" (see Harris, 1979) to substitute victims seems appropriate when society as a whole has been menaced, when the immediate casualties can't be found, or when the victims don't want to accept the offenders' aid. "Creative restitution" (Eglash, 1977), an ideal solution, occurs when offenders, on their own initiative, go beyond what the law or their sentence requires, exceed other people's expectations, and leave the victims better off than they were before the crimes took place.

Usually, wrongs are righted in a straightforward manner. Litterbugs clean up the mess they have made. Adolescent graffiti artists scrub off their spray-painted signatures. Burglars repay cash for the loot they have carted away. Embezzlers return stolen funds to the company.

Occasionally, "client-specific" punishments are tailored to fit the crime, the criminal, and unmet community needs. These sentences provide alternatives to the traditional sanctions of fines and confinement. For example, a drunken driver does several months of voluntary labor in a hospital emergency room to see, first hand, the consequences of his kind of recklessness. A law student caught shoplifting avoids a criminal record by spending time giving legal advice to clients too poor to pay for it. A movie executive, who confessed to forging company checks, produces a film about drug abuse at his own expense. A teenage robber, who preys on the elderly, is ordered to work weekends at a nursing home. Such sentences anger those who are convinced that imprisonment is the answer: "If you do the crime, you must do the time." But such dispositions are favored by reformers who want to reduce prison overcrowding, cut the tax burden of incarceration, and shield first offenders and petty criminals from the corrupting influences of the prison subculture ("Fitting Justice?" 1978; Seligmann and Maor, 1980; "When Judges Make the Punishment Fit the Crime," 1978).

The idea of making criminals repay their victims is an ancient one. The groundswell of support for its revival is due to a recognition of the glaring inadequacies of private insurance coverage, governmental compensation plans, and civil lawsuits as means of recovering losses. Yet the principles on which sentiment for restitution is based are deceptively simple. Thorny problems arise at every turn when theory is translated into practice. Enthusiasm over restitution today is reminiscent of the unfounded optimism that greeted earlier "sweeping reforms" that were intended to restore equity and bring about justice: the substitution of imprisonment for corporal and capital punishment; the establishment of a treatment-oriented juvenile justice system to supplant a punitive one; and the replacement of fixed-term sentences by indeterminate ones. The future of restitution remains uncertain. Its history reveals both its promises and its pitfalls.

The Rise, Fall, and Revival of Restitution

In the ages before formal law and criminal justice, spontaneous revenge was surely the gut reaction to attack. Victims sought to "get even" with aggressors by inflicting physical injuries and by taking back things of value. When possible, victims would counterattack so ferociously that their assailants would end up victimized. But as groups accumulated riches and primitive societies established rules of conduct, the tradition of retaliatory violence gave way to negotiation and reparation. Money or goods changed hands as repayments for wrongful acts in the interest of community harmony. Financial settlements led to truces rather than interminable, escalating feuds.

Compulsory restitution became institutionalized in the societies of antiquity. The Code of Hammurabi decreed that offenders repay victims as much as thirty times the amount of damage they had caused. The laws of Moses specified that a guilty party had to make five-fold restitution to the injured party for stealing an ox. Under Roman law, robbers had to pay back four times the value of what they had taken.

These restitution guidelines went beyond any formula of "an eye for an eye and a tooth for a tooth." Restitution was intended to satisfy victims' thirst for vengeance, as well as to reimburse them for their losses. The transaction was also designed to encourage a lasting settlement ("composition") between the parties in order to avoid any further strife (Schafer, 1970).

By the ninth century in Britain, an offender was supposed to restore peace and harmony by offering payments—a "bot" (or "bote") to the victim and a "wer" (or "wergild") to the victim's kin. An official list spelled out exact penalties attached to specified acts. (For example, a person who knocked out another's teeth would have to pay a certain sum of composition to the injured party, depending on precisely which teeth had been lost.) Private retaliation was permissible only if the offender refused the victim's demands for repayment. Anyone in the community could kill such an outlaw.

But fragmentary historical records confirm the suspicion that in a society with sharply defined classes, restitution worked to the advantage of the upper crust. If they were powerful enough, guilty parties could scoff at the claims of their social "inferiors." If compelled to settle accounts, the affluent could easily make fiscal atonement for even the most outrageous breaches of law through relatively inconsequential composition payments of gold, cattle, land, or other valuables. On the other hand, offenses by the marginal against the mighty were not so readily resolved. The amounts specified were often beyond the grasp of the common folk. Those who could not meet their obligations were branded as outlaws or were forced to sell themselves into virtual slavery. Restitution functioned as one of many mechanisms that made the rich richer and the poor poorer (Geis, 1977).

During the next few centuries, restitution underwent changes. As the power of the feudal aristocracy and of nation-states congealed, royal officials drew up regulations to formalize the process of redressing grievances between subjects. Public involvement in what were formerly considered to be private matters was justified on several grounds: to more effectively preserve peace; to curb brutality, extortion, and exploitation of the weak by the strong; and to raise revenue for the Crown. Offenders became obligated to repay the state for its services, as well as to reimburse their victims for their losses. The nobility extracted a "wite" as a fee for supervising reconciliation between the two parties and for guaranteeing protection to the offenders from any retaliation by the victims or their kin. By the twelfth century, the victim's bot and the kin's wer were shrinking, while the wite paid to the treasury was growing.

The expansion of the state's interest in resolving criminal matters was solidified with the emergence of a category of "bootless" crimes considered so heinous that no transfer of money could restore social equilibrium. The offender had to pay in blood. As the concept evolved, the state as protector of the "King's peace" and "public order" began to define itself as the injured party, in most crimes. Its demands to punish transgressors and to collect fines from them soon crowded out the victim's right to recover damages. Under a law of forfeiture, the Crown could seize whatever property a felon owned (Mueller and Cooper, 1973; Younger, 1977).

In America before the Revolution, criminal acts were viewed primarily as injuries to individuals. Police departments and public prosecutors did not exist. Victims in cities could call for help from nightwatchmen, but they might not be on duty or the offenders could flee beyond their jurisdiction. If victims sought the aid of sheriffs, they were charged a fee. If the sheriffs located the alleged perpetrators, they would charge extra to serve criminal warrants. With the defendants in custody, victims hired attorneys to draw up indictments; then victims either prosecuted the cases by themselves, or hired attorneys at additional fees to handle the prosecution for them. If successful, victims reaped substantial benefits. Persons convicted of theft were required to pay their victims three times as much as had been stolen. If the thieves could not hand over such amounts, they were assigned to their victims as servants until their debts were paid off. If the victims wished, they could sell these indentured servants for a hefty price and had one month in which to find a buyer. After that, they were responsible for the costs of maintaining the offenders in jail; if they didn't pay, the convicts were released.

In the years following the American Revolution, the criminal justice system set up by the British in the colonies underwent substantial changes. Reformers were concerned about the built-in injustices of procedures in which only wealthy victims could afford to purchase law enforcement by hiring sheriffs, private detectives, and attorneys, and by posting rewards. Public prosecutors were established by state and local governments. Prison systems were constructed to house offenders. Crimes became acts against the state. The redress of individual grievances was no longer regarded as the primary function of the criminal justice process (McDonald, 1977).

A distinction developed within English and American common law between "crimes" and "torts" (although this separation never crystallized on the European continent or in Latin American legal systems). Crimes were offenses against the state, and torts were the corresponding wrongful acts that harmed the immediate victims. Criminals were forced by the state to pay their debt to society through fines and other punishments. Victims who wanted to try to force criminals to pay their personal debts were shunted to separate arenas—civil courts rather than criminal courts.

Within the Anglo-American framework, criminal law and civil law have drifted apart. Each has evolved its own codes, rules, administrative practices, and sets of consequences. For instance, in criminal law a higher standard of proof was required—guilt beyond a reasonable doubt—

whereas under civil law a judgment could be won on the basis of a preponderance of the evidence. Of the two branches of law, criminal matters took precedence over civil matters. Maintaining the security of the entire community was deemed more vital than alleviating the financial hardships of private individuals. When suspects were apprehended, the rule was that any civil actions that victims wanted to initiate had to be postponed until criminal proceedings had been resolved. In practice, this usually meant that victims were denied any chance of repayment and had to content themselves with the satisfaction of knowing that the state was making the criminals suffer through harsh punishments.

As soon as restitution fell into disuse, leading figures in legal philosophy and criminology called for its revival. In his book *Utopia* in 1516, Sir Thomas More proposed that offenders labor on public works projects. The English utilitarian philosopher Jeremy Bentham advocated mandatory restitution for property offenses. Bonneville de Marsengy, the French jurist, developed a plan in 1847 that combined restitution with compensation from state funds. A number of criminologists, including the Italian Raffaele Garofalo and the Belgian Adolphe Prins, introduced restitution resolutions at international prison congresses around the turn of the century. Enrico Ferri raised the issue in Italy in the 1920s, and the penal reformer Margery Fry rekindled support for restitution in England during the 1950s (Jacob, 1977; Schafer, 1970).

In 1967, the President's Commission on Law Enforcement and the Administration of Justice recommended restitution by convicts, and it suggested the repeal of laws passed during the Great Depression that crippled prison industries by restricting the sale of inmate-made products. During the 1970s, model sentencing proposals of the American Law Institute, the American Bar Association, and the National Advisory Commission on Criminal Justice Standards and Goals embraced restitution as one of several possible sanctions, as did the U.S. Supreme Court. Reform groups, like the American Correctional Association and the National Moratorium on Prison Construction, also favor restitution. But the implementation of restitution remains haphazard, largely depending on the discretion exercised by individual judges and probation departments (Harland, 1981; Leepson, 1982).

Opportunities versus Obstacles

Possibilities

Restitution is an extremely flexible sanction, which is not being used to its full potential within the criminal justice system. Restitution by the offender to the victim is possible at every juncture, from the immediate aftermath of the crime up until the final moments of parole supervision following a period of imprisonment. (See figure 6-1.)

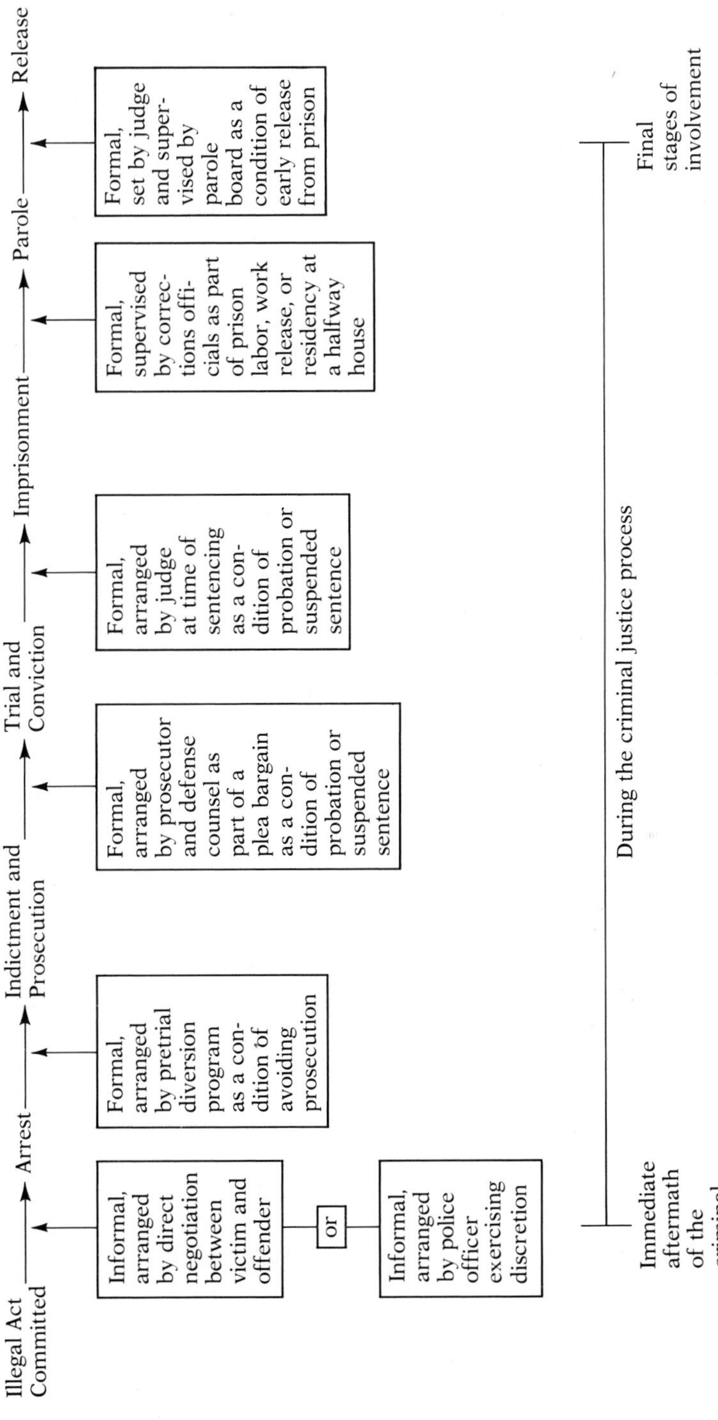
Illegal Act Committed
Arrest
Indictment and Prosecution
Trial and Conviction
Imprisonment
Parole
Release
Informal, arranged by direct negotiation between victim and offender
or
Informal, arranged by police officer exercising discretion
Formal, arranged by pretrial diversion program as a condition of avoiding prosecution
Formal, arranged by prosecutor and defense counsel as part of a plea bargain as a condition of probation or suspended sentence
Formal, arranged by judge at time of sentencing as a condition of probation or suspended sentence
Formal, supervised by corrections officials as part of prison labor, work release, or residency at a halfway house
Formal, set by judge and supervised by parole board as a condition of early release from prison
Immediate aftermath of the criminal act
During the criminal justice process
Final stages of involvement

FIGURE 6-1. Opportunities to make restitution

As soon as an offender is apprehended, an informal restitution arrangement can settle the matter. The victim might negotiate directly with the offender or with a representative. For example, a storekeeper might order a shoplifter to put the stolen item back on the shelf and never return to the premises; parents might offer to pay for their son's act of vandalism in slashing the tires of a neighbor's parked car. Similarly, a police officer can pressure a suspect to make restitution on the spot to the victim in lieu of arrest. In most states, however, serious offenses cannot be resolved in this manner. It is a felony for an injured party to demand or accept from an offender any payment as "hush money" to conceal a serious crime, in return for not pressing charges, or as a motive for discontinuing cooperation with the authorities in an investigation or prosecution. A criminal act is an offense against the state in addition to a particular person and cannot be settled privately (Laster, 1970).

If a suspect is arrested, an agreement can be worked out with a diversion program as an alternative to formal prosecution. If a defendant is indicted, the District Attorney's Office might make restitution a condition for dismissing formal criminal charges. When prosecution is initiated, restitution can be part of the plea bargain struck by the defense lawyer and the district attorney, wherein the accused concedes guilt in return for lesser penalties. Restitution is particularly appropriate as a condition of probation or of a suspended sentence. If incarcerated, a prisoner might get a chance to repay the victim from earnings derived from labor in prison, from an outside job while on work release, or when residing at a halfway house. Restitution can easily be included as a condition of parole, after a period of imprisonment.

Restitution contracts can be administered by the entire spectrum of parties concerned about the crime problem: community groups, private and nonprofit charitable and religious organizations, juvenile courts, adult criminal courts, probation departments, corrections departments, and parole boards.

Five kinds of restitution programs can be recognized (Schneider and Schneider, 1980). In the "basic restitution" model, offenders pay the court, and the court forwards the money to the victims. In the "expanded basic restitution" model, jobs are found for offenders (especially low-income youths). In the "victim assistance" model, projects subsidize the offenders' employment, making it more likely victims will receive full reimbursement. In "victim assistance–offender accountability" programs, settlements satisfactory to both parties are negotiated, sometimes in face-to-face meetings. Finally, in the "community accountability–deterrence" model, a panel of community representatives sets the amount that must be repaid, chooses the jobs that must be done, and schedules the repayments. A few of the hundreds of formal local restitution programs that have sprung up across the country illustrate how versatile repayment arrangements can be (see box 6-1, pp. 184–185).

Limitations

As promising as restitution is, it is not the answer for most victims. Only a small percentage will ever get anything back from those who have harmed them. The problem is directly comparable to the situation faced by victims who seek satisfaction from retribution. Just as most criminals escape punishment, most also evade restitution obligations. The situation has been labeled "funneling," or "shrinkage," and has been likened to a leaky net. At the outset, there are many cases, involving large numbers of victims and criminals, that are appropriate for restitution. But after these cases have been processed by the criminal justice system, only a relative handful of restitution arrangements result. All the other cases have slipped through the net (see figure 6-2).

Not all crimes are reported to the police. A large proportion of offenders (the percentage varies dramatically with the type of crime) immediately drop out of the picture. The police don't respond to some calls, which they deem inconsequential. They fail to solve most property crimes and many violent crimes (with the exception of homicides). So, early in the criminal justice process, most victims have already been eliminated from any chance of receiving restitution.

Some arrestees are not indicted or, if indicted, are never prosecuted because the cases are considered weak and unwinnable in court, or are

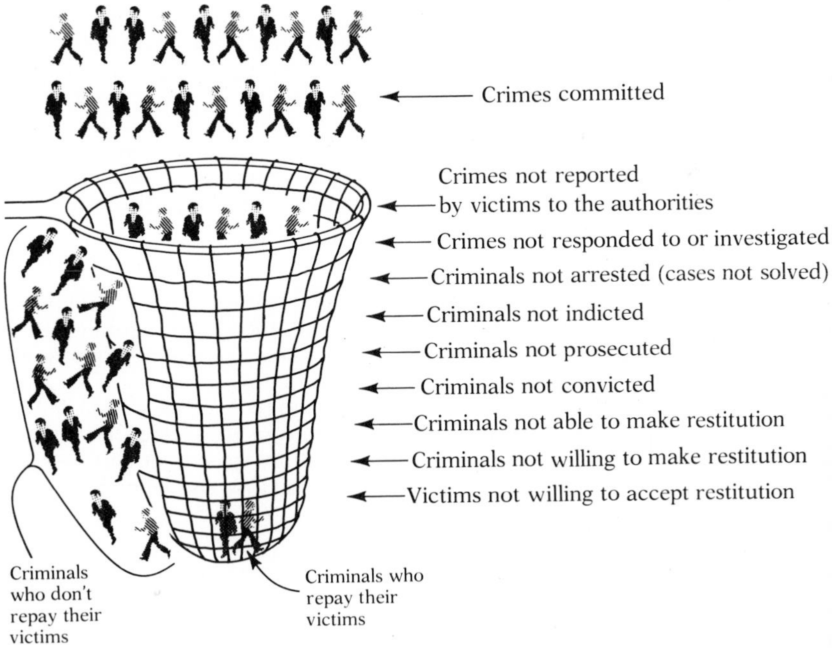

FIGURE 6-2. Funneling, or shrinkage—the leaky net

of a low priority. The overwhelming majority of cases (upwards of 90 percent in urban jurisdictions) are resolved through plea bargains, which involve dropping charges or dropping counts. Many victims are eliminated from consideration in this manner.

Some cases that go to trial result in acquittals, and some convictions are reversed on appeal. Of those who are convicted or who plead guilty, not all are willing or able to repay their victims. Those who are incarcerated discover that prison labor is demeaning and extremely low paid. Work release is a privilege reserved for a select few. Prisoners granted parole have trouble finding any work, let alone a job that pays enough to allow the subtraction of meaningful payments after all the other deductions. In sum, although restitution is often possible, it is not, statistically speaking, probable.

BOX 6-1 Restitution in Action: Where Crime Doesn't Pay

Minnesota

The Minnesota Restitution Center was a community-based residential placement (halfway house) for paroled property offenders. It was set up in 1972 with the help of a federal grant. Restitution contracts were drawn up by four parties: the victim, the offender, a staff member from the center, and a representative of the corrections department. Face-to-face negotiations occurred between the offender and the victim about half the time. A victim who did not want to take part could veto the offender's participation in the program.

Most offenders repaid their victims by making deposits from their earnings into the victims' bank accounts. During the three years of the program's operation, the average amount contracted for by eighty-seven parolees was roughly $400 each. But only about two-thirds of the promised sums typically ever reached victims. Contracts were not completed because some offenders violated the conditions of their parole and were returned to prison; others became fugitives or died; and the rest finished their stint on parole before all they owed had been repaid (Hudson and Chesney, 1978).

Iowa

In 1974, the Iowa Legislature mandated restitution as a condition of either a suspended sentence or probation. Full restitution is not required if the offenders' earning capacity is limited. Offenders can request a hearing about some aspect of the restitution contract they object to, but victims have no similar right. However, victims do not relinquish their right to try to recover additional damages in civil court when they accept (criminal) court-ordered restitution. Defendants who fail to comply in good faith with the restitution agreement can be considered in violation of the terms of their probation, and they risk being imprisoned (Vogelgesang, 1975).

Georgia

In 1975, Georgia, with federal assistance, set up several community restitution

Divergent Goals, Clashing Philosophies

Restitution is often rejected as an option because other considerations come first: punishing offenders to teach them a lesson and to deter potential criminals from following their example; treating offenders so they can be released back into the community as rehabilitated; or incapacitating them through confinement because they are believed to be dangerous. But some advocates of restitution have been advancing this ancient practice as a new form of punishment as well as a new method of rehabilitation. Other champions of restitution emphasize its positive impact on victims. Although all these pro-restitution forces are united in their goal of promoting the adoption of restitution within the criminal justice system, they are divided over priorities. As a result, opposing

---

programs run by the corrections department for probationers and parolees. These halfway houses charge their residents for room and board. The remainder of their earnings goes to their victims, to taxes, to the offenders' families, and to their savings accounts (Read, 1977).

Maryland

The Community Arbitration Program was established in Anne Arundel County in 1975 as a diversion project for juvenile misdemeanants. Restitution settlements are worked out at informal meetings between the youths, their parents, and the victims. A juvenile intake officer, usually a local attorney, serves as an arbitrator, determines the "adjustment," and sentences the youngsters to a specified number of hours of community work. If the offense was serious, if the youths insist they are innocent, or if their parents request a formal hearing, the case is forwarded to the state attorney and then to juvenile court (National Institute of Justice, 1981).

Juvenile Courts across the Country

A survey of 133 juvenile courts selected at random from a total of 3,544 jurisdictions found that in the mid-1970s:

- As much as 86 percent of all juvenile courts in the sample occasionally ordered offenders to make restitution.
- For the past 17 years, on the average, restitution had been a possible sentence.
- An average of 38 percent of all cases involved restitution as part of the sentence.
- About 70 percent of all crimes against property led to restitution obligations.
- In 45 percent of all robbery cases, restitution was ordered.
- In 25 percent of all assault cases, restitution was ordered.
- In 10 percent of all sex offenses, restitution was ordered.
- Most restitution obligations were a condition of probation. Compliance rates were high in most jurisdictions (Schneider, Schneider, Reiter, and Cleary, 1977).

---

camps with divergent aims and philosophies are pushing restitution but are pulling at newly established programs from different directions.

Restitution as a Means of Repaying Victims

Those who advance restitution primarily as a way of helping victims (see Barnett, 1977; McDonald, 1978) argue that the present punitive-oriented criminal justice system offers victims few incentives to get involved. Those who cooperate with the police and prosecutors incur additional losses of time and money for their trouble (for example, attending lineups and appearing in court). They also run a greater risk of retaliation by the offender. In return, they get nothing tangible—only the sense that they have discharged their civic duty by assisting in the apprehension, prosecution, and conviction of a disruptive or dangerous person, generally a social obligation that goes largely unappreciated. The only satisfaction the system provides is revenge. But when restitution is incorporated into the criminal justice process, cooperation really pays off.

Restitution enthusiasts who espouse the cause of victims want to give them formal input into decision making, perhaps even veto power over certain outcomes that threaten their interests. From the standpoint of victims, reimbursement should be as comprehensive as possible. The criminal ought to pay back all stolen cash plus the current replacement value of any lost or damaged property, any outstanding medical bills stemming from crime-related injuries (including psychological wounds attended to by therapists and counselors), any wages lost because of absence from work (including sick days or vacation time used up during the period of recuperation or while cooperating with the police and prosecutors), plus any crime-related miscellaneous expenses (such as the cost of renting a car to replace one that was stolen or the expense of hiring a baby-sitter when testifying in court). It is to the victims' advantage that repayment be as prompt as possible, since they foot the bill in the interim.

Restitution as a Means of Rehabilitating Offenders

Advocates of restitution who are entirely focused on satisfying the victim clash with those who look to restitution as a means of treating offenders. If restitution is to be therapeutic for offenders (see Prison Research, 1976; Keve, 1978), their needs and wants must be given a higher priority than any contradictory demands from the victims. Instead of being punished through suffering for doing something against the law, the wrongdoers must be humanized and sensitized to the disruption and distress that their illegal actions have brought about. Learning about the victim's plight, they realize the injurious consequences and human toll of their deeds. By expending effort, sacrificing time and convenience, and performing meaningful tasks that undo the damage they have caused, they begin to understand their personal responsibilities and social obligations. By making fiscal atonement or contributing services, they can feel cleared of guilt, morally redeemed, and reaccepted. Through their hard work to defray the victim's losses, they can gain a sense of accomplishment and self-respect from their legitimate achievements. Perhaps they will develop work skills, self-discipline, and valuable on-the-job experience as they earn their way back into harmony with a community from which they previously felt estrangement and hostility. Restitution makes reconciliation possible.

If restitution is to be therapeutic, offenders must perceive the obligations as logical, relevant, just, and fair. They must be convinced to voluntarily undertake efforts to reimburse the victim because it is in their own best interest as well as being "the right thing to do."

Predictably, offenders will define their interest as minimizing any penalty for lawbreaking. This includes minimizing restitution, even if it is offered as a substitute for serving time behind bars. Since supervision and restrictions on liberty (either probation or parole) are punishments in themselves, offenders will want to escape the clutches of the criminal justice system as fast as possible. They will want to get the restitution obligation over with as quickly as they can. On this issue they are in accord with the victims, who want speedy reimbursement. However, if the amount of restitution is large and their earnings are modest, offenders may want to stretch out the payments (like a consumer on the installment plan), so that their pay checks are not "taxed" so drastically. But payments that trickle in will aggravate impatient victims, serving as a continuous irritant and reminder of the original incident.

However, the real quarrel over conflicting interests is likely to erupt over the total amount to be repaid. Offenders will underestimate the suffering they have caused, while victims may tend to overestimate their losses. Offenders might grudgingly concede to pay the depreciated value of any stolen or damaged goods (as insurance companies do), but victims could insist on its current replacement value (especially during inflationary times). Victims may want to extract as much as they can from offenders, regardless of the counterproductive consequences this might have on the therapeutic value of restitution. Offenders will probably balk at paying for indirect expenses, maintaining that the victims are trying to reverse roles and victimize them through fraud or exaggeration (see McKnight, 1981). Overburdened and embittered offenders could be driven to commit new crimes to quickly raise cash to pay off their restitution debts (literally robbing Peter to pay Paul), just as prostitutes must work harder to pay off fines imposed by the state. The sensibilities of offenders must be taken into account, since their compliance in shouldering the burden of restitution is the key to the success of this "treatment." The advocates of restitution as a means of rehabilitation want compromise solutions, either negotiated or arbitrated, that are acceptable to offenders even if they are less than fully satisfying to victims.

Restitution as a Means of Punishing Offenders

Victims and their pro-restitution allies also come into conflict with people who advocate restitution as a means of punishment and deterrence. Those who view restitution as an additional penalty (see Schafer, 1977; Tittle, 1978) argue that for too long offenders have been able to shirk their responsibility to the victim. First they should suffer incarceration to pay their debt to society for violating norms that embody cherished values and maintain social stability. Next they should undertake strenuous efforts to repay the specific individuals they have harmed. Only then can their entanglement with the criminal justice system come to an end. The problem with this approach, from the victims' standpoint, is that repayment is delayed for many years. Since few convicts can earn decent wages behind prison walls, the slow process of reimbursement cannot begin until the period of incarceration is over, either when the sentence expires or on the granting of parole. When punishment takes priority over reimbursement, the victims' needs are subordinated to the interests of the state. As long as prison labor is poorly paid, restitution and punishment are incompatible.

Unresolved Issues

Some key questions about the applicability of restitution remain unanswered because of the divergent goals and philosophies of restitution advocates that have just been examined (see Edelhertz, 1977; Galaway and Hudson, 1975; Gottesman and Mountz, 1979; Harland, 1981).

Cases of Shared Responsibility

In a situation where the victim is partly to blame for what happened (as in an aggravated assault that was provoked), it would seem fair to require less-than-full restitution by the offender. But if partial restitution is the solution to cases of shared responsibility, then offenders have an incentive during the negotiation of a restitution contract to derogate victims as having asked for trouble and having deserved their fate. This incentive undermines the therapeutic aspect of making amends as a means of reconciliation. On the other hand, if the victim's precipitation or provocation is disregarded as a mitigating factor, the offender will consider the terms of the settlement unjust.

A Privilege or a Right?

If receiving restitution becomes a right of victims on conviction of the offenders, then victims ought to have an institutionalized role in criminal justice decision making in order to protect their interests. Without mandatory restitution, only a select few enjoy the privilege of being repaid. With it, the discretion of prosecutors, judges, probation departments, and parole boards would be limited—something they oppose.

Restitution by the Not Guilty

Offenders who are not formally convicted may be offered the possibility of making restitution as an alternative to prosecution in diversion programs. But the Thirteenth Amendment to the Constitution prohibits involuntary servitude, except as a punishment for a crime on conviction. Further, the Fourteenth Amendment prohibits the government from taking away a person's property or liberty without due process of law. Hence, accused persons can't be coerced into repaying anyone, and they must be granted the right to challenge their participation in a restitution program once they are in it.

Immediate Payments to Victims

Private insurance companies pay their policyholders reasonably quickly (whether or not anyone is caught and convicted for the crime). A government fund could do likewise, granting the victim immediate reimbursement. Later, the agency could recover the money by garnishing the offender's wages. In some jurisdictions, however, appellate courts have ruled that only direct victims, and not third parties (agencies), can collect restitution (Harland, 1979).

Needs and Abilities

Some programs take into account both the offender's ability to pay and the victim's need for reimbursement. It would be a violation of the equal protection clause of the Fourteenth Amendment to discriminate against an entire class of criminals, denying them the chance to make restitution and avoid imprisonment simply because they lacked marketable skills. (In fact, this problem may have contributed to their involvement in street crime in the first place.) Yet this discriminatory practice is already evident. The typical participant in a restitution program is a white, middle-class, first-time property offender. The reason that poorer, less educated convicts are excluded might be an admissions criterion of "perceived ability to repay the victim" (Hudson and Chesney, 1978).

Businesses are the most common type of victim currently receiving reimbursement. This presents a problem if restitution is viewed as a tool for rehabilitation. Offenders compelled to repay an insurance company, chain store, or another prosperous enterprise may interpret the arrangement as unnecessary and therefore unjust. This may fuel their resentment of the way the criminal justice system works and the way society treats them (Harland, 1981:20). If a "means test" or hardship criterion were imposed on victims, eliminating from eligibility those entities and households that could afford the loss, this problem of perception could be alleviated. But then some well-off victims would feel discriminated against, and some businesses might be viewed as "fair game" by criminals.

Restitution for Violent Crime

Most restitution cases involve crimes against property committed by first-time offenders and petty criminals. If violent offenders are eliminated from consideration, then the possibilities of restitution are slashed dramatically. Although crimes against property outnumber crimes against people by a ratio of about nine to one, most property crimes are never solved, whereas a sizable proportion of violent crimes are cleared by arrest. The history of restitution shows that at various times and places payment schedules have been worked out to resolve nearly every kind of offense, including the most vicious acts. In tort law (civil proceedings), monetary values have been calculated for all sorts of injuries, from loss of prestige to loss of life. In certain cases, the victims (and their kin or survivors) might demand restitution from violent offenders; but in other cases, the injured parties might not want to accept, or permit, restitution as a means of making amends for acts of cruelty and brutality.

Economic Ironies Thwart Restitution Programs

Since the street crime problem is, in large part, an outgrowth of economic ills, it is no surprise that solutions involving restitution collide with economic realities. Repayment takes time and costs money. Restitution is predicated on work. Offenders must have, must be helped to find, or must be given jobs. These jobs must pay reasonably well, to permit restitution installments to be deducted from total earnings. But the U.S. economy cannot provide decent jobs for all who want to earn a living. Besides chronic unemployment, there is a permanent shortage of high-paid positions in government and industry. The following dilemmas that arise when restitution is attempted must be seen within this context of intense competition and relative scarcity:

1. If a job is found or created, then the prospects for the successful completion of the restitution obligation are increased. But if a job cannot be found or created, then unemployed, down-and-out street criminals are denied a chance to make amends.
2. If the wages are low, then the repayment cannot be completed within a reasonable amount of time. When nearly all the fruits of offenders' labor are confiscated and handed over to the victim, their commit-

ment to the job and to repaying the debt is jeopardized. If the job is demeaning, then its therapeutic value as a first step in a new lifestyle built on productive employment is lost. When it is a temporary job, only for the duration of the restitution obligation, then the risk of the offenders' returning to a career of crime is heightened.

3. But, if the positions found or created for offenders are permanent and pay well, then outsiders might object. To some, it will appear that the criminals are being rewarded, not punished, for their misdeeds. Law-abiding unemployed people may be resentful, since they are denied such opportunities and special treatment.

4. If the employer is a government agency or a major corporation, then trade union members might rightfully feel threatened that their civilian labor will be replaced by convict labor, over the long run. If the offenders are put to work in prison industries, then business interests will complain about unfair competition.

5. If adolescents owing restitution are too young to receive working papers, then a job in private industry would violate child labor laws. Only unpaid community service would be permissible. When large numbers of youngsters are put to work cleaning streets, repairing park facilities, maintaining public beaches, and so on, municipal workers feel threatened that their jobs are being farmed out to troubled youth. If the community service work is extremely unpleasant, exhausting, or dangerous, then restitution becomes a smokescreen for forced labor, chain-gang style.

6. When the offenders are destitute and the victims are hard pressed to make ends meet as well, restitution seems most appropriate. But if the offenders are penniless while the victims are affluent, then restitution smacks of exploitation—taking from the poor and giving to the rich. When the offenders are well-off and are allowed to make restitution by drawing on their wealth, instead of by working, it will appear that they are "buying their way out of trouble."

Despite these limitations, conflicts, dilemmas, and ironies, on balance, restitution merits the attention it is receiving. Properly conceived and executed, restitution arrangements can benefit both victims and offenders. In a fraction of cases, victims might legitimately wind up better off than before. In the majority of cases, receiving restitution can help dissipate victims' anguish and alienation and speed their return to normal functioning. After offenders make amends, victims are less likely to feel hostility and demand retribution. The entire community can benefit from the relaxation of divisive internal tensions and the spread of a spirit of reconciliation. Given the emptiness (for victims) of the punishment model and the ineffectiveness (for offenders) of the treatment model, large-scale restitution is worth a concerted try.

Making Criminals Repay Their Victims: Another Route

The Revival of Interest in Civil Lawsuits

- A jury orders a convict serving a prison term for manslaughter to pay the parents of the murder victim $40,000 for the "severe emotional stress" he has caused them.
- A burglar who killed a physician must pay $5 million to the widow, according to a ruling by a civil court judge.
- A jury awards over $500,000 to five black women shot by Ku Klux Klan members during a racially motivated attack (Gest, Solorzano, Shapiro, and Doan, 1982).

Today a growing number of crime victims are no longer content to let the criminal justice system handle their case. Their search for an arena in which to more actively defend their interests has led them to civil court. There, they can take legal matters into their own hands by suing the parties responsible for their plight for all they can get. Litigation lets them seek revenge coupled with restitution.

The victims who exercise this legal option and the lawyers who help them sue have proclaimed themselves the vanguard of the "victim's rights movement." To further the "cause," centers for legal advocacy and technical assistance have sprung up in a number of cities, including Virginia Beach, Washington, Philadelphia, Atlanta, Denver, Kansas City, Sacramento, and Springfield, Massachusetts (Barbash, 1979).

The victim's rights movement views civil lawsuits as a neglected weapon in the battle waged by victims against criminals. It wants to try to hold offenders accountable in two arenas, civil court as well as criminal court. Guilty verdicts in criminal courts cost offenders their freedom. Successful judgments in civil courts cost offenders cash. Lawsuits are a new occupational hazard for professional criminals.

Possibilities and Pitfalls from the Victim's Point of View

Victims considering civil litigation must weigh the advantages and disadvantages of this course of action. One reason civil suits are relatively uncommon is that most victims conclude that the benefits are not worth the risks.

The attractions of civil suits are straightforward. Reimbursement is soothing, and revenge is sweet. Accused persons (called "defendants," as in criminal court) can be sued for actual damages, future expenses, lost income, and the intangible mental wound of pain and suffering. In some jurisdictions, victims (called "plaintiffs" rather than complainants) can collect punitive damages far in excess of their out-of-pocket costs. Litigation looks promising if the offenders have assets, such as homes, cars, savings accounts, paychecks, investments, or inheritances. Most states allow awards to be collected for up to twenty years. Like other personal injury cases, civil suits against offenders are generally taken on by lawyers on a contingency basis. They cost nothing unless a judgment is won. In theory, it's easier to win in civil court than in criminal court because of the less difficult standard of proof: guilt by a preponderance of evidence, rather than guilt beyond a reasonable doubt.

However, there are a number of drawbacks that deter most victims from suing offenders. Civil proceedings are independent of criminal proceedings. The entire case must be tried all over, but this time at the victim's initiative, without the backing of the government and its enormous resources. Top-notch lawyers (who serve as prosecutors in presenting the plaintiff's case) probably won't be interested unless a huge amount of money is at stake. Win or lose, civil suits take years to be resolved. The backlogs and delays are worse than those in criminal courts because litigation is such a popular way of resolving disputes. There are motions, hearings, conferences, depositions, interrogatories, and appeals. In the meantime, the plaintiff (and the defendant as well) undergoes an ordeal marked by suspense, anxiety, frustration, embarrassment, injured pride, and lost earnings. Countersuits by defendants against the plaintiffs are common as acts of harassment or intimidation designed to promote a negotiated settlement. As in criminal court, 90 percent or more of all cases never go to trial. Last-minute, out-of-court settlements are the rule. To lawyers on both sides, such deals are a sure thing, in contrast to the unpredictable verdicts and awards of juries and judges. Most discouraging of all, even in victory there can be defeat. Winning a substantial judgment can still leave the victim behind financially, once the lawyer's sizable percentage fee has been paid. Worse yet, most street criminals don't have what lawyers call "deep pockets" (substantial assets). On the contrary, they are often "judgment proof"—broke or hard to collect from without incurring great expense because they have spent or hidden the spoils of their crimes (Main, 1978).

Suing Third Parties

Even when the perpetrators of a crime are known to be judgment proof, victims still have a chance to recover their losses. Instead of suing those who directly inflicted the injuries, they can go after third parties, either individuals or entities such as businesses or institutions.

The new wrinkle is to allege that a third party is partly to blame for the victim's misfortunes. The legal theory behind the current wave of third-party suits parallels traditional notions of "negligence." The plaintiff argues that the defendant (the third party) had a duty or obligation, that there was a breach of this duty, and that this breach proximately caused injury to the plaintiff. The plaintiff tries to prove that the third party's negligence put the criminal in a position to single out the plaintiff and harm him or her (Carrington, 1977).

Third-party suits can be of two types. The first type is directed against enterprises like private businesses—for example, landlords, innkeepers, and department stores. The second type is aimed at custodial agencies and officials of the criminal justice system, such as parole boards, prison wardens, probation officers, and directors of mental institutions. (See box 6-2.)

BOX 6-2 Landmark Cases of Successful Third-Party Lawsuits

Suits against Enterprises

A motel chain as third party:

In 1974, a well-known singer was raped in a Howard Johnson's motel in Westbury, Long Island, by an unknown assailant who had entered her room by jiggling the lock on sliding glass terrace doors. Badly shaken by the experience and unable to appear on stage, the singer sued the motel chain for lost earnings. Her attorney argued that the motel had shown gross negligence in maintaining security for its guests by failing to provide adequate door locks. A jury rendered a verdict in her favor of $2.5 million. Howard Johnson's agreed to a settlement by not appealing the verdict and paying her $1.5 million.

A department store as third party:

In 1976, a security guard at a drive-in hamburger stand was shot in the head during a robbery. He didn't sue the offender or his employer (the restaurant). Instead, his attorney alleged that the store that had sold the robber the bullet, a branch of Sears, Roebuck in Wilmington, Delaware, was guilty of gross negligence. The guns and ammunition department routinely ignored an obscure state law that required two citizens to vouch for the identity of the purchaser of bullets.

Suits against Criminal Justice Agencies and Officials

Custodial personnel as third parties:

In 1973, a fourteen-year-old girl was abducted from a private school in the Washington, D.C., area, tied to a tree, molested, and then left to freeze to death. The man who killed her had previously attacked another girl from the same school in that way. He had been committed for treatment while under confinement at a nearby psychiatric institute. The victim's parents sued the mental hospital, a psychiatrist, and a probation officer for arranging the release of the offender into an outpatient program without first receiving court approval. They won a judgment of $25,000.

In 1972, a convict with a record of forty felony convictions and seventeen escape attempts was permitted to participate in a "take-a-lifer-to-dinner" program at a prison in Washington. After eating at the home of a prison baker, he escaped, committed an armed robbery, and killed a man. The victim's widow sued the warden both personally and in his official capacity, in addition to the state of Washington, for gross negligence. Her attorney argued that the warden didn't have legislative authority or administrative permission from his superiors to let the inmate out that night. She won a judgment of $186,000, which the state did not appeal.

SOURCE: Carrington, 1977, 1978; Barbash, 1979; Rottenberg, 1980.

Third-party lawsuits against businesses have established new definitions of corporate responsibility and financial liability. The suits never accuse the defendant (business) of intentionally harming the plaintiff, because the executives in charge probably never met the victim and were two or three steps removed from the criminal action. What is alleged is that the defendant's gross negligence created a climate that made the criminal's task easier. The victim's lawyer argues that the enterprise had a general duty to protect invited guests, customers, and clients from crime on the premises, or at least had an obligation to issue warnings about potential dangers (by posting notices). The lawyer argues further that the enterprise should have exercised due care when hiring employees to represent the business in its contacts with the public (Carrington, 1977, 1978).

Victims can win if they can prove in civil court that management did not act to prevent a reasonably foreseeable crime. To prevail, the attorney must convincingly demonstrate that the business firm did not increase security after it received notice of previous crimes on the premises, and that the degree of protection offered did not meet community standards. Most claims fail to meet this test, but the few that successfully do can contribute to the improvement of the safety of the public in places like apartment complexes, shopping centers, bus terminals, parking lots, and hotels (Gest, Solorzano, Shapiro, and Doan, 1982; Newman, 1981a, 1981b; Press and Clausen, 1982).

Third-party lawsuits against custodial agencies and officials also revolve around charges of gross negligence. The plaintiffs allege that the officials (and the agencies that employ and empower them) severely abused their discretionary authority. The crimes are said to have occurred because of official inaction or incompetence that facilitated the offenders' inclination to harm others. Specifically, the charges are that officials failed to properly supervise convicts under their custody or negligently released dangerous persons from court-ordered confinement without warning potential victims about the heightened risks (Carrington, 1978).

Suits against custodial officials and agencies raise important issues. A U.S. Court of Appeals, in rejecting a victim's third-party lawsuit, declared that "there is no constitutional right to be protected by the state against being murdered by criminals or madmen" (Gest, Solorzano, Shapiro, and Doan, 1982:62). The U.S. Supreme Court ruled in 1980 that neither the Constitution nor the Civil Rights Act of 1964 gave the survivors of a murder victim the right to sue a state parole board (Carrington, 1980). In upholding the doctrine of sovereign immunity from liability, the Court argued that government has a legitimate interest in seeking to rehabilitate criminals. All the treatment alternatives to totally incapacitating convicts through maximum-security confinement involve taking a gamble with the public's safety. Halfway houses, therapeutic communities, work release, educational release, furloughs, probation, and parole—all grant conditional liberty to known offenders.

The second guessing that invariably underlies charges of abuse of discretionary authority and of gross negligence assumes that dangerousness can be predicted. It usually can't be. What is predictable is that successful third-party lawsuits by victims against custodial officials and agencies will have a chilling effect on wardens, psychiatrists, parole boards, and others who make decisions regarding confinement and conditional liberty. What might develop in therapeutic relationships is a type of defensiveness comparable to the defensive medicine practiced by doctors afraid of malpractice suits. Fear of legal and financial repercussions will dominate professional judgments and record keeping. Efforts to implement rehabilitation programs might be stifled. Eligible convicts could be barred from such programs because administrators wouldn't want to jeopardize their own careers by releasing them from total confinement. Qualified professionals could be deterred from taking such jobs because of exposure to personal-liability lawsuits unless states protect such custodial employees by a doctrine of sovereign immunity. On the other hand, aggrieved parties need some mechanism to make public officials accountable and to recover losses inflicted by dangerous criminals who should not have been left unsupervised (see Press and Clausen, 1983).

References

BARBASH, FRED. 1979: "Victim's Rights: New Legal Weapon." *Washington Post*, December 17:1.

BARNETT, RANDY. 1977: "Restitution: A New Paradigm of Criminal Justice." In Randy Barnett and John Hagel (Eds.), *Assessing the Criminal: Restitution, Retribution, and the Legal Process*, 1–35. Cambridge, Mass.: Ballinger.

CARRINGTON, FRANK. 1977: "Victim's Rights Litigation: A Wave of the Future?" *University of Richmond Law Review*, 11,3:447–470.

—— "Victim's Rights: A New Tort." 1978: *Trial*, June: 39–41.

—— "Martinez Ruling Won't Bar Suits on Negligent Custodial Releases." 1980: *National Law Journal*, February 11:26.

EDELHERTZ, HERBERT. 1977: "Legal and Operational Issues in the Implementation of Restitution within the Criminal Justice System." In Joe Hudson and Burt Galaway (Eds.), *Restitution in Criminal Justice*, 63–76. Lexington, Mass.: Lexington Books.

EGLASH, ALBERT. 1977: "Beyond Restitution: Creative Restitution." In Joe Hudson and Burt Galaway (Eds.), *Restitution in Criminal Justice*, 91–100. Lexington, Mass.: Lexington Books.

"Fitting Justice?: Judges Try 'Creative' Sentences." 1978: *Time*, April 24:56.

GALAWAY, BURT. 1977: "The Uses of Restitution." *Crime and Delinquency*, 23,1:57–67.

——, and HUDSON, JOE. 1975: "Issues in the Correctional Implementation of Restitution to Victims of Crime." In Joe Hudson and Burt Galaway (Eds.),

Considering the Victim: Readings in Restitution and Victim Compensation, 351–360. Springfield, Ill.: Charles C Thomas.

GEIS, GILBERT. 1977: "Restitution by Criminal Offenders: A Summary and Overview." In Joe Hudson and Burt Galaway (Eds.), *Restitution in Criminal Justice,* 147–164. Lexington, Mass.: Lexington Books.

GEST, TED; SOLORZANO, LUCIA; SHAPIRO, JOSEPH; and DOAN, MICHAEL. 1982: "'See You in Court'—Our Suing Society." *U.S. News & World Report,* December 20:58–63.

GOTTESMAN, ROBERT, and MOUNTZ, LYNNE. 1979: *Restitution: Legal Analysis.* Reno, Nev.: National Council of Juvenile and Family Court Judges.

HARLAND, ALAN. 1979: "Restitution Statutes and Cases: Some Substantive and Procedural Constraints." In Burt Galaway and Joe Hudson (Eds.), *Victims, Offenders, and Restitutive Sanctions,* 151–171. Lexington, Mass.: Lexington Books.

——1981: *Restitution to Victims of Personal and Household Crimes.* Washington, D.C.: U.S. Department of Justice.

HARRIS, M. 1979: *Sentencing to Community Service.* Washington, D.C.: American Bar Association.

HUDSON, JOE, and CHESNEY, STEVE. 1978: "Research on Restitution: A Review and Assessment." In Burt Galaway and Joe Hudson (Eds.), *Offender Restitution in Theory and Action,* 131–148. Lexington, Mass.: Lexington Books.

JACOB, BRUCE. 1977: "The Concept of Restitution: An Historical Overview." In Joe Hudson and Burt Galaway (Eds.), *Restitution in Criminal Justice,* 45–62. Lexington, Mass.: Lexington Books.

KEVE, PAUL. 1978: "Therapeutic Uses of Restitution." In Burt Galaway and Joe Hudson (Eds.), *Offender Restitution in Theory and Action,* 59–64. Lexington, Mass.: Lexington Books.

LASTER, RICHARD. 1970: "Criminal Restitution: A Survey of Its Past History and Analysis of Its Present Usefulness." *University of Richmond Law Review,* 5:71–98.

LEEPSON, MARC. 1982: "Helping Victims of Crime." *Editorial Research Reports,* 1,17:331–344.

MAIN, JEREMY. 1978: "Sue the Bastards." *Money,* November:85–95.

McDONALD, WILLIAM. 1977: "The Role of the Victim in America." In Randy Barnett and John Hagel (Eds.), *Assessing the Criminal: Restitution, Retribution, and the Legal Process,* 295–307. Cambridge, Mass.: Ballinger.

—— 1978: "Expanding the Victim's Role in the Disposition Decision: Reform in Search of Rationale." In Burt Galaway and Joe Hudson (Eds.), *Offender Restitution in Theory and Action,* 101–110. Lexington, Mass.: Lexington Books.

McKNIGHT, DOROTHY. 1981: "The Victim-Offender Reconciliation Project." In Burt Galaway and Joe Hudson (Eds.), *Perspectives on Crime Victims,* 292–298. St. Louis, Mo.: Mosby.

MUELLER, GERHARD, and COOPER, H. 1973: *The Criminal, Society, and the Victim.* Washington, D.C.: National Criminal Justice Reference Service.

NATIONAL INSTITUTE OF JUSTICE. 1981: *Exemplary Projects.* Washington, D.C.: U.S. Department of Justice.

NEWMAN, STEPHEN. 1981a: "Everyday Perils: Your Legal Rights When Danger Strikes." *New York,* November 9:48–50.

—— 1981b: "Who's to Blame if You Get Hurt?" *New York,* August 17:33–34.

PRESS, ARIC, and CLAUSEN, PEGGY. 1982: "Let the Seller Beware." *Newsweek,* August 16:63.

—— 1983: "When Can a Shrink Be Sued?" *Newsweek,* March 7:77.

PRISON RESEARCH EDUCATION AND ACTION PROJECT. 1976: *Instead of Prisons.* Geneseo, N.Y.: Author.

READ, B. 1977: *Offenders' Restitution Programs in Georgia.* Atlanta: Georgia Department of Corrections.

ROTTENBERG, DAN. 1980: "Crime Victims Fight Back." *Parade,* March 16:21–23.

SCHAFER, STEPHEN. 1970: *Compensation and Restitution to Victims of Crime* (2nd Edition). Montclair, N.J.: Patterson Smith.

—— 1977: *Victimology: The Victim and His Criminal.* Reston, Va.: Reston.

SCHNEIDER, ANNE, and SCHNEIDER, PETER. 1980: "An Overview of Restitution Program Models in the Juvenile Justice System." *Juvenile and Family Court Journal,* 31:3–22.

SCHNEIDER, PETER; SCHNEIDER, ANNE; REITER, PAUL; and CLEARY, COLLEEN. 1977: "Restitution Requirements for Juvenile Offenders: A Survey of Practices in American Juvenile Courts." *Juvenile Justice,* 28,4:43–56.

SELIGMANN, JEAN, and MAOR, YVETTE. 1980: "Punishments That Fit the Crime." *Newsweek,* August 4:60.

TITTLE, CHARLES. 1978: "Restitution and Deterrence: An Evaluation of Compatibility." In Burt Galaway and Joe Hudson (Eds.), *Offender Restitution in Theory and Action,* 33–58. Lexington, Mass.: Lexington Books.

VOGELGESANG, BOB. 1975: "The Iowa Restitution in Probation Experiment." In Joe Hudson and Burt Galaway (Eds.), *Restitution in Criminal Justice,* 134–145. Lexington, Mass.: Lexington Books.

"When Judges Make the Punishment Fit the Crime." 1978: *U.S. News & World Report,* December 11:44–46.

YOUNGER, EVILLE. 1977: "Introduction." In the American Bar Association, *Victims of Crime or Victims of Justice?,* 1–5. Washington, D.C.: ABA.

CHAPTER 7

Compensating Crime Victims for Their Monetary Losses

The Need for Compensation

When restitution by the offender is an inadequate or impractical method for financial reimbursement, compensation by a third party is the only alternative. The third party can be either a private insurance company or a government insurance fund.

- A middle-aged man was blinded by assailants. They were caught, convicted, and imprisoned. On their release, they were ordered by the court to pay restitution to their victim for the loss of his eyesight. The arrangement would have required 442 years for the victim to collect the full amount due to him (Fry, 1957).
- A Good Samaritan came to the aid of two elderly women who were being harassed by a drunken youth on a subway train. As his wife and child watched in horror, the man was stabbed to death by the drunk. The killer was captured and sentenced to from twenty years to life in prison. The widow was forced to send her child to live with her mother while she went to work to pay off bills ("The Good Samaritans," 1965).
- A man shot during the course of a robbery was awarded \$30,000 for unpaid medical bills and \$12,000 for wages lost because of his injuries. He received \$600 a month until he was able to go back to work.
- The widow of a murder victim was granted \$1,500 for funeral expenses and \$15,000 for loss of support. She collected \$1,000 a month in death benefits until a maximum of \$20,000 in payments was reached.

The first two cases, which took place in England in 1951 and in New York City in 1965, dramatize the need for special funds to compensate victims for devastating losses. The remaining two cases, from New York's compensation program, illustrate the kinds of aid that are now available. Money can't erase painful memories or cure lingering emotional and physical wounds. Payments are stop-gap measures that counteract the effects of crime without touching its roots. Yet reimbursement can ease the suffering of victims. It is the easiest, simplest, and most direct way of speeding recovery with the aim of making the victim whole again.

Insurance as a Source of Compensation

Private Crime Insurance

Private insurance companies issue policies that can reimburse crime victims for specified expenses and losses. Public victim compensation plans have been designed to pick up those costs that are not covered routinely by private insurers.

Insurance companies make profits in two ways. They adjust their rates continuously so that they take in more in premiums than they pay out in claims. In addition, they invest the money paid in by policyholders in order to collect interest, dividends, and rents.

Private companies offer various policies and charge differing rates. Potential crime victims can take out coverage to insure themselves against a wide variety of hazards. Life insurance policies can pay sizable sums to survivors of murder victims. Some policies (which cost more) contain a "double indemnity" clause, which pays survivors twice as much if the policyholder dies from an accident, including a criminally inflicted injury.

Coverage can also be purchased to offset expenses due to medical bills (health insurance), and lost earnings (income maintenance). Property can be insured against loss or damage. Car and boat insurance covers losses due to theft, vandalism, and arson. Home insurance covers losses due to burglary, some larcenies (of items on porches or in yards, for example), vandalism, arson, and robbery (if the confrontation occurs within the home). Some companies sell robbery insurance that covers losses no matter where the crime occurs. A few offer protection to businesses whose executives might be kidnapped and held for ransom.

Patterns of loss, recovery, and reimbursement. Data from victimization surveys confirm some commonsense predictions about insurance coverage and recovery. First, some types of coverage are more common than others. More people are insured against medical expenses than against property losses. Medical costs are potentially more devastating, and health coverage is often a fringe benefit for full-time jobs. Second, higher-income people are more likely to buy crime insurance than lower-income people (even though poorer people may be exposed to more risks and may suffer higher victimization rates). Third, large losses are more likely to be reimbursed through insurance claims than small ones. Many policies have "deductible" clauses, which stipulate that the victim bears the first $100 or $250 (or some other sum) of the losses and cannot file a claim unless the out-of-pocket expenses exceed this figure (Harland, 1981a:13–15.)

Statistics derived from victimization surveys show that most victims who suffer economic losses do not collect insurance reimbursement (see table 7-1).

TABLE 7-1 Percentage of Crime Victims Who Collected Insurance Reimbursement

*Type of crime**	*Percentage who recovered some or all of their losses through insurance†*
Robbery	2%
Personal larceny	6%
Household larceny	5%
Burglary	16%
Motor vehicle theft	28%

*Only crimes in which something was stolen are counted.

†Insurance recovery can be either partial or full.

SOURCE: Estimates calculated from tables 80 and 81, *Criminal Victimization in the United States.* Washington, D.C.: U.S. Department of Justice, 1982: 66–67.

In vehicle thefts, motorists are repaid by insurance companies in about a quarter of the cases. In nearly all other cases, police find cars abandoned by joyriders or discover parts of cars stolen by professional thieves. (The recovery rate for stolen vehicles has plummeted since the 1960s because of the increase in activity of commercial theft rings.) Besides auto theft, the only type of crime in which insurance plays an appreciable role as a means of recovering losses is burglary. Slightly more than one burglary victim in six collects some money from an insurance policy. But some burglary victims are more likely than others to be reimbursed (see table 7-2).

Statistics concerning patterns of burglary loss, coverage, and recovery show that both the average amount stolen and the percentage of victims insured are positively correlated with family income. That is, the average value of stolen cash and valuables lost in a burglary increases as the victim's family income goes up. Families that earn more have more valuables and thus lose more when burglars break into their homes. Also, since they have more to protect, they have more incentives to buy

TABLE 7-2 Burglary Losses, Coverage, and Recovery

Burglary losses and burglary coverage, by victim's family income, 1973

Victim's yearly family income	*Average amount stolen*	*Percentage of victims insured*
$20,000 or more	$408	52%
$15,000–$19,999	$396	49%
$12,000–$14,999	$264	36%
$10,000–$11,999	$286	36%
$ 7,500–$ 9,999	$285	26%
$ 3,000–$ 7,499	$273	18%
$ 0–$ 2,999	$157	10%

SOURCE: Adapted from *Victimization Surveys and Criminal Justice Planning,* by Wesley Skogan. Washington, D.C.: U.S. Department of Justice, 1978:6. Statistics are from the 1973 National Crime Survey.

Burglary recovery, through insurance and other means, by size of loss, 1974

Total value of loss due to theft	*Partial or full recovery from insurance*	*Partial or full recovery by direct methods**
$1000 or more	31% of victims	11% of victims
$500–$999	26%	10%
$100–$499	17%	9%
$ 25–$ 99	4%	9%
$ 1–$ 24	1%	6%
All burglary victims	11%	10%

*Direct methods refer to police recoveries and repossessions by the victims themselves.

SOURCE: Adapted from *Restitution to Victims of Personal and Household Crime,* by Alan Harland. Washington, D.C.: U.S. Department of Justice, 1981:15–16. Statistics are from the 1974 National Crime Survey.

protection. Hence, higher-income people are more likely to be insured than lower-income people. For example, only one family in ten is insured in the lowest income category, whereas about half of all families in the higher-income category are covered. (Presumably, the rich are fully insured, but the data are unavailable.) Recoveries of stolen goods by the police or by victims themselves rarely occur; victims who lose a lot have a slightly better chance of getting partial or full recovery than victims who lose a little (whose cases are assigned very low priorities by the police and whose lost goods are difficult to positively identify and return). For losses of less than $100, insurance is of no use to nearly all victims, probably because of deductible clauses. In sum, although insurance may allow some victims to recover substantial amounts of what they originally lost, insurance provides relief for relatively few burglary victims.

Similar conclusions can be drawn about insurance coverage for other crimes. Many victims discover that they are unprotected or inadequately covered. They are compelled to absorb losses that heighten their anger and suffering. A small percentage is economically ruined, often because of huge medical bills and lost earnings. Perhaps public insurance is the answer for these victims.

Federal Crime Insurance

One irony of the insurance-for-profit business is that those who face the greatest risks are sometimes denied coverage. The insufficiency and unfairness of private insurance underwriting practices first received public attention during the late 1960s.

The National Advisory Panel on Insurance in Riot Affected Areas, part of the National Advisory Commission on Civil Disorders, was appointed by President Lyndon Johnson in 1967 to examine the plight of inner-city residents and businessmen who had suffered losses during ghetto rebellions. The panel cited a general lack of insurance availability as a contributing factor in urban decay—the closing of businesses, the drying up of jobs, the abandonment of buildings, and the exodus of residents from high-crime areas. In 1968, Congress followed some of the panel's recommendations and granted relief to victims of insurance "red-lining" (denial of coverage).

As part of the Housing and Urban Development Act, the secretary of the newly created department was authorized to set up a program to reinsure private insurance companies against property losses arising from civil disorders. Fair Access to Insurance Requirements (FAIR) plans were drawn up to make sure that property owners were not denied fire damage coverage solely because the neighborhood had a high rate of arson cases. Inner-city homeowners and businessmen had complained to their legislators that insurance companies were reluctant to extend policies or write new ones in the wake of the fires that had gutted riot-torn areas.

In 1970, the Federal Insurance Administration reported to President Richard Nixon and Congress that crime victims in poor neighborhoods could no longer bear the full financial burden of either their policy premium costs or their uninsured losses. Congress amended the 1968 act that had created the reinsurance fund for fire coverage to permit the federal government to offer "affordable" burglary and robbery insurance directly to urban homeowners, tenants, and businesses in locales where such coverage from private companies was either unavailable or exorbitantly expensive. State regulatory agencies and private insurers were to be encouraged to change their practices, and federal intervention to assist actual and potential crime victims was to be a last resort (Bernstein, 1972:521–523).

Once the government begins to sell insurance coverage to those who are prudent enough to purchase it before disaster strikes, it becomes reasonable to ask whether public funds can be set up to bail out families that are economically ruined by serious crimes. Government compensation programs are being designed to aid victims who find themselves in that kind of financial crisis, either because they had no insurance coverage at all or because their policies permitted only partial reimbursement of staggering losses.

The History of Victim Compensation by Governments

The earliest reference to governmental compensation for crime victims can be found in the ancient Babylonian Code of Hammurabi (about 1775 B.C.), which is considered to be the oldest written body of criminal law. The code instructed territorial governors to replace a robbery victim's lost property if the criminal was not captured; in the case of a murder, the governor was to pay the heirs a specific sum in silver from the treasury. In the centuries that followed, restitution by the offender to the victim replaced compensation by the state to the victim. But it, too, faded away during the Middle Ages, leaving the victim with little redress except to seek to recover losses by suing the offender in civil court.

Interest in compensation revived when the prison reform movement in Europe during the 1800s focused on the suffering of convicts and, in so doing, indirectly called attention to the plight of their victims. Jeremy Bentham, a major figure in the Classical School of criminology, argued that those who had been victimized, either in their person or their fortune, should not be abandoned to their fate. The society to which they had contributed, and which ought to have protected them, owed them an indemnity. The three leading criminologists of the rival Italian Positivist School, Cesare Lombroso, Enrico Ferri, and Raffaele Garofalo, also endorsed compensation (and restitution) at several International Penal Congress meetings held at the turn of the century. But these resolutions did not lead to any concrete actions.

Legal historians have uncovered only a few instances of special funds set aside for crime victims—one in Tuscany after 1786, another in Mexico starting in 1871, and one beginning in France in 1934. Switzerland and Cuba also experimented with victim compensation (MacNamara and Sullivan, 1974; Schafer, 1970; Silving, 1959).

Margery Fry, an English magistrate, is widely acknowledged as the prison reformer who sparked the revival of interest in compensation in Anglo-Saxon legal systems in the late 1950s. Because of her efforts, a government commission investigated different schemes for reparations in Britain in 1963. Developments were swifter in the Commonwealth country of New Zealand; a Criminal Injuries Compensation Tribunal was established that same year. Britain set up its program in 1964. Several Australian states and Canadian provinces followed suit during the next few years.

The Origins of Compensation in America

Supreme Court Justice Arthur Goldberg was instrumental in popularizing the issue in the United States in 1964, after initial proposals for compensation plans had been criticized by distinguished scholars in law journals in 1959. Goldberg argued that society should assume some responsibility for making whole again those whom the law has failed to protect. Soon, many victimologists and criminologists joined the ranks of compensation advocates, although a few remained among the most vehement opponents. Ideological, social, economic, legal, and administrative aspects became subjects for debate. Some well-known political figures came to accept the argument that compensation was long overdue: senators Ralph Yarborough, John McClellan, Mike Mansfield, Hubert Humphrey, and Edward Kennedy, and governors Nelson Rockefeller, Edmund Brown, and Marvin Mandel. National and state commissions began to examine philosophical objections, potential costs, and practical problems (Brooks, 1972; Edelhertz and Geis, 1974).

The proposals of political leaders, the suggestions of scholars and professionals, and the pressures of a few interest groups were necessary but not sufficient to trigger action. The growth of public enthusiasm for helping crime victims paved the way for the first programs. They were based on the liberal philosophy of President John Kennedy's New Frontier and President Lyndon Johnson's Great Society of creating governmental programs to solve social problems. Also, considerable disenchantment with the traditional remedies of seeking satisfaction through either punishment or restitution promoted experimentation in this direction.

Widely publicized incidents of brutality and tragedy inspired pro-victim legislation in those states where conditions were ripe. In 1965, California became the first to initiate compensation to crime victims who had been injured and to the dependents of murder victims, as part of its public assistance system. In 1966, New York created a special board to allocate money. In 1967, Massachusetts made provisions for the court and the state Attorney General's office to grant financial aid.

A few interest groups have come forward to encourage the acceptance of reparation plans. The American Bar Association has enthusiastically endorsed compensation legislation, partly as a matter of justice but also because it provides a new field of specialization for lawyers and an additional source of claims and fees. The International Association of Chiefs of Police has also supported these plans, hoping that they will be linked to provisions for better benefits to the families of policemen severly injured or killed in the line of duty. Law enforcement interest groups have also anticipated that compensation could be a measure to increase public cooperation with the police, as well as to reduce frustration with the police for failing to prevent or solve crimes. Some politicians have sponsored compensation legislation so that they will be perceived by the voters as "doing something about the crime problem." To date, private insurance companies have not felt threatened by the entrance of nonprofit government agencies into this marginal area of their business (Edelhertz and Geis, 1974; Meiners, 1978).

State Compensation Programs

Similarities and Differences

In thirty-three states, the question of whether to compensate crime victims has been resolved. But the programs vary in structure, procedures, and sources of financing, reflecting the diversity among the states in size, population, and resources and the differing rationales from which the programs were derived. They do, however, share a number of important features (see table 7-3).

TABLE 7-3 Which Crime Victims Can Apply for Compensation?

Eligible	*Ineligible, eliminated*
All crime victims ↓	
Victims of violent crimes against persons ↓	→ Victims of non-violent crimes against property
Victims or Good Samaritans who were injured ↓	→ Victims who were not physically wounded
Victims who required medical attention and/or missed work ↓	→ Victims who did not need medical attention and/or did not miss work
Victims whose bills and lost earnings were not reimbursed by private or public insurance ↓	→ Victims who had adequate insurance coverage or received sick pay
Victims who were totally or largely innocent ↓	→ Victims who were largely responsible for their own suffering
Innocent victims of violent crimes whose injuries led to out-of-pocket expenses for medical care or lost earnings; and needy dependents of innocent victims who died from their wounds (pool of potential recipients of compensation)	

All of the programs grant reimbursements only to innocent victims. Offenders (and their accomplices) responsible for violent acts are automatically ruled ineligible for any reparations. Compensation boards investigate for evidence of victim facilitation, precipitation, and provocation, or any other signs of contributory misconduct. If it is established that the victim in some manner and to some degree was to blame for the commission of the crime, the grant can be reduced in size or disallowed entirely.

Another common feature is that the programs deal only with the most serious crimes, which result in injury or death. They do not repay victims for property that is damaged or lost in thefts, burglaries, or robberies. They reimburse victims only for their "out-of-pocket expenses" (bills not covered by collateral sources, such as worker's compensation or private insurance, like Blue Cross). The payments can be for medical expenses (to doctors, emergency rooms, clinics, hospitals, psychiatrists, counselors, rehabilitation therapists), and for earnings lost because of missed work. If victims die as a result of their injuries, their families are eligible for assistance with reasonable funeral and burial costs and, sometimes, a death benefit or pension for surviving dependents. Each program requires that all claims be fully documented with bills and receipts.

All state programs prohibit double recoveries. Any money collected from insurance policies or other government agencies is deducted from the compensation board's final award. In the statistically unusual cases in which offenders are caught, found guilty, and forced to make restitution to their victims, state programs subtract this money too.

An assailant does not have to be caught and convicted in order for a victim to receive compensation. But the burden of proof falls on the victim to provide evidence that a violent crime did indeed take place. The victim must report the crime to the police and must cooperate with any investigation and prosecution in order to maintain eligiblity for an award.

Although the thirty-three state programs have these basic features in common, they differ significantly in a number of ways: how long victims can wait before telling the police about the crime; how long victims can take before submitting an application for reimbursement; how much victims must lose in order to be eligible for an award; how much victims can collect; where the money comes from; whether offenders must repay victims out of any profits from their notoriety; whether victims must be financially ruined in order to get aid; whether the program will lend victims money to cover immediate expenses before hearing their case; whether the program will pay victims to hire a lawyer to represent them before the board; and whether victims who are out-of-state visitors or commuters are covered. (See table 7-4.)

When the programs were set up, special boards were created to review

TABLE 7-4 Variations in State Compensation Programs

State*	Year started	Reporting deadline (Days)	Filing deadline (Years)	Minimum loss	Maximum award allowed	Source of funding	Repay from profits?	Must show hardship?	Grants emergency loans?	Pays attorney fees?	Pays out-of-state residents?
Alaska	'72	5	2	$ 0	$25,000	Tax	Yes	No	Yes	Yes	Yes
California	'65	None	1	100	25,000	Pen.	No	No	Yes	Yes	No
Colorado	'82	3	1½	25	1,500	Pen.	No	No	Yes	—	No
Connecticut	'79	5	2	100	10,000	Pen.	No	No	Yes	Yes	Yes
Delaware	'75	None	1	25	10,000	Pen.	No	No	No	Yes	Yes
Florida	'78	3	1	0	10,000	Pen.	No	Yes	Yes	Yes	No
Hawaii	'67	None	1½	0	10,000	Tax	No	No	Yes	Yes	Yes
Illinois	'73	3	1	200	15,000	Tax	Yes	No	No	Yes	Yes
Indiana	'78	2	3 mos.	100	10,000	Both	No	No	Yes	Yes	No
Kansas	'78	3	1	100	10,000	Tax	No	Yes	No	Yes	Yes
Kentucky	'76	2	1	100	15,000	Both	Yes	Yes	Yes	No	Yes
Maryland	'68	2	6 mos.	100	45,000	Both	No	Yes	Yes	Yes	Yes
Massachusetts	'69	2	1	100	10,000	Tax	Yes	No	No	Yes	No
Michigan	'77	2	1 mo.	100	15,000	Tax	No	Yes	Yes	Yes	No
Minnesota	'74	5	1	100	10,000	Both	Yes	No	Yes	No	Yes
Missouri	'82	2	1	200	25,000	Pen.	No	No	Yes	—	No
Montana	'78	3	1	0	25,000	Pen.	Yes	No	No	Yes	Yes
Nebraska	'79	3	2	0	10,000	Tax	Yes	No	Yes	No	Yes
Nevada	'75	5	1	100	5,000	Pen.	Yes	Yes	No	Yes	No
New Jersey	'71	90	1	100	25,000	Both	No	No	Yes	Yes	Yes
New Mexico	'81	30	1	0	12,500	Tax	No	No	Yes	—	No
New York	'66	7	1	0	No limit	Tax	Yes	Yes	Yes	Yes	Yes
North Dakota	'75	3	1	100	25,000	Tax	No	No	Yes	Yes	Yes
Ohio	'76	3	1	0	25,000	Pen.	No	No	Yes	Yes	Yes
Oklahoma	'81	3	1	0	10,000	Both	Yes	No	Yes	—	Yes
Oregon	'78	3	6 mos.	250	23,000	Tax	No	No	Yes	No	Yes
Pennsylvania	'77	3	1	100	25,000	Pen.	No	No	Yes	Yes	Yes
Tennessee	'76	2	1	100	50,000	Pen.	No	No	Yes	Yes	Yes
Texas	'80	3	6 mos.	0	50,000	Pen.	Yes	Yes	Yes	Yes	No
Virginia	'76	2	6 mos.	100	10,000	Pen.	No	Yes	Yes	Yes	Yes
Washington	'75	3	6 mos.	0	15,000	Both	No	No	No	Yes	—
West Virginia	'81	3	2	0	20,000	Pen.	No	No	No	—	Yes
Wisconsin	'77	5	2	0	12,000	Tax	No	No	Yes	Yes	Yes

Key to terms and symbols:

Year Started: when the program began to consider claims

Reporting Deadline: the number of days a victim can wait before telling the police about the crime

Filing Deadline: the time limit, in years, after which applications will not be considered.

Minimum Loss: costs must exceed this amount

Maximum Award Allowed: upper limit for all money granted to reimburse victims or their dependents for all kinds of expenses

Source of Funding: whether the money comes from general tax revenues or from penalties imposed on convicted offenders, or from both sources

Repay from Profits?: whether convicted offenders have to repay victims from profits derived from the publicity surrounding the crime

Must Show Hardship?: whether a financial means test is used to eliminate victims who can "afford" their losses
Grants Emergency Loans?: whether immediate reimbursement is allowed, before claims are resolved
Pays Attorney Fees?: whether the expenses of hiring a lawyer are reimbursed, in addition to other losses
Pays Out-of-State Residents?: whether visitors and commuters are covered as well as residents
—: information was not available.

*Georgia has had a compensation program for injured Good Samaritans since 1967. During 1983, compensation programs began to operate in Iowa, Louisiana, Rhode Island, and South Carolina. The District of Columbia and the Virgin Islands have programs, but Puerto Rico doesn't.

SOURCES: Austern et al., 1979; Gaynes, 1981; Leepson, 1982; McGillis and Smith, 1983; Meuerer, 1979; NOVA, 1983.

claims in most states. In the remainder, either the worker's compensation division or a court agency was empowered to process applications and make awards.

Three states do not impose a time limit on reporting the incident that caused the injuries and losses, but all jurisdictions have a filing deadline, ranging in length from one month to two years after the event.

In twenty states, bills must exceed a minimum loss, usually set at $100 but ranging from $25 to $250, which is comparable to a "deductible" clause in an insurance policy. The intent is to discourage the filing of minor claims that would cost more to process than the victim is requesting. In thirteen states, however, even the smallest claims are considered. The most generous states pay out as much as $50,000 to victims with huge bills and severe losses. In Hawaii and Tennessee, a victim can receive compensation for "pain and suffering" due to mental anguish or nervous shock. In Colorado, a victim can't collect more than $1,500, regardless of the size of the loss. In nine states, only those who can demonstrate serious financial need are eligible for awards. Other innocent victims are considered capable of affording their losses. Most programs grant low-interest or no-interest emergency loans to victims who desperately need money. Lawyers who represent victims can have their fees paid by the program in the majority of states, although some try to avoid an adversary format at hearings. In most jurisdictions, visitors and commuters are covered, but a few states stipulate that they will pay the victim only if the victim's home state has a comparable compensation program. Californians can be repaid by their state fund regardless of where they are victimized.

In every state except California and Delaware, a victim is automatically ineligible for reimbursement if he or she is related to the offender. Many states also eliminate from consideration any victim who resides in the same household as the offender. These family exclusion provisions can be waived in several states by the board "in the interest of justice."

Only twelve of the thirty-three states, generally those with the older programs, rely exclusively on general tax revenues to provide funds. Seven states collect money both from the public and from convicted persons. States like Montana, which derive their compensation funds from "penalty assessments," earmark a portion of traffic fines, bail forfeitures, and restitution earnings to aid victims. Connecticut collects an extra ten dollars from all misdemeanants and fifteen dollars from felons. In specific cases, convicted offenders may be compelled through the process of "subrogation" to repay the government for the money it has paid out to the victim. Although most states permit subrogation, it is rarely imposed, because few offenders have the means to reimburse the government.

Also on paper but rarely invoked are "Son of Sam" statutes. Just like penalty assessments, these provisions have been added to existing programs in eleven states in recent years. Named after New York's "44 Caliber Killer," they require that all the money that criminals derive from selling the rights to their stories be deposited in escrow accounts and held by the compensation boards until their victims are repaid for their losses. The intent of these provisions is to compel offenders who gain notoriety to make restitution to their victims from the profits they reap from royalties for movie reenactments of the crime, books, magazine articles, interviews, or other media presentations.

At the start of the 1980s, the average claimant throughout the nation received about $2,000, or approximately $.18 per taxpayer in those states with compensation programs. California anticipated giving out about $15 million to more than six thousand victims in 1982; North Dakota expected to handle about a dozen claims during that year (Austern et al., 1979; Carrow, 1980; Garofalo and Sutton, 1977; Gaynes, 1981; Geis, 1983; Leepson, 1982; NOVA, 1983).

Compensation programs set up in Great Britain, Australia, and Canada in the 1960s and in Austria, Denmark, France, West Germany, Ireland, the Netherlands, and Norway in the 1970s operate along somewhat similar lines. In Iceland, Sweden, and Switzerland comprehensive social welfare legislation covers most losses of crime victims. Some of these countries do not have special programs exclusively for crime victims. The most complete protection in the Western world is offered in New Zealand, which in 1972 abolished the victim compensation program it had pioneered in 1963 and absorbed it within a universal accident insurance system. Everyone in New Zealand (even visitors) is covered for losses arising from any kind of accident, including criminal victimizations. The nature of the event, the reason why it occurred, and the responsibility for it do not affect the compensation decisions (European Committee on Crime Problems, 1978; Meiners, 1978).

Pros and Cons: The Debate Continues

Although no strong lobby has emerged in opposition to reparations, there are skeptics and critics. As of 1983, seventeen states and the federal government still offered no assistance. A debate continued over the wisdom and practicality of setting up these programs and adequately funding them. (Brooks, 1972; Carrow, 1980; Childres, 1964; Gaynes, 1981; Geis, 1976; Meiners, 1978; Schultz, 1965; U.S. House, 1980; Wolfgang, 1965.)

Arguments in Favor of Compensation

Three separate arguments have been advanced by compensation advocates (who embrace different philosophies and represent groups with diverse interests). These rationales appear in declarations of policy or purpose in the preambles of the thirty-three existing state statutes, and they are supposed to guide the practices, procedures, and daily operations of the programs. These justifications picture compensation as (1) an additional type of social insurance, (2) another facet of public assistance for the underprivileged, and (3) a way of meeting an overlooked governmental obligation to all citizens.

Proponents of the "shared risk" rationale view compensation as the latest facet of a comprehensive social insurance system that has been developing in the United States since the Great Depression of the 1930s. All of these public welfare insurance programs are intended to enable people to cope with the hazards that threaten stability and security in everyday life: health problems—Medicaid and Medicare; disability and death—Social Security; on-the-job accidents—worker's compensation; and loss of work and earnings—unemployment compensation. The premiums for these state-run compulsory insurance plans are derived from taxation. Criminal injury insurance, like the other types of coverage, provides protection against dangers that are reasonably certain to harm some members of society but that are unpredictable for any individual. All taxpayers contribute to the pool to spread the costs and share the risks that would otherwise burden the victims alone.

The "welfare" approach holds that the state has a humanitarian responsibility to assist crime victims, just as it helps other disadvantaged groups. The aid is given because of the social conscience of concerned citizens and as a symbolic act of mercy, compassion, and charity, but not as insurance coverage or part of any legal obligation. According to this theory, victims do not have a right to compensation, so major eligibility restrictions and payment limits are permissible.

The remaining argument for compensation is that the government is responsible for the protection of its citizens because it monopolizes, or reserves for itself, the right to use force to suppress crime and to punish offenders. Since citizens are not routinely allowed to carry weapons for their own defense against criminal attacks—although special authorization is available for certain occupations—the state is obliged to protect people and their property. Private vengeance is forbidden, and offender restitution is unusual. Thus, the government has made it difficult for victims to recover their losses. If, then, the police are incompetent, negligent, or simply unable to prevent crime, it becomes the state's responsibility to make reparation to the victims. Within the social contract that has developed between the state and its citizens, victims can hold the state liable for damages when it fails to fulfill its obligations to them. This is termed the "tort" rationale. If the logic of this argument is extended, all victims, regardless of their economic standing and the type of loss they have suffered, ought to have a right to compensation. The state owes them reparations to make them whole again.

Besides these rationales, several additional arguments have been advanced to encourage public acceptance of compensation. Some sociologists and criminologists contend that the "system" (the social institutions, economic and political arrangements, prevailing relationships) generates crime by perpetuating bitter competition, poverty, discrimination, unemployment, and insecurity, which breed greed, desperation, and violence. Therefore, society through its governmental bodies owes crime victims compensation as a matter of social justice.

Some advocates note that both public opinion and expert opinion support the concept of reimbursing victims. Citing poll results, they urge that legislators respond to the will of the majority and enact these popular programs.

Certain champions of the victim's cause like to compare the treatment accorded to criminals with the neglect shown to innocent victims. They charge that it is blatantly unfair to attend to many of the medical, educational, vocational, legal, and emotional needs of criminals (albeit minimally, and sometimes against their will) at public expense while injured victims are left to fend for themselves. They suggest that the "imbalance" in the criminal justice system can be partially corrected by implementing compensation programs.

Some pragmatists who favor compensation anticipate that it will help reduce crime by enlisting greater cooperation from victims as complainants and witnesses. Laws can be more effectively enforced and criminals brought to justice if victims are required to assist the authorities by pressing charges, marshaling evidence, and giving testimony against their assailants as preconditions for collecting their money. Since citizens are reluctant for financial reasons to become involved as Good Samaritans to stop a crime in progress and to rush to the aid of victims, compensation programs might elicit more bystander intervention.

Challenges to Compensation

There are several arguments against victim compensation. Some reject it on the basis of their political philosophy; some fear its potential costs; and others object to its possibly undesirable effects on crime rates and the criminal justice system.

The earliest American opponents of compensation generally looked with alarm at what they considered to be the spread of "governmental paternalism" and "creeping socialism." They contended that tax-funded crime insurance undermined the virtues of rugged individualism, self-reliance, personal responsibility, independence, saving for emergencies, and calculated risk taking. They considered any expansion of the welfare state and the growth of new, powerful, and remote bureaucracies as greater evils than the neglect of crime victims. Private enterprise could write more effective and efficient policies than governmental bodies for individuals and families who had enough prudence and foresight to purchase protection in advance, before tragedy struck.

Some skeptics predict that the practice of compensation will increase rather than decrease the crime rate. Criminal injury insurance, like fire, auto, and theft coverage, is vulnerable to fraud. Deserving applicants are hard to distinguish from false victims who have staged incidents, inflicted their own wounds, and padded their bills. Offenders, if they care at all, might feel that they are not hurting their victims too badly, since the government will pay their bills. Some people, lulled by the knowledge that crime-related expenses will be covered by insurance, may act carelessly, irresponsibly, even recklessly. In these ways, compensation may contribute to the temptation–opportunity pattern that characterizes some criminal activities. Public outrage about crime and the plight of victims might diminish, but the root causes of lawlessness will remain. Victim participation in criminal justice proceedings could improve, but the indifference of witnesses might be reinforced. If compensation boards hold additional rounds of hearings at which nonvictim witnesses must testify, then bystanders might become convinced that the only way to avoid thankless obligations is to see nothing and do nothing.

Most contemporary critics do not dispute the merits of compensation programs but object to their establishment on financial grounds. They believe that it is unfair to compel taxpayers to subsidize the losses of crime victims as well as the huge costs of maintaining the criminal justice system—the police, courts, and prisons. Compensation funds must dole out more money each year for a number of reasons. Medical expenses continue to climb. The crime rate for certain acts of violence, like murder and rape, appears to be rising, generating an ever-increasing pool of eligible claimants. Applications for reimbursement pile up as programs receive publicity and victims learn of their rights. The number of awards, the average size of the awards, and the overall operating expenses grow each year, according to the annual reports of the various state compensation boards.

Merits and Demerits: Policy Questions and Administrative Issues

Victims, program administrators, politicians, and criminologists have praised certain features of the thirty-three state compensation programs and assailed other aspects of their rules and practices. But there is no consensus about the merits and demerits of the existing efforts.

The fundamental issue that divides experts and laypersons alike is whether more victims should receive more money or whether program costs should be held down. Controversies surround certain eligibility requirements and benefit restrictions. Critics charge that they undermine any spirit of equity and social justice, but defenders contend that they are necessary to avoid escalating payouts and fraudulent claims. Practically every rule is debatable: the financial hardship test, the penalty for shared responsibility, the family member exclusion, the denial of awards for pain and suffering, the property loss omission, the attorney's fee provision, the minimum loss requirement, and penalty assessments. (Hudson and Galaway, 1975; Reiff, 1979; Carrow, 1980; Lamborn, 1981; Gaynes, 1981; Harland, 1981b; Leepson, 1982; McGillis and Smith, 1983.)

The hardship test. Is it fair to conclude that victims with modest savings and investments don't need help with their out-of-pocket expenses? Realistic concerns regarding unpredictably expensive programs made this restriction a necessary concession to assure the passage of compensation bills by a number of state legislatures. Financial stress tests are intended to screen out those victims who supposedly can "afford" to absorb crime-inflicted losses. They are justified only under the welfare rationale: limited public resources provided as a matter of grace must be channeled to the most desperate victims. Unfortunately, any association of compensation reimbursements with "charity" often conjures up a "welfare handout" stigma that discourages some eligible victims who are neither poverty-stricken nor well-to-do from applying for benefits. Those who dare press a claim are often subjected to some of the same indignities inflicted on the needy seeking public assistance. Their itemized expenses are viewed with suspicion, they wait for hours in inhospitable offices, the processing of their applications is repeatedly delayed, and they are frequently pressured to return to work so their benefits for lost earnings can be canceled.

Critics of the eligibility test point out that victims from the most privileged strata in society are likely to reject compensation in favor of the other remedies—civil lawsuits against perpetrators or third parties, if possible; comprehensive insurance coverage (accident, disability, income maintenance); sick leave with pay during recuperation; and tax deductions for unreimbursed crime losses. In the event of death, their dependents are usually in line for a substantial inheritance and life insurance benefits. The net effect of the hardship test is to eliminate victims drawn from the ranks of the working poor and the middle class. The ironic consequence of spending time to determine eligibility by investigating the victims' finances is an administrative overhead that partially offsets any savings from enforcing the hardship requirement.

The penalty for shared responsibility. A great many victimologists have challenged the notion of the entirely guilty offender and the totally innocent victim (although the opposite stereotypes of the fully responsible victim and the provoked offender are equally misleading). Compensation boards have attempted to assess the victims' contribution to the crime, if any, and have sought to exercise discretionary authority by reducing or denying claims by initiators or escalators of lawless acts. On theoretical grounds, these reductions in compensation are justifiable according to each of the three leading rationales. The social insurance risk-sharing argument assumes that people are randomly susceptible to criminal attack; but randomness no longer holds when victims single themselves out by their own actions. The duty of the state to repay victims it has failed to sufficiently protect is diminished, if not entirely relieved, when the victims actively participate in the incidents leading to their injury or death. The welfare and moral responsibility rationale for compensation is undermined if the criminal act arises directly from the lawless behavior of the victim (for example, a man robbed and wounded while visiting a prostitute or seeking to buy illicit drugs). But in any given episode of criminal violence, the degree of culpability, if any, that can be attributed to victims through their facilitation, precipitation, or provocation is ethically difficult, time-consuming, and costly to determine. The processing of claims could be speeded up and overhead costs slashed if a no-fault standard were adopted, as it has been for auto accidents and worker's compensation claims. But some object that such a policy might not sufficiently encourage prudence and might unjustly reward those who had brought about their own misfortunes.

The family exclusion cause. The provision that a victim related to the offender is automatically ineligible for compensation is very common but of questionable fairness. Wives battered by their husbands, children physically abused by their parents, and brothers and sisters orphaned by the violent acts of other members of their household can't apply. The exclusion saves programs a great deal of money, because family quarrels account for many violent outbursts and deaths. The family/relative/household exclusion is also designed to protect the fund from those who would conspire to defraud it through staged incidents and false claims about how an injury actually occurred. Dishonesty or, worse yet, brutality should not be rewarded by granting money to the family and thus indirectly to the offender. But can these goals be achieved without such blanket exclusions? Critics of the family exclusion rule suggest that payments could be limited to medical bills if victims fully cooperated in the prosecution of the offender. The "unjust enrichment" clause provides an adequate basis for denying awards that would benefit offenders much more than their victims, and the provision mandating reductions if the victims share some of the blame could be invoked when provocation or collusion was established. In these ways, deserving victims could be identified and compensated, and undeserving victims rejected.

Reimbursement for pain and suffering. Another issue still to be resolved is whether to pay victims for any pain and suffering they might endure. Only two states permit victims to apply for money to help heal this invisible and intangible wound. Awards for pain and suffering set by judges and juries in civil court are intended to punish the wrongdoer as much as to soothe the victim. It is difficult to translate pain and suffering into dollars, because each case is unique, and objective criteria can't be established. But a steadfast refusal to recognize pain and suffering as real wounds means that most programs can offer no financial assistance to victims of robberies, sexual assaults, and rapes unless they sustain physical injuries. Critics of this proviso commend those states that consider mental and nervous shock as a legitimate medical problem and permit victims to submit their bills for psychological or psychiatric help.

Payments for property losses. All programs prohibit awards for damaged or lost property, except for eyeglasses, hearing aids, dentures, and other health-related devices essential to the physical well-being of the victim. Those who justify property loss exclusions calculate that reimbursements would be too costly, since the recovery rate for most stolen items other than automobiles is very low. They also point to the possibility of outright fraud. It is easier to fake a break-in or inflate a claim by overstating the value of stolen goods than it is to feign a physical injury or collect for a self-inflicted wound. Besides, other remedies are available: private insurance, federal crime insurance, and income tax deductions for uninsured property losses. Since a property loss lacks the compelling emotional impact of a physical injury that impairs a victim's ability to run a household or earn a living, programs don't provide such coverage. The result is that low-income families who can't afford insurance premiums and don't itemize their tax deductions get no relief from their economic distress if someone steals what little they have. A similar point is raised by those who question why "small" losses are deductible or are not even considered, even though they may loom as major disasters to hard-pressed victims (the rationale is to reduce processing costs and avoid backlogs).

The source of funds. Advocates of the trend toward raising money through penalty assessments argue that adequate funds can be obtained at no cost to taxpayers. This method is attractive to legislators at a time when state budgets face severe fiscal restraints and compensation programs are threatened with cuts or freezes. The tapping of this alternative funding source also appeals to those who opposed compensation as an unfair additional financial burden imposed on innocent citizens who already foot the tax bill for the criminal justice system. But the penalty assessment method can be criticized as a convenient tax levied on an unpopular group. The major offenders who should be repaying their victims generally don't or can't. The added penalties are extracted from the multitude of petty offenders processed for traffic offenses, minor violations, and property crimes. Many from this group are desperately poor already. It is difficult and costly to try to collect extra fines from them or to extract money from prisoners' wages. Furthermore, from a legal standpoint it is not sound to hold an entire class of people, labeled "offenders," financially responsible for the losses of a diverse group, labeled "victims" (in contrast to a restitution obligation which imposes the burden of reimbursement to a particular victim on the specific offender who caused the harm). (Thorjaldson and Krasknik, 1980.)

Attorney fees. Compensation boards that permit the repayment of attorney's fees admit that this feature induces victims to hire an attorney. The justification offered is that a lawyer performs valuable services by efficiently and accurately completing applications and eloquently presenting the victim's case. But critics argue that a reliance on a lawyer fosters a more formal adversarial climate that results in complicated procedures and favors more privileged victims who can afford to retain an attorney at their own initial expense.

Victimologists have grappled with most of these controversial issues. Their recommendations are in some cases more generous or pro-victim than those that politicians are willing to enact (see box 7-1).

In sum, compensation programs are under fire from different quarters. Administrators and legislators are being pressured to make changes along a number of dimensions by various interest groups, advocates, opponents, and observers.

BOX 7-1 Victimologists Take a Stand

At the 1975 International Study Institute, victimologists from around the world passed resolutions that addressed some of the controversial issues regarding compensation (Viano, 1976: 624–625):

- Adequate compensation should include financial grants for "pain and suffering."
- Maximum and minimum levels of reimbursement impose arbitrary restrictions on the principle of fair and adequate compensation.
- Regardless of any shared responsibility for the crime, victims ought to be allowed to apply for reimbursement for direct damages. Victim precipitation can be a reason for reducing or denying any money for pain and suffering.
- A family relationship between the offender and the victim should not be a basis for ruling certain applicants automatically ineligible. But the victim should bear the burden of proof that no collusion or fraud exists and must cooperate fully with the criminal justice system.
- The victim's financial situation should be taken into account in determining how much should be repaid, but compensation should not be limited to those who pass a hardship test.
- Needy victims should be offered free legal aid to prepare their claims.

Successes and Failures: Evaluating Compensation Programs

Many of the arguments about the "rightness" of compensation hinge on judgments about what type of financial help crime victims require and on assumptions about the ability of programs to meet these needs. Now that a number of states have operated programs for fifteen years or more, a substantial body of data has become available for analysis. Evaluation studies can provide benchmarks to justify or rule out new procedures and requests for more funds. Assessments of the efficiency of administrative practices contribute to efforts to eliminate delays, minimize overhead, and iron out inequities. Evaluation as a means of improving service delivery is especially important during periods when the public clamors for additional government aid but is not willing to pay the taxes for it. The differences between the state programs can be taken as an asset. Each jurisdiction is a "laboratory" in which a social experiment is in progress, with various approaches to the same goal being tested.

Revealing How Programs Work

Process evaluations center on the programs' internal operations. They analyze variables like the volume of work, indicated by the number of inquiries received, applications reviewed, and awards granted; productivity, as measured by the number of decisions, the average processing time for a claim, the size of the backlog of outstanding claims, and the time elapsed from decision to payment; overhead costs, calculated as average expenditure per claim or per award, and the ratio of administrative costs to benefits paid out; and decision-making patterns, as revealed by the types of reimbursement made and the reasons for denying claims. Process evaluations also involve developing profiles of the typical claimants and recipients in terms of their sex, race, age, income, and other attributes. Analyzing data bearing on these questions allows evaluators to provide useful feedback to administrators and board members about the trends and patterns that characterize their efforts.

Statistics made public by the New York State Crime Victims Compensation Board for its fourteenth year of operation show that over two-thirds of claimants were turned down. The most frequent reasons for denying reimbursement were that the applicant had failed to divulge the required financial background data about income and expenses and that the type of loss was not covered by the program (the expenses were not for medical bills or lost earnings). Of the awards that were made, much of the money went to repay out-of-pocket hospital and doctor bills. The bulk of the benefits paid to dependents of victims who died from their wounds was for support rather than for funeral and burial costs. (See table 7-5.)

Detecting the Effects of Programs

Impact evaluations clarify the consequences of a program for its clients and the communty. These studies compare a program's intentions with its actual accomplishments. To determine whether compensation really eases the financial stress experienced by crime victims, the ratio of award payments to submitted losses could be calculated. To assess a program's impact on the participation of compensated victims in the criminal justice system, those who did and did not receive aid could be compared with regard to their attendance rates as witnesses in police lineups and court trials.

The prevailing diversity of structures and procedures in different state programs provides opportunities to test out which arrangements work best under which conditions. The findings of research and evaluation studies can have important consequences for the future of compensation. Discoveries of successes and failures can help to resolve the ongoing debates over the pros and cons of compensating crime victims with public funds and the merits and demerits of particular rules and practices (Carrow, 1980; Chappell and Sutton, 1974).

Some preliminary impact evaluations of compensation programs have yielded findings that turn out to be disappointments for administrators. It was hoped that the prospect of reimbursement would increase the public's degree of cooperation with law enforcement. But a study of reporting rates for violent crimes in states with programs compared with

TABLE 7-5 Decisions Made by the New York State Crime Victims Compensation Board

Overview		
Reimbursement granted	2,496	(31%)
Reimbursement denied	5,670	(69%)
Total decisions, 1980–1981	8,166	
Types of awards		
To repay losses from personal injuries	$3,732,154	(65%)
To compensate for death of a family member	$2,018,395	(35%)
Total benefits paid out	$5,750,549	
Of the benefits paid out to reimburse losses for injuries:		
To cover out-of-pocket medical expenses		61%
To compensate for lost earnings		35%
Of the benefits paid out to compensate for death:		
To provide support to family members		64%
To cover out-of-pocket funeral expenses		35%
Reasons for denying reimbursement		
No information was supplied by the victim to the board about finances and losses.		44%
The type of loss was not compensable.		18%
The victim withdrew the application.		7%
The victim would be covered by worker's compensation for lost earnings.		6%
The victim would be covered by Medicaid for hospital and doctor bills.		3%
The victim was not completely innocent.		4%
The victim did not cooperate with the police or the board.		3%
The victim was harmed by a member of the family or household.		2%
The victim could not prove that paying the bills would cause a serious financial hardship.		2%
The person who filed the claim was ineligible.		2%
The victim was not physically injured.		1%
Other miscellaneous reasons		7%

SOURCE: *Annual Report, 1980–81* of the New York State Crime Victims Compensation Board.

states without programs showed no appreciable differences in the extent to which victims in cities told the police about their misfortunes (Doerner, 1978). Research into the attitudes of claimants in Florida who were granted awards compared with those whose requests were denied revealed that getting repaid did not significantly improve the attitudes of victims toward the police, prosecutors, or judges (Doerner, 1980).

An evaluation of the New York and New Jersey programs concluded that claimants were more alienated from the criminal justice system after applying for compensation than nonclaimants. Instead of serving as a means of reducing public discontent with the police and courts, compensation programs provoked additional frustrations. Applicants' expectations probably rose when they first learned about the chance of reimbursement, but these hopes were consistently dashed when most claimants, for a variety of reasons, were turned down or were granted awards insufficient to let them come out even. Only about a third of the claimants in the two states received any money during the late 1970s. Three-quarters indicated that they would not apply for compensation again if they were victimized a second time, largely because of their displeasure over delays and eligibility requirements, their treatment by program administrators, incidental expenses, inconveniences, and, ultimately, the inadequacy of their reimbursements (Elias, 1983a).

The enactment of victim compensation programs can be viewed as an exercise in "symbolic politics" (Elias, 1983b). The public is favorably impressed by the foresight and concern shown by policymakers and legislators toward victims. Unaware that the majority of claimants are turned down and that the remainder are largely dissatisfied with the extent of reimbursement, the public is led to believe that an effective "safety net" has been constructed to cushion the blows of violent crime. At their current insufficient levels of funding, compensation programs serve more to "pacify" victims than to genuinely restore them to their financial condition before the crime occurred.

Congressional Debates over Federal Aid to Crime Victims

Although Congress has considered many compensation bills since 1965, it has failed to enact any legislation to ease the financial burdens of crime victims. The story behind Congress's inaction is instructive, since victims ostensibly have no opponents, only supporters, among Democrats and Republicans.

The first victim compensation bill, introduced in Congress in 1965 by Senator Ralph Yarborough (D–Tex., ADA=71),[1] pertained only to the federal jurisdiction over the District of Columbia. Senator Yarborough justified his bill by contrasting the treatment of victims to the handling of criminals. He complained that society takes care of the accused but does little for the person left lying in the street. In succeeding years he offered similar bills covering victims in Washington, D.C., and other federal territories, as did Representative Frank Horton (R–N.Y., ADA=80) in 1969 and Representative Abner Mikva (D–Ill., ADA=88) in 1972. But none of these was voted on by Congress.

[1]In addition to political party and state, the "liberalism score" of each member of Congress will be given. Lobbies and special interest groups, including the American Conservative Union and its liberal counterpart, Americans for Democratic Action (ADA), rate the voting record of senators and representatives every year. The ADA scores are listed annually in *ADA World,* with high scores approaching 100 denoting a liberal voting record. These scores indicate whether it was liberals or conservatives who sponsored and supported pro-victim legislation.

Federal Aid to State Programs

In 1971, bills intended to encourage the spread of victim compensation programs to more states by providing federal funds for part of the programs' costs were introduced to Congress by senators Vance Hartke (D–Ind., ADA=81), Walter Mondale (D–Minn., ADA=100), and Mike Mansfield (D–Mont., ADA=78). Senator Mansfield's proposal was the most restrictive, or least generous, of the three. It received serious consideration by the Senate Judiciary Committee. The bill called for a Federal Violent Crimes Compensation Board to determine eligibility and awards for claimants injured on federal property. States setting up similar plans could be reimbursed for up to 75 percent of their outlays through the Law Enforcement Assistance Administration. Good Samaritans received preferential treatment compared with that of innocent victims, who first had to prove severe financial stress before they could collect up to $50,000 for lost earnings and medical expenses.

In 1972, the Subcommittee on Criminal Laws and Procedures of the Senate Judiciary Committee held hearings on Senator Mansfield's bill (S.750) and related measures. The legislative proposal was endorsed by representatives of state compensation boards already in operation, governors of these states, consumer groups, the American Bar Association, and the International Association of Chiefs of Police. No interest group or lobby opposed the bill. However, the Justice Department of the Nixon administration recommended defeat of the compensation bill at that time, because it was undertaking a study of the potential of restitution by the offender as a means of reparation (Kleindienst, 1972:19). In his speeches Senator Mansfield used all three rationales that had been developed as arguments for the justness of compensation: that compensation schemes are by no means revolutionary but simply follow the precedent of worker's compensation to aid industrial accident victims; that citizens are owed compensation for their losses when the state fails in its obligation to protect them; and that society has a moral duty to take care of people beset by tragic misfortunes. He also predicted that the possibility of repayment would encourage bystanders to take risks and intervene in behalf of crime victims (Mansfield, 1972:127–133).

The Senate committee wrote a favorable report of S.750 and noted that only seven states had initiated compensation programs without federal backing, surmising that the remainder were deterred by a fear of unknown costs. Senator Roman Hruska (R–Neb., ADA=5) opposed the bill on the Senate floor, imploring the body to give the subject greater study. Senator Sam Ervin (D–N.C., ADA=10), another critic, asserted that the size of the federal debt was too huge to permit such a costly new program. He also argued that there was no more justification for compensating innocent victims of violent crime than there was for compensating victims of nonviolent acts such as fraud. The bill passed the Senate on a roll-call vote of 60 to 8. It was then consolidated into a comprehensive-aid-to-victims package, which also authorized group life insurance benefits for public safety officers and cash pensions to their survivors, made it a federal crime to harm a public safety officer, and strengthened civil remedies for victims of racketeering. This package was attached to a bill providing drug and alcoholism treatment to prisoners. The entire legislative package (HR.8389) was passed by the Senate unanimously, but it was not acted on by the House Judiciary Committee, so it died ("Omnibus Crime Victims Bill," 1972:783–785).

In 1973, senators Mansfield (1973 ADA=85) and Mondale 1973 ADA=95) sponsored a very similar crime victims aid bill (S.300). Senator Strom Thurmond (R-S.C., ADA=0) opposed the act because it encroached on the responsibility of state governments to handle their own crime problems. Senator Hruska (1973 ADA=0) contended that private insurance companies could provide adequate coverage against crime-inflicted health-care costs and lost earnings. He charged that the bill would grant a type of "welfare" to the middle class, since the wealthy were excluded from coverage by hardship tests and the poor had little to lose and could get reimbursed from public assistance funds. S.300 was approved by a voice vote and was attached to a bill previously passed by the House increasing furloughs for federal prisoners. But the House refused to accept it as an amendment, so the Senate incorporated it into an omnibus aid to crime victims package. As in 1972, the Senate passed the bill (93 to 1), but the House Judiciary Committee failed to act on it ("Crime Control Amendments," 1973:370–371).

The House of Representatives paid serious attention to the possibility of compensation for the first time when the Subcommittee on Criminal Justice of the Judiciary Committee held hearings on the Victims of Crime Act of 1977 (HR.7010). Speakers for the American Bar Association, a judge's group, the National District Attorneys Association, the U.S. Conference of Mayors, the National League of Cities, the National Conference of State Legislatures, the National Council on Crime and Delinquency, existing state compensation boards, and senior citizen's groups endorsed the proposals, with some modifications. A speaker for the Department of Justice under the Carter administration recommended lower payment limits to victims and a reduced federal reimbursement formula. But the Judiciary Committee reported favorably on a bill that authorized up to $50,000 per victim and up to 50 percent of a state program's payout costs (excluding administrative overhead). Seven committee Republicans and two Democrats appended dissenting views to the report. They denounced federal aid to state compensation programs as "illogical, arbitrary, and unfair," because they viewed the federal government as having no liability to citizens hurt by violations of state laws. They were concerned about escalating costs and angry that the bill was more generous than the Justice Department had recommended (U.S. Senate, 1977).

The debate on the House floor led to several changes in the Judiciary Committee's version of the compensation bill. An amendment by

Representative Charles Wiggins (R–Calif., ADA=5) was accepted that cut the federal reimbursement rate from 50 percent to 25 percent of payout costs, excluding administrative expenses. An amendment by Representative Lamar Gudger (D–N.C., ADA=35) that diminished the maximum grant a victim could get from $50,000 to $25,000 was adopted.

Supporters of the bill argued that federal funds would serve as an incentive to the twenty states that already had programs to expand their benefits and to the remaining thirty states to initiate compensation plans. Representative Peter Rodino (D–N.J., ADA=85) observed that many of the innocent victims of violent crime were elderly and poor and simply could not afford to purchase insurance or absorb the loss. Representative James Mann (D–S.C., ADA=25) predicted that the prospects of compensation would increase the likelihood of citizen cooperation with police and prosecutors. Other proponents anticipated that program costs could be held down and fraud minimized by ceilings on awards, prohibitions on double recovery (from insurance policies as well as state funds), requirements for offender restitution, and exclusions on property losses.

Opponents voiced concern that states with a low crime rate would end up paying for the compensation granted to victims in states with a high crime rate. Representative Robert McClory (R–Ill., ADA=10) viewed compensation as a confession by law enforcement authorities that they were unable to control the crime problem. Representative Wiggins warned that public service advertising would lead to a jump in the number of claimants, and he said he feared that someday repayment for lost property would be permitted (Hager, 1977:2027).

The bill was approved 192 to 173 on a roll-call vote and was sent to the Senate Judiciary Committee ("Victims of Crime," 1977:570–571).

In 1978, the Senate Judiciary Committee reported its version of a compensation bill (S.551). The proposed legislation set the maximum award a victim could receive at $50,000. The committee report asserted that the criminal justice system ought to protect the interests of the innocent victim as well as society as a whole and the offender. The report viewed federal aid to state compensation programs as consistent with other financial assistance from Washington to the states to further law enforcement.

A compromise Victims of Crimes Act of 1978, with a $35,000 award ceiling, was worked out by a House–Senate conference committee. It passed the Senate on a voice vote, but the House killed it on a roll-call vote. Representative Wiggins (1978 ADA=20) condemned the bill as "only the tip of an iceberg." Other opponents objected that an amendment had been deleted that would have set up escrow accounts to benefit victims of federal crimes from the profits accruing to notorious criminals. The House vote was 184 in favor and 199 against the compromise version ("Crime Victims Aid," 1978:196–198).

In 1979, the Criminal Justice Subcommittee of the House Judiciary

Committee drew up a financially less generous bill (HR.4257) sponsored by representatives Robert Drinan (D–Mass., ADA=100) and Rodino (1979 ADA=63). State programs could differ in various ways but had to meet eleven criteria to be eligible for federal aid. Among the criteria were allowing crime victims to appeal award decisions; not forcing them to accept "welfare" instead of compensation; permitting programs to recover money gained by victims from offenders in successful civil suits; imposing restitution by offenders to victims instead of compensation, if possible; charging convicted defendants at least five dollars to help sustain the compensation fund; and setting up escrow accounts to repay victims or their dependents from the book royalties and movie rights enriching convicts in highly publicized cases.

The committee reported favorably on the bill in 1980. It noted that twenty-seven states had operating programs and eleven others had partial or pending programs that would be activated if federal aid came through. The Congressional Budget Office predicted that only 1.7 percent of violent crime victims suffer monetary losses and meet state requirements for eligibility, and that the average reimbursement would be less than $3,000.

Yet eleven of the thirty-one members strongly opposed the bill and signed statements of dissent attached to the Judiciary Committee's report. "Now is not the time, nor is this bill the proper governmental vessel, for such an uncertain and unnecessary legislative journey," the critics wrote. Although some of them were supporters of compensation plans in their own states, as congressmen they felt they had a duty to taxpayers to vote no, since they perceived that the nation had grown weary of any further growth in federal spending. The siren song of an ever-enlarging federal "big brother" was undermining self-reliance, they contended. Like a skyrocket, once fired, this program's costs would only go higher and higher. Undertaking this spending commitment would mean a head-long plunge into another fiscal tunnel so blind that there was not even a light at the end (U.S. House, 1980).

The committee approved the bill by voice vote in June 1979 and issued its written report with dissenting views in February 1980. The bill was not acted on during the remainder of the session of the 96th Congress. A more generous bill (S. 190), allowing for maximum grants of $35,000 and prohibiting state compensation boards from applying hardship tests to eliminate most claimants, was before the Senate Judiciary Committee. But the Senate was waiting for the House to act, since the Senate had approved compensation bills in the previous four Congresses, dating back to 1971. A victim compensation program that covered only federal crimes and jurisdictions was incorporated into the controversial, massive criminal code reform bill (S. 1722), which failed to pass in 1980 (Cohodas, 1980).

A statistical analysis of congressional votes on all these bills over the years since 1965 reveals that Democrats, particularly liberal Democrats, have tended to favor allocating federal aid to reimburse crime victims. Republicans, especially conservative Republicans, have tended to oppose spending federal tax dollars on state compensation programs. The exceptions to these patterns were usually conservative Democrats, generally from Southern states, who sided with conservative Republicans against compensation plans; and some liberal Republicans, often from Northern states, who joined with liberal Democrats in support of these pro-victim legislative initiatives. Ideology has proven itself to be somewhat more important or reliable as a determinant or predictor of voting behavior than party affiliation (Karmen, 1981).

During 1981, 1982, and 1983, Congress did not give any serious attention to victim compensation legislation. Instead, in 1982 it passed a bill ordering offenders to make restitution to victims of federal crimes whenever possible. Under the Reagan administration's economic policies, federal aid to state programs was cut back severely, and any plans for new spending initiatives from Washington were shelved by Congress.

In 1983, Congress considered a Crime Victims' Assistance Act introduced by senators John Heinz (R–Pa.) and Charles Grassley (R–Ia.), and a Victims of Crime Act sponsored by representatives Peter Rodino and Howard Berman (D–Calif.). Despite some minor differences, both bills shared several key features. First of all, victim assistance programs in the various states would be funded by the proposed legislation as well as victim compensation funds. Secondly, both initiatives would not cost taxpayers additional money. The funding would be derived from revenues already coming into the Treasury, and from the proceeds of new penalty assessments levied on convicts. Specifically, the sources would be: all fines collected in federal criminal cases; all forfeitures (of bail, property) in federal criminal cases; taxes collected by the Internal Revenue Service on pistol and revolver sales; a new penalty assessment imposed on people convicted of federal crimes (called a "compensation fee"); and extra fines imposed on criminals who profited substantially from their crimes ("Legislative Update," 1983 [April and June]). The sponsors hoped that by shifting the financial burden from taxpayers to offenders, Congress finally would approve a bill to help states compensate victims. But it didn't.

References

AUSTERN, DAVID; GALAWAY, BURT; GODEGAST, RICHARD; GROSS, RICHARD; HOFRICHTER, RICHARD; HUDSON, JOE; HUTCHINSON, THOMAS; and YOUNG-RIFAI, MARLENE. 1979: *Compensating Victims of Crime—Participant's Handbook,* Criminal Justice Utilization Program. Washington, D.C.: University Research Corp.

BERNSTEIN, GEORGE. 1972: "Report on the Federal Crime Insurance Program." In U.S. Senate, Committee on the Judiciary, Subcommittee on Criminal Laws and Procedures, Congress, 1st session, 521–529. Washington, D.C.: U.S. Government Printing Office.

BROOKS, JIMMY. 1972: *Criminal Injury Compensation Programs: An Analysis of Their Development and Administration.* Ann Arbor, Mich.: University Microfilms.

BUREAU OF JUSTICE STATISTICS. 1982: *Criminal Victimization in the United States, 1980.* Washington, D.C.: U.S. Department of Justice.

CARROW, DEBORAH. 1980: *Crime Victims Compensation: U.S. Department of Justice Program Model.* Washington, D.C.: U.S. Government Printing Office.

CHAPPELL, DUNCAN, and SUTTON, PAUL. 1974: "Evaluating the Effectiveness of Programs to Compensate the Victims of Crime." In Israel Drapkin and Emilio Viano (Eds.), *Victimology: A New Focus* (Volume 2), 207–220. Lexington, Mass.: Heath.

CHILDRES, ROBERT. 1964: "Compensation for Criminally Inflicted Personal Injury." *New York University Law Review,* 39:455–471.

COHODAS, NADINE. 1980: "Legislation to Compensate the Victims of Crime Stalled Again in Congress." *Congressional Quarterly Weekly Report,* 38,6:343–344.

"Crime Control Amendments." 1973: *Congressional Quarterly Almanac,* 29:370–372.

"Crime Victims' Aid." 1978: *Congressional Quarterly Almanac,* 34:196–198.

DOERNER, WILLIAM. 1978: "An Examination of the Alleged Latent Effects of Victim Compensation Programs upon Crime Reporting." *LAE Journal,* 41:71-80.

——— 1980: "Impact of Crime Compensation on Victim Attitudes toward the Criminal Justice System." *Victimology,* 5,2:61–77.

EDELHERTZ, HERBERT, and GEIS, GILBERT. 1974: *Public Compensation to Victims of Crime.* New York: Praeger.

ELIAS, ROBERT. 1983a: "Alienating the Victim: Compensation and Victim Attitudes." *Journal of Social Issues.* Forthcoming.

——— 1983b: "The Symbolic Politics of Victim Compensation." *Victimology.* Forthcoming.

EUROPEAN COMMITTEE ON CRIME PROBLEMS. 1978: *Compensation of Victims of Crime.* Strassburg, Austria: Author.

FRY, MARGERY. 1957: "Justice for Victims." *Observer* (London), November 10:8. Reprinted in *Journal of Public Law,* 1959,8:191–194.

GAROFALO, JAMES, and SUTTON, PAUL. 1977: *Compensating Victims of Violent Crime: Potential Costs and Coverage of a National Program.* Washington, D.C.: U.S. Government Printing Office.

GAYNES, MINDY. 1981: "New Roads to Justice: Compensating the Victim." *State Legislatures,* November-December:11–17.

GEIS, GILBERT. 1976: "Compensation to Victims of Violent Crime." In Rudolph Gerber (Ed.), *Contemporary Issues in Criminal Justice,* 90–115. Port Washington, N.Y.: Kennikat.

——— 1983: "Victim Compensation and Restitution." *Encyclopedia of Crime and Justice,* 1604–1608. New York: Free Press.

"The Good Samaritans." 1965: *The New York Times,* November 20:34.

HAGER, BARRY. 1977: "Aid for Victims of Crime: Federal or State Effort?" *Congressional Quarterly Weekly Report,* 35,40:2027.

HARLAND, ALAN. 1981a: *Restitution to Victims of Personal and Household Crimes.* Washington, D.C.: U.S. Department of Justice.

——— 1981b: "Victim Compensation: Programs and Issues." In Burt Galaway and Joe Hudson (Eds.), *Perspectives on Crime Victims,* 412–417. St. Louis, Mo.: Mosby.

HUDSON, JOE, and GALAWAY, BURT. 1975: *Considering the Victim: Readings in Restitution and Victim Compensation.* Springfield, Ill.: Charles C Thomas.

KARMEN, ANDREW. 1981: "Crime Victims and Congress." Unpublished paper delivered at the convention of the Academy of Criminal Justice Sciences, Philadelphia, February.

KLEINDIENST, RICHARD. 1972: "Letter to the Judiciary Chairman, Senator Eastland." In U.S. Senate, Committee on the Judiciary, Subcommittee on Criminal Laws and Procedures, *Hearing—Victims of Crime,* 92nd Congress, 1st Session, 19. Washington, D.C.: U.S. Government Printing Office.

LAMBORN, LEROY. 1981: "Victim Compensation Programs: An Overview." In Burt Galaway and Joe Hudson (Eds.), *Perspectives on Crime Victims,* 418–422. St. Louis, Mo.: Mosby.

LEEPSON, MARC. 1982: "Helping Victims of Crime." *Editorial Research Reports,* 1,17:331–344.

"Legislative Update." 1983: *NOVA* (National Organization for Victim Assistance) *Newsletter,* 7,4(April):2–3.

"Legislative Update." 1983: *NOVA Newsletter,* 7,6(June):3.

MacNAMARA, DONAL, and SULLIVAN, JOHN. 1974: "Making the Victim Whole: Composition, Restitution, Compensation." In Terence Thornberry and Edward Sagarin (Eds.), *Images of Crime: Offenders and Victims,* 79–90. New York: Praeger.

MANSFIELD, MIKE. 1972: "Statement." In U.S. Senate, Committee on the Judiciary, Subcommittee on Criminal Laws and Procedures, *Hearings—Victims of Crime,* 92nd Congress, 1st Session, 127–133. Washington, D.C.: U.S. Government Printing Office.

McGILLIS, DANIEL, and SMITH, PATRICIA. 1983: *Compensating Victims of Crime: An Analysis of American Programs.* Washington, D.C.: U.S. Department of Justice.

MEINERS, ROGER. 1978: *Victim Compensation: Economic, Political, and Legal Aspects.* Lexington, Mass.: Heath.

MEUERER, EMIL, Jr. 1979: "Violent Crime Losses: Their Impact on the Victim and Society." *Annals, American Academy of Political and Social Science,* 433(May): 54–62.

NATIONAL ORGANIZATION FOR VICTIM ASSISTANCE (NOVA). 1983: *Victim Rights and Services: A Legislative Directory, 1983.* Washington, D.C.: NOVA.

NEW YORK STATE CRIME VICTIMS COMPENSATION BOARD. 1982: *Annual Report, 1980–81.* Albany, N.Y.: Author.

"Omnibus Crime Victims Bill Approved by Senate." 1972: *Congressional Quarterly Almanac,* 28:783–786.

REIFF, ROBERT. 1979: *The Invisible Victim.* New York: Basic Books.

SCHAFER, STEPHEN. 1970: *Compensation and Restitution to Victims of Crime* (2nd edition). Montclair, N.J.: Patterson Smith.

SCHULTZ, LEROY. 1965: "The Violated: A Proposal to Compensate Victims of Violent Crime." *St. Louis University Law Journal,* 10:238–250.

SILVING, HELEN. 1959: "Compensation for Victims of Criminal Violence—A Round Table." *Journal of Public Law,* 8:236–253.

SKOGAN, WESLEY. 1978: *Victimization Surveys and Criminal Justice Planning.* Washington, D.C.: U.S. Government Printing Office.

THORJALDSON, SVEINN, and KRASKNIK, MARK. 1980: "On Recovering Compensation Funds from Offenders." *Victimology,* 5:20–30.

U.S. HOUSE COMMITTEE ON THE JUDICIARY. 1980: *Victims of Crime Act of 1979: Report, together with Dissenting and Separate Views.* 96th Congress, 2nd Session, February 13. Washington, D.C.: U.S. Government Printing Office.

U.S. SENATE COMMITTEE ON THE JUDICIARY. SUBCOMMITTEE ON CRIMINAL JUSTICE. 1977: *Hearings-Victims of Crime: Compensation.* Serial 56. Washington, D.C.: U.S. Government Printing Office.

VIANO, EMILIO. 1976: *Victims and Society.* Washington, D.C.: Visage.

"Victims of Crime." 1977: *Congressional Quarterly Almanac, 33:570–571.*

WOLFGANG, MARVIN. 1965: "Victim Compensation in Crimes of Personal Violence." *Minnesota Law Review,* 50:229–241.

CHAPTER 8

Victims in the Future

Many proposals will be put forth in the near future to make the criminal justice system more responsive and accountable to its primary clients, victims. But a heated debate will develop over what rights crime victims should be guaranteed. Another controversy will erupt over who should pay for their services and benefits.

In disgust and dismay, some victims and their allies are seeking alternative, informal ways of meeting their needs. One substitute for the formal court process that will receive increasing attention is dispute resolution at neighborhood justice centers. Its theme is to engage the antagonistic parties in negotiations that lead to a compromise solution and reconciliation. But there are rumblings about victims turning toward another kind of informal "solution" to their conflicts with criminals: the old-fashioned, uncompromising, retaliatory violence of vigilantism. Any revival of vigilantism would represent a clear failure of the criminal justice system, its informal alternatives, and the pro-victim movements to adequately satisfy the emotional, physical, and financial needs of crime victims.

Toward a Bill of Rights for Crime Victims

To reform simply means to improve, to correct faults, and to end abuses. Different activists and organizations agree that reform of the criminal justice system is needed, but they disagree over goals, priorities, and methods. One focus of attention will be on drawing up a bill of rights for victims. The controversy will center on the issue of "at whose expense?" Two possibilities exist. The first is to grant rights to victims by denying privileges and benefits to suspects, defendants, and prisoners. The second is to improve the welfare of victims at the expense of the privileges and options enjoyed by criminal justice officials and agencies.

The firm conviction that crime victims need to be guaranteed certain rights flows from an appreciation of how they have been neglected, exploited, and denied services in the past. The specific rights they might benefit from are derived from assessments of the problems they face with the police, in hospitals, in court, at work (with employers), at home (with landlords), in the streets (with offenders and their friends), and in the media (with regard to their reputations and their privacy). Various proposals for extending victims' rights (see Carrington, 1975; Grayson, 1981; Reiff, 1979) have led to legislative initiatives.

Tipping the Scales toward the Victim

The point of view that victims' rights ought to be gained at the expense of privileges and benefits currently enjoyed by "criminals" (more accurately: suspects, defendants, and prisoners) is based on the belief that the scales of justice have been tipped too much in recent years toward the accused or convicted and away from the victim. Whittling away the (alleged) advantages enjoyed by offenders would restore balance to the system, according to partisans of this outlook. They believe that one reason the crime problem has intensified is that it has become much more difficult to punish offenders. Their goal is to increase the ability of the state to convict offenders and thereby to improve the lot of victims, who must rely on the state to avenge them. From this perspective, a victim's bill of rights would contain provisions to raise the conviction rate, stiffen penalties, close "loopholes" that permit the guilty to escape their just deserts, and eliminate acts of unwarranted leniency (see table 8-1, pp. 232–233).

Some of the rights granted to victims at the expense of suspects, defendants, and prisoners have altered the balance between the two conflicting parties, but other recently affirmed rights have been available to victims all along. The flurry of legislative activity surrounding victim impact statements and offender restitution obligations illustrates the current trend toward formally spelling out the rights of crime victims.

Judges have had common law authority for many decades to invite victims to address the court before a sentence is pronounced, and to order offenders to make restitution to those they have harmed. A Philadelphia judge has noted that while she routinely offered victims the opportunity to voice their views at sentencing hearings, they seldom chose to speak out (Forer, 1980). Similarly, many judges pass up opportunities to impose restitution. The passage of legislation that permits victims to file impact statements and enables judges to decree restitution as a condition of probation, prison labor, or parole simply provides statutory reinforcement for common law traditions. Some state legislatures have gone further in the direction of guaranteeing these rights, gained at the expense of offenders, by making victim impact statements and restitution mandatory in all relevant cases.

Since 1982 for example, in Maryland, judges must consider the physical, mental, and financial harm suffered by the victim if the victim voluntarily fills out a questionnaire as part of the presentencing report. The impact statement requests that all economic losses be itemized and inquires about the extent of any insurance reimbursement. The victim is asked whether the incident in any way impaired his or her ability to earn a living, caused an unwanted change in lifestyle, or strained family relationships. The victim is also asked to identify any physical injuries or emotional problems that can be traced back to the crime. At the end of the form, space is provided for opinions about the functioning of the criminal justice system and suggestions for an appropriate sentence for the offender. All of the victim's answers must be affirmed as true under penalty of perjury (NOVA, 1983:40).

In most states, the victim impact statement is developed by the probation officer who also investigates the offender's past arrests and convictions, employment history, family background, educational attainment, finances, and personal habits. In some states, victims have the option of either delivering their statements orally in court or submitting them in writing. A few states restrict impact statements to sentencing for serious felonies such as rape or murder (in which case the victim's family would have a direct channel to express their feelings). Arizona permits a victim to be represented by a lawyer at a presentence hearing (NOVA, 1983:4–5). In Connecticut, since the enactment of an impact statement requirement in 1981, court officials estimate that victims appear at about 3 percent of all sentencing hearings. When they do come to court, it is usually to demand restitution rather than retribution (Press and LaBrecque, 1983).

In Delaware, a mandatory restitution statute requires police to prepare a statement of loss for the judge, who must order restitution or else state for the record the reasons for denying the victim the right to reimbursement. Money paid to the court by the offender first goes to pay off the penalty assessment that supports the state's compensation fund. Then the victim receives restitution. Finally, a portion of the offender's earnings is earmarked for court costs and fines. In Nevada, making restitution is not mandatory as a condition of probation or parole, but if it is imposed by a judge, failure to keep to the payment schedule constitutes a violation of the terms of probation or parole and is grounds for revocation and imprisonment (NOVA, 1983:11,16).

Civil liberties groups consider many of these newly enacted "rights" potentially unconstitutional. In the name of rushing to the aid of victims, the power of the state has been greatly strengthened. But lifting the

TABLE 8-1 Victims' Rights Gained at the Expense of Offenders' Rights

Subject	*Proposals*	*Enacted where, when*
Bail	Deny bail to suspects accused of serious crimes if their freedom is believed to endanger their victims or the community at large. Require judges to state for the record why bail is justified each time they grant it.	California, 1982*
Protection from intimidation	Increase the penalties for intimidating victims or witnesses, and enforce court orders of protection with greater vigilance.	Pennsylvania, 1980; Rhode Island, 1980; Oklahoma, 1981; Wisconsin, 1981; Nebraska, 1981; federal jurisdictions, 1982;† California, 1983; Minnesota, 1983
Pleas	Restrict plea bargaining as a way of resolving major felony cases, or involve victims in the process.	Indiana, 1981; California, 1982
Defenses	Restrict the use of two defenses: "not guilty by reason of insanity" and "diminished capacity" (due to intoxication or drug use).	California, 1982; Connecticut, 1982; Hawaii, 1982; Idaho, 1982; Montana, 1982
Evidence	Permit all relevant evidence gathered by the police in good faith to be admissible in trials instead of excluding whatever was gathered illegally.	California, 1982
Sentencing	Permit victims to press for greater penalties and restitution by including their views in presentencing victim impact statements, along with reports of their losses.	Illinois, 1978; New Jersey, 1980; Ohio, 1980; Connecticut, 1981; Indiana, 1981; Kansas, 1981; Nevada, 1981; New Hampshire, 1981; Arizona, 1982; California, 1982; Maryland, 1982; New York, 1982; federal jurisdictions, 1982; Minnesota, 1983

restraints on the authority of government officials to punish citizens is not the same as empowering victims to pursue their legitimate interests. Victims and state officials often have differing, even opposing, interests. According to the critics, these anti-offender and pro-prosecutor measures undermine the foundations of the U.S. justice system. The principles that a person is innocent unless proven guilty and that the burden of proof is shouldered by the state are subverted when bail is denied to suspects, when illegally obtained evidence can be used against defendants, and when the victim's thirst for revenge is exploited by the government to enhance its punitive powers. Opponents of these measures also question the practicality of restricting plea bargaining and of imprisoning more people for longer periods of time. Additionally, they point out that

Youth	Send young adults to prisons rather than juvenile institutions if they commit serious crimes, and hold juveniles responsible for full adult penalties for serious crimes.	New York, 1978; California, 1982
Restitution	Impose restitution as a mandatory condition of probation or parole, or require the judge to cite reasons why it was not ordered.	New Jersey, 1980; Wisconsin, 1981; California, 1982; Delaware, 1982; Utah, 1982; federal jurisdictions, 1982
Appeals	Permit victims to appeal sentences imposed on offenders that seem to be too lenient.	California, 1982
Parole	Permit victims to argue against parole at hearings and to oppose commutations of sentences by governors.	Massachusetts, 1982; California, 1982; Arkansas, 1983
Abuser's tax	Raise money to pay for victim compensation and victim–witness assistance programs by taxing felons, misdemeanants, and traffic law violators.	California, 1974; Minnesota, 1974; Connecticut, 1980; Nevada, 1981; Montana, 1981; Colorado, 1981; Oklahoma, 1981; Texas, 1981; Missouri, 1981; Tennessee, 1981; Ohio, 1981; Pennsylvania, 1981; West Virginia, 1981; Virginia, 1981; Florida, 1981; Maryland, 1981; Delaware, 1981; New Jersey, 1981; Iowa, 1982; New York, 1982; Kentucky, 1982; Washington, 1982; Rhode Island, 1982; South Carolina, 1982

*Part of a proposition passed by California voters that was entitled a Victim's Bill of Rights
†Part of an Omnibus Victims Protection Act of 1982 passed by Congress and signed into law by the president

SOURCES: Cohodas, 1982; Gest and Davidson, 1982; Leepson, 1982; Lindsey, 1982; New York State Assembly Task Force on Crime Victims, 1982; Press and Contreras, 1982; Reilly, 1981; Shipp, 1982; Victim/Witness Resource Center, 1982; NOVA, 1983; "From the States: Minnesota," 1983.

these "rights" can be exercised by only a small percentage of victims who are fortunate enough to have their cases solved by the police. For the overwhelming majority of property crime victims and for most victims of violence, these are empty rights, since no one is even arrested in their cases.

Making the Criminal Justice System Serve Its Clients

The alternative approach to designing and implementing victim's rights starts from the premise that the suffering of victims must be minimized through governmental programs. The criminal justice system has a responsibility to its clients even if it cannot catch their offenders. Society, or, more accurately, the social system, is partly at fault for the crime problem and bears an obligation to help victims get back on their feet. The forms of assistance and support offered to certain victims in particular jurisdictions ought to be guaranteed to all victims in all parts of the country. The preoccupation with punishing offenders must not interfere with efforts to restore victims to the condition they were in before the crime occurred (see table 8-2, pp. 236–237).

As tables 8-1 and 8-2 indicate, most of the proposals that have been enacted into law on the state and federal levels have advanced victims' rights at the expense of the rights of suspects, defendants, and convicts (rights that had been established by Supreme Court rulings in cases brought by civil rights and civil liberties groups). Only a few of the proposals that aid victims at the expense of criminal justice agencies or the public treasury (taxpayers) have been enacted. One major reason for the inactivity on this front is the fear on the part of state legislators that such mandated entitlements would be very costly. Where would the money come from to pay for an expansion of the "safety net" to catch victims toppled from their social positions by offenders?

Financing Victim Services

An ironic situation is developing. Although the enthusiasm for helping victims is growing, the willingness to pay for the necessary services is declining. There are many imaginative programs and experiments, but there is not much government support.

The future of existing programs is in doubt. Many rape crisis centers, shelters for battered women, victim–witness assistance programs, and restitution projects were originally funded with federal "seed money." Financing was arranged through the Law Enforcement Assistance Administration of the Department of Justice, the Urban Initiatives Anti-Crime Program of the Department of Housing and Urban Development, and the Office of Domestic Violence and the National Center for the Prevention and Control of Rape of the Department of Health and Human Services. Besides volunteers, staff members were drawn from Comprehensive Employment and Training Act (CETA) workers and from Action. Severe budgetary cutbacks have compelled these federal agencies to discontinue the aid they were providing to the fledgling field of victim assistance.

Victim services programs have turned to state and local governments for funding as the federal government's priorities have shifted from social spending to military spending. But a fiscal problem—if not a crisis—exists in many states, counties, and municipalities. Tax reduction movements are demanding across-the-board relief (including for high-income people and prosperous businesses), so the ability of local government to raise sufficient revenues for existing expenses is severely restricted. Additional responsibilities and outlays are particularly unwelcome at such times. Competition is keen over portions of a shrinking pie.

Social programs intended to improve the welfare of crime victims have suffered most visibly during the fiscal crisis of the early 1980s. Budgetary cutbacks have taken their toll in a number of ways. Some shelters for battered women, crisis centers for rape victims, and victim–witness assistance programs have been forced to shut their doors. Others struggle along, overcrowded, understaffed, and underfunded.

Since 1980, fourteen state legislatures have passed bills ensuring the funding of victim and witness assistance programs at the county and municipal levels. The trend has been to raise the money for these services by levying penalty assessments on all convicted offenders rather than by taxing the general public. In Alaska, Nebraska, New York, and Wisconsin, victim services are funded solely from general revenues. In California, Connecticut, Florida, Missouri, Oklahoma, and Pennsylvania, services are supported entirely from penalties and fines. Both sources of money are tapped in Kentucky, Minnesota, New Jersey, and Washington (NOVA, 1983). In Washington, the "abuser's tax" is fifty dollars for all people convicted of felonies and twenty-five dollars for misdemeanors. In California, an additional four dollars in penalty assessments is collected for every ten dollars in fines, for traffic tickets as well as for more serious violations of the law (Leepson, 1982).

Even with this new source of funds, victim services and victim compensation programs face financial hard times. In Rhode Island, the compensation fund ran out of money when it awarded victims twice as much as it took in from penalty assessments (Associated Press, 1983). In other states, benefits have been cut and claimants must wait years to receive their awards.

As a last resort, some victim assistance programs have sought private donations and rely on volunteers for staffing (President's Task Force, 1982).

Determining New Directions for Victims' Rights and Services

In the foreseeable future, victimologists and victim advocates will focus their attention on three themes: first, identifying groups whose rights are not being respected and whose needs are not being adequately met; second, devising new rights to safeguard the interests of crime victims; and third, improving the quality of services offered to victims. Three groups that are currently neglected in terms of rights and services are rural victims, arson victims, and victimized members of deviant groups. Proposals to guarantee the rights of victimized children as complainants within the criminal justice system are likely to merit a great deal of attention in coming years, along with initiatives to respect a victim's right to privacy. In the realm of service delivery, integrating existing programs

TABLE 8-2 Victims' Rights to Assistance, Services, and Reimbursement

	Proposals	*Enacted where, when*
To be informed	Read victims their rights as soon as they report a crime. Inform them of all services, opportunities, and obligations at this time. Provide information in writing about assistance programs, crisis intervention counseling, compensation plans, restitution projects, civil lawsuits, tax deductions, and other courses of action open to them. Furnish numbers to call, forms to file, and advocates to consult with at police stations, hospital emergency rooms, district attorney's offices, and courthouses.	Wisconsin, 1980; Nebraska, 1981; Minnesota, 1983
To sue	Permit victims to sue the government in civil court for breach of contract if their "right to know" as outlined above is violated.	
To notification	Give victims as much advance notice as possible of criminal justice proceedings which they are required to attend, and tell them promptly of any changes in schedule.	Wisconsin, 1980; Nebraska, 1981; Washington, 1981
To know about their case	Keep victims posted about the progress of their cases and the outcome of important proceedings. Advise them if a warrant is issued for someone's arrest, a suspect is in custody, bail is granted, a plea is negotiated, a conviction is secured, probation is granted, incarceration is begun, the offender is furloughed, parole is granted, or the prison term expires.	Washington, 1981; Oklahoma, 1981; Nebraska, 1981; Minnesota, 1983

will be tried. The establishment of the role of victim advocate within an integrated system is likely, as well.

The rights of victims residing in rural areas are not adequately addressed, and the kinds of assistance available to them are severely restricted in comparison to the aid offered within metropolitan areas. The response times for police and ambulance services are much longer in the countryside surrounding small towns than in cities. The problems arise from low population densities, transportation difficulties over great distances, and a lack of nearby emergency and criminal justice facilities (Young, 1982).

Every year there are some 75,000 fires in residential buildings that are

To intercession	Upon request, intercede with employers who would otherwise seriously penalize victims for missing work because of court appearances. Intercede with creditors, like landlords or banks, who demand payments and won't make allowances for crime-related losses.	Wisconsin, 1980; Washington, 1981
To witness fees	Pay victims (and witnesses for both the prosecution and the defense) fees at least equivalent to the minimum wage for the time they must spend in court.	Washington, 1981
To separate facilities	Provide victims and prosecution witnesses with separate waiting rooms from those used by defendants and spectators, to avoid intimidation, embarrassment, and confrontation.	Wisconsin, 1980; Washington, 1981
To return of property	Promptly return stolen property that was recovered by the police (if it is being held as evidence; permit photographs to substitute for the impounded items, whenever possible).	Wisconsin, 1980; Kansas, 1981; Nebraska, 1981; Washington, 1981
To crucial property	Restore essential personal property such as eyeglasses or crutches to victims who are elderly, handicapped, or destitute.	
To tax breaks	Treat all crime-related medical expenses that are not covered by health insurance as fully tax deductible.	
To reimbursement	Make up unreimbursed losses, preferably through restitution or a civil lawsuit, but as a last resort through state-funded victim compensation.	

SOURCES: Hudson, 1980; New York State Assembly Task Force on Victims, 1982; NOVA, 1983; "From the States: Minnesota," 1983.

set by arsonists. Each fire causes an average of $6,000 worth of property damage. About 1,000 people die and 10,000 are injured annually in fires that are intentionally started. Most are "third party," or incidental victims who are not the intended targets of the arsonist. (In many tenement blazes, the primary or direct victims, the owners of the buildings, are not victims but criminals. They have paid others to burn down their failing businesses in order to collect insurance reimbursement. In such cases, the innocent victims are the tenants of apartments in these buildings.) The motives of the criminals include: to collect insurance reimbursement, to force tenants to move, to maliciously destroy property, to retaliate against an owner or tenant, or to cover up evidence of another crime. The victims of an arson fire share the same problems of other victims: physical injuries, emotional disturbances, lost property, and lost earnings. However, they also face unusual hardships in their dealings with the criminal justice system. For example, after a tenement fire, arson victims may be unable to enter their apartments to retrieve money, checkbooks, clothing, and other valuables, so they need emergency financial assistance. Because their immediate concern is to find shelter, they may leave the scene of the crime without providing authorities with a forwarding address, and thus become "lost." Since fire marshals cannot immediately determine the cause of the blaze, the burned out tenants may not realize that they are victims of a criminal act and are thereby eligible for certain forms of aid. If they are not eyewitnesses, the displaced tenants can play no role in the investigation and prosecution of the case, and thus won't be offered services by victim–witness assistance programs. Even if they have valuable information to contribute, they may "fall through the cracks" of the overlapping jurisdictions of fire marshals and police investigators. If they are not adequately insured, they cannot turn to state compensation programs to get reimbursement for devastating losses (Victim/Witness Assistance Project, 1983).

In many tenement blazes, the primary or direct victims, the owners of the buildings, are not victims but criminals. They have paid others to burn down their failing businesses in order to collect insurance reimbursement. In such cases, the innocent victims are the tenants of apartments in these buildings. Realizing the plight of tenant victims, community activists in thirty neighborhoods across the country have organized a National Arson Prevention and Action Coalition. It tries to smother arson-for-profit schemes by developing early warning systems to identify high risk buildings that can then be guarded by tenant patrols or police and fire marshal stake-outs. The founders of the coalition researched the history of the burned buildings on their blocks in Boston and discovered that the targets of insurance fires set by professional "torches", hired by unscrupulous landlords, had these characteristics: they were run-down, with many violations of health and safety codes; they were not owner-occupied; the buildings had had many owners over a short period of time; the owner was in arrears on mortgage payments and property taxes; some apartments were already vacant; the building was insured far in excess of its current market value; and there had been a rash of suspicious small fires before the major blaze (Lafferty, 1981).

Victimologists have been directing their attention toward the plight of particularly vulnerable groups, such as those who are physically weak (children, the aged) or are at a social, economic, or political disadvantage (women, minorities, workers, consumers). Yet a relatively unexplored area is the victimization of deviants—people assigned a low social status, such as prisoners, mental patients, prostitutes, alcoholics, drug addicts, homosexuals, and members of religious cults (see MacNamara and Karmen, 1983; and Fattah, 1981). The exploitation and oppression of socially stigmatized and ostracized groups have caused their members to organize in defense of their rights, but their special needs as street crime victims have gone largely unattended: homosexuals are assaulted, prostitutes robbed, and drunks "rolled," for example. When, as a last resort, individuals from disvalued groups turn to the criminal justice system for help, they find themselves treated as "second-class" complainants. The authorities view them primarily as victimizers and troublemakers rather than as victims with legitimate claims for protection and service.

In the recent past, the elderly have received extra consideration within the criminal justice system. In the near future, victims at the opposite end of the age spectrum are likely to gain special privileges. The rights of child victims need to be safeguarded because their experiences within the criminal justice system are particularly anxiety-provoking. Sometimes they are deemed too young to testify in cases of child abuse, sexual abuse, or school violence, but if they do appear in court as witnesses for the prosecution, they may be subjected to a humiliating cross examination by defense attorneys to destroy their credibility. In recognition of their special vulnerability, the specific rights they may be granted include the use of language they can understand when explaining their role in the criminal justice process, and the use of videotapes of their testimony and cross examination in lieu of personal appearances in court, if the judge has good cause to believe direct participation would be traumatic ("Wisconsin Considers: Should Children Have Rights Too?," 1983).

A number of states have begun to permit court proceedings to be televised. The immediate impact of the presence of cameras on the testimony of victims and witnesses (of all ages) and the long-term effects of the resulting publicity are not known. It is likely that guidelines will be developed to safeguard the rights of victims and witnesses to dignity and privacy. They may gain the right to refuse to be televised or photographed in court to prevent their plight from becoming a public spectacle ("Policy Issues: On Cameras-in-the-Courtroom," 1983).

Victimologists have uncovered the debilitating effects of "second wounds" delivered by victim-blamers long after the crime. In response, a number of proposals will be presented to state legislatures that will guarantee other facets of a victim's right to privacy, confidentiality, and protection from unwanted publicity. These issues were dramatized in Rhode Island when staff members of a rape crisis center burned records on the steps of a courthouse as the director was sentenced to jail for ignoring a subpoena for case notes from the center's files. They argued that if confidentiality could not be assured, victims would not benefit much from counseling because of their reluctance to openly discuss deeply personal feelings; and that if notes about the fears, desires, and fantasies of rape victims under extreme duress were revealed to defense lawyers, the intensely private material could be used to discredit the testimony or character of the victims on the stand during a trial. In 1981, Pennsylvania and Minnesota passed laws to exempt sexual assault counselors (nurses, social workers, volunteers, and former victims) from testifying or turning over case files without the victim's consent. Some states will implement the recommendation of the President's Task Force on Victims of Crime that the privilege of confidentiality now shielding the files of psychiatrists and psychologists be extended to other designated counselors who serve all kinds of victims, beyond just rape (NOVA, 1983:6).

In the near future, efforts will be made to integrate existing victim services. At the present time, service providers tend to be highly specialized. Some projects help victims of a particular crime (rape, wife-beating) or of a particular kind (women, the elderly, children) or with a particular problem (crisis intervention, witness assistance, restitution). Among service providers, a controversy rages over the advantages and disadvantages of working with groups that are differentiated by the type of crime that befell them, the kind of background they come from, and by which phase within the criminal justice process they have entered (Young, 1982). The trend is toward centralizing services within comprehensive programs.

A rivalry has arisen between competing agencies representing the criminal justice system and the mental health system. In the coming years, it is probable that community mental health centers will develop greater expertise in addressing the problems of crime victims. These centers have already reached out to people with acute needs, such as potential suicides, drug abusers, and teenage runaways. It is likely that victims of interpersonal violence of all kinds, including military conflicts (prisoners of war, combat veterans), political conflicts (hostages of terrorists, survivors of concentration camps), and street crime, share common aftereffects that require similar treatments. One major task will be to identify appropriate indicators of the effectiveness of the services victims receive (see Salasin, 1981).

In the future, the role of victim advocate will gain greater importance. As crime victims are granted more formal rights and become eligible for a wider array of services, it will be necessary for them to ally with knowledgeable persons to ensure that they get all the privileges and benefits to which they are entitled. An experimental program in a neighborhood near the University of Chicago in which a public-interest lawyer was available to safeguard victims' interests might serve as a model for empowering such advocates within the criminal justice process (see Becker, 1980, for the accomplishments and shortcomings of this experiment).

Informal Justice: Resolving Disputes and Achieving Reconciliation

Settling Conflicts through Mediation and Compromise

- A husband and wife who are separated and awaiting a divorce meet by chance on the street. An argument ensues, and he begins to hit her. An onlooker calls the police, and the man is arrested for assault.
- Two college roommates decide that they will no longer share their off-campus apartment. They cannot decide who owns the television set they purchased jointly. One night the roommate who moved out breaks into the apartment and takes the set. The other roommate discovers the burglary and wants her arrested.
- Two suburban homeowners continually quarrel over a parking spot on the street between their houses. One slashes the tires of the other's car. In return, his neighbor sets a fire in his garage.
- Two boys are in love with the same girl. After a high school prom they fight, and one boy's tooth is broken.
- Two friends spend an evening drinking and playing poker. One accuses the other of cheating, grabs all the money, and leaves.

As of 1982, more than 180 dispute resolution centers were dispensing informal justice in cases concerning vandalism, trespassing, assault, thefts committed by juveniles and first-time offenders, domestic quarrels, neighborhood conflicts, landlord–tenant disagreements, and merchant–customer complaints. Interpersonal disputes between people who know each other and who jointly share responsibility for violations of the law, as in the cases above, clog the courts but may not be appropriate for the win all/lose all adversarial process (Alper and Nichols, 1981). (See box 8-1.)

There is a movement toward informality throughout the criminal justice system. In practice, informality is marked by a preference for unwritten, flexible, commonsense, discretionary procedures tailored to fit particular cases. As an ideology, informality is characterized by an antipathy toward rigid hierarchy, bureaucratic impersonality, and professional domination. The growing interest in informal justice is nourished by several beliefs: that centralized governmental coercion has failed as an instrument of social change; that people must solve their own problems in decentralized, community-controlled forums; that nonstranger conflicts ought to be diverted from the formal adjudication process whenever possible; that both punishment and rehabilitation have failed to "cure" offenders; and that criminal justice officials and agencies primarily serve the state's interests, or their own, to the detriment of both offenders and victims. Enthusiasm for informal alternatives is fed by perceptions that the crime rate is rising while criminal courts are paralyzed, civil courts are swamped with frivolous lawsuits,

BOX 8-1 Taking Out the "Garbage"?

The majority of violent crimes are committed by complete strangers. But in a substantial number of cases, the offenders are known to their victims. The proportion varies by crime: In 24 percent of all robberies (from 1973 to 1979), victims report that the perpetrators were not complete strangers or persons known only by sight. Family members, other intimates, acquaintances, classmates, colleagues, and neighbors were responsible for 35 percent of all forcible rapes, 44 percent of all aggravated assaults, and 47 percent of all simple assaults (Rand, 1982).

These incidents are more likely to be resolved by the criminal justice system than cases involving strangers. A study of cases handled by courts in New York City during the mid-1970s ascertained that the offender and the victim had a prior relationship of some sort, in 21 percent of all auto theft cases in which charges were pressed, in 36 percent of robberies, in 39 percent of burglaries, in 69 percent of assaults, and in 83 percent of rape indictments.

Victims may take these cases very seriously, but criminal justice officials generally do not. Their perception is that too many people "waste" the courts' resources to resolve their personal matters and to settle scores with petty antagonists. Prosecutors, in particular, distinguish between these "junk," or "garbage," cases involving prior relationships and "real crimes" committed by strangers that merit attention. Prosecutors contend from past experience that victims who know their offenders are less likely to press charges after arrests have been made or to testify in court. Most of the time, victim noncooperation arises because the victim and offender have reconciled their differences rather than because of a fear of reprisal.

Prosecutors prefer to dispose of the "garbage" cases quickly, anticipating that complainants will soon have a change of heart. When they are not dismissed entirely, prior-relationship felony cases are routinely plea-bargained down to misdemeanor convictions. Judges hand down much lighter sentences in prior-relationship cases. (Silberman, 1978:358–363; Vera Institute of Justice, 1977:1–22).

What these findings demonstrate is that victims of nonstranger offenders are not well served by the police, prosecutors, and judges, and their needs are not well attended to by the criminal justice system.

---

and prisons and jails are dangerously overcrowded. As a pragmatic response to such economic and political realities, informality beckons as a solution to the government's fiscal crisis. Dispute resolution centers can relieve the overburdened criminal justice system at a time when demands for more services are clashing with demands for less taxation. However, the critics of informality warn that the coercive apparatus of the state can be extended in new ways over more people under the guise of cutting back on formal governmental intervention into everyday life (Abel, 1982).

The first experiments with mediation as a technique of conflict resolution for criminal and civil matters were launched at the start of the 1970s. The American Arbitration Association set up a program in Philadelphia, and the City Prosecutor's Office in Columbus, Ohio, began a joint venture with a law school. By the end of the 1970s, about one hundred "neighborhood justice" projects were under way. Many originally received seed money from the LEAA. Some recently established centers are funded under the 1980 federal Dispute Resolution Act, and others are paid for by comparable state laws. The majority of dispute resolution programs are sponsored by and attached to a criminal justice system agency, usually a prosecutor's office or a local court. The others are run by private, non-profit organizations (like the American Arbitration Association or the Institute for Mediation and Conflict Resolution), a local bar association, or a municipal or county government. The nature of the parent agency profoundly shapes the operations of the dispute resolution center (McGillis, 1982).

Most of the cases referred to centers are diverted from the criminal justice system. Community associations, schools, and religious institutions direct some disputants to centers, and the remainder are "walk-ins" who have heard about the services. Almost always, the disputants know each other. Many are members of the same family, lovers, neighbors, or former friends. Other are schoolmates, fellow workers, tenants and their landlords, or customers quarreling with businessmen. Most of the clients referred to dispute resolution centers are not drawn from the middle and upper strata (Garofalo and Connelly, 1980).

The adversary system that underlies criminal and civil proceedings has been likened to a "zero sum game." At each stage, points are won by one party at the expense of the other. At the end of the contest there must always be a winner and a loser. The victorious side is pleased with the outcome, while the defeated side is embittered. The conclusion of the battle leaves the two parties more alienated and polarized than at the outset.

The "moot model" of informal justice rejects the constraints of a guilty–innocent, wrong–right, pin-the-blame/deny-responsibility framework. The person who brings the matter to the attention of the intermediaries is called the complainant; the other party invited to the proceedings is the respondent. The disputants examine their differences in an atmosphere as free from coercion as possible. They educate each other by presenting their own versions of their conflict. The intent is to look to the future rather than to dwell on the past. The goal is to achieve reconciliation and to restore harmony to their community (Prison Research,1976).

The mediator plays a central role in dispute resolution, replacing the prosecutor, defense attorney, and judge. As a neutral third party, the mediator promotes discussion, solicits viewpoints, and helps people who are at odds to discover areas of common interest. The mediator guides the disputants to work out a mutually acceptable compromise solution.

Mediation lies at the middle of a continuum bounded by conciliation and arbitration. In conciliation, the third party plays a more passive role by simply facilitating communication between the disputants and by bringing them together for face-to-face negotiations. In arbitration, the third party plays a more active role and imposes what he or she considers to be a fair settlement on disputants who are deadlocked and unable to arrive at their own compromise solution.

At dispute resolution centers, hearings are scheduled at the convenience of the participants, not the staff. The use of private attorneys is discouraged. The rules of evidence are minimized. Witnesses are not sworn in. Mediators do not wear robes or sit above others. Nontechnical language is used, and only limited records of the proceedings are kept.

A typical hearing involves one or two mediators, the disputants, and perhaps a witness. The voluntary participation of the disputants is underscored at the outset. Both parties are reminded that they can withdraw at any point and take their grievances to another forum, like a police station, the prosecutor's office, criminal court, or civil court. Each disputant is then invited to tell his or her side of the story without interruption. The mediator asks questions to clarify and amplify points. Then a series of caucuses is held. The two parties tell the mediator what arrangements they are willing to accept and what accommodations they are inclined to make. When an understanding is arrived at, a contract is drawn up detailing in plain English the terms they have agreed to abide by in the future. Both parties take a copy home and are urged to return to the center if the concessions and promises are not kept. Although the centers have no authority to directly enforce the terms of the contracts, the threat of returning to the criminal justice system can coerce compliance. (Arbitration awards are collectible in civil court.)

Both complainants and respondents find dispute resolution to be a satisfactory method, according to several preliminary evaluations of selected projects. Most disputants leave the centers believing that their disagreements have been settled. Mediators receive higher ratings for fairness than judges, and the mediation process meets with more approval than adjudication. The compromise solutions worked out at centers are adhered to more faithfully than court-ordered dispositions of criminal and civil cases (Cook, Roehl, and Sheppard, 1980; Garofalo and Connelly, 1980). (See table 8–3.)

Encouraging preliminary findings like these have secured the future of "storefront" justice. In 1980, Congress passed the Dispute Resolution Act to further such experiments. However, only New York State had enacted legislation providing substantial funding to new and existing programs (Freedman and Ray, 1982).

Pros and Cons from the Victim's Point of View

From the victim's perspective, dispute resolution offers several advantages over adjudication in criminal or civil court for certain kinds of cases.

Informal justice has proven to be speedier, cheaper, and more accessi-

TABLE 8-3 Dispute Resolution: What's in it for Victims?

*Terms of compromise agreements**

Provision	*Percentage of mediated settlements containing this provision*
Stop harassment	
Of complainant, by respondent	15%
Of respondent, by complainant	1%
Of each other	71%
Of a third party	8%
Total	95%
Limit or terminate relationship	
Respondent stays away from complainant	15%
Complainant stays away from respondent	5%
Contact only at specified times or places	4%
Never see each other again	21%
Total	45%
Behavioral restrictions	
Respondent will exercise self-restraint	22%
Complainant will exercise self-restraint	10%
Total	32%
Restitution	
Respondent will make restitution	18%
Complainant will make restitution	2%
Total	20%
Other outcomes	
Complainant concedes respondent is innocent of any criminal charge	3%

*Felony cases mediated at the Brooklyn Dispute Resolution Center, 1977–1978; $n = 144$.

Complainants' reactions to dispute resolution and to court adjudication†

Issue	*Mediated at dispute resolution center*	*Adjudicated in Brooklyn criminal court*
Outcome was fair	77%	56%
Outcome was satisfactory	73%	54%
Had opportunity to tell story	94%	65%
Mediator/judge was fair	88%	76%
Respondent's/defendant's behavior has improved	62%	40%
Respondent/defendant still causing problems	19%	28%
Complainant had to call police again	12%	13%

† n varies by group and issue from 55 to 160 people.

SOURCE: Adapted from *Mediation and Arbitration as Alternatives to Criminal Prosecution in Felony Arrest Cases: An Evaluation of the Brooklyn Dispute Resolution Center*, by Robert Davis, Martha Tichane, and Deborah Grayson. New York: Vera Institute of Justice, 1980:47;50–51;55–56;61–62.

ble than formal proceedings. Cases are handled sooner, cost less in terms of time and money, and are heard at times and places convenient to the participants. Incidents can be explained that otherwise would be too trivial to interest the police or prosecutors. Smoldering disputes that might flare up again and result in escalating violence and counterviolence can be smothered. Complainants who might otherwise never get a chance to air their grievances are given an opportunity to ventilate their feelings. Victims who don't want to insist that an arrest be made or that charges be pressed now have an additional option. Victims who dread the public spectacle of testifying and being cross-examined in open court can choose the center's hearings behind closed doors. They can represent themselves rather than accept the services of a prosecutor who looks after the state's interests or, in civil court, a private attorney who looks only for financial gain.

Most important from the victim's viewpoint, the settlement can be seen as a vindication if the respondent apologizes in writing and undertakes restitution as an admission of responsibility for harm caused. Such settlements can provide a sound basis for reconciliation for people who want to—or have to—learn to get along with each other within their community in the future.

From the victim's point of view, dispute resolution also has its disadvantages. Because the "moot model" consciously abandons the presumptions of guilt and innocence that underly the labels "offender" and "victim" and terms both parties "disputants," a completely innocent victim might find informal justice unsatisfactory. Although the process stigmatizes defendants less by calling them "respondents," it might leave "complainants" who believe themselves to be totally innocent more vulnerable to criticism. The complainants' conduct is more open to scrutiny, especially in the absence of rules of evidence and cross-examination. The notion of shared responsibility is frequently invoked by mediators, who view disputes as outgrowths of misunderstandings and the pursuit of self-interest by both parties. In order to reach an accommodation, complainants might be pressured to concede more responsibility (fault, involvement) than they feel they should. The entire notion of compromise solutions as a means of achieving reconciliation rests on the practice of both parties giving in, to varying degrees, from their original demands. Complainants who insist that they are absolutely blameless will feel cheated that their cases have been diverted from the criminal justice system, because this symbolizes a withdrawal of governmental support (prosecutorial power) from their side.

For those victims who are intent on revenge, the greatest drawback of dispute resolution is that the process is not punishment oriented. The centers are not authorized to convict offenders, publicly humiliate them with the stigma of the label of "criminal," fine them, or confine them in a penal institution. Such retaliation isn't allowed, in order to improve the chances of reconciliation, but some victims don't want to be reconciled with their antagonists—at least not until they have had the satisfaction of "getting even" (Garofalo and Connelly, 1980).

Informal Justice: Vigilante Style

When Victims Take the Law into Their Own Hands

There is another kind of "informal justice," which centers on revenge rather than reconciliation. It has a long and bloody history and may reappear with disturbing frequency in the future. It is vigilantism—"back-alley justice," or "curbstone justice," in common parlance. Although it is a forbidden alternative to the formal criminal justice system, it appeals to many people on the gut level. Several popular movies have capitalized on this yearning for sweet revenge with fictionalized accounts of victims lashing out, striking back, and making criminals pay for their misdeeds in blood. The transparent plots have been so emotionally gripping that audiences stand up and cheer as vicious thugs get their "just desserts":

- A fashion model is raped by her younger sister's music teacher. She has him arrested and presses charges, but she loses the case, her boyfriend, and her lipstick modeling contract. Only days after the teacher is acquitted, he rapes his student (her younger sister). Convinced that the system has failed her and would fail her sister as well, the model grabs a rifle and makes sure he will never molest anyone else again—*Lipstick* (1976).
- His wife murdered and his daughter raped and traumatized, a mild-mannered architect is transformed into an avenging angel of death who rids Manhattan's Upper West Side of muggers. His method is simple but courageous: offering himself as bait, he guns them down once they signal their intentions—*Death Wish* (1974).
- Another round in his one-man war against criminals is triggered when his daughter is raped a second time. He roams the sleazy sections of Los Angeles, seeking out villains to bludgeon, shoot, and electrocute—*Death Wish II* (1982).
- A devoted family man who owns a delicatessen in a crime-ridden section of Philadelphia organizes neighbors into a street patrol that clashes with troublemakers—*Fighting Back* (1982)

The phrases used in the newspaper ads and coming attractions for such films capture the spirit of vigilantism: "When the cops won't, and the courts can't . . . he will give you justice! Deadly force—when nothing else will do!"—*Deadly Force* (1983). "Tired of bucking the system that is supposed to make the streets safe, they patrol while you sleep, bringing about true justice!"—*Vigilante* (1983).

From a victimological standpoint, vigilantism is characterized by a reversal of roles. Victims become the victimizers and physically harm the people who previously made them suffer. The offenders who formerly had the advantage within the relationship, are compelled to assume a subordinate position and receive harsh punishment for their earlier crime. The process is an "informal" brand of "justice" because the victims and their accomplices (or the accomplices alone, acting in behalf of the victims) dispense with all the rules of the criminal justice game. The delicate balance between the rights of victims and defendants, hammered out through centuries of conflict and compromise among advocates of law and order and of civil liberties, is overturned, and the suspect is denied all due-process rights and guarantees. (The history of vigilantism is littered with cases of mistaken identity, in which the wrong person was made to pay a high price for someone else's misdeeds.) The state's role as arbitrator between the parties to the conflict is eliminated. The victims and their accomplices assume the roles normally played by the judge, prosecutor, jury, and, ultimately, executioner. They use force, sometimes deadly force, excessively, without the constraints that limit the police, to take a suspect into custody and to extract a confession. Physical punishments, including capital punishment, are imposed in the heat of passion. Unlike the other kind of informal justice arrived at through mediation at neighborhood centers, vigilantism is not directed toward a peaceful resolution of an antagonistic relationship through negotiation and compromise; its intent is to forcefully settle matters in a manner that mirrors the original act of violence.

Vigilantism is usually defined as "taking the law into one's own hands." But the expression does not capture the essence of this type of reaction to crime. Vigilantes don't take the law, they break the law. They don't act in self-defense, which is legal; they retaliate in an aggressive fashion after the crime is consummated, which is illegal. They inflict physical punishments not permitted under law. And in their wrath, they may impose a penalty much more severe than the law allows—death for a noncapital offense. Their disregard for the "technicalities" of due process mocks the entire legal system. Vigilante "justice" is too swift, too sure, and too harsh. Launched in the name of restoring law and order, it undermines social stability by trampling on the highest law in the land, the Constitution, and in particular, the Bill of Rights. Carried out to vindicate the victim, it generates new victims. Vigilantism is criminal violence in response to criminal violence.

Frontier Origins

Vigilantism is a worldwide phenomenon. In the thirteen American colonies it first broke out as a frontier reaction to marauding criminal bands in South Carolina. In the late 1700s, a "vigilance committee" led by a Colonel Lynch in Virginia developed a reputation for the public whippings it staged. Its escalating violence against lawbreakers gave rise to the terms *lynch law* and *lynchings.*

Over the course of American history, the vigilantes' call to action was issued at times and places where "honest, upright citizens" became enraged and terrified about what they considered to be an upsurge of criminality and a breakdown of law enforcement. Closely identifying with victims, vigilantes feared that they were next if they didn't take drastic measures. Hence, "red-blooded, able-bodied, law-abiding" men banded together and pursued outlaws who were threatening their families, property, and way of life. Led by individuals from the local power elite, with a solid middle-class membership, vigilance committees singled out people at the bottom of the social hierarchy for attack. They lashed out at alleged cutthroats, bushwackers, road agents (robbers), cattle rustlers, horse thieves, and desperadoes of all kinds. They also crusaded against people they maintained were troublemakers, parasites, drifters, idlers, sinners, "loose" women, "uppity" members of subjugated groups, "outside agitators," and anarchist and communist "subversives." The targets of their wrath were blacklisted, banished (run out of town), flogged (whipped), tarred and feathered, mutilated, and sometimes brutally murdered (Burrows, 1976).

From 1767 to 1909, 326 short-lived vigilante movements peppered American history, mostly as Western frontier phenomena, claiming 729 lives (Brown, 1975). From 1882 until as recently as 1951, spontaneous lynch mobs killed 4,730 people, mostly black men, particularly in rural areas of the Deep South (Hofstadter and Wallace, 1970). Very few of these self-appointed executioners ever got into legal trouble for their lawless deeds.

Vigilantes portrayed themselves as true patriots and dedicated upholders of moral codes and sacred traditions. The manifestos of vigilance committees were crowned with references to "the right to 'revolution,'" "popular sovereignty," and personal survival as "the first law of nature." Just as they held criminals fully accountable for their transgressions, these rugged individualists held themselves personally responsible for their own security. If duly constituted authority could not be relied on for protection, they would shoulder the burden of law enforcement and the obligation to punish offenders. The vigilante credo boils down to a variation of "the end justifies the means"—it is necessary to break the law in order to preserve the rule of law.

Most vigilante actions were defended in the name of avenging victims and punishing common criminals. But in retrospect other motives may have been paramount. Teaching lawbreakers a lesson and making an example out of them to deter other would-be offenders was the goal the men in the mob attacks cited to rationalize their own criminality. But vigilantes probably had other motives as well: to quash rebellions; to reassert control over rival racial, ethnic, religious, or political groups; to intimidate subordinates back into submission; and to impose the dominant group's moral standards on outsiders, newcomers, and marginal members of the community (Brown, 1975).

The Drift Back toward Vigilantism

- Late on a Saturday night, an unruly customer stabs to death the owner of a grocery store in a Brooklyn neighborhood. As the killer flees, a hue and cry is heard up and down the street. A crowd gathers, catches up with the suspect, and sets upon him. By the time the police arrive, he is so badly beaten that his eye must be removed by doctors at a hospital emergency room (Davila, 1982).
- A 10-year-old girl is abducted from her bedroom at four in the morning. Twelve hours later she comes running back to her apartment in a housing project in Buffalo, New York, and tells her father the name of the man who kidnapped and raped her. The father and two dozen of his friends surround the accused man and begin to punch and kick him. In a fit of rage, the father stabs him. The father is arrested, and the district attorney tells the press, "The reason we have a system of laws is to prevent vigilante-style justice. We cannot turn over our system of justice to the streets. The consequences would be catastrophic." But the father reports that strangers come up to him and say, "We saw you on TV. We're 100 percent with you" (Winerip, 1983).
- Four men repeatedly rape a woman on a pool table in a bar in New Bedford, Massachusetts. Other patrons drink and watch. The four alleged rapists and two witnesses who encouraged the attack and helped hold the victim down are arrested. Several days later, three thousand angry people march through the town demanding, among other things, that more of the bystanders be indicted (Press, Taylor, and Clausen, 1983).

These cases illustrate opposite problems. The first two represent outbreaks of spontaneous vigilantism, in which outraged bystanders overreact and use more force than the law allows to subdue a suspect. The third incident typifies a more common situation, in which bystanders underreact and fail to give aid and comfort to a crime victim.

Most people would agree that, ethically, eyewitnesses to a crime in progress have a duty to rush to a phone to call the police. Legally, however, witnesses are not required to inform the authorities and cannot be punished for their inertia. Unless they participate in the illegal act, they are not accessories. There was an old common law offense known as "misprision of a felony" (failure to furnish the police with information about a serious crime) but it has fallen into disuse. Under civil law as well, eyewitnesses to a tragedy usually bear no obligation to intervene to rescue strangers. In Vermont, a bystander can be fined up to $100 for failing to "reasonably assist" a gravely endangered person, but as of 1982 no one had ever been punished for passivity. In 1983, a disturbing incident in Minnesota prompted the passage of a Good Samaritan law: ten people stood by for forty minutes as a 13-year-old girl was subdued and raped, until finally an 11-year-old boy alerted the police. Other states are likely to follow suit and enact legislation that will make it a crime not to come to the aid of a person in distress, at the minimum by summoning help (Press, Taylor, and Clausen, 1983; Haimes, 1983).

It is questionable whether new laws can compel onlookers to render assistance to someone who has been harmed in their presence. Social psychological experiments indicate that the most plausible explanation for spectator inaction is that people are confused by what they see and are untrained about what to do and how to help. In a large crowd, witnesses just watch because each person is waiting for someone else to take charge. Some additional reasons why eyewitnesses become immobilized include their fears of being injured, performing ineffectively, making things worse, embarrassing themselves, and becoming entangled in a process that will ultimately cost them time and money. According to experimental evidence, those who do intervene tend to be braver, stronger, appropriately trained, or simply infuriated by the sight of a crime underway (Haimes, 1983; Latané and Darley, 1970; Takooshian, 1980).

When the opposite problem, spontaneous vigilantism, erupts, it usually breaks out in tightly-knit, ethnically homogeneous neighborhoods, in which passersby share a sense of closeness and community. Bystanders intentionally injure a street crime suspect when they are confident that their interpretation of the event is correct—that they witnessed a crime and are sure who is to blame (Shotland, 1976). Some incidents in which the police use unnecessary force to take a suspect into custody (cases of police brutality) or employ deadly force without justification might be embodiments of "police vigilantism," in which patrol officers assume the role of judge, jury, and executioner (Kotecha and Walker, 1976).

A type of political violence that represents the historical link to the vigilante movements of the past is embodied in the terrorist acts of Ku Klux Klansmen and neo-Nazis. They lash out at people and groups they define as "troublemakers" and "the criminal element." Other similar far right wing groups openly proclaim their intention to revive the "night-rider" tradition to "rid society of undesirable elements" (see Burrows, 1976; Madison, 1973).

Vigilantism is envisioned by a new breed of rugged individualists, the "survivalists." Whereas the old-time vigilantes banded together to defend their community during a breakdown of law and order, the survivalists are intent only on personal (and family) well-being. (See box 8-2.)

Yet vigilantism is talked about much more than it is carried out. Any impression that vigilante groups have sprung up to drive away street criminals results from media hype. The label "vigilante" (which was formerly a term accepted with pride, but now is hurled as an epithet) crops up as an exaggeration for shock value in accounts by journalists and public officials about citizen anti-crime activities.

When civilians fortify their homes and arm themselves against possi-

BOX 8-2 *Survivalists—Ready to Rise from the Ashes*

There are from a few thousand to perhaps several tens of thousands of Americans who have absolutely no intention of allowing themselves to be victimized in any way. These "survivalists" are stocking up, battening down, digging in, and preparing for the worst. They are getting ready to weather natural disasters like volcanic eruptions or earthquakes and are bracing for upheavals of human origin like deadly pollution, nuclear warfare, and massive rioting. In their collapse-of-civilization scenarios, their immediate enemies will be the panic-stricken urban hordes who will surge out of concrete jungle death traps in a desperate search for food and shelter. Survivalists vow that there will be no looting, raping, or murdering at their expense, at least not as long as their ammunition holds out.

Ideologically, the survivalist movement draws sustenance from several diverse currents. It espouses a self-defense, self-reliance ethos that dates back to the vigilantism of frontier days. It taps ultraconservative doctrines of individual responsibility and military preparedness in the face of bureaucratic ineptness, governmental paralysis, and subversive conspiracies. And it resonates with fundamentalist religious prophecies about the imminence of a "Judgment Day." Clearly, the survivalist mentality is also a product of the times—an age of diminishing expectations amidst a culture of narcissistic self-absorption. Beleaguered individuals feel crushing economic, political, and social pressures bearing down on them. Signs of danger, decay, and doom seem everywhere, as powerful forces beyond understanding and control run amok. The best strategy for personal survival appears to be to keep options open and to be ready to jump into the lifeboat ahead of everyone else. Survivalists act on the basis of widespread fears and cynical, pessimistic beliefs.

A mini-industry has sprung up to cater to those with intense concerns about the hard times ahead. There are survivalist newsletters, magazines, do-it-yourself guidebooks for all kinds of subsistence activities, elaborate menus of freeze-dried and dehydrated foods, well-stocked weapons dealers, survival training courses, and even custom-built homes with greenhouses and underground shelters (DeWan, 1980; Langway, Copeland, Reese, and Maier, 1980; Lasch, 1982).

---

ble intruders, that is not vigilantism but simply the exercising of legitimate self-defense precautions (a huge debate rages over whether such measures may be counterproductive and endanger family members rather than guarantee their safety). When neighbors organize citizen patrols and ride around in cars equipped with two-way radios, that's not vigilantism either. (The first such crime watch patrol in 1964 in a Brooklyn community was quickly dubbed a "vigilante group" by politicians and police officials, but the concerns of authorities have subsided. Federal money has sponsored such local efforts to supplement law enforcement, and police departments have provided training and equipment to civilian patrols.) Tenant and subway patrols (like the "Guardian Angels") also have been misrepresented in the media and by suspicious police union leaders as vigilante groups. They are not, so long as they confine their activities to reporting incidents, helping victims, and making citizen's arrests of suspects. If they do not cross the line and dish out "back-alley justice," then they are not vigilantes (Marx and Archer, 1976).

But genuine vigilantism of the Old-West and Deep-South varieties may make a comeback if victims and their supporters conclude that only civilian violence can quell criminal violence.

A survey of community leaders across the nation ("It's Time to Retaliate," 1982:2–4) confirmed that an extremely hard line toward criminals is being advocated. Swift and sure punishment is "in"; rehabilitation and the more "understanding" (of the offenders' problems) treatments are decidedly out of favor. Public confidence in the ability of government to protect lives and property is rapidly dwindling. Instead of placing their faith in the police, courts, and prisons, anxious people are counting on locks, alarms, and guns. Grass-roots organizations are being encouraged to cultivate the image that their neighborhoods are "crime-conscious villages" that are risky places for criminals.

Opportunistic politicians seeking to capture the pro-victim, anti-crime vote and ride it to higher office have rekindled the vigilante impulse with their overblown rhetoric. Their inappropriate analogy of "waging war on crime" has become a household phrase. In this "war," victims are the casualties, the "criminal element" is the enemy, and criminal justice personnel are the troops. Their overstatements about how the "war" is being "lost" because the criminal justice system has "broken down" spread panic. Their oversimplified analysis that the police are "handcuffed" by needless rules, that judges are "too soft," and that prisoners are "coddled" prompts distraught victims and their allies to mobilize their own forces lest they be overrun by invaders. Desperate acts of retaliation loom as reasonable solutions to stave off military defeat and rout the enemy.

The emotional attraction of the vigilante "solution" to the street crime problem rests on the notion that retaliation in kind is what "justice" is all about. Because the criminal justice system rarely imposes punishments that directly match the harm inflicted by offenders, it fails to deliver this kind of "justice" to victims and their supporters. Vigilantism appeals to those who passionately believe that victims must "get even" or "pay back" criminals who terrorized them and made their lives miserable.

The vigilante impulse is held in check at present by counterideologies. The tenets of professionalism, embraced by law enforcement officials, spurn any tolerance of vigilantism because of a conviction that experts, not ordinary citizens, ought to control the criminal justice process. A more potent barrier to a vigilante resurgence is the civil liberties doctrine of respect for due-process safeguards and constitutional guarantees. Vigilante "justice" has been exposed as too informal—it is unleashed spontaneously and arbitrarily against marginal individuals and scapegoated groups; too certain—innocent victims of mistaken identity and of frame-ups are railroaded in "kangaroo courts"; and too severe—ugly passions and sadistic urges erupt when violent mobs inflict cruel punishments (see Karmen, 1983).

Vigilantism is no solution to the crime problem. As an informal alternative to the formal criminal justice process, it ironically turns things upside down, or inside out. In a reversal of roles, victims wind up as victimizers, and victimizers experience what it is like to be a victim of a violent crime. There are enough offenders already. Victims shouldn't join their ranks.

References

ABEL, RICHARD. 1982: *The Politics of Informal Justice* (Volume 1: *The American Experience).* New York: Academic Press.

ALPER, BENEDICT, and NICHOLS, LAWRENCE. 1981: *Beyond the Courtroom.* Lexington, Mass.: Lexington Books.

ASSOCIATED PRESS. 1983: "Crime Victims' Fund a Victim of Its Success." *The New York Times,* August 4:A12.

BECKER, THEODORE. 1980: *Victims and Their Lawyer: A Study of Victim Advocacy.* Unpublished Ph.D. dissertation, Northwestern University. Ann Arbor, Mich.: University Microfilms International.

BROWN, RICHARD. 1975: *Strain of Violence: Historical Studies of American Violence and Vigilantism.* New York: Oxford University Press.

BURROWS, WILLIAM. 1976: *Vigilante!* New York: Harcourt Brace Jovanovich.

CARRINGTON, FRANK. 1975: *The Victims.* New Rochelle, N.Y.: Arlington House.

COHODAS, NADINE. 1982: "Five Anti-Crime Bills Cleared, Major Measures Still Stalled." *Congressional Quarterly Weekly Report,* October 9:2643–2644.

COOK, ROYER; ROEHL, JANICE; and SHEPPARD, DAVID. 1980: *Neighborhood Justice Centers Field Test.* Washington, D.C.: U.S. Department of Justice.

DAVILA, ALBERT. 1982: "No Curbs on Street Crime." *The New York Daily News,* December 17:5.

DAVIS, ROBERT; TICHANE, MARTHA; and GRAYSON, DEBORAH. 1980: *Mediation and Arbitration as Alternatives to Criminal Prosecution in Felony Arrest Cases: An Evaluation of the Brooklyn Dispute Resolution Center (First Year).* New York: Vera Institute of Justice.

DeWAN, GEORGE. 1980: "Ready for Doomsday." *Newsday,* October 16:II/3.

FATTAH, EZZAT. 1981: "Becoming a Victim: The Victimization Experience and Its Aftermath." *Victimology,* 6,1:29–47.

FORER, LOIS. 1980: *Criminals and Victims: A Trial Judge Reflects on Crime and Punishment.* New York: Norton.

FREEDMAN, LAWRENCE, and RAY, LARRY. 1982: *State Legislation on Dispute Resolution.* Washington, D.C.: American Bar Association.

"From the States: Minnesota." 1983: *NOVA Newsletter* 7, 10 (October): 3, 7.

GAROFALO, JAMES, and CONNELLY, KEVIN. 1980: "Dispute Resolution Centers: Part I—Major Features and Processes; Part II—Outcomes, Issues, and Future Directions." *Criminal Justice Abstracts,* September:416–610.

GAYNES, MINDY. 1981: "New Roads to Justice: Compensating the Victim." *State Legislatures,* November–December:11–17.

GEST, TED, and DAVIDSON, JOANNE. 1982: "Easing the Pain for Crime Victims." *U.S. News & World Report,* June 21:45.

GRAYSON, ROBERT. 1981: "Criminal Justice vs. Victim Justice: A Need to Balance the Scales." *The Justice Reporter,* 1,4:1–8.

HAIMES, RAYMOND. 1983: "Some Reasons Why 'Helpless Bystanders' Just Don't React." *Newsday,* August 24:56.

HOFSTADTER, RICHARD, and WALLACE, MICHAEL. 1970: *American Violence: A Documentary History*. New York: Knopf.
HUDSON, PAUL. 1980: "A Bill of Rights for Crime Victims." *Victimology*, 5,2: 428–437.
"'It's Time to Retaliate!' Nation's Leaders Advocate." 1982: *Crime Control Digest*, April 19:2–5.
KARMEN, ANDREW. 1983: "Vigilantism." *Encyclopedia of Crime and Justice*, 1616–1618. New York: Free Press.
KOTECHA, KANTI, and WALKER, JAMES. 1976: "Vigilantism and the American Police." In Jon Rosenbaum and Peter Sederberg (Eds.), *Vigilante Politics*, 158–174. Philadelphia: University of Pennsylvania Press.
LAFFERTY, ELIZABETH. 1981: "Arson for Profit Sweeps Poor Urban Areas." Pacific News Service, December 9:1.
LANGWAY, LYNN; COPELAND, JEFF; REESE, MICHAEL; and MAIER, FRANK. 1980: "The Doomsday Boom." *Newsweek*, August 11:56.
LASCH, CHRISTOPHER. 1982: "Why the 'Survival Mentality' Is Rife in America." *U.S. News & World Report*, May 17:59–60.
LATANÉ, BIBB, and DARLEY, JOHN. 1970: *Unresponsive Bystander: Why Doesn't He Help?* New York: Appleton-Century-Crofts.
LEEPSON, MARC. 1982: "Helping Victims of Crime." *Editorial Research Reports*, 1,17:331–343.
LINDSEY, ROBERT. 1982: "Anti-Crime Measure Passes, Causing Confusion on Coast." *The New York Times*, June 10:B23.
MacNAMARA, DONAL, and KARMEN, ANDREW. 1983: *Deviants: Victims or Victimizers?* Beverly Hills, Calif.: Sage.
MADISON, ARNOLD. 1973: *Vigilantism in America*. New York: Seabury Press.
MARX, GARY, and ARCHER, DANE. 1976: "Community Police Patrols and Vigilantism." In Jon Rosenbaum and Peter Sederberg (Eds.), *Vigilante Politics*, 129–157. Philadelphia: University of Pennsylvania Press.
McGILLIS, DANIEL. 1982: "Minor Dispute Processing: A Review of Recent Developments." In R. Tomasic and M. Feeley (Eds.), *Neighborhood Justice: Assessment of an Emerging Idea*, 60–76. New York: Longman.
NATIONAL ORGANIZATION FOR VICTIM ASSISTANCE (NOVA). 1983: *Victims Rights and Services: A Legislative Directory*. Washington, D.C.: NOVA.
NEW YORK STATE ASSEMBLY TASK FORCE ON CRIME VICTIMS. 1982: *Proposals for Victim's Rights Legislation*. Albany, N.Y.: Author.
"Policy Issues: On Cameras-in-the-Courtroom." (1983) *NOVA Newsletter*, 7,1 (January):5–6.
PRESIDENT'S TASK FORCE ON VICTIMS OF CRIME. 1982: *Final Report*. Washington, D.C.: U.S. Government Printing Office.
PRESS, ARIC, and CONTRERAS, JOE. 1982: "A 'Victims' Bill Of Rights.'" *Newsweek*, June 14:64.
———, and LaBRECQUE, RON. 1983: "Giving Victims a Say in Court." *Newsweek*, March 14:51.
———; TAYLOR, JOHN; and CLAUSEN, PEGGY. 1983: "The Duties of a Bystander." *Newsweek*, March 28:79.
PRISON RESEARCH EDUCATION AND ACTION PROJECT (PREAP). 1976: *Instead of Prisons*. Geneseo, N.Y.: Author.
RAND, MICHAEL. 1982: "Violent Crime by Strangers." *Bureau of Justice Statistics Bulletin*. Washington, D.C.: U.S. Department of Justice.
REIFF, ROBERT. 1979: *The Invisible Victim*. New York: Basic Books.
REILLY, JAMES. 1981: "Victim Rights Legislation." *The Prosecutor*, October:18–20.
SALASIN, SUSAN. 1981: *Evaluating Victim Services*. Beverly Hills, Calif.: Sage.
SHIPP, E. R. 1982: "New Act to Require Lawbreakers to Help Pay Cost of Court System." *The New York Times*, May 13:B6.

SHOTLAND, LANCE. 1976: "Spontaneous Vigilantism: A Bystander Response to Criminal Behavior." In Jon Rosenbaum and Peter Sederberg (Eds.), *Vigilante Politics*, 30–44. Philadelphia: University of Pennsylvania Press.

SILBERMAN, CHARLES. 1978: *Criminal Violence, Criminal Justice.* New York: Random House.

TAKOOSHIAN, HAROLD. 1980: "Looking Crime in the Eye, We Avert Our Gaze." *The New York Daily News*, December 28:49.

VERA INSTITUTE OF JUSTICE. 1977: *Felony Arrests: Their Prosecution and Disposition in New York City's Courts.* New York: Author.

VICTIM/WITNESS ASSISTANCE PROJECT. 1983: *Arson Victims: Suggestions for a System Response.* Washington, D.C.: American Bar Association.

VICTIM/WITNESS RESOURCE CENTER. 1982: "New Help for Victims and Witnesses: States Pass Model Legislation." *Report*, October:4–6. Washington, D.C.: Aurora Associates.

WINERIP, MICHAEL. 1983: "Rape Case: Vengeance and Furor." *The New York Times*, August 1:B1.

"Wisconsin Considers: Should Children Have Rights Too?" 1983: *NOVA Newsletter*, 7,4 (April):1–2.

YOUNG, MARLENE. 1982: "Crime Victim Assistance: Programs and Issues in the United States." Unpublished paper delivered at the Fourth International Symposium on Victimology, Tokyo, Japan, August, 1982.

Name Index

Subject Index